M A S T E R
M E D I A
L I M I T E D

DATE DUE

## Other Books by John Tepper Marlin:

LET'S GO: STUDENT GUIDE TO EUROPE

CITY HOUSING

THE WEALTH OF CITIES

PRIVATIZATION OF LOCAL GOVERNMENT ACTIVITIES:
LESSONS FROM JAPAN

THE BOOK OF AMERICAN CITY RANKINGS

CONTRACTING MUNICIPAL SERVICES

BOOK OF WORLD CITY RANKINGS

# CITIES OF OPPORTUNITY

FINDING THE BEST PLACE TO WORK, LIVE
AND PROSPER IN THE 1990'S AND BEYOND

BY

## JOHN TEPPER MARLIN

WITH

DAVID LAMPE,

DAVID CACERES, LOUISE HARPMAN AND LILY SHANG

MASTERMEDIA and colophon are registered trademarks of
MasterMedia Limited

Library of Congress Cataloging-in-Publication Data

Marlin, John Tepper.
   Cities of opportunity.

   Bibliography: p.
   Includes index.
   1. Cities and towns—United States—Handbooks,
manuals, etc.   2. Quality of life—United States—
Handbooks, manuals, etc.   I. Title.
HT123.M2985   1988        306'.0973        88-9323
ISBN 0-942361-07-5
ISBN 0-942361-06-7 (pbk.)

Designed by Irving Perkins Associates, Inc.
Manufactured in the United States of America

10   9   8   7   6   5   4   3   2   1

To all the people who are making the difficult decision of where they should work—graduating seniors, final-year graduate students, mid-career professionals considering future options, retirees, or transferred employees. May you all make a decision you can live with, and may you live with your decision.

# ACKNOWLEDGMENTS

The author would like to acknowledge his debt to the following: the four interns who worked so hard on collecting the data for each of the forty-two metro areas in the book; the individuals and writers throughout the country who assisted us in the collection and organization of the information (see notes for further acknowledgments by name); the board of directors of the National Civic League and its president, John Parr, for providing the facilities, time and encouragement to work on this book; the author's wife, Alice, and children, J. J. and Caroline, for welcoming this book into their home like another (uninvited) member of the family; and Susan Stautberg and her able colleagues at MasterMedia, for encouraging the author to write this book, helping to finance it with an advance and bringing her resources to it when needed.

We are indebted to David Birch of M.I.T. and Cognetics, Inc., in Cambridge, Mass., for his advice on selecting the CITIES OF OPPORTUNITY (his helpful recent book is referenced in Chapter 3 and elsewhere) and to Sara Noble of *Inc.* magazine for giving us early access to data prepared for *Inc.*'s 1988 "Metro Hot Spots" issue.

# CONTENTS

# FOREWORD

SENATOR TERRY SANFORD
*North Carolina*

It is fascinating reading: the best places to work, live and prosper. Why is that important? I remember when I was finishing law school, right after World War II, I was free to select my town, and I was looking for the best place to "seek my fortune." I knew what I wanted to do. So where was the best place to start? The place I chose is not listed in this book, but it might well have been forty years ago. I was looking for a spirit of entrepreneurship, a sense of community, a place with hopes and plans, a place growing but not booming. I found it.

Now, the author of this book, the accomplished and experienced John Tepper Marlin, makes this kind of selection easier for those who are fortunate enough to be able to choose the place where they might work, live and prosper. This book, he says, "is totally dedicated to helping couples . . . facing a career decision with options involving more than one city."

The book certainly does that. For a decision of such magnitude, it is worth the time for any couple to pore over this book. I have found in it, however, another function, maybe, I cautiously suggest, even more significant.

I think every mayor, every chamber of commerce leader, every person devoted to community betterment should study the findings.

For example, I have long been convinced that the creativeness of small business, the risk-taking of the entrepreneur, gives a zest and stability to the economy that is not equaled by large companies. And so, we learn, a city's economic strength is enhanced by a strong small business sector. The question for community leaders is how is it that some places are more conducive to the flourishing of small business than others? This book is worth studying for clues to the answer.

The author is an officer of the National Civic League, which, among many other projects, conducts the program that annually selects and designates the All-America Cities. Perhaps unconsciously, perhaps deliberately, he covers in his study the elements that mark an All-America City. One main purpose of this program is to hold up civic accomplishment for other communities to witness, to learn from. This book does that.

Another group of people who are actively engaged in looking for ideal cities in which "to work, live and prosper" is that vast army of scouts who are are constantly searching for new sites for the location of branch plants, industry and business. The economic development professionals will find in this book many leads that will make them look good in the eyes of their clients.

The author and his associates may have had in mind the lucky couples exploring the options for their own well-being, but I predict this book, so full of success stories, will be bootlegged into countless corporate suites, industrial development and chamber of commerce offices, and council rooms of municipalities. It has a strong message for all of them.

# FOREWORD

SENATOR RICHARD G. LUGAR
*Indiana*

When I declared my candidacy for mayor of Indianapolis in 1967, I was a thirty-four-year-old lifetime resident of the city. Although many talented business and professional persons who had graduated from the Indianapolis public schools in the 1950s had moved to other locations during years in college or the armed services, a substantial number remained in their hometown.

As relatively young parents and neighborhood leaders on the fringe of overall civic leadership, we had watched the riotous scenes of racial violence in Detroit and Los Angeles on television. We were certain that inner-city decline surrounded by accelerating outer-city growth would condemn all of us who were young and hopeful to political and economic civil war throughout all of our days in Indianapolis.

After we captured City Hall, we formulated a plan to consolidate Indianapolis with the rest of Marion County, which surrounds the former inner-city, to be led by one mayor, one council, with the combined city-county moneys available for budget consideration. City-county authorities sorted out the best use of land and allocation of vital community resources for services, including roads, sewage line extensions and environmental cleanups.

All of this occurred prior to the efforts to rate cities and their services by John Tepper Marlin and the Council on Municipal

Performance or the publication of this capstone volume on city performance and prospects entitled *Cities of Opportunity*.

This book addresses a vital element of economic efficiency and planning, namely, the perfection of choice through accurate and comprehensive information. A great strength of our nation's growth has been the willingness of citizens to relocate and to become productive participants in each new environ within a short period of time. For those who are mobile by choice or necessity, the courage of John Tepper Marlin and his associates in measuring so many critical distinctions among cities will come as an unexpected windfall during traumatic moments of employment decisions and dislocation. Others have sought to categorize the urban good and bad in the past, but no one has provided so many dramatic details. Furthermore, the author operates from the explicit premise that provision of better job opportunities is the first incentive a city must offer to prospective inhabitants.

My own experience as a mayor renewed my faith that the most ambitious of plans was possible in the political and economic reform of a city if its citizens were fully employed. Tough problems of civil rights, police and fire departments, the location and financing of schools, medical services, sports arenas and environmental controls were relatively easy to tackle when unemployment was 3 percent or less in the city.

To some extent, each city is always at the mercy of either good or bad fiscal and monetary policies at the federal level, but it is evident that many cities offer job opportunities that are superior to those available at the national level. The ability to do this consistently over the span of years is worthy of a bright spotlight.

The political and business leadership of cities should be accountable for results. City dwellers who have no intention or prospects of moving on and hometown businesses with firmly implanted fixed assets will draw stimulus from John Tepper Marlin's periodic report cards and even more from the comprehensive conclusions of *Cities of Opportunity*.

In 1967, I had no inkling that a book like this would appear. My team proceeded with fundamental reforms because our family roots, businesses, farms and strong social ties were in Indianapolis. We were aware of magnificent scenery, weather and major-league sports elsewhere, but our sense of place and personal development was in the center of Indiana. I suspect that this is still true of most potential city leaders.

In 1988, I am thrilled to read about Indianapolis. I share the pride of its great mayor, William H. Hudnut III, who has served ever since I completed my term of office in 1975. This book will spur Indianapolis on to even greater achievements and generate an explosion of interest in city performance and opportunity everywhere.

The quality of life in most cities will improve if leaders and all other citizens consider carefully their objective situations. The mysteries of why small businesses seek certain environments and why services are more readily available in some locations than others may yield to solutions based on facts.

A generation ago, President Lyndon Johnson proposed a substantial investment of federal resources in 5 major model cities projects. In subsequent years, the focus of this program spread to 150 cities. Presently, federal assistance to cities is on the wane. This will continue during years in which Americans are genuinely alarmed about federal budget deficits.

*Cities of Opportunity* comes along as most cities are required for fiscal and other reasons to rethink their strategies of the past. It outlines the appropriate analytical procedures as well as the implications for planning of those reviews. An America in which most cities are properly prepared through conscious effort to offer better jobs and services to longtime residents and prospective newcomers is a country devoutly to be wished for and encouraged through political and civic wisdom and efforts.

# PREFACE

This book opens with a story about a hypothetical couple named Bob and Carmen. Carmen announces she has been offered a putatively better job in another city. They must both explore all of their options to negotiate their best possible future.

As the dedication indicates, this book is designed for couples in Bob and Carmen's situation—or graduating seniors, or second-year M.B.A.s, or third-year law students, or fourth-year medical students, or retirees, job changers, or anyone facing a career decision—to help them identify and sort through their geographical options involving more than one city.

**WHY CITIES EXIST.** Surveys consistently show that people would rather live in the country than in the city. For anyone in doubt, check the freeways on vacations—in their free time, people head for the country. Urban living is associated with crime, high costs, problems in the schools, disease and addiction.

So why would anyone go to these places? Two answers. First, the need for company. People say that cities make them miserable, to a factor of 15 on a hypothetical Misery Index of 100. But they also say loneliness makes them even more miserable, to a factor of 40.

The second answer is more important. People go to cities for a job. Unemployment jumps up to 90 on the Misery Index. The need for jobs outweighs any public prejudice against cities. Over the centuries cities have become above all markets where goods and services are bought and sold. By and large, the bigger the city, the more specialized the markets are and the greater the opportunity for interesting work at a good level of compensation.

HOW JOBS ARE CREATED.  In 1776 Adam Smith argued that the wealth of a nation should not be measured by how much gold the king has in his vaults, but rather by how productive its work force is. The wealth of nations is in its people at work. Smith advised kings (and queens) to get out of the way of individuals who are willing to take risks to create jobs. President Reagan in recent years has been acting on this advice, reducing the federal role—except for defense spending, which more than doubled between 1980 and 1988.

On the other hand, the role of state and local governments has a lot to do with who is up to the job challenges of the next couple of decades. Jobs are requiring higher and higher levels of skills. Fewer and fewer people are being recruited to be typists; more and more, the need is for people who can handle word processors. Local governments must focus on making sure that the products of their schools are up to the skill needs of the next century. Individuals considering a move must consider whether a city has adequate educational facilities for their children.

Higher education is playing an increasing role in job creation as well. One research institution can be the breeding ground for jobs for an entire state. High-innovation businesses (a much broader category than high-tech businesses) are a major source of new jobs. These businesses rely heavily on having a research institution to develop and disseminate new ideas.

Above all, this book will show that small businesses are the key to job creation in cities—a point to be remembered not only by cities themselves but by people looking at cities as possible creators of jobs for themselves. Cities that are attractive to entrepreneurs are going to grow; those that are not, won't.

WHY ME?  What makes me think I can help someone decide where to find a job? Answer: Thinking and writing about cities has been my own job for the past fifteen years, as president of the Council on Municipal Performance and vice president of the National Civic

League; this was preceded by nine years as a federal government economist and economics professor. I was trained as an economist at Harvard, Oxford and George Washington universities. As a diplomat's son I made five intercity career-related moves and on my own I made two such moves. I know the pangs of departure and the trepidation of arrival, as well as the joys of discovery.

My previous books comparing cities include the first edition of the best-selling *Let's Go Student Guide to Europe* (with Lois Dean and Gordon T. Milde, 1961); ratings of the economies of 31 U.S. cities in *The Wealth of Cities* (1974); ratings of the 100 largest U.S. cities on 397 variables in *The Book of American City Rankings* (with James S. Avery, 1983); and comparisons of 105 world cities in the *Book of World City Rankings* (with Immanuel Ness and Stephen Collins, 1986).

For *Cities of Opportunity* I had the help of four outstanding Harvard students over the summer of 1987: David Lampe, David Caceres, Louise Hartman and Lily Shang. Lampe stayed on to work for the National Civic League year-round, and his hard work and good humor were of invaluable aid in wrestling this book to the mat in the fall of 1987 and beginning of 1988.

As a basic, timely measure of cities' economic strength, we have tracked the monthly metro area employment data prepared by the Federal Bureau of Labor Statistics (BLS). We arranged with the BLS for some special printouts of this information, which are described in Chapter 2. In late summer 1987 we also conducted an opinion survey of urban experts, and at relevant points we provide a summary of their answers for reader consideration.

We fleshed out this predictive information with a wide range of data bearing on what it's like to live in each of the cities and what kinds of people will find it most satisfying to work in them. We wrote to every mayor and chamber of commerce in the cities we decided to include, asking for data, and we also contacted many independent experts. Later, we sent our report on each city back to these correspondents so that they could review it for accuracy and emphasis, and we have sought fairness and objectivity in responding to their concerns.

The reader should keep a few things in mind to make the best use of this book. We have done our best to provide accurate information on each city, but much of the raw data are from outside sources, such as the cities themselves; furthermore, what may be completely accurate at time of writing may not be so by the time you read it. Please take pains to verify any information that you think is especially important in making your decision on where to work or invest.

We believe that our approach to the subject matter is well supported, but a certain amount of opinion must be introduced in a book of this sort, even while we strive for objectivity.

In particular, we have made decisions relating to the choice of cities to be included in this book. We decided not to make this choice solely on the basis of any one index. We left some room for turnaround situations. This decision was quite frankly a subjective one, open to change based on new information. Undoubtedly other cities have legitimate claims to be in this book; we will look at such claims when we update the book.

The best advice we can give you is: read the book thoughtfully, and then go visit the cities that interest you. See for yourself.

Here, then, are the fruits of our labors. We hope they help you, America's Bobs and Carmens (or foreign nationals considering moving to a U.S. city) in your lifetime decision making about where to work and live.

# CITIES
# OF
# OPPORTUNITY

# 1

## WHY THIS BOOK NOW?
### MOVING IN AMERICA

Carmen Sandiego comes home one evening and somewhat nervously explains to her husband, Bob Cratchit, "The office wants to transfer me to a branch on the West Coast where they have been having problems. They made it clear that if I say no, they will be disappointed and even annoyed; but they realize it might be a difficult move for us and they are talking about negotiating some terrific benefits in addition to a nice raise."

"Hey, that's great, I think," Bob responds cautiously, trying to look pleased, "and I suppose I'll be able to pick up some work there, too."

"Bob," Carmen interjects, "I don't expect you to settle for any old job. But your skills will be in demand there as much as here. The benefits they are talking about start with a couple of round-trip tickets each and a month off to check out housing and a job for you. And they will pay for the brokerage fee when we sell our house."

"Carmen, I'm not worried. Let's tell your office OK, and I'm sure I'll land on my feet."

Truthfully, Bob and Carmen *should* worry. Or at very least they should follow Gertrude Stein's advice: "Don't worry, so long as you worry." The facts for couples such as Bob and Carmen are scary. They are facing a 36 percent (.2 × 1.8) likelihood that at least one

3

of them will be looking for work again by the end of the first year, because *one in five workers changes jobs every year*—half of them involuntarily (employer doesn't like worker's performance or eliminates the job), half voluntarily (worker doesn't like the job). So Bob and Carmen need to pay careful attention to the overall job market in the city they are moving to, *even if they think they have lined up secure jobs.*

To be sure, career-related moves are nothing new. Since Adam and Eve, human beings have been forced out of one environment to make their way in another. Moses and his followers spent forty years hunting for the right spot to settle in. Jesus and the early Christians made repeated moves—for safety and to do their work more effectively.

Today, with a majority of married couples (56 percent) pursuing dual careers, patriarchal decision making about moves has been replaced by a more collaborative approach requiring a high level of understanding of risks and opportunities. *Intercity career transfers are turned down by one out of five working couples because the spouse couldn't find a satisfactory new job.* Of the four out of five couples that do opt for the transfer, many (presently 700,000 nationwide) end up with one spouse working in a different city— long-distance commuter couples.

So companies are now having to do a lot of negotiating about employee job moves. Yet both sides of the negotiations commonly come to the table with very little of the data they need—a situation that in other business settings would raise questions about the competence of the bargainers. Employers need to understand better the options available to, and personal risks faced by, individuals today, and to work within this framework to offer attractive relocation packages. Individuals need to know in depth the positive and negative features associated with different cities, so they can make effective (not to mention *impressive!*) arguments for sweeter transfer arrangements. Did you know, for example, that some companies pay the real estate broker's fee *at both ends* of a move and also provide *temporary financing* for the new home until the old one is sold? Did you know that women who have worked in more than one city recite distinct differences in the degree of professional respect women are accorded in different types of cities?

This book offers facts, opinions and predictions to help answer relocation-related questions. For example, it shows that some cities may have a good quality of life but don't have good prospects for generating a high volume of the crucial new small business jobs that are the basis for future job prospects. Bob and Carmen need information about a city's economic base, small business growth, new developments that may affect the area's future, public services and neighborhoods.

You will find here information on trends in forty-two metro areas that we have selected as "cities of opportunity" on the basis of size, small business growth and other factors. We advise you about who will find it easiest to succeed in each city, and where to break in. We explain the limited laws needed to make it in each city. As Mark Twain wrote: "In Boston they ask, 'How much does he know?' In New York they ask, 'How much is he worth?' In Philadelphia, 'Who were his parents?' " This book expands on this theme.

## Our Focus: Personal Opportunity

Our focus is on economic opportunity for individuals. We are interested in finding measures that so far as possible will be reliable for predicting future job growth.

We also pay some attention to the quality of life because it is another consideration for people contemplating a move, and it is also one of the things that contributes to job growth. However, we do not attempt to aggregate quality-of-life measures into the "most livable city" type of nonsense. We abide by Nobel Prize–winner Wassily Leontief's assertion that aggregation to a single quality-of-life index is professionally indefensible because the weights people assign to different components of such an index are personal. We also think that many aspects of quality-of-life indicators are secondary to most people's basic concern of finding a good job. We place the priority in this book on where the jobs are and will be in 1995 and 2000.

## Freedom to Move: The American Privilege

In 1776, when the United States was first created, a book like this would not have found many buyers. America's pioneers tended to stay more or less where they were born, or move once to a stakehold. Moving was difficult and dangerous. This has been the case in most parts of the world in most periods of history. Migrations have occurred largely to escape tyranny or famine. Some countries make it very difficult for people to move, requiring passes or permits. Others have cultural barriers that inhibit mobility.

These factors are not totally absent from today's United States, but our country's residents surely have more real freedom of movement than any other people on earth, today or at any other period of world history. The continued existence of a common currency, the absence of internal trading barriers, the ease of travel and communication, and the expansion of national industrial, commercial and financial institutions—not to mention the melting-pot effect of university education and military training—all contribute to an extraordinary voluntary mobility for American citizens that constitutes the Great American Privilege.

All in all, the average American moves an astonishing eleven times during his or her lifetime, according to the U.S. Census Bureau. In the 1983–84 Census survey year, in a country with just 97 million people in the work force, 39 million Americans moved. It's not just moving down the block, either. Of the 39 million Americans on the move, 6 million—over 15 percent—moved to a different *state*. As U.S. and world society reels from one future shock to another, the pace of mobility is likely to increase. This will present many *problems* as well as opportunities.

## When Americans Move

Americans move from a comfortable existence merely to obtain a more comfortable one, although sometimes a desire to escape domestic or community tyranny of one form or another (nagging and gossip are nonviolent but nonetheless effective forms of persecution) may play a part. People facing either adolescent rebellion or a mid-life crisis or retirement often feel that a change of city might help them lead a happier life. It could be true (although retiree-movers should note that being near their grandchildren is powerfully related to the happiness of elderly people).

People move to go away to college, to take a first job, to start a business or political career, to find a new job after being terminated (or finding themselves dissatisfied, underutilized or in the wrong place for their future career development), or to find a retirement home. Even those who don't move are greatly affected by the mobility of others, because the movers may be their parents, siblings or children.

The highest rate of moving occurs among young adults. While an average of 17 percent of all Americans move to another home each year, the figure is 34 percent for those between the ages of twenty and twenty-four, and 30 percent for those twenty-five to twenty-nine years of age. Going away to college doesn't count as moving by Census standards, or the figures would be even higher. But college does seem to open up horizons to young people, and they are more mobile after graduation than they might otherwise be.

Mobility is also increased by years of military service; as with college students, military personnel on their discharge may stay where they are—some military bases are located in nice spots such as Norfolk (48,000 on the world's largest naval base), San Diego (41,000 on its naval base), San Antonio (36,000 on one base), and El Paso (25,000 on one base)—or move to a city to which they have been exposed during their service. It's just as well that young people get some options before they start their careers, because where a person starts out is very important for future success. As we shall see later, economic opportunity is greater in certain cities as well as in certain professions (the combination of city and profession is important!).

Then, in mid-career, many Americans must move because of the restructuring of corporate America, which is causing wholesale moves of headquarters companies (for example, J. C. Penney from New York to the Dallas area, Mobil Oil from New York to Fairfax County), the elimination of companies through merger or acquisition (once-proud RCA, for example, is now swallowed up by General Electric, which eliminated many RCA jobs), or simply retrenchment to cut costs. Wall Street's precipitous drop on Black Monday 1987 created a whole group of people whose fortunes have been wrecked and who welcome an opportunity to start afresh in another city.

## Marital Status and Job-Related Moves

As we saw in the case of Bob and Carmen, the problems of career changes are becoming more complex for two-career couples, which are today the rule rather than the exception. As a consultant observes: "Besides the fact that the husband and wife may each have developed a satisfying career that he or she may regret leaving, the family may have developed a life-style that requires two salaries.

"The spouse to the employee offered the transfer may have to accept a position at a lower salary, or be willing to wait for an indefinite period to gain employment equal to what was left behind. In addition, for many corporate families, transferring is synonymous with promotion and more prestigious housing, which may not be possible with today's economy."

Unsurprisingly, some people who make major moves suffer from depression. According to an Atlanta area psychiatrist, "everyone needs to be aware that existing problems in the family tend to be magnified during periods of change." He urges every effort to allow children to finish their school year. Beyond that, "it may be helpful for one of the family members to move into the community ahead of time to help orient the family to new schools, shopping areas, playgrounds and so forth, thus helping to lessen the 'groping in the dark' feeling."

In response to the problems, some pioneering companies are becoming more flexible in their handling of reassignments, and are relying on in-house staff and real estate companies to provide relocation guidance to staff being transferred. Increasingly, companies recognize that while it is easy to make an employee feel welcome and at home at the office, it is harder for the employee's family members to adjust to the change. Making new friends is hard for everyone in the family, and schoolchildren must in addition adjust to curriculum differences.

All this in turn means that two-career couples have more corporate sympathy and options than they used to. The best information should be available to potential transferees and job-seekers (as well as their employers!) not only for their own benefit but also for the sake of the efficiency of the job market and ultimately the American economic system in general.

# Jobs Mean Opportunity
## JOB GROWTH IN CITIES

"You're right," said Bob, his right eyelid twitching, "I should be able to get just as good a job on the West Coast. Still, I don't know them and they don't know me. It might not work out. What are the general job prospects out there? Who are the big employers?"

"Let's find out," said Carmen.

### Jobs as Opportunity

The word *opportunity* comes from the Latin god Opportunus, protector of harbors. Something was opportune when the winds were favorable for a sailing (Opportunus had a Greek antecedent, Palaemon, and a Christian successor, St. Christopher). Opportunity implies both good conditions for and, above all, good timing for prosperity. The sophisticated Romans had two different words for what we call luck. One is *opportunitas*, luck that you can see coming and just have to take advantage of; the other is *occasio*, an unpredictable event. We are interested in *opportunitas*, the kind of luck that is more predictable.

Or, as Gary Palmer reportedly said when he won a golf game with a remarkable wedge shot into the 18th hole and his opponent called him lucky: "Yes, it was lucky. And the more I practice, the luckier I get."

9

When Americans think of opportunity for themselves, mostly they think of the opportunity of getting a good job when they are ready for it—whether that job is high up in a big company or at the head of a small business. So a key measure of a city of opportunity is how many jobs are available in a particular month in a metro area, as defined by the federal government and explained in detail in the Notes at the end of this book. As of September 1987, the top ten metro employers are (the envelope, please): New York, 4.1 million jobs; Los Angeles–Long Beach, 4 million; Chicago, 3 million; Philadelphia, 2.2 million; Washington, D.C., 2 million; Detroit, 1.9 million; Boston, 1.7 million; Atlanta and Houston, 1.4 million each; and Dallas, 1.3 million. The complete list of the top 100 is provided below:

TABLE 2.1.    LARGEST 100 METRO AREAS, BY NUMBER OF JOBS (SEPT. 1987)

| Rank | Metro Area | Nonagricultural Jobs (000 Omitted) |
|------|------------|-----------------------------------|
| 1. | New York, N.Y. | 4,115.5 |
| 2. | Los Angeles–Long Beach, Calif. | 4,039.7 |
| 3. | Chicago, Ill. | 2,989.7 |
| 4. | Philadelphia, Pa.–N.J. | 2,162.1 |
| 5. | Washington, D.C.–Md.–Va. | 2,048.7 |
| 6. | Detroit, Mich. | 1,873.5 |
| 7. | Boston, Mass. | 1,723.3 |
| 8. | Atlanta, Ga. | 1,387.7 |
| 9. | Houston, Tex. | 1,376.6 |
| 10. | Dallas, Tex. | 1,306.6 |
| 11. | Minneapolis–St. Paul, Minn. | 1,274.4 |
| 12. | Nassau–Suffolk, N.Y. | 1,127.6 |
| 13. | St. Louis, Mo.–Ill. | 1,110.8 |
| 14. | Anaheim–Santa Ana, Calif. | 1,101.8 |
| 15. | Baltimore, Md. | 1,070.5 |
| 16. | Newark, N.J. | 955.4 |
| 17. | San Francisco, Calif. | 939.0 |
| 18. | Seattle, Wash. | 937.5 |
| 19. | Cleveland, Ohio | 910.2 |
| 20. | Phoenix, Ariz. | 902.4 |
| 21. | San Diego, Calif. | 868.9 |
| 22. | Pittsburgh, Pa. | 856.3 |
| 23. | Miami–Hialeah, Fla. | 814.8 |
| 24. | Denver, Colo. | 801.4 |
| 25. | Tampa–St. Petersburg, Fla. | 782.4 |
| 26. | San Jose, Calif. | 780.8 |
| 27. | Kansas City, Mo.–Kans. | 718.4 |

TABLE 2.1.   LARGEST 100 METRO AREAS, BY NUMBER OF JOBS (SEPT. 1987)(*cont.*)

| Rank | Metro Area | Nonagricultural Jobs (000 Omitted) |
|------|-----------|-----------------------------------:|
| 28. | Milwaukee, Wis. | 695.8 |
| 29. | Cincinnati, Ohio | 687.8 |
| 30. | Columbus, Ohio | 662.6 |
| 31. | Indianapolis, Ind. | 609.7 |
| 32. | Riverside–San Bernardino, Calif. | 604.4 |
| 33. | Charlotte–Gastonia, N.C.–S.C. | 568.2 |
| 34. | Portland, Oreg. | 558.0 |
| 35. | Sacramento, Calif. | 551.2 |
| 36. | Norfolk–Virginia Beach, Va. | 549.9 |
| 37. | Fort Worth–Arlington, Tex. | 517.8 |
| 38. | New Orleans, La. | 511.9 |
| 39. | San Antonio, Tex. | 496.0 |
| 40. | Hartford, Conn. | 481.4 |
| 41. | Orlando, Fla. | 477.5 |
| 42. | Nashville, Tenn. | 464.5 |
| 43. | Rochester, N.Y. | 460.7 |
| 44. | Greensboro–Winston-Salem, N.C. | 459.6 |
| 45. | Salt Lake City–Ogden, Utah | 453.6 |
| 46. | San Juan, P.R. | 453.2 |
| 47. | Ft. Lauderdale–Hollywood, Fla. | 451.5 |
| 48. | Dayton–Springfield, Ohio | 437.5 |
| 49. | Louisville, Ky.–Ind. | 437.5 |
| 50. | Buffalo, N.Y. | 436.1 |
| 51. | Richmond–Petersburg, Va. | 431.0 |
| 52. | Memphis, Tenn.–Ark.–Miss. | 417.5 |
| 53. | Albany–Schenectady, N.Y. | 405.4 |
| 54. | Oklahoma City, Okla. | 403.9 |
| 55. | Birmingham, Ala. | 394.3 |
| 56. | Jacksonville, Fla. | 392.6 |
| 57. | Raleigh–Durham, N.C. | 380.7 |
| 58. | Austin, Tex. | 357.1 |
| 59. | Honolulu, Hawaii | 356.5 |
| 60. | Monmouth–Ocean, N.J. | 321.4 |
| 61. | West Palm Beach–Boca Raton, Fla. | 319.6 |
| 62. | Providence, R.I. | 319.4 |
| 63. | Grand Rapids, Mich. | 309.7 |
| 64. | Greenville–Spartanburg, S.C. | 307.4 |
| 65. | Tulsa, Okla. | 300.6 |
| 66. | Omaha, Nebr.–Iowa | 298.7 |
| 67. | Harrisburg–Lebanon, Pa. | 297.5 |
| 68. | Syracuse, N.Y. | 296.6 |
| 69. | Las Vegas, Nev. | 288.9 |
| 70. | Toledo, Ohio | 288.8 |

TABLE 2.1.  LARGEST 100 METRO AREAS, BY NUMBER OF JOBS (SEPT. 1987) (cont.)

| Rank | Metro Area | Nonagricultural Jobs (000 Omitted) |
|---|---|---|
| 71. | Scranton–Wilkes-Barre, Pa. | 286.6 |
| 72. | Wilmington, Del.–Md.–N.J. | 273.7 |
| 73. | Allentown–Bethlehem, Pa. | 273.2 |
| 74. | Akron, Ohio | 269.2 |
| 75. | New Haven–Meriden, Conn. | 253.0 |
| 76. | Jersey City, N.J. | 246.2 |
| 77. | Knoxville, Tenn. | 246.1 |
| 78. | Springfield, Mass. | 242.6 |
| 79. | Tucson, Ariz. | 242.1 |
| 80. | Albuquerque, N.M. | 233.8 |
| 81. | Little Rock, Ark. | 230.9 |
| 82. | Gary–Hammond, Ind. | 219.1 |
| 83. | Wichita, Kans. | 216.4 |
| 84. | Columbia, S.C. | 216.3 |
| 85. | Baton Rouge, La. | 215.1 |
| 86. | Fresno, Calif. | 206.7 |
| 87. | Des Moines, Iowa | 206.2 |
| 88. | Paterson–Clifton, N.J. | 206.0 |
| 89. | Oxnard–Ventura, Calif. | 202.6 |
| 90. | Bridgeport–Milford, Conn. | 199.8 |
| 91. | Madison, Wis. | 199.1 |
| 92. | Worcester, Mass. | 198.6 |
| 93. | Lansing–East Lansing, Mich. | 197.0 |
| 94. | Youngstown–Warren, Ohio | 195.7 |
| 95. | Trenton, N.J. | 194.0 |
| 96. | Charleston, S.C. | 187.8 |
| 97. | El Paso, Tex. | 187.7 |
| 98. | Fort Wayne, Ind. | 186.2 |
| 99. | Chattanooga, Tenn. | 185.6 |
| 100. | Lancaster, Pa. | 181.1 |

So is bigger always better? For many types of small businesses, a bigger city is preferable to a smaller one because greater variety and supply of services are constantly on tap. But bigger doesn't always mean more opportunity. When New York City was insolvent in the mid-1970s, it was a terrible place to find a job. After Black Monday, October 19, 1987, New York's securities firms and banks have been chopping back their staffs—not a good time to look for work on Wall Street. Timing is still an essential aspect of opportunity and job growth even though in a large city opportunities are being created with more frequency. Detroit was Layoff City for years, because of Japanese and European competition, but in recent years has staged a comeback. Houston and Dallas are still in the doldrums because of the drop in oil prices but could soon turn around. How do we pick among these cities? Do smaller cities sometimes offer more opportunity (not to mention a more human scale and a stronger quality-of-life advantage)?

The rest of this book seeks answers to these questions. We look at the prospects for major cities and many intermediate-size cities, and discuss the pros and cons of smaller cities as well. Often a city has pockets of opportunity for certain kinds of people even if the overall growth prospects are not encouraging. The specialized medical centers in Houston may thrive even when the oil companies are pulling in their horns and office vacancy rates hit new highs. Above all, we stress the idea that jobs come and go in cycles and that you must be aware of these cycles.

## City Cycles, Pendulums and Chain Letters

Today's growth city may be tomorrow's ghost town. That's a fact of life. The problem with economic growth is that it feeds on itself and can tend toward boom-and-bust cycles—or a pendulum effect. A common precipitating industry is construction, which can have a chain letter effect. The chain letter (pyramid, Ponzi) scheme produces rapid growth but at each stage requires more and more input (people, money). Its growth sooner or later screeches to a halt.

The first round of growth in any city creates demand for new housing and office space, which in turn generates new jobs and more demand for new housing and office space. The construction industry grows along with real estate speculation until the bubble bursts. The United States went through an office-building boom in the first half of the 1980s, which came to a halt in 1986, when the national average office vacancy rate rose to 14 percent in central business districts of major cities and 23 percent in the metro areas outside the central business districts.

New construction in 1987 has slowed dramatically, especially in the hardest hit metros, those heavily dependent on oil and agriculture, from Louisiana and Texas through Oklahoma up to Colorado. The drop-off in new office building (which experts at the real estate firm of Cushman & Wakefield predict will persist through the end of the 1980s) should reduce vacancy rates and bring down the speculative fever to long-range sustainable levels.

The impact of a reversal of speculative land purchase and office building is a drastic job drop in the construction industry. Dallas, for example, between September 1986 and September 1987 lost 35,000 jobs, a 2.6 percent decline. Dallas rated 100th of the top 100 metro areas in change in employment. Does that mean Dallas is not a city of opportunity? No, because the city has an aggressive cadre of business entrepreneurs, and they will probably see to it that new jobs are created. For example, J. C. Penney has been lured to the Dallas suburb of Plano, bringing with it 3,000 direct jobs and many more indirect ones.

## The Multiplier-Accelerator and the High-Beta City

It may be helpful to bear in mind the "Multiplier-Accelerator" theory, a concept from economics that is used to explain business cycles. When an external (for example, federal) investment is made, the funds injected into the local economy have a multiplied effect because the money continues to flow through the system as residents spend it in successive transactions.

The higher level of spending is then accelerated further because it induces new investment—for example, in construction to create space for new employees. This accelerator is very fragile. Cities with high accelerators, a readiness to expand, have very volatile economies. The growth prospects are good but are accompanied by risk. We say of a high-growth, high-risk firm that it has a high "beta" (the measure of the steepness of the slope of its stock price in relation to some average of stock prices). We can similarly say of a city that it has a high beta in its tendency to expand . . . and contract.

Sometimes a high-beta city or area will come a cropper. Texas did just that at the end of 1987, but the high energy level of entrepreneurs in the state is waiting, ready to seize on the next growth industries. For that reason we bet that Texas is still full of cities of opportunity.

## The Myth of the Steady Company/City

The myth of the steady job and steady company goes along with that of the steady city: "Sound companies grow steadily. Get a steady job at a steady company in a steady city."

In fact, companies, even big ones, lurch along from idea to idea—a new technology or a new market. The cities they operate in are affected by these lurching actions. A company offers a new product or markets old products in a new way. It expands to the limit (and beyond—beware the risk of failure from overexpansion). At the limit, it cuts back.

Then it must repeat the process or decline. That is the essence of what Joseph A. Schumpeter in *Capitalism, Socialism, and Democracy* has called the "process of creative destruction" of capitalism. Companies that grow steadily are usually churning with ideas and experimentation internally. Of the firms with the highest job growth rates in a study David Birch of Cognetics, Inc., did in the 1970s, only 12 percent had been high-growth firms in the previous three-year period. A much larger proportion, 20 percent, had been heavy job *losers* in the earlier period. Also, 22 percent of the big employment generators in a subsequent two-year period were establishments that had shrunk in both earlier periods. Companies with small job changes showed the greatest risk of dying.

A vivid example of one year's disaster being the next year's top performer may be seen in the stock market. In 1986 Bethlehem Steel dropped 59 percent, the Dow Jones Average's worst performer. In 1987 it soared 168 percent, the Dow's best performer. The same thing happened to Union Carbide in 1984–85 and Allied Chemical in 1978–79. If you had invested in the five worst-performing stocks in the Dow basket at the end of 1986, you would have gained over 45 percent in 1987. Trouble is, it wouldn't have worked in 1985–86; timing is everything.

The same observations could be made about cities. Seldom do high-growth cities fade into oblivion. If the source of their business income suffers, as has happened recently in oil- or mining-based cities (such as those in areas of Colorado, Louisiana and Oklahoma), entrepreneurs must look for new opportunities. The biggest danger is to have a city dependent on a narrow range of activities with a relatively small band of entrepreneurs creating the jobs for armies of workers, as was the case in Pittsburgh or Cleveland or Detroit. When foreign competition undercuts the manufacturers' economics, the city has an inadequate cadre of job creators to put it back on track.

## Strategic Recommendations

For individuals, the implication of all this is that it makes strategic sense to try to determine which stage cities, and the companies in them, are in, and to go for the ones that appear to be on the upswing. Catch the wave—catch cities and companies in the early stage of a good new industry based on a new product or marketing idea. Quit a city or company that you think is backing a bad industry, product or marketing idea, or is overexpanding. Don't be the first or last on board. But remember: Yesterday's (or today's) big losers may be tomorrow's big winners. As Birch says, "Those who feel they are playing it safest often end up being the sorriest."

For companies and cities, the strategic message is that those prepared to cut back drastically are the most likely to grow rapidly in a later period. They have more control over their costs and their activities. The most encouraging indicator that Wall Street firms will successfully weather their expectations of bleaker days is the speed with which many of them reined in their expenditures after (and even before!) Black Monday. Similarly, the best evidence that New York City is not headed for a repeat of its mid-1970s fiscal disasters is the speed with which the city cut back its work force, imposing a job freeze within a week after Black Monday.

In 1948 the people of Manchester, New Hampshire, hanged Royal Little, CEO of Textron, in effigy for closing the company's inefficient plant in their town. At the time, Little said that the townspeople would eventually bless him for not letting the community drift along in a dead-end industry. So they did, thirty-five years later, with a banquet in his honor, because the emptied mills in time became homes to high-tech companies that are providing more and better jobs for the children of the low-paid factory workers.

CHANGE IN JOBS  "This strategic advice is all very well," you may say, "but how do we catch the wave?"

Aha. The simplest approach is to look at recent job growth patterns. Of the 100 largest areas, in 1984–85 (September to September) only five metros saw a decline in jobs; it was a boom year except for those most affected by the drop in oil prices (New Orleans, Oklahoma City, Houston) or cutbacks in electronics (San Jose). In 1985 and 1986, eleven metros had a decline in jobs, with steel industry metros joining the now further depressed oil/energy cities. In the latest year, 1986–87, seven metro areas saw a decline in jobs, with the steel metros (Pittsburgh, Allentown–Bethlehem) hiring again.

An average of the three years is shown in Table 2.2, ranking the 100 largest metro labor markets by their nonagricultural job growth rates. (Note that several markets tied in the rankings.) The five metro areas with the fastest job growth rates are Riverside–San Bernardino (in the greater Los Angeles consolidated metro statistical area) with a 7.7 percent average annual growth rate; Orlando with a 6.9 percent rate; West Palm Beach–Boca Raton (that is, Palm Beach County), 6.3 percent; Las Vegas, 6 percent; and San Diego, 5.3 percent.

At the other end of the chart, seven metro areas had a negative growth rate during the period; of them, six were suffering at least in part from setbacks in the oil industry. The other was San Jose, suffering from retrenchment in the Silicon Valley's electronics manufacturing. Bottom-ranked Oklahoma City was beset by damage due not only to the oil industry but also to farm incomes.

TABLE 2.2.   ANNUAL NONAGRICULTURAL JOB GROWTH, 1984–87

| | | Avg. Annual % Growth | |
|---|---|---|---|
| Rank | Metro Area | 9/84–9/87 | 9/86–9/87 |
| 1. | Riverside–San Bernardino, Calif. | 7.7 | 7.2 |
| 2. | Orlando, Fla. | 6.9 | 6.6 |
| 3. | West Palm Beach–Boca Raton, Fla. | 6.3 | 7.1 |
| 4. | Las Vegas, Nev. | 6.0 | 8.0 |
| 5. | San Diego, Calif. | 5.3 | 4.4 |
| 6. | Sacramento, Fla. | 5.0 | 4.3 |
| 7. | Phoenix, Ariz. | 4.9 | 1.8 |
| 8. | Anaheim–Santa Ana, Calif. | 4.7 | 4.5 |
| 8. | Fort Wayne, Ind. | 4.7 | 4.6 |
| 8. | Jacksonville, Fla. | 4.7 | 4.0 |
| 11. | Raleigh–Durham, N.C. | 4.5 | 2.7 |
| 12. | Columbus, Ohio | 4.3 | 3.8 |
| 12. | Atlanta, Ga. | 4.3 | 2.3 |
| 14. | Cincinnati, Ohio | 4.2 | 3.7 |
| 15. | Seattle, Wash. | 4.1 | 4.1 |
| 15. | Tucson, Ariz. | 4.1 | 0.2 |
| 17. | Oxnard–Ventura, Calif. | 4.0 | 3.4 |
| 17. | Trenton, N.J. | 4.0 | 3.1 |
| 19. | Washington, D.C.–Md.–Va. | 3.9 | 2.6 |

# Cities of Opportunity

TABLE 2.2.  ANNUAL NONAGRICULTURAL JOB GROWTH, 1984–87 (continued)

| Rank | Metro Area | Avg. Annual % Growth | |
|------|-----------|:-----------:|:-----------:|
| | | 9/84–9/87 | 9/86–9/87 |
| 20. | Charleston, S.C. | 3.8 | 3.1 |
| 20. | Indianapolis, Ind. | 3.8 | 4.2 |
| 20. | Monmouth–Ocean, N.J. | 3.8 | 2.2 |
| 20. | Tampa–St. Petersburg, Fla. | 3.8 | 2.5 |
| 24. | Fort Lauderdale–Hollywood, Fla. | 3.7 | 3.2 |
| 25. | Charlotte–Gastonia, N.C. | 3.6 | 3.7 |
| 25. | Nashville, Tenn. | 3.6 | 2.3 |
| 27. | Hartford, Conn. | 3.5 | 3.5 |
| 27. | Norfolk–Virginia Beach, Va. | 3.5 | 2.7 |
| 29. | Toledo, Ohio | 3.4 | 4.1 |
| 29. | Worcester, Mass. | 3.4 | 3.7 |
| 31. | Richmond–Petersburg, Va. | 3.3 | 2.8 |
| 32. | Lancaster, Pa. | 3.2 | 3.4 |
| 32. | Wilmington, Del. | 3.2 | 3.9 |
| 34. | Albuquerque, N.M. | 3.1 | 2.3 |
| 34. | Birmingham, Ala. | 3.1 | 3.7 |
| 34. | Detroit, Mich. | 3.1 | 0.6 |
| 34. | Lansing–East Lansing, Mich. | 3.1 | 1.7 |
| 38. | Dayton–Springfield, Ohio | 3.0 | 2.3 |
| 38. | Honolulu, Hawaii | 3.0 | 2.8 |
| 40. | Harrisburg–Lebanon, Pa. | 2.9 | 3.4 |
| 40. | Madison, Wis. | 2.9 | 3.2 |
| 42. | Columbia, S.C. | 2.8 | 0.7 |
| 42. | Greenville–Spartanburg, S.C. | 2.8 | 1.9 |
| 42. | Memphis, Tenn.–Ark.–Miss. | 2.8 | 1.7 |
| 42. | Nassau–Suffolk, N.Y. | 2.8 | 1.6 |
| 46. | Albany–Schenectady, N.Y. | 2.7 | 2.7 |
| 46. | Philadelphia, Pa.–N.J. | 2.7 | 2.6 |
| 46. | Portland, Oreg. | 2.7 | 5.1 |
| 49. | Louisville, Ky.–Ind. | 2.6 | 2.3 |
| 49. | New Haven–Meriden, Conn. | 2.6 | 2.7 |
| 51. | Bridgeport–Milford, Conn. | 2.5 | 3.4 |
| 51. | El Paso, Tex. | 2.5 | 0.7 |
| 51. | Greensboro–Winston-Salem, N.C. | 2.5 | 2.2 |
| 51. | Los Angeles, Calif. | 2.5 | 2.8 |
| 51. | Springfield, Mass. | 2.5 | 4.0 |
| 56. | Salt Lake City–Ogden, Utah | 2.4 | 1.0 |
| 56. | Grand Rapids, Mich. | 2.4 | 1.9 |
| 56. | Des Moines, Iowa | 2.4 | 3.4 |
| 59. | Wichita, Kans. | 2.3 | 4.7 |
| 59. | Fort Worth–Arlington, Tex. | 2.3 | 1.2 |
| 59. | Providence, R.I. | 2.3 | 1.9 |
| 62. | Boston, Mass. | 2.1 | 2.6 |

TABLE 2.2.   ANNUAL NONAGRICULTURAL JOB GROWTH, 1984–87 (continued)

| Rank | Metro Area | Avg. Annual % Growth | |
|------|-----------|:---:|:---:|
| | | 9/84–9/87 | 9/86–9/87 |
| 62. | Buffalo, N.Y. | 2.1 | 2.3 |
| 62. | Chattanooga, Tenn. | 2.1 | 2.7 |
| 62. | Fresno, Calif. | 2.1 | 2.8 |
| 62. | Minneapolis–St. Paul, Minn. | 2.1 | 2.6 |
| 62. | San Antonio, Tex. | 2.1 | 0.4 |
| 62. | Youngstown–Warren, Ohio | 2.1 | 2.4 |
| 69. | Baltimore, Md. | 2.0 | 1.2 |
| 69. | Jersey City, N.J. | 2.0 | 2.5 |
| 69. | Little Rock, Ark. | 2.0 | 1.9 |
| 69. | Syracuse, N.Y. | 2.0 | 0.7 |
| 73. | Austin, Tex. | 1.9 | −1.3 |
| 73. | Miami–Hialeah, Fla. | 1.9 | 2.7 |
| 75. | Chicago, Ill. | 1.7 | 0.6 |
| 75. | Cleveland, Ohio | 1.7 | 2.3 |
| 75. | San Juan, P.R. | 1.7 | 3.3 |
| 78. | Scranton–Wilkes-Barre, Pa. | 1.6 | 0.4 |
| 79. | New York, N.Y. | 1.5 | 1.6 |
| 79. | Omaha, Neb.–Iowa | 1.5 | 1.7 |
| 81. | Akron, Ohio | 1.4 | 2.0 |
| 81. | Milwaukee, Wis. | 1.4 | 2.1 |
| 81. | St. Louis, Mo. | 1.4 | 0.7 |
| 84. | Allentown–Bethlehem, Pa. | 1.3 | 3.2 |
| 84. | Kansas City, Mo.–Kans. | 1.3 | −0.4 |
| 84. | Newark, N.J. | 1.3 | 1.1 |
| 84. | Paterson–Clifton, N.J. | 1.3 | 1.0 |
| 84. | Rochester, N.Y. | 1.3 | 0.9 |
| 89. | Knoxville, Tenn. | 1.2 | 1.8 |
| 90. | San Francisco, Calif. | 1.1 | 1.5 |
| 91. | Dallas, Tex. | 0.8 | −2.6 |
| 92. | Gary–Hammond, Ind. | 0.6 | 5.4 |
| 93. | Pittsburgh, Pa. | 0.4 | 1.4 |
| 94. | Baton Rouge, La. | −0.4 | 0.5 |
| 94. | San Jose, Calif. | −0.4 | 1.6 |
| 94. | Tulsa, Okla. | −0.4 | 0.0 |
| 97. | Denver, Colo. | −0.6 | −0.2 |
| 98. | New Orleans, La. | −1.4 | −0.8 |
| 99. | Houston, Tex. | −2.5 | 0.6 |
| 100. | Oklahoma City, Okla. | −1.8 | −1.0 |

Note that the second column shows the most recent trends. All of the steel towns (Allentown, Gary, Pittsburgh) show an uptick because the steel industry had a good year. Dallas did worse in

1986–87 than in the prior two years, but Denver, Houston and Tulsa were doing marginally better.

INDUSTRY DEPENDENCE AND OUTLOOK    Table 2.2 shows clearly that certain metros are in a down cycle. If you believe that oil prices are going to climb back up again and that the oil/energy industry will recover soon, you may well want to migrate to one of these areas. It's relatively easy to determine which ones they are. They have a large proportion of workers under the category of *mining*. The metros with more than 1 percent of employment in this category in September 1987 are (in order of total metro employment): Houston, 4.6 percent; Dallas, 1.4 percent; Denver, 1.9 percent; New Orleans, 3.1 percent; Oklahoma City, 2.7 percent; Tulsa, 4.8 percent; Wichita, 1 percent; Oxnard–Ventura, 1 percent. Check these names against Table 2.2 and note the correspondence. Oil prices dropped from $26 a barrel to under $10 by the middle of 1986; severe layoffs followed, and the worst is seen as being over. Optimists are projecting a price of $18 a barrel for oil in 1988, but pessimists note that OPEC didn't get its act together at the end of 1987, so that oil could drop to as low as $13 a barrel, $5 a barrel below what companies need to make a profit (at press time the price is $14 a barrel).

Moving up toward sea level from mining to *construction* . . . A metro with a large number of workers in construction is on a growth binge. The question to be asked is how long the area's density, traffic and air quality can sustain such growth. The metros with the highest proportion of workers in construction—that is, over 7 percent—are dominated by those in the states of Arizona, California and Florida: Phoenix, 7.6 percent; Tampa–St. Petersburg, 8.2 percent; Riverside–San Bernardino, 8.9 percent; Orlando, 7.1 percent; Fort Lauderdale, 8 percent; Jacksonville, 7.2 percent; West Palm Beach–Boca Raton, 10 percent; Tucson, 8.5 percent; Albuquerque, 7.3 percent; Baton Rouge, 9.4 percent; Charleston, S.C., 7.9 percent. If you are interested in construction you may want to check these cities out—or opt to be a contrarian and avoid them because building activity is already so frenetic!

Metros dependent on *manufacturing* have been given a lift in 1987 by the drop in the value of the dollar, making it harder for overseas manufacturers to sell in the United States and easier for American manufacturers to sell abroad. The three metros with the *lowest* proportion of workers in manufacturing are Washington, D.C., 4.2 percent; Honolulu, 4.6 percent; and Las Vegas, 3 percent. The metros with the *greatest* proportion of workers in manufacturing—that is, over one-fourth—are Detroit, 25.2 percent; San Jose, 34 percent; Charlotte–Gastonia, 26.8 percent; Rochester, N.Y., 29 percent; Greensboro–Winston-Salem, 33.2 percent; Grand Rapids, 30.6 percent; Greenville–Spartanburg, 32.4 percent; Allentown–Bethlehem, 28.2 percent; Gary–Hammond, 25.2 percent; Wichita, 27.4 percent; Paterson–Clifton, 29.7 percent; and Bridgeport–Milford, 30.4 percent. The biggest turnaround stories in the 1987 stock market were in the steel industry, which has trimmed back and retooled sufficiently to be competitive, especially with the help from a weaker dollar; whether demand for steel will hold up in 1988 will depend on the success of the U.S. auto industry and other heavy users. Auto employment at the end of 1987 was up 200,000 over mid-1982, but was down nearly 50,000 from its 1984–85 peak even though production is higher than ever. Americans are expected to buy 10 million cars and 5 million light trucks in 1988. After two bad years in 1985 and 1986, U.S. semiconductor makers made a profit in 1987 as a result of a U.S.–Japanese trade agreement and the weaker dollar. You can be sure key people in the steel, auto and other manufacturing-based metros know about fluctuations in the value of the dollar. Your assessment of the future of these metros should relate to your expectations about the future of the dollar in world markets.

In the *wholesale and retail trade* industry, six metros pass the very stringent test of having over 27 percent of their employees in this line of work and qualify as Shoppers' Paradises: Atlanta, 27.9 percent; Nassau–Suffolk, 27.3 percent; Tampa–St. Petersburg, 27.2 percent; Fort Lauderdale, 29.6 percent; Memphis, 27.9 percent; Monmouth–Ocean, 27.9 percent. Some trade-oriented metros didn't make this short list because they concentrate either on the wholesale or the retail side. Fort Worth, for example, tends to be a wholesale warehouse for the region but is less strong than Dallas on the retail side. For 1988, retailers expect a slow start in the aftermath of the stock market crash, with possibly stronger growth later in the year. The spread of "hypermarkets" (combining sale of food and other goods under one roof) and multiple in-store boutiques may provide some room for enterprise and growth.

Metros with more than 8 percent of employees in *transportation and public utilities* tend to have an important airport, port or rail center (not to mention possibly a battery of missiles): Atlanta, 8.1 percent; Newark, 8.4 percent; San Francisco, 8.4 percent; Miami–Hialeah, 8.2 percent; Denver, 8.1 percent; Charlotte–Gastonia, 8.7 percent; New Orleans, 8.2 percent; Memphis, 9 percent; Omaha, 8.2 percent; Jersey City, 12.4 percent. Airlines made about $1 billion in profits in 1987 and are expected to do the same in 1988, depending on labor settlements (increasing concentration makes the airlines a juicy target) and oil prices (fuel is a major cost). With the dollar so weak, a surge of foreign tourists to the United States and more domestic vacationing are expected in 1988.

Hartford (16.5 percent) and New York (14.1 percent) dominate the metros with a high proportion of workers in the *finance, insurance and real estate* industries. New York had 578,500 workers in this sector in the month before Black Monday. There is a good chance that the number will drop below 500,000 in 1988. Other metros with more than 9 percent of employees in this industry: Dallas, 9.9 percent; San Francisco, 12 percent; Jacksonville, 9.6 percent; Omaha, 10.1 percent; Des Moines, 13.2 percent. At the end of 1987 the four largest banks in the world were all Japanese. Japanese firms were investing more aggressively in U.S. companies and real estate—expect this trend to continue. Within the United States, expect some new regional banks, unburdened by Latin American debt, to move up several notches into the top ten while some New York banks drop down in importance (Citicorp, Morgan Bank and Bankers Trust are expected to maintain their preeminence).

An odd fact: New York is one of only six metros with over 30 percent of its employees in the *services* industry. (If that is the case, why is it so hard and expensive to get service in New York?) Here is the list of the top six: New York, 30.4 percent; Washington, D.C., 31.4 percent (one-upmanship); Boston, 32 percent; San Diego, 30.6 percent; Orlando, 32.2 percent; Las Vegas, 47.9 percent. Services are a key source of future jobs. But the $450 billion health-care services industry is unlikely to continue its past rate of job growth because of severe government cost-containment measures and higher labor costs. Large health-maintenance organizations such as U.S. Healthcare and Maxicare will probably grow at the expense of smaller HMOs.

When times get tough, it's good to have the stability of federal and state *government* jobs (drawing on a tax base beyond city limits) in an area. The metros with more than one-fourth of their employees in government jobs are Washington, D.C., 27.1 percent; Sacramento, 29.5 percent; Albany–Schenectady, 26.7 percent; Austin, 27.1 percent; Columbia, 26.6 percent; Baton Rouge, 25.7 percent; Madison, 29.5 percent; Lansing, 31.8 percent; Trenton, 28.4 percent; Charleston, 26.1 percent. Metro areas with between one-fifth and one-fourth of their employees in government jobs area Riverside–San Bernardino, 20.2 percent; Norfolk–Virginia Beach, 22.8 percent; San Antonio, 22 percent; Salt Lake City–Ogden, 20.8 percent; Richmond–Petersburg, 20.7 percent; Oklahoma City, 23.7 percent; Raleigh–Durham, 22.7 percent; Honolulu, 20.9 percent; Harrisburg–Lebanon, 22.2 percent; Tucson, 20.5 percent; Fresno, 21.1 percent; El Paso, 21 percent. (Metro areas are listed in order of total population within each grouping.)

## Summing Up

A city of opportunity is one that is poised to grow in the next ten years and therefore provide a good living for its workers. Cities tend to concentrate in certain types of activities. For career purposes you need to understand what a city's areas of specialization are, what the prospects are for these activities and what key factors should be monitored.

# 3

## ENTERPRISE MEANS JOBS
### WHERE JOBS COME FROM

"Carmen, dear," Bob said after some thought, "let's try to plan things so that we don't have to move again soon. If we are going to move, let's think of it as a permanent one. Let's make sure that where we are going has growth potential—that it's a place where jobs will be plentiful in five or ten years."

"How can anyone predict such a thing?" Carmen asked.

"Small business growth trends," Bob suggested.

"Who keeps track of *that*?"

### Enterprise: Small Business Creates Job Opportunity

In his fables, Aesop said that opportunity has "hair in front but is bald behind"—it's easier to catch hold of it as it comes toward you than when it's getting away. In other words, since timing is of the essence, opportunity is something to be anticipated and planned for—that is, to be predicted.

Predicting future opportunity in a metro is difficult and risky. We look primarily at one fundamental measure—growth in small business enterprise. This is indicated by the recent formation and growth rate of small firms. We put this figure in the context of the

## Figure 3.1  Framework for Opportunity

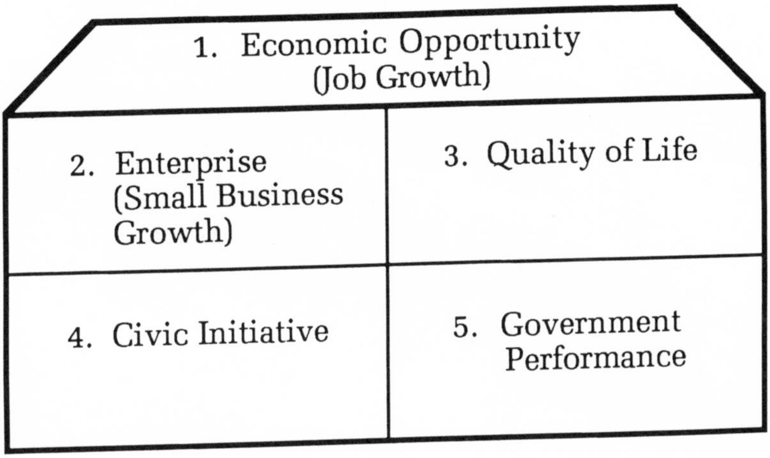

| 1.  Economic Opportunity (Job Growth) | |
|---|---|
| 2.  Enterprise (Small Business Growth) | 3.  Quality of Life |
| 4.  Civic Initiative | 5.  Government Performance |

change in overall jobs (Table 2.2) by combining this number with the two numbers for small business growth.

Overall job growth and small business enterprise constitute numbers 1 and 2 in Figure 3.1. In Chapters 4 through 6 that follow, we explore other nonjob issues, such as quality of life (number 3), government services that underpin it (number 5) and the keystone element of civic initiative (number 4)—the civic infrastructure that must be linked to effective government.

PREDICTIVE VALUE  Economists speak of indicators as being lagging, leading or coincident. A *lagging* indicator follows some other event. A thunderclap, for example, is a lagging indicator of a lightning bolt. A figure for completed new housing units is a lagging indicator of new housing permits. A *leading* indicator is one that theoretically or historically (or both) predicts the direction and extent of another indicator. Thus, a lightning bolt is a leading indicator of a thunderclap. A measure of housing permits ought to, and does, predict a measure of completed housing units some months later. Housing permits is a leading indicator of completed new housing units. An indicator of housing finance commitments might be a *coincident* indicator of new housing permits, meaning that the two move closely together.

Generally, people want the longest possible notice of something they are interested in. That is why housing permits are watched carefully—they measure the first major step of the housing construction process.

Applying this principle to the task of predicting cities of opportunity, we can see the value of a measure of enterprise and of government performance as tools for predicting the future success of a city.

Quality of life contributes to job growth and therefore *leads* it, but it is a *lagging* indicator in relation to government performance. The cultural and health facilities, low crime rates and so forth that loom large in such indicators are the result of prior periods of government actions.

Small business growth is predictive of future overall job growth and is a *leading* indicator. A measure of civic initiative such as the existence of a participatory planning program (for example, Goals for Dallas) may be a superleading indicator, superpredictive of a community's future because it is widely accepted as a fundamental feature of strong community initiative. If measures of civic initiative are still frail, they are nonetheless immeasurably important.

ENTERPRISE PREDICTS JOB OPPORTUNITY   In a sense, you can find economic opportunity anywhere. As Emerson wrote: "No great man ever complains of want of opportunity." Two shoe salesmen in a developing country wired home about their prospects. One cabled: "They don't wear shoes here. I'm coming home." The other cabled: "We have a giant untapped market to ourselves. Send help."

But it sure is easier to succeed if success is all around you. A key to reliable future prosperity is small business, since big companies may leave or falter. We like the *Inc.* magazine index of small business growth (new start-ups and proportion of young companies with high growth rates) as a measure of enterprise and therefore a predictor of future job growth.

Jane Jacobs, author of *The Death and Life of Great American Cities*, and others have written extensively on the economics of cities. Popular theories of growth include: growth by substituting for imports; growth by expanding "export" industries; growth by nurture of infant industries. But they all add up to entrepreneurship, enterprise—a significant group of people creating new businesses.

We pursue a simple theory that a city grows by attracting and

nurturing enterprising people in small and medium-size businesses. In other words, a city becomes a magnet for certain kinds of
people. As Montaigne wrote in his *Essays*: "Not only each country,
but each city has its own particular decorum." A clientele of people
favoring the decorum in each city grows up—or, more likely, many
overlapping clienteles—for the arts, for sports, for government
services, for professional services.

THE MYTH OF THE BIG COMPANY    The myth of the big company is the
idea that bigger means more secure: "Don't consider a job at a firm
employing fewer than 500 people."

In fact, that approach would rule out over half of all job prospects. Companies employing over 500 people account for only 38
percent of employment; the smaller companies employ 62 percent.

Of all new jobs in 1981–85, *88 percent* were created by enterprises with under 20 employees. Enterprises with under 100
employees created 105 percent of net new jobs; enterprises with
100 employees or more *lost* a net of 5 percent. The Fortune 500
overall reduced its work force by nearly 3 million people between
1980 and 1986. The percentage of employees being laid off (7.3
percent) is lowest among companies with under 20 employees; it is
highest among companies with 100 to 499 employees, followed by
companies with 5,000 or more employees.

A better strategy is not to rule out smaller companies. Get high
job security by developing a high level of skills and flexibility. A
first job with a large employer may be a means to an end. It should
not be thought of as a secure spot.

## The Importance of Small Business

Small business is a crucial component of a city's economy because
it is the source of future jobs. Small business (defined by the U.S.
Small Business Administration as an employer with fewer than
500 workers) has been leading in overall job growth nationally as
well. In the year ending September 1985 it grew 5.9 percent,
compared to only 0.6 percent overall for large business.

According to the Bureau of Labor Statistics, small business has
outpaced large business in construction (small business jobs grew
by 7.5 percent while large business shrank 1.8 percent); in transportation (4.7 percent versus −0.1 percent); in wholesale trade

(3.7 percent versus 2.4 percent); in retail trade (5.0 percent versus 4.5 percent); in finance (6.1 percent versus 3.2 percent); and in services (7.5 percent versus 1.7 percent). The total percentage growth for small businesses was 5.1 percent, compared with a dismal 0.7 percent for large businesses.

The ten fastest growing industries dominated by small business are, according to The State of Small Business, 1986: (1) radio, television, video and music stores, which grew 15.4 percent; (2) computer and data-processing services, 14.2 percent; (3) credit reporting and collection, 13.7 percent; (4) sanitary services, 11.5 percent; (5) masonry, stonework and plastering, 11.3 percent; (6) carpentry and housing, 11.2 percent; (7) engineering and architectural services, 10 percent; (8) real estate agents and managers, 9.9 percent; and (9) mailing, reproduction and stenographic, and (10) nonresident building construction, both of which grew at 9.2 percent.

By contrast, the ten fastest growing sectors dominated by large business are: (1) air transportation, which grew 10.1 percent; (2) accounting, auditing and bookkeeping, and (3) medical services and health insurance, 8.6 percent; (4) personnel supply services, 7.9 percent; (5) personal credit institutions, 7.8 percent; (6) miscellaneous general merchandise, 7.3 percent; (7) services to buildings, and (8) security brokers and dealers, 6.9 percent; (9) grocery stores, 5.4 percent; and (10) elementary and secondary schools, 4.8 percent. (The slowest were petroleum and coal products, which declined 8.9 percent each.)

SMALL BUSINESS FORMATION AND GROWTH   Small business formation data are generally derived from Dun & Bradstreet reports. State figures are regularly tracked—for example, in The State of Small Business, 1986. Connecticut had an increase in new incorporations from 1984 to 1985 of 38.1 percent, which gave it the number-one ranking. New York led in the actual number of new business incorporations with 72,083, but it ranked twenty-fifth in percent growth. Florida followed New York with 71,649 and was ranked eighteenth. The state that did worst, Arkansas, had fewer new incorporations in 1985 than it did in 1984.

David Birch has taken the tracking process to a higher degree of precision, identifying smaller areas than states and keeping track of individual businesses over time. He has developed two valuable measures: the ratio of significant (surviving) new small businesses to population ("birth rate") and the ratio of small businesses that expand their employment above a significant rate ("growth rate") to population.

TABLE 3.1.   ENTERPRISE: SMALL BUSINESS GROWTH, 1982–87

| | | Per 1,000 Pop. | | |
|---|---|---|---|---|
| | | Birth Rate | Growth Rate | Combined: Small Business Growth |
| 1. | Austin, Tex. | 6.8 | 4.0 | 10.8 |
| 2. | Dallas–Fort Worth, Tex. | 5.3 | 3.9 | 9.2 |
| 2. | Phoenix, Ariz. | 5.0 | 4.2 | 9.2 |
| 4. | Raleigh–Durham, N.C. | 4.6 | 4.5 | 9.1 |
| 5. | Orlando, Fla. | 4.9 | 4.0 | 8.9 |
| 6. | Atlanta, Ga. | 4.6 | 4.2 | 8.8 |
| 7. | Washington, D.C. | 4.2 | 4.4 | 8.6 |
| 8. | Nashville, Tenn. | 4.2 | 4.2 | 8.4 |
| 8. | San Diego, Calif. | 4.1 | 4.3 | 8.4 |
| 10. | El Paso, Tex. | 5.5 | 2.7 | 8.2 |
| 11. | Tucson, Ariz. | 4.3 | 3.7 | 8.0 |
| 12. | Albuquerque, N.M. | 3.7 | 4.1 | 7.8 |
| 12. | San Antonio, Tex. | 4.2 | 3.6 | 7.8 |
| 14. | Boston, Mass. | 2.8 | 4.6 | 7.4 |
| 15. | Charleston, S.C. | 4.1 | 3.2 | 7.3 |
| 15. | Baltimore, Md. | 3.4 | 3.9 | 7.3 |
| 15. | Tampa–St. Petersburg, Fla. | 3.9 | 3.4 | 7.3 |
| 18. | Greensboro, N.C. | 3.2 | 4.0 | 7.2 |
| 18. | Richmond, Va. | 3.1 | 4.1 | 7.2 |
| 20. | Norfolk, Va. | 3.7 | 3.4 | 7.1 |
| 21. | Houston, Tex. | 4.2 | 2.8 | 7.0 |
| 21. | Jacksonville, Fla. | 3.6 | 3.4 | 7.0 |
| 21. | Las Vegas, Nev. | 4.1 | 2.9 | 7.0 |
| 21. | Memphis, Tenn. | 3.2 | 3.8 | 7.0 |
| 25. | Denver, Colo. | 3.9 | 3.0 | 6.9 |
| 25. | Minneapolis–St. Paul, Minn. | 3.5 | 3.4 | 6.9 |
| 25. | Los Angeles, Calif. | 3.5 | 3.4 | 6.9 |
| 25. | Anaheim, Calif. | 3.5 | 3.4 | 6.9 |
| 29. | Charlotte–Gastonia, N.C. | 3.3 | 3.5 | 6.8 |
| 30. | San Francisco, Calif. | 2.8 | 3.9 | 6.7 |
| 30. | Columbus, Ohio | 2.9 | 3.8 | 6.7 |
| 30. | Fort Wayne, Ind. | 2.8 | 3.9 | 6.7 |
| 33. | Indianapolis, Ind. | 3.0 | 3.6 | 6.6 |
| 33. | Seattle, Wash. | 3.7 | 2.9 | 6.6 |
| 33. | Miami, Fla. | 3.8 | 2.8 | 6.6 |
| 33. | Columbia, S.C. | 3.8 | 2.8 | 6.6 |

TABLE 3.1.   ENTERPRISE: SMALL BUSINESS GROWTH, 1982–87 (continued)

| | | Per 1,000 Pop. | | |
| --- | --- | --- | --- | --- |
| | | Birth Rate | Growth Rate | Combined: Small Business Growth |
| 33. | West Palm Beach, Fla. | 3.8 | 2.8 | 6.6 |
| 38. | Bridgeport, Conn. | 2.6 | 3.9 | 6.5 |
| 39. | Wilmington, Del. | 2.7 | 3.8 | 6.5 |
| 40. | Knoxville, Tenn. | 3.6 | 2.8 | 6.4 |
| 41. | Kansas City, Kans.–Mo. | 3.2 | 3.1 | 6.3 |
| 41. | Philadelphia, Pa. | 2.5 | 3.8 | 6.3 |
| 43. | Baton Rouge, La. | 3.3 | 2.8 | 6.1 |
| 43. | Salt Lake City, Utah | 3.2 | 2.9 | 6.1 |
| 43. | Grand Rapids, Mich. | 2.8 | 3.3 | 6.1 |
| 43. | Greenville, S.C. | 3.3 | 2.8 | 6.1 |
| 43. | Lancaster, Pa. | 2.3 | 3.8 | 6.1 |
| 48. | Worcester, Mass. | 2.4 | 3.6 | 6.0 |
| 48. | Cincinnati, Ohio | 2.7 | 3.3 | 6.0 |
| 50. | New Haven, Conn. | 2.2 | 3.7 | 5.9 |
| 50. | Dayton, Ohio | 2.5 | 3.4 | 5.9 |
| 50. | Birmingham, Ala. | 3.0 | 2.9 | 5.9 |
| 53. | Detroit, Mich. | 2.6 | 3.2 | 5.8 |
| 53. | Albany, N.Y. | 2.1 | 3.7 | 5.8 |
| 53. | Lansing, Mich. | 2.5 | 3.3 | 5.8 |
| 56. | Rochester, N.Y. | 2.5 | 3.2 | 5.7 |
| 56. | Sacramento, Calif. | 2.8 | 2.9 | 5.7 |
| 56. | Omaha, Nebr. | 2.8 | 2.9 | 5.7 |
| 56. | New York, N.Y. | 2.6 | 3.1 | 5.7 |
| 56. | Wichita, Kans. | 2.7 | 3.0 | 5.7 |
| 61. | Honolulu, Hawaii | 2.5 | 3.1 | 5.6 |
| 61. | Portland, Oreg. | 2.5 | 3.1 | 5.6 |
| 61. | St. Louis, Mo. | 2.2 | 3.4 | 5.6 |
| 61. | Little Rock, Ark. | 2.7 | 2.9 | 5.6 |
| 61. | Madison, Wis. | 2.9 | 2.7 | 5.6 |
| 61. | Toledo, Ohio | 2.4 | 3.2 | 5.6 |
| 67. | Chicago, Ill. | 2.4 | 3.1 | 5.5 |
| 68. | Milwaukee, Wis. | 2.4 | 3.0 | 5.4 |
| 68. | Cleveland, Ohio | 2.2 | 3.2 | 5.4 |
| 68. | Louisville, Ky. | 2.7 | 2.7 | 5.4 |
| 71. | Chattanooga, Tenn. | 3.3 | 1.9 | 5.2 |
| 72. | Hartford, Conn. | 2.3 | 2.8 | 5.1 |
| 73. | Tulsa, Okla. | 2.8 | 2.1 | 4.9 |
| 73. | Pittsburgh, Pa. | 2.3 | 2.6 | 4.9 |
| 73. | Providence, R.I. | 1.9 | 3.0 | 4.9 |
| 76. | New Orleans, La. | 2.6 | 2.2 | 4.8 |

TABLE 3.1.   ENTERPRISE: SMALL BUSINESS GROWTH, 1982–87 (*continued*)

| | | Per 1,000 Pop. | |
| | | Birth Rate | Growth Rate | Combined: Small Business Growth |
|---|---|---|---|---|
| 77. | Youngstown, Ohio | 2.5 | 2.2 | 4.7 |
| 78. | Springfield, Mass. | 1.9 | 2.7 | 4.6 |
| 78. | Syracuse, N.Y. | 2.1 | 2.5 | 4.6 |
| 80. | Buffalo, N.Y. | 1.7 | 2.8 | 4.5 |
| 80. | Harrisburg, Pa. | 1.7 | 2.8 | 4.5 |
| 82. | Allentown, Pa. | 1.8 | 2.5 | 4.3 |
| 82. | Fresno, Calif. | 2.0 | 2.3 | 4.3 |
| 84. | Oklahoma City, Okla. | 2.6 | 1.5 | 4.1 |
| 85. | Scranton, Pa. | 1.5 | 2.4 | 3.9 |
| 86. | Des Moines, Iowa | 2.2 | 1.6 | 3.8 |

Note that Table 3.1 relates small business growth to population. A city such as Pittsburgh, which rates poorly (that is, 2.2 high-growth firms per 1,000 residents, versus 4.7 in Austin) in the 1981–85 data that served as two of the three components of the April 1987 *Inc.* metro small business activity index, has just as many high-growth firms as top-ranked Austin and Orlando. The trouble with Pittsburgh is that it is a larger metro area; the entrepreneurship is less evident because it is mixed in with a greater number of older companies.

## Overall Ranking of City Opportunity

To generate an overall picture of the cities of opportunity in the context of other large cities, the Dun & Bradstreet/Birch/*Inc.* data for 1982–87 are combined with the BLS data to provide a growth index that is two-thirds weighted toward small business formation and growth and one-third weighted toward job growth. This is essentially the approach used by *Inc.* magazine, except that since we view the BLS data as more coincident and the D&B/Birch/*Inc.* data as a leading indicator, we have not gone as far back as *Inc.* did in its 1987 "Metro Hot Spots" issue, when it made the beginning and ending dates of the three sets of numbers the same (1981–85). The results are shown in Table 3.2.

TABLE 3.2.   CITIES OF OPPORTUNITY, RANKED
(The Cities of Opportunity are in boldface)

|  | | Job Growth 1984–87 % | Small Business Growth 1982–87 (per 1,000 pop.; see Table 3.1) | Score |
|---|---|---|---|---|
| 1. | **Orlando, Fla.** | 6.9 | 8.9 | 15.8 |
| 2. | **Phoenix, Ariz.** | 4.9 | 9.2 | 14.1 |
| 3. | **San Diego, Calif.** | 5.3 | 8.4 | 13.7 |
| 4. | **Raleigh–Durham, S.C.** | 4.5 | 9.1 | 13.6 |
| 5. | **Atlanta, Ga.** | 4.3 | 8.8 | 13.1 |
| 6. | **Las Vegas, Nev.** | 6.0 | 7.0 | 13.0 |
| 7. | **West Palm Beach, Fla.** | 6.3 | 6.6 | 12.9 |
| 8. | **Austin, Tex.** | 1.9 | 10.8 | 12.7 |
| 9. | **Washington, D.C.** | 3.9 | 8.2 | 12.1 |
| 9. | **Tucson, Ariz.** | 4.1 | 8.0 | 12.1 |
| 11. | **Nashville, Tenn.** | 3.6 | 8.2 | 11.8 |
| 12. | **Jacksonville, Fla.** | 4.7 | 7.0 | 11.7 |
| 13. | Fort Wayne, Ind. | 4.7 | 6.7 | 11.4 |
| 14. | Charleston, S.C. | 3.8 | 7.3 | 11.1 |
| 14. | **Tampa–St. Petersburg, Fla.** | 3.8 | 7.3 | 11.1 |
| 16. | **Columbus, Ohio** | 4.3 | 6.7 | 11.0 |
| 17. | **Albuquerque, N.M.** | 3.1 | 7.8 | 10.9 |
| 18. | **El Paso, Tex.** | 2.5 | 8.2 | 10.7 |
| 18. | **Sacramento, Calif.** | 5.0 | 5.7 | 10.7 |
| 18. | **Seattle, Wash.** | 4.1 | 6.6 | 10.7 |
| 21. | Norfolk, Va. | 3.5 | 7.1 | 10.6 |
| 22. | Richmond, Va. | 3.3 | 7.2 | 10.5 |
| 23. | **Charlotte–Gastonia, N.C.** | 3.6 | 6.8 | 10.4 |
| 23. | **Indianapolis, Ind.** | 3.8 | 6.6 | 10.4 |
| 25. | **Cincinnati, Ohio** | 4.2 | 6.0 | 10.2 |
| 26. | **Dallas–Fort Worth, Tex.** | 0.8 | 9.2 | 10.0 |
| 27. | **San Antonio, Tex.** | 2.1 | 7.8 | 9.9 |
| 28. | **Memphis, Tenn.** | 2.8 | 7.0 | 9.8 |
| 29. | **Greensboro, N.C.** | 2.5 | 7.2 | 9.7 |
| 29. | Wilmington, Del. | 3.2 | 6.5 | 9.7 |
| 31. | **Boston, Mass.** | 2.1 | 7.4 | 9.5 |
| 32. | **Anaheim, Calif.** | 4.7 | 4.7 | 9.4 |
| 32. | Columbia, S.C. | 2.8 | 6.6 | 9.4 |
| 32. | **Los Angeles, Calif.** | 2.5 | 6.9 | 9.4 |
| 32. | Worcester, Mass. | 3.4 | 6.0 | 9.4 |
| 36. | **Baltimore, Md.** | 3.2 | 6.1 | 9.3 |
| 36. | Lancaster, Pa. | 3.2 | 6.1 | 9.3 |
| 38. | Birmingham, Ala. | 3.1 | 5.9 | 9.0 |
| 38. | Bridgeport, Conn. | 2.5 | 6.5 | 9.0 |

TABLE 3.2. CITIES OF OPPORTUNITY, RANKED (*continued*)
(The Cities of Opportunity are in boldface)

| | | Job Growth 1984–87 % | Small Business Growth 1982–87 (per 1,000 pop.; see Table 3.1) | Score |
|---|---|---|---|---|
| 38. | **Philadelphia, Pa.** | 2.7 | 6.3 | 9.0 |
| 38. | Toledo, Ohio | 3.4 | 5.6 | 9.0 |
| 38. | **Minneapolis–St. Paul, Minn.** | 2.1 | 6.9 | 9.0 |
| 43. | Dayton, Ohio | 3.0 | 5.9 | 8.9 |
| 43. | **Detroit, Mich.** | 3.1 | 5.8 | 8.9 |
| 43. | Greenville, S.C. | 2.8 | 6.1 | 8.9 |
| 43. | Lansing, Mich. | 2.8 | 6.6 | 8.9 |
| 47. | **Hartford, Conn.** | 3.5 | 5.1 | 8.6 |
| 47. | Honolulu, Hawaii | 3.0 | 5.6 | 8.6 |
| 49. | Albany, N.Y. | 3.0 | 5.6 | 8.5 |
| 49. | Grand Rapids, Mich. | 2.4 | 6.1 | 8.5 |
| 49. | Madison, Wis. | 2.9 | 5.6 | 8.5 |
| 49. | **Miami, Fla.** | 1.9 | 6.6 | 8.5 |
| 49. | New Haven, Conn. | 2.6 | 5.9 | 8.5 |
| 49. | **Salt Lake City, Utah** | 2.4 | 6.1 | 8.5 |
| 55. | Portland, Oreg. | 2.7 | 5.6 | 8.3 |
| 56. | Louisville, Ky. | 2.3 | 5.7 | 8.0 |
| 56. | Wichita, Kans. | 2.3 | 5.7 | 8.0 |
| 58. | **San Francisco, Calif.** | 1.1 | 6.7 | 7.8 |
| 59. | **Kansas City, Kans.–Mo.** | 1.3 | 6.3 | 7.6 |
| 59. | Knoxville, Tenn. | 1.2 | 6.4 | 7.6 |
| 59. | Little Rock, Ark. | 2.0 | 5.6 | 7.6 |
| 62. | Harrisburg, Pa. | 2.9 | 4.5 | 7.4 |
| 63. | Chattanooga, Tenn. | 2.1 | 5.2 | 7.3 |
| 64. | **Chicago, Ill.** | 1.7 | 5.5 | 7.2 |
| 64. | **New York, N.Y.** | 1.5 | 5.7 | 7.2 |
| 64. | Omaha, Nebr. | 1.5 | 5.7 | 7.2 |
| 64. | **Providence, R.I.** | 2.3 | 4.9 | 7.2 |
| 68. | Cleveland, Ohio | 1.7 | 5.4 | 7.1 |
| 68. | Springfield, Mass. | 2.5 | 4.6 | 7.1 |
| 70. | Rochester, N.Y. | 1.3 | 5.7 | 7.0 |
| 70. | St. Louis, Mo. | 1.4 | 5.6 | 7.0 |
| 72. | Milwaukee, Wis. | 1.4 | 5.4 | 6.8 |
| 72. | Youngstown, Ohio | 2.1 | 4.7 | 6.8 |
| 74. | Syracuse, N.Y. | 2.0 | 4.6 | 6.6 |
| 75. | Buffalo, N.Y. | 2.0 | 4.5 | 6.5 |
| 76. | Fresno, Calif. | 2.1 | 4.3 | 6.4 |
| 77. | **Denver, Colo.** | −0.6 | 6.9 | 6.3 |
| 78. | Des Moines, Iowa | 2.4 | 3.8 | 6.2 |

TABLE 3.2.   CITIES OF OPPORTUNITY, RANKED (continued)
(The Cities of Opportunity are in boldface)

| | Job Growth 1984–87 % | Small Business Growth 1982–87 (per 1,000 pop.; see Table 3.1) | Score |
|---|---|---|---|
| 79. Allentown, Pa. | 1.3 | 4.5 | 5.8 |
| 80. Baton Rouge, La. | −0.4 | 6.1 | 5.7 |
| 81. Scranton, Pa. | 1.6 | 3.9 | 5.5 |
| 82. Pittsburgh, Pa. | 0.4 | 4.9 | 5.3 |
| 83. **Houston, Tex.** | −2.5 | 7.0 | 4.5 |
| 83. Tulsa, Okla. | −0.4 | 4.9 | 4.5 |
| 85. New Orleans, La. | −1.4 | 4.8 | 3.4 |
| 86. Oklahoma City, Okla. | −1.8 | 3.8 | 2.0 |

Of the eighty-six metros, forty-two are identified as cities of opportunity. They include all of the top twelve on the list and all but two of the top twenty. The excluded cities tend to be smaller; our thinking was that smaller cities are less diversified and lack some of the amenities to be reviewed in Chapter 4. On the other end of the table, we have included only two of the bottom nineteen on the list; these two were picked because we believe that the oil/ energy downturn responsible for their decline is temporary and that enterprise is strong enough in the two cities to find new avenues for job creation.

Besides using Birch's data and BLS figures, we did our own survey of experts in government and regional economic activity. A sample of the results follows.

FUTURE INDUSTRY GROWTH   We asked questionnaire respondents which of the fastest-growing industries they thought would continue to be strong. They responded essentially that communications and biotechnology would become much more important, while computers and health care would continue their rapid growth. See Table 3.3 for a summary of their answers. The first column shows the ranking of actual 1986–87 growth rates in each industry. The second column shows the ranking produced by averaging predictions of the expert panel as to the near-term growth of each industry. Finally, the third column shows the average scores themselves (out of a possible maximum of 10).

TABLE 3.3. FUTURE INDUSTRY GROWTH (EXPERT SURVEY)

| Industry | 1986–87 Growth Rank, Actual | Predicted Future Rank | Score/10 |
|---|---|---|---|
| Communications | 12 | 1 | 8.32 |
| Biotechnology | 11 | 2 | 8.00 |
| Computer/Data Processing | 2 | 2 | 8.00 |
| Health Services | 4 | 4 | 7.89 |
| Financial Services | 6 | 5 | 7.53 |
| Entertainment (A/V) | 1 | 6 | 7.32 |
| Sanitary Services (Waste) | 4 | 7 | 6.68 |
| Real Estate | 8 | 8 | 6.26 |
| Engineering/Architectural | 7 | 9 | 6.05 |
| Credit Reporting/Collection | 3 | 10 | 5.74 |
| Manufacturing | 9 | 11 | 4.68 |
| Heavy Industries | 10 | 12 | 3.83 |

PREDICTED SURPRISES   The idea may seem oxymoronic (if a city is *expected* to do well, how can it be a surprise if the city *does* well?). We asked respondents to pit themselves against conventional wisdom and tell us which of the top eighty metros will surprise us with their economic strength.

One city stood out above all the others (see Table 3.4). Out of a maximum possible score of 100, Indianapolis got 30, named by over half the respondents. The other cities mentioned by more than one respondent are Boston (17 out of 100); Chicago (15); Baltimore (14); Memphis, Pittsburgh and Sacramento (12 each); Raleigh-Durham and Seattle (10); Nashville and New York (9); Cleveland (8); Greensboro, Milwaukee, San Francisco and Atlanta (7); San Diego (6). Scores below 6 are not shown.

TABLE 3.4. PREDICTED SURPRISES (EXPERT SURVEY)

1. Indianapolis (30)
2. Boston (17)
3. Chicago (15)
4. Memphis
4. Pittsburgh
4. Sacramento (12)
7. Raleigh–Durham
7. Seattle (10)
9. Nashville
9. New York City (9)

TABLE 3.4.   PREDICTED SURPRISES (EXPERT SURVEY) (continued)

11. Cleveland (8)
12. Atlanta
12. Greensboro
12. Milwaukee
12. San Francisco (7)
16. San Diego (6)

## Summing Up

Future metro jobs depend on today's small business enterprise. Measuring the formation and growth of small businesses provides a basis for predicting the future economic prospects of metros. However, we don't rely on this measure exclusively, because we believe some cities are suffering from temporary setbacks and have excellent prospects over a ten-year time span.

# 4

# QUALITY-OF-LIFE CONSIDERATIONS
## QUALITY OF SERVICES AND CIVIC
## INFRASTRUCTURE

Bob had another thought. "What's it going to be like living out there? What kind of life-style will we have to adapt to? I'm not strong on eating barbecued beef outside every day."

"Look, I've been thinking about some of the same kinds of things," Carmen replied. "More basic things, if you want to know. Like, will I be able to find day care, a·place where I will feel comfortable leaving a child? We are just going to have to find out, that's all."

Besides visiting a community, Bob and Carmen can glean some answers to their life-style questions by perusing various numbers relating to the quality of life provided for each metro area in Chapter 7. There Carmen will also find the leads she is seeking on day-care availability.

Quality-of-life data are provided by chamber of commerce brochures, convention and visitors bureau handouts, and relocation fact sheets. What officials and local newspapers care to measure reveals their values—what they consider important. Local communities will always find something to brag about. The poorest community can highlight its spiritual qualities, its low cost of living, availability of services. A community with polluted air and water can focus on its strong economy. A community with unemployment will emphasize its unharried pace, clean air, lack of congestion.

Community indicators are nothing new. The Bible abounds with measures of relative strength (numbers of soldiers) and prosperity (numbers of sheep, cattle, slaves, units of treasure). The Greek historians made constant comparisons of the different city-states, using such measures as size of armies, numbers of ships, games won, treasures amassed and beautiful structures built.

Today, these numbers by which a community is measured have come to be called quality-of-life indicators, defined by the U.S. government as "statistics of direct normative interest" (that is, numbers that implicitly reflect values) that "facilitate concise, comprehensive and balanced judgment about the condition of major aspects of a society."

A "social index" is a combination of several such indicators, and certain types of combinations are legitimate and meaningful. But an "overall quality-of-life indicator," such as Rand McNally has been producing for American cities, invalidly combines several social indices into one single number for each city. Quality of life is in the eye of the beholder, and collapsing a variety of social indices into a single figure is too subjective to be meaningful.

Thus, an opera lover might feel a prisoner anywhere outside the major cities that have regular opera programs. On the other hand, a nature lover might feel a prisoner in the opera-rich cities because of the long travel time to open space.

## Measuring Quality of Life

The effort to measure the quality of life has a distinguished history. In the nineteenth century, Herbert Spencer, best known for popularizing theories of evolution and inventing the term *survival of the fittest*, worked with three friends, all bachelors like him, to develop a comparative measure of the quality of life in England and New Zealand (and possibly other countries). England won in literature, science, music and art, and was given three extra points for "accessibility to the Continent."

Spencer's group eventually voted: New Zealand 301, England 110. They awarded New Zealand 40 points for healthfulness, 35 for the naturalness of local occupations and 20 for climate—plus 100 points for the likelihood of marriage. One of the four did emigrate and died in a boat accident soon after landing in New Zealand.

In 1931, journalist H. L. Mencken proudly confessed to be on the trail of the worst, as appears to be true of some journalists today. In his magazine *The American Mercury* he and C. Angoff surveyed data to determine "the worst American state." They applied 106 indicators into five social indices for each state. While clearly seeking to entertain, the authors did a remarkable scholarly job of assembling the data. Their conclusions were admirably couched in caveats and apologies that less careful successors would do well to reread.

Some of the indicators Mencken and Angoff used could no longer be used today. Example: compliance with Prohibition laws (guess which way the indicator was used!). Other factors that we would expect to see used today, such as air quality, were not yet recognized as social problems. They used the homicide rate as an indicator—a good measure, but probably not as good for most purposes today as the robbery rate.

Later scholars have gone to smaller and smaller units of study. State analysis was preferred to national because states play more of a role in providing services than the national government. But states in turn became viewed as poor territorial units by which to observe social well-being, since one or two large cities may influence the average for each state. Comparisons among cities (or metro areas) are most useful, because by and large city residents fight the same traffic, ride the same buses, face the same crime, drink the same water and breathe the same air. State averages mask local realities.

## The Livability/Opportunity Paradox

Quality-of-life indicators and economic indicators often work together. A good quality of life attracts good employees. However, a paradox also occurs. A city that ranks high on crude measures of livability may well rank poorly on economic opportunity. Cities with a long history and with strong unions may have a solid physical and cultural infrastructure and high incomes, all of which adds to their quality of life. But the same factors that appeal to employees may make communities unattractive to entrepreneurs seeking a place to establish a business.

New Orleans, for example, has great history and culture but has been cursed by having had a relatively easy life. Herodotus said of Athens that its poor farmland forced its people to become hustling traders. Conversely, Adam Smith explained the decline of Spain by the easy living its people had from mining gold. Mississippi River trade just floated down to New Orleans and the city's people became rich with very little effort. When competition came from the canals and the railroads, New Orleans was too laid-back to act quickly. It has a legacy of unique traditions and facilities, but a weak entrepreneurial group compared to other cities.

Allentown, Buffalo, Cleveland, Detroit, Pittsburgh, St. Louis and Youngstown exemplify the same problem. They had been doing so well from their auto, steel and heavy manufacturing industries that they failed to act quickly to modernize their operations in the face of foreign competition. Only the severe drop in the dollar is putting them back on their feet.

It is no accident that fast-growing communities have quality-of-life problems. Older cities in decline actually have two advantages: (1) with time they have built up many of the amenities that rate highly in quality-of-life surveys, while (2) suspension of much of their industrial output is a last-resort (in the absence of modernization and addition of pollution-control equipment) way to clean up the local air and water. The true environmental test of heavy-industry towns will be how they handle the new low-dollar expansion.

### Growth Potential

We can identify three groups of cities. First, for reasons we have seen, some cities may have a good quality of life but have modest internally generated (from enterprise) job growth potential, like New Orleans, Pittsburgh and St. Louis. Second, some cities like Portland and San Francisco have great growth potential that residents wish to control for quality-of-life considerations. Portland has gone through a period of seeking to control the influx of new migrants, while San Franciscans are trying to prevent further building of skyscrapers ("Manhattanization"). Third, some cities are both livable and experience growth. A prime example is Boston, though its economy is vulnerable to possible cutbacks in "Star Wars" and other defense contracts.

Fourth, some cities are suffering from the drop in oil and other energy prices—Austin, Dallas, Denver and Houston—and are vigorously fighting off recession. They have collected large numbers of entrepreneurs who are actively working on turning their cities around. While the turnaround will be rapid if oil and other energy prices rise dramatically, enough is going on in these cities that on a ten-year cycle they can be expected to turn around even if oil prices do not soar. The reasons for optimism are the high level of local enterprise and the attitudes of business people in these cities—no one is just waiting for higher oil prices; people are intelligently finding new things to do.

## Government Performance

Quality of life is related to government performance, one of the two underground elements of the Framework for Opportunity in Figure 3.1 on page 25. Many of the things that make people proud of their community have to do with their government. Julius Caesar counted troops and bounty; presumably for Romans these facts added to the quality of their life. Similarly, St. Paul, on a different level, counted converts in each city.

In the Middle Ages, when church and state were intertwined, people willingly contributed to the construction of large churches. At the same time, as cities increasingly competed for trade, governments sought to give their traders an edge. So the United States was discovered by chance because the queen of Spain financed an Italian explorer to seek out new trade routes.

Government performance has been studied intensively by people such as Herbert Simon (before he went into the managerial research that won him a Nobel Prize). Government can improve the quality of a community's life. But it can't control some things, like the weather; it's hard for Atlanta to compete with Denver for accessibility of skiing, or for Phoenix to compete with San Diego for surfing (although a Phoenix company is trying, with an artificial surf-maker). Even the quality of services depends on factors not always under short-term control of government—education, for example, depends crucially on parent cooperation. For those seeking to contribute to the well-being of their communities (that is, those who want to fight rather than switch—the flowers as opposed to the butterflies), what can be changed is a crucial area of focus. Government services are a key focus for civic activity, and the purpose of concentrating on service delivery measures is that these can become a motivating factor for improvement of services over time.

Examples of key services commonly looked at for comparing communities with one another or over time: education, housing, transportation, safety and health care. Taxes are also commonly measured to indicate the cost of providing services. Over time some indicators have come to be looked at as "bellwether" measures. For example, in the public safety arena, the crime of robbery is such a measure because it is both a crime of violence (provoking fear for one's life) and a crime of property (providing a motive for stranger-to-stranger crime); other crimes of violence (rape, murder, assault) are less likely to occur among total strangers.

Edward Chandler has shown in *The Visible Hand* how improvements in accounting were essential preconditions, and stimuli, for modern business management techniques. These techniques became firmly established in manufacturing entities before they did in service operations. Government operations—a subset of the services industry—seem slowest to adapt fully to the techniques. The eminent management consultant Peter Drucker has said that the need for government to so adapt is the greatest management challenge for the remainder of this century.

## Civic Initiative

Finally, we come to the remaining one of the five elements of the framework shown in Figure 3.1, civic initiative (labeled 4). Quality of life depends ultimately on developing a strong civic community to help maintain a balance between *development* (private enterprise) and *amenities* (culture, infrastructure, parks). Some of the older cities are at an advantage here, because they usually have strong civic communities. The civic infrastructure plays the same role in ensuring good government that an entrepreneurial infrastructure plays in ensuring economic growth.

Civic initiative backs up government performance and helps build a better quality of life. The civic sector must maintain its independence from government because the civic community can create effective government but government cannot create an effective citizenry.

A city with a weak civic community cannot plan collectively for its future and will be more likely to be surprised down the road by destructive intergroup warfare. After all, Detroit won the job of being the headquarters of the auto industry because it had an aggressive Chamber of Commerce years ago that sold the auto entrepreneurs on locating there. The cities with a strong infrastructure today are going to get the jobs of tomorrow.

**MEASURES OF CIVIC INITIATIVE** We can best consider measures of civic initiative by examining the results of its absence—the picture of urban decay resulting from poor government planning and services and a related failure of job growth to keep pace with population growth. (See Figure 4.1.)

By contrast, a city deservedly proud is one that has built up a good quality of life—based on a government that performs in delivering services and healthy job growth, backed up by civic initiative and healthy job growth based on small business enterprise. See Figure 4.2 for a picture of Civic Pride, showing ten components of civic initiative.

## Figure 4.1  Urban Decay

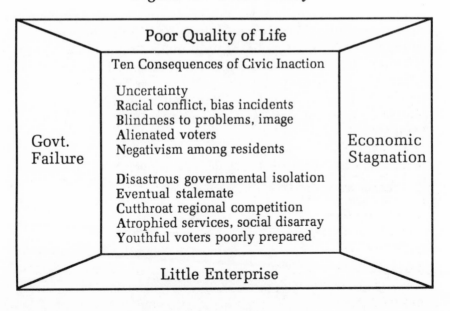

Poor Quality of Life

Ten Consequences of Civic Inaction

Uncertainty
Racial conflict, bias incidents
Blindness to problems, image
Alienated voters
Negativism among residents

Disastrous governmental isolation
Eventual stalemate
Cutthroat regional competition
Atrophied services, social disarray
Youthful voters poorly prepared

Govt. Failure

Economic Stagnation

Little Enterprise

## Figure 4.2  Civic Pride

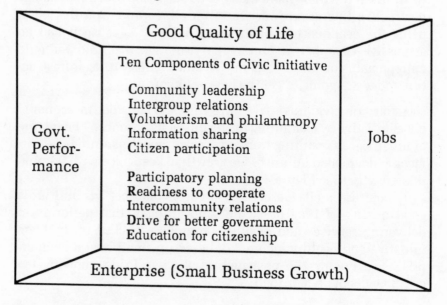

Good Quality of Life

Ten Components of Civic Initiative

Community leadership
Intergroup relations
Volunteerism and philanthropy
Information sharing
Citizen participation

Participatory planning
Readiness to cooperate
Intercommunity relations
Drive for better government
Education for citizenship

Govt. Performance

Jobs

Enterprise (Small Business Growth)

## Survey Results

In our expert survey we asked respondents to rate the eighty largest metros on their civic infrastructure. On this measure, the winning city is Minneapolis–St. Paul, with a score of 35, nearly half the maximum possible score of 75. Atlanta is second (24), Indianapolis third (20). The others with a score over 5: San Francisco (17); Boston, Dallas–Fort Worth, Baltimore (13 each); Seattle (12); Pittsburgh (9); and Houston and San Diego (8 each). (See Table 4.1.)

TABLE 4.1.  STRONGEST CIVIC INFRASTRUCTURE (EXPERT SURVEY)

1. Minneapolis–St. Paul (35 out of max. possible 75)
2. Atlanta (24)
3. Indianapolis (20)
4. San Francisco (17)
5. Baltimore
5. Boston
5. Dallas (13)
8. Seattle (12)
9. Pittsburgh (9)
10. Houston, San Diego (8)

## Neighborhoods/Communities

Just as each city has a clientele, each *neighborhood* within a city has a clientele searching for a particular quality of life in relation to cost. We make an effort to describe key neighborhoods and their characteristics for each city. In a 600-square-mile city such as Houston, people say they identify more with the distinct community they live in than with downtown, which may be an hour's drive away. In a more compact city such as New York, someone's strongest identity may be the apartment complex, one of 10,000 block associations or one of the nearly sixty community boards.

"Neighborhoods" in a metro area may mean separately incorporated cities, as we will discuss when we get to individual cities in Chapter 7. (Someone in Las Vegas responded to our question about neighborhoods by suggesting that "neighborhoods" has a suspiciously East Coast smell to it in a part of the world where you may want to take out the car to drop by and see your next-door neighbor.)

## Summing Up

Quality of life has to be an important factor in a relocation decision. But no one can rely on someone else's weighting of such factors. Consider which ones are most important to you, and check them out. Don't neglect an important factor, such as the quality of civic initiative, even though it may be hard to measure.

# 5

# BECOMING BETTER OFF
## CHANGING CAREERS, TOO

"When you figure in all the costs of pulling up stakes in one place and hammering them in somewhere else, I wonder whether we will really be better off," Bob said glumly.

"I'm not sure," replied Carmen. "Let's go through the figures."

This chapter is about the economic reasons for a move. Will it actually improve the standard of living you have been accustomed to, or live up to your expectations?

**Personal Reasons**

Before looking at the economic consideration, we hasten to say that few people move exclusively to improve their living standards. The predisposition to move may follow from personal considerations—divorce, for example. When no children are involved (or sometimes because they are involved), it could make sense for one of two partners to move out of town and seek a new social environment free from unpleasant past associations. Another reason might be health—a person's doctor may suggest a more healthful climate. Elderly people who retire to Florida argue that their life expectancy is considerably longer in the warmer climate.

Whatever the initial motivation, economic factors will commonly soon come into play, because the person who decides to move to another city will presumably have to make a living in the new location, and job availability must be explored. The considerations for someone not reliant on a job are almost inverse—communities with higher unemployment and lower incomes permit a fixed income to buy more goods and services.

## Individual Economic Needs

Individuals often move primarily to improve their economic situation. The frontier caravans heading west were motivated by the incentive of free land, gold or oil strikes, or just by the lure of better-paying jobs.

Today, the prospects for free land are not what they were, but land prices vary so much across the country that a Kentucky farm may look almost free to a cabin-fevered New York corporate lawyer with a craving for the rural life, and by extension a home in a middle-size city looks cheap compared to one in a major metro area.

Metals and energy prospecting have been institutionalized and concentrated to the point that the potential for individuals isn't what it was, either.

The real economic bases for moving are three: (1) to be exposed to the best in a profession (whether it be law, medicine, publishing, communications, the arts), regardless of short-term income, to improve one's *lifetime* earning potential or perform at one's personal best, or both; (2) to increase one's salary relative to the cost of living, either by increasing one's income or reducing one's costs, or both; or (3) to move to a location that is growing rapidly in order to maximize the potential for one's small business or sales incentive arrangements.

## Switching Careers

The predisposition to move may also imply a predisposition to change careers. The shift of locale can be accompanied by a change in career. David Birch has attempted to determine what career changes are likely to be beneficial. He assumes certain aptitudes and skills based on the existing job of a potential career-switcher, and then ties them to likely new jobs for the would-be switcher (and the training costs for potential new jobs).

Some people, he

concludes, can only suffer salary-wise from a switch—doctors and lawyers, for example.

If we define *more than adequately paid jobs* as ones that would cost their holders $3,000 or more a year to leave, the following types of jobholders are best advised not to switch: scientists, physicians, technicians ("other"), lawyers, managers/administrative ("other"), sales/insurance/real estate, craft/supervisors, craft/public utilities.

Similarly, if *adequately paid jobs* are ones that would not benefit their holders to leave (they can't do better by switching), the following jobholders should think twice before planning a change, though they might not suffer greatly by a switch: engineers, medical workers, computer specialists, writers/artists, professional workers ("other"), public administrators, sales ("other"), craft/construction, craft/metalwork, craft/mechanics, operatives/metal, operatives ("other"), operatives/transportation, services/protective.

However, those in *underpaid jobs* should think seriously about a change. They can do better by $1,000 to $2,999 a year: science technicians, registered nurses, teachers (secondary, college, adult, other), accountants, secretaries, clerical, craft/auto mechanics, crafts ("other"), services/building management, laborers/helpers. Renewed national interest in the importance of education may raise teacher salaries. Teachers may in any case value the contribution they make to America's youth too much to switch. Three other reasons for remaining a teacher: (1) June, (2) July, and (3) August.

Those in *extremely underpaid jobs* need to ask themselves seriously why they are stuck and whether they can't escape from jobs when they apparently can improve their salaries by $3,000 or more a year just by switching jobs: practical nurses, social scientists, managers of food and lodging establishments, sales clerks, secretaries, office computer operators, services (food, health, personal).

SERVICES (THE McDONALD'S MYTH)   A myth to worry about is that white-collar service jobs are the only way to go and that service jobs are to be avoided—that one shouldn't work for McDonald's because it has only dead-end jobs.

The fact is, it depends on your age, education and experience. White-collar jobs indeed continue to grow and are projected to increase from 52.2 percent of all jobs in 1980 to 54.9 percent in

1995. By contrast, blue-collar jobs (which grew temporarily to 40 percent in World War II) continue trending downward, from 31.7 percent to 26.3 percent (as does agriculture).

But services are growing even faster than white-collar jobs, continuing their steady uptrend from 13.3 to 16.1 percent (a larger percentage point increase from a much smaller base) of the labor force. Helpers or "extenders" (substitutes) for high-paid lawyers, doctors, dentists, computer experts and other executives under pressure of health-care and legal cost containment are all in great demand. The Bureau of Labor Statistics predicts the fastest growing occupations between 1986 and 2000, ranked by percent growth (new jobs in parentheses): paralegal, 104 percent (64,000); medical assistants, 90 percent (119,000); physical therapists, 88 percent (83,000); physical and corrective therapy assistants, 82 percent (29,000); data-processing equipment repairers, 80 percent (56,000); home health aides, 80 percent (111,000); podiatrists, 77 percent (10,000); computer systems analysts, 76 percent (251,000); medical records technicians, 75 percent (30,000); employment interviewers, 71 percent (54,000); computer programmers, 70 percent (335,000); radiology technicians, 65 percent (75,000); dental hygienists, 63 percent (54,000); dental assistants, 57 percent (88,000); physician assistants, 57 percent (15,000); operations and systems researchers, 54 percent (21,000); occupational therapists, 52 percent (15,000); operators of peripheral data-processing equipment, 51 percent (24,000); data entry keyers, 51 percent (24,000); optometrists, 49 percent (18,000).

So the best strategy is: If you are early in your career, don't rule out getting a start in a service job. Someone who has been a gas station attendant or franchise worker for a while is more liable to make a good impression, and reap useful management insights, than someone who has never had a finger dirtied. Consider a service-type job as a bridge to something in management. McDonald's may be an excellent first job for many people (don't stay too long if you don't get promoted!), and in any case most service jobs aren't dead-end fast-food functions. Look at paramedical, paralegal and computer services. You don't have to go through long years of training to garner some of the high salaries in these fields. The training may be surprisingly brief or inexpensive, and may be paid for by an employer.

THE MANUFACTURING-IS-DEAD MYTH   Because manufacturing has been on the decline in major metros for the past few decades, it is viewed as a dead-end industry. Not necessarily so. It depends.

It is true that Birch predicts only about 17 percent of private nonagricultural jobs will be in manufacturing by 1995, versus 8 percent in finance, insurance and real estate. But the falling dollar is rescuing many firms that were on the ropes. We have already mentioned that Bethlehem Steel went from being the stock market's worst performer in 1986 to being its best performer in 1987.

Birch identifies a group of "trend buckers"—traditional manufacturing firms that have managed to stay competitive. Now, with the drop in the U.S. dollar (not to mention creation of U.S. subsidiaries of Japanese manufacturers), the outlook for trend buckers is even more promising. Birch may well have overestimated finance and underestimated manufacturing; the BLS prediction of at least 20 percent manufacturing, less than 7 percent F.I.R.E. (finance, insurance, real estate) seems more probable in early 1988 than Birch's forecast.

The better strategy, instead of ruling out manufacturing, is to figure out what events a firm's success would depend on, and then evaluate the likelihood of these events. Look for job opportunities in pockets of activity, regardless of broad category.

THE HIGH-TECH MYTH   Another prevalent myth is: "High-tech is where the jobs are. It's the only place to be."

In fact, high-tech accounts for only 2.8 percent of all jobs, according to the BLS definition—computers, communications equipment, electronic components, drugs, radio and television-receiving equipment, aircraft, measuring and controlling devices, medical instruments. It has accounted for only one in eight new jobs in the U.S. economy in the last twenty years and one-quarter of Inc. magazine's fastest growing companies. Innovation is more than high-tech. It means creating a new function or replacing an existing function more efficiently; the innovation is to do this with a new device or procedure, or rearrange or assemble an existing device or procedure. The other six high-innovation sectors Birch identifies are: (1) information-age group—information processing such as Federal Express, computer software services; (2) trend buckers, contrarians—Florida Steel; (3) leisure-time group—travel services (airlines, charters), sporting goods; (4) energy group—oil and gas and coal; (5) baby boom/Yuppie/women-in-the-labor-force group—home entertainment, restaurants, natural foods, Ben & Jerry's Ice Cream, colleges and universities, women's business clothing, etc.; (6) aging group—health care, travel.

A better strategy is to look for innovative firms generally, not just high-tech firms.

## Business Needs

Small business owners often move to areas where supply of workers is better, costs are lower or sales opportunities are stronger. A move may simply be to expand.

The most common reason of all for moving—particularly for people in their thirties and forties—is that their company moves them, either from headquarters to a branch, from one branch to another, or from a branch to headquarters.

CORPORATE REASSIGNMENT Corporations often ask key employees to move to the field because it strengthens management's understanding of its business for senior executives to have been in the field environment and because it is helpful for people who have been at headquarters to be available for branch staff. They also routinely promote branch managers to headquarters positions.

Increasingly, however, corporations have run into employee resistance to reassignment. One approach to this situation is to invoke navy standards, making it very clear that outright refusal by an employee to move may mean the end of an employee's prospects for promotion. Another common corporate approach is to invoke the carrot as well as the stick, piling on the benefits and offering an employee a choice of locations, especially when the employee's spouse is working.

McGraw-Hill has one of the best employee-relocation services in the country. It has to, since it moves 250 to 300 employees per year, more than one person every working day. The man who handles the whole operation is quite appropriately a former traffic management officer for the U.S. military, Nathan S. Dwarica.

In his job he helps individuals who are being reassigned find new housing, and he arranges for the move, operating as realtor-advisor, insurance advisor and appraiser. Most moves are within the United States, among the company's 200 branches. McGraw-

Hill has very specific, detailed relocation policies. Every possible concern that may arise during relocation is addressed. Everyone is helped by the plan equally with no preferred treatment for anyone.

"People are relocated by the company on the basis of their job," says Dwarica. "The company decides whether the employee is promotable and can do the job in a different environment. The prime age group is forty to fifty; second is twenty-five to thirty-five. Median salary for those being moved is about $60,000—clerical staff is almost never moved (replacements are hired locally). Then a cost package is assembled that has to be approved by the company. Costs include the closing costs for sale of the employee's residence, closing costs for purchase of a new residence, transportation of personal belongings, temporary living quarters, and sometimes mortgage-assistance loans."

McGraw-Hill lends approximately $1 million a year from a revolving fund to its relocating employees. The average cost passed on to McGraw-Hill from the relocation is about $35,000 for a homeowning transferee and would be higher if prudent cost control procedures were not exercised.

We asked Dwarica what companies he deals with, since this might be useful for someone else without his experience approaching the task of moving.

"One of the things we have to do is buy the employee's house. We want to do this through a third party, so that an objective price can be established. We use Coldwell Banker, a relocation company."

We asked: "What about the actual moving?" "We use Reliable/International Van Lines, based in Elizabeth, New Jersey. They are a subsidiary of Allied Van Lines. They can handle a move anywhere in the world."

"Insurance?" "For homeowner insurance, we use Barood Agency, based in New Brunswick, New Jersey. They shop around different insurance companies to find the best deal. For the insurance to cover the actual move, inland marine insurance, we use Hartford Insurance."

## Who Should Move?

"Don't move," Dwarica says, "if you suffer from mental strain of any kind or have a child who does—moving will add to the pressures." Moving out of a region is harder on older people; and younger people, while more mobile, tend to want to move in only one direction, toward larger cities. This may not be the best way to go for everyone.

"People moving to New York City must consider whether they are going to earn enough to afford the expensive life-style and real estate," Dwarica warns. He thinks a minimum family income of $80,000 a year is needed for a family to live comfortably in the Big Apple metro. Prospective transferees don't want to hear this; most of them are initially attracted to a New York move because it usually means a promotion. Yet they must face up to the fact that they will probably have to settle for a reduced life-style even on a higher income, whether it be a cramped apartment in Manhattan and private school tuition, or a pitifully overpriced house with so-so schools in the near suburbs, or a costly house and long commute from the greener suburbs. Dwarica labels this life-style sacrifice as "the cost of promotion."

## Corporate Relocation

An employee can turn down a reassignment request and get away with it, but what if the company itself moves? In that case, it may well be a choice between following the company or leaving it.

To facilitate thinking about the likelihood of a company's moving, it may help to know how corporations decide where they will locate. Usually they call in a consultant, even when executives have a pretty good idea of where they want to move. The reason is that a consultant is widely viewed as being more dispassionate and analytical about a move, and his or her recommendation is therefore used to shift the focus of attention from emotional issues to economic ones.

A consultant typically starts by reviewing the client company's activities to see what the potential cost savings might be from a move to several possible locations, and what the main labor, transportation and other requirements would be. The client's preferences regarding a new location are also identified.

RATIONALE FOR CORPORATE MOVES  If the potential cost savings look promising and other requirements are met, the corporate client may decide that a move is desirable. Then the consultant zeroes in on specific sites—buildings being offered for rent or sale—and tries to determine which ones would best meet the client's preferences at the lowest cost.

The better known relocation consultants will look at dozens of variables relating to different sites, mostly costs and subdivisions of costs (different types of labor, different types of other costs). As many as 400 numbers may be generated for a site, although no one in the business pretends that more than a few will be decisive. As few as 3 numbers may make the difference in determining the final site.

A large company has fewer options than a smaller one because of its need for large numbers of workers. But smaller companies have their own special needs—for readily accessible ancillary services. A large company must be near a large, quality labor pool, but it can be on the outskirts of a metro area—the option selected by Mobil (outskirts of Washington, D.C.) and J. C. Penney (Plano, Texas, an outer suburb of Dallas)—gaining access to the metro labor pool without the cost of downtown real estate and traffic. This option is less viable for many kinds of small businesses that require the accessibility to support services only found downtown or in a city-size suburb.

Displaced employees tend to be cynical about the reasons for a move, and argue that the crucial variable is the distance between the site and the chief executive's home or hometown.

Among site requirements, the local environment or quality of life is quite important since most companies need a faithful few to continue working for them. They need to provide a good quality of life if they are to keep these people. Public schools, for example, are important for getting good people to work for the company at its new location.

Costs are an important reason to move, especially now that labor costs for service and high-tech businesses are looming larger. Besides labor costs, a company must pay special attention to infrastructure and livability in the new place.

The downside risk is misplacement—not accurately evaluating the business environment or moving to a location that is undesirable to those essential for the company's welfare. Whole operations can be crippled if crucial people decide not to go to the new location.

IMPORTANCE OF LABOR QUALITY   In preparing this book we spoke with many urbanologist colleagues. Those in the relocation area have stressed the importance of labor quality as an increasingly important concern of corporate managers.

We visited two officers—C. Ford Harding and Gene DePrez—of the Fantus Company, a national relocation firm headquartered in quiet, suburban Millburn, N.J. They said that in recent years corporations have been primarily interested in relative costs for personnel, in order to save on labor costs. Their next most important considerations are local quality of life and availability of talent (either local or recruitable).

But to put this corporate interest in perspective, they identify three kinds of functions that account for the vast majority of corporate moves:

1. Manufacturing plants. Primary corporate concerns about a new location are adequate labor, low taxes, utilities and real estate costs.
2. Administrative offices. Primary corporate concerns: quality and cost of labor, and availability of support services.
3. Control center, regional offices. Primary corporate concern: ability to reach out regionally (must be in a major metro area that serves as a regional center).

The Fantus officers say they are seeing signs that corporations are becoming more concerned about quality of labor and less concerned about its cost. Jobs are becoming more skilled as automated factories require alert staff while permitting higher compensation. The costs of employee error in such plants are high, and the significance of employee salaries is becoming relatively less important as transportation costs soar.

We also called on Karen Gerard (formerly an economist with the Chase Manhattan Bank and then New York City Deputy Mayor for Economic Development) at the New York City–based relocation consulting firm of Moran, Stahl and Boyer, and her remarks tended in the same direction.

She cites five major factor groupings in relocation analysis:

1. Business economics (cost savings).
2. Organizational impact—what will happen to the organization after a move.

3. Business environment of the new location.
4. Livability of the new location.
5. The business and economic base of the new location.

Companies grow after relocation, she says, because of factors relating to the location, not because the company by itself lures people to the new spot. For example, she says Boston's Route 128 firms prospered because they located near a pool of high-quality employees, not because any one firm moved such employees to the area. The bottom line for a company contemplating relocation is: Labor quality in a city is of utmost importance.

For an individual planning a move, this means: Think about the labor quality of the place you are planning to go to. You are safer in the long run to be one of many competent people in the work force, just another little fish in a large lake, rather than a big fish in a little pond—the danger of the pond is that it could dry up!

## Summing Up

An individual must consider an entire package to determine if he or she will be better off after a move, whether the move is from one city to another or from one job to another, or (quite possibly) both at the same time. In making relocation decisions, companies must face the same concerns as individuals, with the same goal of economic and quality-of-life improvement. Increasingly, corporations are looking for quality labor—they are chasing good workers as much as workers are seeking good employers!

# 6

## YOUR BEST MOVE
### WOMEN, MINORITIES, TIME-OF-LIFE FACTORS

"**Do** you want to know what's really bothering me?" Carmen asked Bob. "I'm wondering if men take women seriously as professionals out there. Not to mention the fact that English is my second language."

"Maybe you will be treated *better*," Bob offered.

This chapter is about certain special kinds of problems faced by individuals contemplating a move. What's the social environment? Will special noneconomic considerations—such as a higher degree of racial, religious or ethnic pressure—make the city unpleasant to live in? Will it be hard for a woman to advance in the city?

These are reasonable fears. Cities take on a clientele of their own. Birds of a feather flock together. A heavy-industry town, for example, takes on certain characteristics simply because of the way its companies are organized. Heavy industry is highly centralized, with clear hierarchies, and the employee pool tends to be heavily male and unionized. So labor unions are relatively strong and management is relatively macho in a heavy industry town.

Such a community is likely to be less attractive than others to small entrepreneurs, who would pick among several communities of comparable size the one with the lowest prevailing labor rates. Similarly, a relatively macho management style is likely to be less appealing to women professionals seeking employment. Surveys cited in this chapter will show that these *a priori* hypotheses are borne out by the experiences of women in these cities.

In sum, how much opportunity a city presents to an individual depends on the kind of person he or she is and the type of work he or she is seeking. As in other areas, some types of work make more sense to seek than others.


## Best Cities for Women

Women as a rule find it harder to get senior management positions in heavy industry compared to other types of work. Companies in the heavy industry sector tend to be more male oriented in their hiring and promotion practices. By extension, cities dependent on heavy industry for many jobs are not as attractive to women as those where it is less important. Combine with this fact the previously mentioned problem of heavy-industry towns for small business—that union-driven high wages keep labor costs too high for entrepreneurs—and a picture that what's bad for women is also bad for small business emerges.

Judging from a 1985 survey by *Savvy* magazine and our own opinion survey, women are still ducks out of water in communities that have historically depended on heavy industry for much of their economy. The macho legacy creates a work environment that can often prove uncomfortable for women.

*Savvy* asks: "Do you still hear the terms 'honey' and 'little lady'?" Why put up with it, the magazine continues, "when you could enjoy the stimulating, encouraging climate of an Atlanta or a Denver?"

The two best cities for women in 1985, according to *Savvy*, were New York and Los Angeles, perhaps reflecting the importance of publishing and entertainment, fields where barriers to women have fallen long ago, in these two cities. In the next tier were San Francisco; Washington, D.C.; Chicago; Atlanta; and Minneapolis–Saint Paul. The third tier ("honorable mention") were Anchorage; Austin; Tampa; Denver; Stamford, Connecticut; and Portland, Maine.

The worst cities for women, according to *Savvy*, were New

Orleans, Cincinnati, Tulsa, Birmingham, Indianapolis and Buffalo. Cities that were changing for the better: Houston, Nashville, Burlington (Vermont, where the article's writer is based), Columbus and Pittsburgh. (An update of *Savvy's* report is scheduled for its September 1988 issue.)

We asked our expert panel both whether a city would be good economically for women and whether it would be good socially. On the economic side, New York City and Washington, D.C., were considered the most promising, followed by San Francisco and Boston (see Table 6.1).

TABLE 6.1. BEST CITIES FOR WOMEN, ECONOMICALLY (EXPERT SURVEY)

1. New York City, Washington, D.C. (40 each out of possible 75)
3. San Francisco (26)
4. Boston (22)
5. Chicago (19)
6. Atlanta (13)
7. Denver, Los Angeles (6)

A study by the Council on Economic Priorities, released in late 1987, ranked these brand-name consumer companies as top employers of women (in our metro areas): (1) *New York* area: Merck (Rahway, N.J.), Avon, Xerox (Stamford, Conn.), IBM (Armonk, N.Y.), Exxon, Pfizer; (2) *Philadelphia* area: Campbell Soup (Camden, N.J.); (3) *Boston* area: Digital Equipment (Maynard, Mass.), Polaroid; (4) *Wilmington:* Dupont; (5) *Milwaukee–Racine:* Johnson Wax (Racine); (6) *Los Angeles:* Arco; (7) *Oakland:* Clorox; (8) *Detroit:* Ford, GM, Kellogg; (9) *Minneapolis:* General Mills, Pillsbury; (10) *Cincinnati:* Procter & Gamble; (11) *Chicago:* Quaker Oats, Sara Lee. Note that no southern-based cities are included.

Going back to our expert survey, the top four cities for women on the social side were the same as for the economic rating except for Minneapolis–Saint Paul, which came in fifth (see Table 6.2).

TABLE 6.2. BEST CITIES FOR WOMEN, SOCIALLY (EXPERT SURVEY)

1. New York, San Francisco, Washington, D.C. (12 each)
4. Boston (10)
5. Minneapolis–Saint Paul (4)

## Best Cities for Blacks

Cities with black mayors and large black populations are more likely to have stores, restaurants and clubs that cater to the needs of black executives and their families. The best cities for blacks economically were viewed as Atlanta; New York; Washington, D.C.; Chicago and Detroit, four of which had black mayors at the time of the survey; the other, New York, had a black borough president. (See Table 6.3.)

TABLE 6.3.   BEST CITIES FOR BLACKS, ECONOMICALLY (EXPERT SURVEY)

1. Atlanta (45 out of possible 70)
2. New York and Washington, D.C. (31 each)
4. Chicago (21)
5. Detroit (17)
6. Los Angeles (14)
7. San Francisco (12)
8. Milwaukee (7)
9. Baltimore (6)

Another way of looking at the question is to review how many black-owned small businesses are in each city relative to the black population. On this measure, using 1982 business data and 1980 population data, figures for black businesses per 1,000 black population show California at the top, the Northeast cities mostly at the bottom.

TABLE 6.4.   BLACK BUSINESS POPULATION

| Metro Area | Black Businesses per 100,000 Pop. |
| --- | --- |
| Los Angeles | 24.9 |
| San Francisco | 24.0 |
| Houston | 23.1 |
| Washington, D.C. | 22.0 |
| San Diego | 19.4 |
| Dallas | 18.7 |
| Atlanta | 16.6 |
| Columbus, Ohio | 16.1 |
| Indianapolis | 16.0 |
| Raleigh–Durham | 15.2 |

The best cities for blacks socially showed some changes from the economic list. Atlanta was at the top again, but New York dropped out (it has never had a black mayor) and Los Angeles moved up behind Washington and ahead of Detroit. All four cities have black mayors. (See Table 6.5.)

TABLE 6.5.   BEST CITIES FOR BLACKS, SOCIALLY (EXPERT SURVEY)

1. Atlanta (27 out of possible 36)
2. Washington, D.C. (11)
3. Los Angeles (6)
4. Detroit (5)

## Best Cities for Asians

For Asians, our panel rates the West Coast at the top socially (San Francisco, Los Angeles, Seattle), along with New York. Again, as with blacks, the experts' view relates to the availability of Asian cuisine, recreational facilities, religious institutions and so forth on the West Coast and in New York.

TABLE 6.6.   BEST CITIES FOR ASIANS, SOCIALLY (EXPERT SURVEY)

1. San Francisco (28 out of possible 39)
2. Los Angeles (17)
3. New York, Seattle (5 each)

## Best Cities for Hispanics

Hispanics will account for one-fifth to one-half of U.S. population growth in the next twenty-five years. The Hispanic presence will become increasingly evident in the large U.S. cities. Our panel concludes that the best cities for Hispanics, economically, are those in which a large proportion of Hispanics already reside: Los Angeles, San Antonio, Miami, New York. Two of the four have Hispanic mayors. These cities have many Hispanic-run and -owned businesses where the language of management is Spanish or is bilingual. That improves the odds that an employee for whom Spanish is the mother tongue will be able to advance in the organization. (See Table 6.7.)

TABLE 6.7.   BEST CITIES FOR HISPANICS, ECONOMICALLY (EXPERT SURVEY)

1. Los Angeles (40 out of possible 70)
2. San Antonio (38)
3. Miami (34)
4. New York (15)
5. San Francisco (14)
6. Houston, San Diego (9 each)
8. El Paso (7)


For formation of Hispanic businesses, Miami is the best area overall, with 42.9 Hispanic businesses per 1,000 Hispanics (1982 data). New York and Chicago are the worst with 8.2 and 7.9 respectively (out of forty-one major metros). After Miami: Tampa (33.8); Washington, D.C. (25.2); Houston (21.8); San Francisco (21.7); San Antonio (21.5); Austin (20.5); El Paso (20.2); Anaheim (18.6); Albuquerque (18.3); Sacramento (18.2).

On the social side, our expert panel views the best cities for Hispanics as those where Hispanics have already established a large presence: Los Angeles, Miami, San Antonio. (See Table 6.8.)

TABLE 6.8.   BEST CITIES FOR HISPANICS, SOCIALLY (EXPERT SURVEY)

1. Los Angeles, Miami, San Antonio (15 each out of possible 39)
4. El Paso (7)
5. New York (6)


## Best Cities for Singles

No attempt was made to determine whether any cities were especially promising for singles economically. However, we did ask whether certain cities were better socially. The same four cities that ranked best for women socially and economically were considered the best socially for singles: San Francisco, New York, Boston and Washington, D.C. (See Table 6.9.)

TABLE 6.9.   BEST CITIES FOR SINGLES, SOCIALLY (EXPERT SURVEY)

1. San Francisco (14)
2. New York (13)
3. Boston (6)
4. Washington, D.C. (4)

## Best Cities for Young Marrieds

The best community for young marrieds is likely to be similar to that for singles. The life-style of young marrieds doesn't necessarily change a great deal from that of young unmarrieds until they have their first baby. As the time to raise children approaches, young marrieds need to start shifting their focus to the next category—parents with young children.

PARENTS WITH YOUNG CHILDREN   Commuting time is a key factor for parents of young children, along with the quality of school systems and the availability of child care. Suburban residential living commonly offers good quality public schools and lawns to mow. Of the 13 million American households with incomes of over $50,000 in 1985, 61 percent opted to live in suburban communities—40 percent in metro areas of over 1 million and 21 percent in metro areas of under 1 million. (Of the remaining 39 percent of such households, 17 percent live downtown in metro areas over 1 million, 11 percent downtown in metro areas under 1 million and 11 percent outside of metro areas.)

However, suburban living usually requires a relatively long, commonly unpleasant and uncomfortable daily commute, which takes time away from family or work, or both. It may also pose a child-care problem (where are the people in suburban communities who want to do this work inexpensively?).

Not that all suburban communities are rich, either. While 1985 per capita income in Kenilworth, outside of Chicago, was $49,000, it was only $5,000 to $6,000 in Ford Heights and Robbins, two other Chicago suburban communities.

Central-city living cuts down the commuting time and provides a variety of child-care options, but is commonly associated with poor schools, necessitating costly private school tuition. The bigger the city, the starker the contrast between inner city and suburban public schools.

One way some people have their cake and eat it too is to live and work in the suburbs. But skeptics wonder whether large companies that move their head offices to suburban or even exurban locations can maintain their dynamism. A study by William H. Whyte, author of *The Organization Man*, of companies that left

New York shows that a disproportionate number were subsequently swallowed up by other companies.

## Best Cities for People over Fifty

People over fifty, with children commonly grown up, in college or independent, are back in the singles phase, but this time with an eye to the final stage of retirement. People in this age group should beware of the myth of retirement as a job creator—the belief that in a place (company, city) where a lot of people are nearing retirement, many jobs will open up lower down.

The fact is, less than 3 percent of jobs open up through death or retirement. Most open up through the job-creating power of new firms. Many jobs die with their holders because their functions have become obsolescent; no one is ready to take their place because the demand isn't there. The real need is for innovation-based workers with the flexibility to be retrained at a moment's notice.

A better strategy: (1) For an individual, focus on remaining flexible in the job market. Learn broad skills and areas of knowledge that won't get out of date. (2) For government (federal, state, local), encourage individuals to remain flexible by providing tax advantages for creating an Individual Training Account—a vested fund to be used like an IRA account, but for training rather than retirement—as Pat Choate, author of *Retooling the American Workforce*, has suggested.

## Best Cities for Retirees

This book is not meant primarily for retirees. Some of the factors that make a community desirable for a young career person make it undesirable for a retiree—high incomes, for example, are good for a worker, because salaries are by and large more important than intercity differences in the cost of living. However, high income levels are bad for someone on a fixed income, because services are more expensive to buy. High unemployment is bad for a job-seeker, good for someone seeking service workers.

At age sixty-five, 14 percent of all Americans move. The figure is higher for better-educated, higher-income people (of those earning more than $50,000 a year, 24 percent move). The largest single motivation for moving is a better climate—45 percent move for that reason.

On the other hand, a key factor (studies show) in determining the happiness of grandparents is whether or not they live near their grandchildren. Of those who move at age sixty-five, 22 percent do so to be closer to relatives. So tension is likely to persist in the future for grandparents seeking low-cost, healthful retirement living and wanting to be near their grandchildren.

## Regional Opportunities

The United States is uniquely resilient because it has both a high degree of entrepreneurship, in contrast to most of Europe, and a high degree of self-generated innovation, in contrast to most of Asia. In the decade ending 1997, the United States is predicted to grow to 95 million private sector jobs (up 15.7 percent).

But where in the United States should one move to? The answer is that opportunities exist in every region of the country. Differences within regions are more significant than differences among regions. Prospering Minneapolis differs more economically from its struggling Minnesota neighbor Duluth than from a healthy city in the West, South or East.

A few years ago, people were urged to despair of the Northeast and migrate to the Sunbelt. A myth was afoot that the Northeast was dead, that the Sunbelt was where America's future lay, and the eastern unemployed should start walking west.

In fact, between 1982 and 1985, the West and Plains states together created only 2.2 million jobs. Meanwhile, the South created 2.9 million jobs and the Northeast-Midwest 3 million jobs. Predicted growth (assuming no widespread water shortages, which would favor the North): South, 41 percent; Northeast-Midwest, 31 percent; West and Plains, 28 percent. These predictions were made before the major drop in oil prices that has hurt the South and the drop in the dollar that has benefited the industrial North-Midwest. A better strategy is not to take a regional position at all but to look for *pockets* of growth; above all, don't write off the Northeast or Midwest.

EXPERTS DISPUTE THE REGIONAL APPROACH   Our expert relocation contacts endorsed this conclusion. At Fantus they said the "hot"

metro areas among relocation consultants (in August 1987) were
Atlanta, Greenville–Spartanburg, the North Carolina metro areas,
Tampa, northern New Jersey and New England. They stressed that
some cities may price themselves out of the market.

The word from Moran, Stahl and Boyer is that the popular places
are California, the South and Southwest, but that the future will be
less determined by regions as smaller areas within regions assume
more importance. For example, sections of the Northeast are doing
better than entire other regions.

Our contact recommended as cities of opportunity some
"sleepers"—cities not currently flourishing but with all the necessary amenities to thrive: Wilmington, Delaware; Louisville, Kentucky; and Providence, Rhode Island. Of these three, we have
included Providence.

McGraw-Hill's relocation expert feels the hot areas for relocating
are Houston, which he believes will come back within the next
three to five years; Washington, D.C., because of its importance as
our capital; and California. He's also very positive about the southeastern city of Atlanta as well as the North Carolina metro areas.
The Southwest, he says, really just gets the overflow from Texas.

NEW ENGLAND (including Boston, Massachusetts; Providence,
Rhode Island; Hartford, Connecticut—three cities of opportunity).

Salaries have been rising and unemployment has dropped to the
point where labor shortages in some areas have been serious. This
is good for employees, especially new entrants with strong technical skills, but is bad for employers, who don't have needed skills
available, and isn't so great for the region in the longer term.

The other major concern is that the region is highly dependent
on military spending. An arms control agreement, especially one
that cuts down on spending for "Star Wars" (the Strategic Defense
Initiative), would call in the Faustian bargain that the Boston area
and several Connecticut cities have made with the defense
spenders.

Providence is benefiting from the prosperity of its neighbors and
its relatively higher availability of labor.

MIDDLE ATLANTIC (New York—one city of opportunity)

Samuel M. Ehrenhalt, regional commissioner of the Bureau of
Labor Statistics, has long warned about the vulnerability of the
New York economy to a downturn in the stock market, as manufac-

turing jobs have dropped out in favor of financial services jobs. His warnings were borne out by the aftermath of Black Monday, October 19, 1987. Nonetheless, New York still offers unique opportunities for people wishing to start careers in finance, law, accounting, communications, fashion, dance and music.

MIDDLE WEST (North Central: Chicago, Illinois; Cincinnati and Columbus, Ohio; Minneapolis–Saint Paul, Minnesota; Detroit, Michigan; Indianapolis, Indiana; and Kansas City, Missouri–Kansas—seven cities of opportunity)

Manufacturing employment is improving, but with use of robots and computerization of factory processes, fewer people are being hired. Employers are finding labor costs less significant than transportation and are looking for more skilled people than in the past. With new emphasis by the federal government on containing health-care costs, this industry is a weaker employer than in the past. Education will be a strong employer for the next few years in cities like Chicago. The setback for the financial services industry will be felt in Chicago as well as New York.

SOUTHEAST (South Atlantic and East South Central: Baltimore, Maryland; Washington, D.C.; Atlanta, Georgia; Memphis and Nashville, Tennessee; Charlotte, Greensboro and Raleigh–Durham, North Carolina; and Jacksonville, Tampa–St. Petersburg, Miami, Orlando and West Palm Beach, Florida—thirteen cities of opportunity)

This region has been moving away from manufacturing, toward provision of services. The extractive industry in Louisiana is depressed, as it is in Texas and Oklahoma. Textile manufacturers have seen their fortunes improve recently, after having been hard hit by foreign competition.

SOUTHWEST (South Central: Austin, Dallas, Houston, El Paso and San Antonio, Texas; Albuquerque, New Mexico—six cities of opportunity)

The drop in oil prices caused a similarly precipitous drop in real estate prices in Texas. Austin's prices were still declining as of the fourth quarter of 1987. Dallas–Fort Worth is helped by the wholesale/distribution role played by Fort Worth and the greater diversification of the Dallas economy compared to Houston. Albuquerque has been adding distribution jobs.

MOUNTAIN STATES   (Denver, Colorado; Salt Lake City, Utah; Las Vegas, Nevada—three cities of opportunity)

Denver is suffering from overbuilding, with high vacancy rates. A bright spot in Denver is expansion of employment at the airport. Salt Lake City is benefiting from growth in the state in the areas of food processing, metals and aerospace. Las Vegas is growing rapidly as the glitter of the Strip continues to draw.

FAR WEST   (Anaheim, Los Angeles, San Francisco, San Diego and Sacramento, California; Phoenix and Tucson, Arizona—seven cities of opportunity)

With shakeouts and increasing competitiveness in the computer industry, Silicon Valley has become more of a known quantity, with less in the way of blue-sky expectations. Los Angeles is benefiting from aerospace contracts, and demand for secretaries is especially strong (other job categories showing strength are paralegals, systems analysts and cable installers, according to the state's Economic Development Department). Phoenix and Tucson are in a building slump, as developers wait for existing vacancies to be filled.

NORTHWEST   (Pacific: Seattle, Washington—one city of opportunity)

As Boeing's employment moves up, Seattle prospers. Technically trained people are also in demand for environmental consultants and waste management companies.


## Summing Up

A move must take into account differences in receptiveness that different groups of people face in different cities. Mormons, for example, are likely to be more at home in Salt Lake City than in Boston. Based on a survey of experts and on published data, women get along best in three entertainment-based cities—Los Angeles, New York and Washington—and least well in cities that have relied on heavy manufacturing or oil for a large part of their employment. Blacks are best off in a city where blacks have achieved high elective office. Asians are likely to adapt most quickly in the two largest Pacific cities, Los Angeles and San Francisco. The top three cities for Hispanics are Los Angeles, San Antonio and Miami. Looking at the country regionally, stars burn brightly or fade in every sector—the important factor is not the region but the type of industry on which the metro depends.

# 7

## THE CITIES OF OPPORTUNITY

This long chapter provides information on each of the cities of opportunity, in alphabetical order. For each city, the following information is provided:

METRO STATISTICAL AREA (MSA) POPULATION. A CMSA (Consolidated Metro Statistical Area) is a very large agglomeration of two or more cities that would themselves be large enough to form a metro area. A PMSA (Primary Metro Statistical Area) is one of the metro areas in a CMSA. (From Census Bureau)

POPULATION GROWTH, 1980–86. Total growth in population over six years. (From Census Bureau)

COUNTY in which metro area is located.

EMPLOYMENT, MSA or PMSA, 9/87. (From Bureau of Labor Statistics) (see Table 2.)

AVERAGE TEMPERATURE in degrees Fahrenheit.

YEARLY RAINFALL in inches.

HUMIDITY (average) in percentage.

COST OF LIVING; 100 = U.S. average. (From American Chamber of Commerce Research Association.)

## KEYS TO THE CITY

**Small Business Growth:** Sum of (1) birth rate ratio of small business formation to population, and (2) growth rate ratio of high-growth small businesses to population. (3) Index: sum of birth rate and growth rate (rate out of 86 metro areas): derived from D&B/Birch/Inc. data, 1982–87 (Table 3.1).

**Average annual job growth (9/84–9/87):** Overall metro job growth, 1984–87 (September to September). Rank of metro area out of the largest 100 metro areas (based on total jobs) is provided in parentheses and is taken from Table 2.2.

**Keys to Prosperity:** Pivotal industries and forces impacting on them.

**Key Developments:** New buildings, other real estate developments, major metro projects or positive events.

**Key Life-Style Trends:** What people do—recreational options unique to the metro area.

## WHY OPPORTUNITY KNOCKS

Why the city is in the book—opportunities for employment, forecasts of growth areas, historical background where relevant.

## QUALITY OF LIFE

**Weather:** Temperature, rainfall, snowfall, regional climatic aberrations.

**Education:** Primary, secondary, vocational, university.

**Neighborhoods:** What kinds of people are attracted to what parts of the city?

**Politics/Government:** How is the metro area run? What are the local points of controversy?

**Transportation:** How hard is it to get around? How expensive? How convenient?

**Health Care:** Local hospitals, clinics, hospices, special programs.

**Child Care:** Where to find a nurturing facility or caregiver for children.

**Housing:** Cost and prevalence of local housing.

**Public Safety:** Robberies per 100,000 city residents.

**Cultural Attractions:** Museums, performing arts, festivals.

**Sports/Recreation:** Spectator, participatory and family sports. Parks.

**Taxes:** State and local tax burden.

## WHERE TO BREAK IN

Major employers, product/service, number of employees.

## SUMMING UP: OPPORTUNITY FOR WHOM?

What types of people will find this metro area a satisfying place to live, professionally and domestically?

# Albuquerque, New Mexico

MSA POPULATION (7/86): 474,400 (75th largest)
POPULATION GROWTH 1980–86: 12.9%
COUNTY: Bernalillo
EMPLOYMENT (9/87): 233,800
AVERAGE TEMPERATURE: 56.8°F
YEARLY RAINFALL: 7.77 inches
HUMIDITY: 28% (39th most humid)
COST OF LIVING: 103.1

## KEYS TO THE CITY

**Small Business Growth:** birth rate, growth rate, growth index (rank/86):  3.7  4.1  7.8  (12th)

**Average Annual Job Growth (9/84–9/87):** 3.1% (34th/largest 100)

**Keys to Prosperity:** Defense spending (SDI and air force base), high-tech industry. The city offers many opportunities to science professionals (especially atomic physicists), since the federal government shows few signs of withdrawing from the strategic arms race. Companies interested in defense contracts have followed the bomb researchers and continue to create employment opportunities in Albuquerque. However, defense spending is peaking.

**Key Developments:** New industrial parks, development of the city's West Side, planned City Performing Arts Center and expansion of city convention center.

**Key Life-Style Trends:** Albuquerque's association with "the Bomb" dates back to the Los Alamos lab north of the city (its location was a secret for a long time; mail went to an Albuquerque post office box) and the Trinity testing site to the south. Both locations are immortalized in the city's National Atomic Museum. The city offers ample sun and outdoor recreation but is short on the kind of cultural attractions offered by older, larger cities.

72

## WHY OPPORTUNITY KNOCKS IN ALBUQUERQUE

Founded in 1706 as an outpost of the then expansive Spanish empire, Albuquerque is the population and business center of New Mexico. Nestled between the Rio Grande River and the Sandia Mountains, Albuquerque became, in the 1880s, a trade and transportation center and was admitted to the Union in 1912. In the 1940s, Albuquerque's proximity to the Los Alamos A-bomb facilities and the Trinity testing site put the city on the map and triggered a growth spurt that continues to this day and shows few signs of abating.

Albuquerque is expanding so rapidly that the Greater Albuquerque Chamber of Commerce claims to see a new business starting up every day and a new office building going up every week. Most of the new jobs are created through the expanding high-tech industry, and high-tech business is among the top employers in the Albuquerque metro area. Expansion is so important to Albuquerque that in January 1987 Governor Garrey Carruthers declared that his first priority would be business growth.

Albuquerque's West Side has flourished and grown so much that there is a great deal of public interest in making it a city in itself. Irvine, California, is a good example of a city that grew in this way. A recent Coldwell Banker report also supports this view that the prime area for expansion in the entire region is Albuquerque's West Side. Rio Rancho, a large residential development, reported 22.3 percent growth from 1970 to 1980, and that momentum has continued into the 1980s. Along with the population growth, the area's infrastructure has expanded to the point that many people begin to think that the West Side could become an independent city.

Low tax rates have attracted many companies that were interested in reducing costs. Also, the availability of venture capital has encouraged new small business growth in Albuquerque. Albuquerque now has approximately 10,000 small businesses. According to *The State of Small Business, 1986*, small business is far outstripping large business in terms of percentage job growth.

Many large businesses have been drawn by the availability of the modern facilities of the new industrial and research parks, as well as the vast human and technical resources made available by the cooperation of the University of New Mexico and the Center of Technical Excellence and Technological Innovation. Albuquerque has long received substantial federal money for the building and testing of weapons. U.S. Senator Bingaman of New Mexico has announced that the Defense Department is currently asking for $54 million in federal aid to build a new weapons depot in the Manzano Mountains near Albuquerque. This facility will also be used for future Strategic Defense Initiative (SDI) and Kirtland Air Force Base programs, and will lead to more government money pouring into the area to fund greater educational programs.

## QUALITY OF LIFE

**Weather:** In the 1920s, Albuquerque enjoyed economic growth based principally on its dry, warm, pleasant climate, especially attractive to people recovering from respiratory diseases. Although tuberculosis is not now epidemic, Albuquerque—and, indeed, most of New Mexico—continues to be popular among fans of warm sunshine and low humidity. Albuquerque experiences hot summer weather, with 90° F days the norm during the months of July and August. Winters are cold, too, with approximately three months worth of freezing days, but snowfall is light, averaging ten inches per year.

**Education:** Albuquerque has good educational facilities. The University of New Mexico is its largest institution, serving over 24,000 students. Other universities and colleges such as the University of Albuquerque, Parks College and Albuquerque Technical-Vocational Institute are very business and technology oriented and do their part to provide workers for the ever-growing industries. Master's degrees in business administration are very popular for an area that had its largest job growth in corporation managers and officers. There are ten libraries in the city; Albuquerque Public Library is the largest branch, with more than 400,000 volumes. Bernalillo County, of which Albuquerque is the seat, has a public school enrollment of approximately 73,000 students and a pupil/teacher ratio of 18.5 to 1; an ongoing effort to improve the quality of public education has succeeded in increasing the number of public school teachers.

**Neighborhoods:** Albuquerque is a city of neighborhoods, with over 150 neighborhood associations, some organized in the 1920s. Neighborhood coalitions regularly provide input to city government on land use and planning issues. The character of neighbor-hoods varies from Old Town, which has existed since the 1700s, to rural agricultural areas and suburban communities. Historic Route 66, which passes through Albuquerque, is currently the site of many redevelopment projects and prosperous revitalization efforts. Upscale neighborhoods include Glenwood Hills (north-east) and Four Hills (southeast), while established working-class communities include Academy Acres and Paradise Hills (both northeast). Taylor Ranch, located in the northwest portion of the city, is a moderate- to upper-middle-income neighborhood. The South Valley is an unspoiled rural area, just outside the city limits, that's noted for the generous spacing of its residences, many with provision for horses.

**Politics/Government:** Since 1974 Albuquerque has operated with a mayor-council form of government, with a full-time mayor and a nine-member, part-time districted city council. The mayor is elected by the citizens at large, while the council members are elected by their constituent districts.

The mayor is designated as the head of city government, but the extent of the mayor's authority is prescribed by the city charter. The council is the official legislative arm of government and is respon-sible for passage of all policy decisions. The mayor is responsible for day-to-day operations of the city and also has veto power over council-passed bills. As Albuquerque strives to outfit itself with all the trappings of a first-class city—performing arts facilities, museums—the city administration finds itself finessing projects through the city council, countering the objections of the socially conscious.

**Transportation:** Albuquerque is already beginning to feel the strain of rapid economic and population growth: the city's two interstate highways are daily choked with heavy commuter traffic. The pressure of downtown traffic is alleviated by municipal bus-ing. Travel to points outside the city is accomplished through Greyhound and Trailways service, Amtrak (which supplies two departures daily) and the Albuquerque International Airport (which is served by sixteen airlines, providing a total of 120 flights a day).

**Health Care:** In addition to Albuquerque's ten general medical and surgical hospitals, the city is served by four psychiatric hospitals and several medical centers with fifty or more physicians with established practices.

**Child Care:** Working parents in need of day care should consult their employers first, but the Children's Center (505-881-9565) can offer solutions to parents.

**Housing:** Subject to frequent fluctuation and currently soft, the Albuquerque housing market has most recently generated the following averages: condos, $68,515 (two bedrooms, two bathrooms); houses, $90,000 (three bedrooms, two bathrooms); apartments, $400 to $450 (per month, two bedrooms, two bathrooms).

**Public Safety:** Compared to many of the cities in our study, Albuquerque is relatively safe, registering 1,248 robberies in 1986, equivalent to 343 robberies per 100,000 of population.

**Cultural Attractions:** Albuquerque has six museums, including the National Atomic Museum, the city's recently built Museum of Natural History, the Ballooning Museum and the Albuquerque Museum, which concentrates on city history. In addition, there are many small art galleries, especially in Old Town. A City Performing Arts Center is in its earliest planning stages, but it's controversial because it's considered by some an extravagance in the face of pressing social issues.

**Sports/Recreation:** Fans of spectator sports will have to content themselves with minor-league baseball, the Albuquerque Dukes, and horseracing at Albuquerque Downs. Participants, however, have a variety of options: golf, hunting, fishing, swimming, tennis, skiing, skating and bowling. Greater Albuquerque (Sandoval, Bernalillo and Valencia counties) has 159 public parks, 257 tennis courts, thirteen golf courses and seventeen public swimming pools.

**Taxes:** Residential property within incorporated Albuquerque is assessed at one-third of market value and taxed at a rate of $52.416 for each $1,000. New Mexico has a graduated state income tax, but Albuquerque levies no tax on income; the effective sales tax is 5.25 percent.

## WHERE TO BREAK IN

For individuals interested in relocating to the Albuquerque area, we recommend contacting alumni and intrafield professional or trade organizations. Here is a partial list of the area's largest employers. For more information, call the Albuquerque Chamber of Commerce at 505-764-3700.

| Firm/Organization | Product/Service | No. Employees |
|---|---|---|
| Albuquerque Public Schools | education | 7,400 |
| Kirtland Air Force Base (civilian) | government | 7,100 |
| Sandia National Laboratories | research and development | 6,963 |
| Kirtland Air Force Base (military) | government | 5,226 |
| University of New Mexico | education | 5,000 |
| City of Albuquerque | government | 4,200 |
| State of New Mexico | government | 3,908 |
| Southwest Community Health Services | general medical and surgical hospital | 2,936 |
| Mountain Bell | telephone utility | 2,106 |
| Lovelace Medical Center | general medical and surgical hospital | 1,920 |
| Sperry Aerospace & Marine Group | research/engineering | 1,850 |
| Public Service Company of New Mexico | electric utility | 1,663 |
| General Electric | jet engine component mfg. | 1,500 |
| University of New Mexico Hospital | teaching hospital | 1,432 |
| U.S. Post Office | government | 1,367 |
| Sunwest Bank | banking | 1,203 |
| Veterans Administration Hospital | health care | 1,120 |
| Digital Equipment Corp. | computers | 1,000 |
| GTE Communications | telecommunications | 800 |

The largest employers are government, retail and wholesale trade, and education and the service fields. Unemployment is approximately 8 percent, down from the 9 percent of 1986. Monthly unemployment is anywhere from 18,000 to 21,000 people. Significant growth has occurred in eating and drinking establishments, retail, business services, health services, recreation, and electronics.

## SUMMING UP: OPPORTUNITY FOR WHOM?

By 1995 Albuquerque is expected to add approximately 50,000 jobs to its present employment figure of 227,900. By then, the number of women in the work force will exceed the number of men, and the largest segment of the work force will be between the ages of twenty-nine and forty. The most common job openings in the Albuquerque area are currently for corporate managers and officers, for whom 1,800 positions open annually. The strength of Albuquerque's retail, services and construction sectors should help generate additional employment opportunities in the finance and real estate sectors. The city benefits from a high concentration of stable, high-paying government employment, which serves as a buffer for the retail and services sectors during economic recession.

# Anaheim, California

ANAHEIM–SANTA ANA PMSA POPULATION (7/86): 2,166,800. Part of Los Angeles–Anaheim–Riverside CMSA population of 13,074,800 (2nd largest).

POPULATION GROWTH 1980–86: 12.1%

COUNTY: Orange

EMPLOYMENT (9/84): 1,101,800

AVERAGE TEMPERATURE: 64.8°F

YEARLY RAINFALL: 14.05 inches

HUMIDITY: 53% (30th most humid)

COST OF LIVING: 107.3

## KEYS TO THE CITY

**Small Business Growth:** birth rate, growth rate, growth index (rank/86):   3.5   3.4   6.9   (25th)

**Average Annual Job Growth (9/84–9/86):** 4.7% (8th/largest 100)

**Keys to Prosperity:** Tourism (Disneyland plus major convention center), strong Chamber of Commerce, high-tech move-in to twelve business parks.

**Key Developments:** Business parks.

**Key Life-Style Trends:** Anaheim Stadium seats 70,000 and is home to two pro teams; Orange County continues to attract residents, but high housing prices are squeezing young marrieds out of Orange and into neighboring Riverside, which is less congested and has cheaper housing. Anaheim's large stadium and many recreational facilities and museums, in addition to Disneyland and Knott's Berry Farm (featuring Snoopy), add to the traffic and area diversions. The congestion problem is being attacked by the area Quality of Life Coalition.

## WHY OPPORTUNITY KNOCKS IN ANAHEIM

The typical American thinks of Anaheim as a pleasant area where Disneyland is located. Disneyland has indeed been a major local attraction since 1955. It has brought in business and scads of people: The population of Anaheim grew from a mere 14,556 in 1950 to 104,184 in 1960. Businesses began to realize that Anaheim was indeed a good location—a livable community strategically placed close to Los Angeles.

Today Anaheim has the West's largest convention center (685,000 square feet). In 1986 Orange County attracted 34.5 million visitors, people who poured an estimated $4.9 billion into the economy. Attendance at 1986's 294 conventions reached 925,352. In 1987, 283 future conventions were booked, breaking a record. Tourism accounts for roughly 10 percent of the county's economy, with 117,000 people employed by the industry in 1986, a figure that is increasing by 4,000 jobs a year. The impact of this industry on Orange County is evident when one looks at local tax receipts. State tax receipts are nearly $100 million and local tax receipts are $50 million.

But Anaheim is not all of Orange County; it is only the largest of the twenty-six cities that compose it. Other cities include Newport Beach, Irvine, Laguna Beach, Costa Mesa, Balboa and Buena Park. In all, Orange County encompasses 780 square miles, 45 of which are in the City of Anaheim. It officially separated from Los Angeles in 1899. Anaheim is some 26 miles from Los Angeles, in the heart of the Los Angeles–San Bernardino–San Diego market triangle, one of the largest and fastest growing areas in the United States.

Any city of genuine opportunity has some economic diversity, and Anaheim is not a one-mouse town; it has strong support services for its businesses. For example, the United States Chamber of Commerce has judged the Anaheim Chamber to be one of the ten best in the country. The Chamber has invited high-tech industry to join the business community and has received a positive response. Redevelopment of some parts of the city is under way, and new efforts are being made to attract international business. Of course, the city's Chamber strongly promotes tourism and related services. Good civic promotion had already helped to make Anaheim known throughout the world, even before Disneyland opened.

But tourism is by no means the only economic sector on which Orange County, and for that matter much of the Los Angeles area, has staked its future. High-tech industry—and, for many local corporations, especially Department of Defense–generated industry—has driven much of the area's growth and economic development. The termination or significant scaling back of the Strategic Defense Initiative, for example, could have potentially devastating "fallout" for high-tech workers and corporations in the area. A recent study by the Council on Economic Priorities (*Star Wars: The Economic Fallout*) predicts that the Los Angeles–Riverside–Orange County area, which receives the single largest chunk of SDI-related contracts, could be in for a nasty turn of fate if the program on which they've banked so heavily is halted. Moreover, it is unclear just how well other high-tech industries, like aerospace, could fill the gap so opened.

Growing traffic is a major problem. Developers have had the upper hand in the past in furthering their own construction goals. Now a group calling itself the Quality of Life Coalition, attempting to coordinate new development to traffic improvements, would forbid occupancy of developments, even if they had been approved prior to the proposal, until minimal traffic standards were met on the roads. Developers agree that the problem demands immediate attention.

Now that Orange County has emerged as the fifth most densely populated metro area in the country, the progrowth/antigrowth controversy is bound to intensify. Although Los Angeles has grown rapidly and has been developed to the point that it now possesses a central-city character, the usual pattern of development in the L.A. area has been, and continues to be, in the form of "pockets." One such growth pocket is unquestionably Orange County, with which more residents are beginning to identify in opposition to L.A. itself. Once a so-called bedroom community for Los Angeles, Anaheim and cities like it have eliminated the need for many workers to commute by establishing their own industries. Nonetheless, as the number of industries—and residents—increases, Orange County's traffic problems will reach crisis levels, and the county could lose the spread-out suburban qualities that have traditionally been its draw.

Anaheim has twelve business parks: Anaheim Business Park, Canyon West, Canyon Commercenter, Crescent Corporate Center, East Anaheim/Dunn Business Park, Kaiser Anaheim Center, Lakeview/LaPalma Business Center, LaPalma Business Center, Lease-All LaPalma, Martens Business Park, Riverbend Industrial Center and the Santa Fe Corporate Center. Business parks are essential to this growing and diversifying economy.

Anaheim has forty-one bank offices, twenty of them savings and loans. Major investment brokers serve Anaheim with a finance, real estate and insurance industry that employs 6.5 percent of the wage and salary workers in Orange County and is growing. There are five permanent and sixteen temporary employment agencies serving the area.

---

## QUALITY OF LIFE

**Weather:** Located in the Greater Los Angeles metro area, Anaheim has a mild climate characterized by few extremes in either temperature or precipitation. Total annual rainfall averages thirteen inches, with most rain occurring November through March. Humidity is also low, with average afternoon humidity around 50 percent in July. Average monthly temperature in January is 52.5°F, and the average monthly temperature in July is 71.4°.

**Education:** Anaheim has twenty-one elementary schools, eight junior high schools and eight high schools. There are nine colleges and universities in the area: California State University, Fullerton; Cypress College, Cypress; Fullerton College, Fullerton; Golden West College, Huntington Beach; Irvine Valley College, Irvine; Orange Coast College, Costa Mesa; Rancho Santiago College–Santa Ana Campus, Santa Ana; Saddleback College, Mission Viejo; and the University of California, Irvine. All of these higher education institutions offer summer programs and do community work.

**Neighborhoods:** The more affluent sections of Anaheim are Anaheim Hills, popular among established professionals and businessmen, and Westmont. Central Anaheim, located downtown, is older (most homes are eighty or more years old), primarily Hispanic, and lower to medium income. West Anaheim is the oldest part of the city, but most residential construction is between twenty-five and forty years old; the neighborhood is considered upper-middle-class.

**Politics/Government:** Of the registered voters, 55 percent are Republican. U.S. Attorney General Edward Meese is the former sheriff of Orange County, former president Richard M. Nixon was born in Orange County and Ronald Reagan has always had a power base in Orange County.

**Transportation:** Part of the Los Angeles air travel hub, Anaheim is within forty-five minutes of four major airports. Movement within the city is aided by municipal bus service, and intercity land travel is provided by Greyhound, Trailways and Amtrak, which offers six departures daily. Anaheim is no stranger to Southern California's celebrated freeway traffic, but most residents still consider their cars a necessity to free movement around the expansive region.

**Health Care:** Anaheim has six general hospitals, one rehabilitation hospital, one sanitarium, four convalescent hospitals and twenty-one rest homes.

**Child Care:** Working parents in need of licensed day care can consult Kid Care (714-543-2273), a resource, information and referral service associated with Children's Home Society. Further information on the quality, availability and general state of child care in the Orange County/Anaheim area is supplied by the Orange County Area United Way (714-971-7300).

**Housing:** The average three-bedroom, two-bathroom house sells for $150,000 in Orange County; one- and two-bedroom apartments rent for between $400 and $750 a month. The single-family, unattached home is the housing form of choice in Anaheim and most of Orange County.

**Public Safety:** Employing our bellwether crime evaluation standard of reported 1986 robberies per 100,000 city residents, Anaheim emerges as a very safe community with a low 283 robberies per 100,000 of population.

**Cultural Attractions:** Anaheim offers the performing arts in ten theaters as well as numerous dinner/theater places and nightclubs. One of those ten theaters is the 3,000-seat Orange County Performing Arts Center, a new development that is expected to increase entertainment opportunities in the area. The area's six museums include Mission San Juan Capistrano, an original Spanish mission, and Movieland, where 230 wax replicas of the stars are on display.

**Sports/Recreation:** If sports interest you, the 70,000-seat Anaheim Stadium is home to two professional teams—the California Angels (baseball) and the Rams (football). Other facilities include golf, tennis, racing, motorcross races, horseback riding, and ice- and roller-skating. Nearby Mission Viejo, whence champion diver Greg Louganis hails, has some of the nation's best aquatic facilities.

Disneyland is one reason many people have gone to Anaheim, and America's most popular amusement park still makes dreams come true for those who visit it. Knott's Berry Farm, which features Charles Schulz's Snoopy, is not very far from the enchanted kingdom and is the nation's third most popular theme park. Catalina Island is not far away, and is a place where one can hike, sunbathe, swim or shop. In Anaheim, one is never too far from Los Angeles, San Diego or Palm Springs. Anaheim has over 400 restaurants, 60 of them in the immediate area of the Anaheim Convention Center.

**Taxes:** California has a graduated income tax similar in structure to the federal income tax. The effective sales and use tax in Anaheim is 6 percent. Residential property in Anaheim is taxed at an average rate of $1.1225 for each $100 of assessed valuation; property tax rates have been stable in Anaheim for some twenty years.

---

## WHERE TO BREAK IN

For individuals interested in moving to the city of Anaheim, we include a list of the area's major employers. For more information, call the Anaheim Chamber of Commerce at 714-758-0222.

| Firm/Organization | Product/Service | No. Employees |
|---|---|---|
| Rockwell International | electronic engineering | 10,000 |
| Pacific Bell | telephone utility | 8,600 |
| Disneyland | theme park          winter: | 3,500 |
|  |                              summer: | 7,500 |
| Karl Karcher Enterprises | restaurants | 2,760 |
| City of Anaheim | government | 2,575 |
| Anaheim Union High School District | education | 2,190 |
| Northrop Corp. | electromechanical products | 1,750 |
| Disneyland Hotel | hotel | 1,600 |
| Interstate Electronics | military electronics | 1,500 |
| California Computer Products | data-processing engineering | 1,350 |

| Firm/Organization | Product/Service | No. Employees |
|---|---|---|
| Kwikset, Div. of Emhart Corp. | lock sets | 1,350 |
| Anaheim Hilton & Towers | hotel | 1,300 |
| Anaheim City School District | education | 1,100 |
| Anaheim Memorial Hospital | general medical and surgical hospital | 1,000 |
| Martin Luther Hospital | general medical and surgical hospital | 850 |
| Century Data Systems (Xerox) | memory disk drives | 800 |
| Lear Siegler, Inc. | data products | 590 |

## Summing Up: Opportunity for Whom?

The median age of Anaheim residents is thirty and one-half years. Of the population, 24.9 percent are under eighteen years old, 14.5 percent are eighteen to twenty-four, 19.4 percent are twenty-five to thirty-four, 19.0 percent are thirty-five to forty-nine, and 22.2 percent are over fifty. The median income in 1980 was $23,000. The county has the highest per capita income in the Los Angeles area at $20,914.

The proportions of workers in the different industries indicate the relative importance of each. Retail and wholesale trade, manufacturing and services employ the bulk—roughly 65 percent—of the people of Orange County. Government and state and local work occupies the next largest portion, 19.8 percent.

Tourism is important to the area, but Anaheim is more than Donald Duck. A big piece of the economy is in military contracting, especially "Star Wars" research, a possible weakness. But the area's many business parks harbor companies in a diversified range of well-positioned enterprises.

# Atlanta, Georgia

MSA POPULATION (7/86): 2,560,500 (13th largest)
POPULATION GROWTH 1980–86: 19.8%
COUNTY: Fulton
EMPLOYMENT (9/87): 1,387,700
AVERAGE TEMPERATURE: 60.8°F
YEARLY RAINFALL: 48.34 inches
HUMIDITY: 62% (19th most humid)
COST OF LIVING: 111.0

## KEYS TO THE CITY

**Small Business Growth:** birth rate, growth rate, growth index (rank/86): 4.6   4.2   8.8   (6th)

**Average Annual Job Growth (9/84–9/87):** 4.3% (12th/largest 100)

**Keys to Prosperity:** Central to the growing southland, Atlanta's burgeoning businesses have left Coca-Cola in fourth place in number of employees, after Lanier, Bellsouth Corp. and Southern Bell. Major growth industries: finance, computers, business services.

**Key Developments:** The airport is now a hub, the nation's second busiest.

**Key Life-Style Trends:** Atlanta has come a long way since Scarlett O'Hara's day. Black leadership is solidly in control in Atlanta's City Hall, and race relations are good (though many whites have moved to comfortable suburban locations). Atlanta's government is also solidly probusiness, which may help explain why Atlanta was the number-one choice of business executives queried in 1987 about where they would most like to locate or relocate a branch of their business.

## WHY OPPORTUNITY KNOCKS IN ATLANTA

When it comes to corporate headquarters, Atlanta is best known as the home of the makers of the famous carbonated beverage Coca-Cola. But this city's strong services and trade sectors make it currently the nation's fourth largest new job market, having added 62,000 new jobs between September 1985 and September 1986. With a high success rate for new small businesses, and no single industry dominant, Georgia's state capital is an attractive relocation spot.

Atlanta's booming services sector is exemplified by successful new companies such as Advanced Telecommunications, a new long-distance telephone company, and Sahlen & Associates, a private investigation firm. As the southeast headquarters for over seventy federal agencies and the home of its own city and state agencies, Atlanta is also a locus for steady government employment.

In addition, Atlanta is a leader in air transportation. The city's William B. Hartsfield International Airport is the nation's second busiest, serving as a major hub for some eighteen airlines.

Atlanta's first major industries were textiles and agriculture, which continue in importance though they share the local work force with banking, insurance and real estate firms. High-paying and increasingly high-tech, Atlanta's manufacturing is led by corporations such as IBM, AT&T, Lockheed-Georgia, General Motors and the Ford Motor Company, all of which have regional headquarters in the city. Atlanta is the national headquarters of Delta Airlines, and Eastern Airlines also has a significant presence in the city. A booming retail sector is supported by high employment concentrations in the communications, utilities, health-care and education industries.

## QUALITY OF LIFE

**Weather:** Its elevation of 1,050 feet above sea level makes Atlanta the nation's second highest large city. Nonetheless, although the local climate does experience four distinct seasons, Atlanta is generally a warm, humid area where going from place to place is a matter of trading one air-conditioned space for another.

**Education:** Public education in the Atlanta area is supplied by twenty-four districts with a total of 650 schools enrolling 413,946 pupils. The area has 187 private and parochial schools, with a combined enrollment of 38,020 pupils. Atlantans have access to a variety of colleges and universities whose combined programs run the gamut of professional training, including law, medicine, business and engineering. The city has 89,336 students enrolled in postsecondary educational programs, distributed among five two-year colleges (two private, three public) and twenty four-year colleges and universities (sixteen private, four public). Among Atlanta's higher educational institutions are Emory University, Atlanta University, the Georgia Institute of Technology, Georgia State University, Oglethorpe University and Agnes Scott College.

**Neighborhoods:** Atlanta's midtown area, which borders the business district, is high-rise and high rent, but also contains most of the city's charming, older apartment buildings. The city's trendy Buckhead neighborhood contains most of the bars, restaurants and nightclubs, and is also a fairly high-cost housing market. The Little Five Points neighborhood is popular among punk rockers, and Virginia Highland is well-Yuppified.

**Transportation:** Atlanta motorists are frustrated by heavy commuter traffic. Public transportation is provided by municipal bus service and a light-rail system known as MARTA (Metropolitan Atlanta Rapid Transit Authority). Intercity transportation is facilitated by Amtrak and by the Hartsfield International Airport, with a total of 765 flights daily.

**Health Care:** Atlanta's health care is of high quality and low cost. Health-care facilities include five teaching hospitals, two medical schools, seven cardiac rehabilitation centers and three hospices.

**Child Care:** Child care in the Atlanta area is supplied by 591 licensed day-care centers, 890 family day-care homes, and 100 summer camps and preschools. Refugee, emergency and school-age child care is available. Referral and matching services are provided by Childcare Solutions, a community group.

**Politics/Government:** Atlanta has a mayor-council form of government. The office of mayor is currently held by Andrew Young, a progressive black who served as the United States Ambassador to the United Nations under Jimmy Carter. Atlanta is distinguished as the first major American city to elect two black mayors in a row (Maynard Jackson served prior to Young). In presidential politics, the city generally sides with the Democrats (in 1980, over 52 percent of all votes were cast for Carter).

**Housing:** The average three-bedroom, two-bathroom home sells for about $94,000 in Atlanta; a one-bedroom apartment may be rented for between $350 and $550 a month.

**Public Safety:** Crime rates in Atlanta are higher than the national average, with 699 violent crimes and 6,092 property crimes reported for 1984. In 1986 the city had 1,218 reported robberies per 100,000 city residents.

**Cultural Attractions:** Atlanta's cultural attractions include a lively variety of museums, music and dance. The High Museum of Art features Renaissance, Baroque, and nineteenth-century European, American and Far Eastern works. The city's Nexus Gallery, operated by Nexus, Inc., serves as a contemporary arts center. The annual Atlanta Arts Festival, held each fall in Piedmont Park, hosts exhibitions of crafts and visual and performing arts. The Atlanta Symphony performs in Symphony Hall and offers outdoor concerts in Chastain Park. Other attractions are the Atlanta Ballet Company and the Alliance and Fox theaters, which produce Broadway-style shows. The Academy Theater features dramatic productions, and Seaberg's Skeleton Theater has an avant-garde reputation. Additionally, the city's Theatrical Outfit performs experimental scripts, and Just Us produces scripts by black playwrights.

**Sports/Recreation:** Atlanta is no slouch in professional sports, serving as home for the Falcons (football), Braves (baseball) and Hawks (basketball).

**Taxes:** State and local taxes are fairly low, with an area tax bite of 3.82 percent of average household income. Atlanta's cost of living is also relatively low: 43 percent lower than New York's, 15 percent lower than Los Angeles's, 10 percent lower than Dallas's and 5 percent lower than Baltimore's.

---

## WHERE TO BREAK IN

For individuals interested in relocating to Atlanta, here is a listing of selected large employers in the area. For more information, call the Atlanta Chamber of Commerce at 404-688-4910.

| Firm | Product/Service | No. Employees |
|------|-----------------|---------------|
| Lanier Business Products, Inc. | office equipment | 5,100 |
| Bellsouth Corp. | telephone utility | 4,500 |
| Southern Bell | communications | 2,000 |
| Coca-Cola Co. | soft drink bottling | 1,400 |
| Georgia-Pacific Corp. | wood/lumber products | 1,300 |
| Southern Co. | electric utility | 1,280 |
| American Family Life Assurance | accident and health insurance | 900 |
| Hayes Microcomputer Products, Inc. | semiconductor products | 600 |
| Sun Life Group of America, Inc. | life insurance | 538 |
| National Data Corp. | management consulting | 500 |

## SUMMING UP: OPPORTUNITY FOR WHOM?

The fifteen-county Atlanta metro area has a work force of 1,022,054 and an unemployment rate of 6.5 percent. The area's major growth industries are computer, aerospace and communications equipment manufacturing; health care; communication; wholesale and retail trade; government; education; and financial services. We provide the distribution of Atlanta's work force among six basic nonagricultural industrial categories.

| Industry | Share of Work Force (in %) |
|----------|----------------------------|
| Services | 22 |
| Retail trade | 18 |
| Government | 14 |
| Manufacturing | 14 |
| Wholesale trade | 10 |
| Finance, insurance and real estate | 8 |

Atlanta's services and high-tech manufacturing sectors should continue to generate employment opportunities for accountants, persons with clerical skills, computer programmers, bankers, electrical engineers, electronics technicians, health-care professionals and educators.

# Austin, Texas

MSA POPULATION (7/86): 726,400 (53rd largest)
POPULATION GROWTH 1980–86: 35.4%
COUNTY: Travis
EMPLOYMENT (9/87): 357,100
AVERAGE TEMPERATURE: 68.1°F
YEARLY RAINFALL: 12.31 inches
HUMIDITY: 53% (30th most humid)
COST OF LIVING: 104.3

## KEYS TO THE CITY

**Small Business Growth:** birth rate, growth rate, growth index (rank/86): 6.8  4.0  10.8  (1st)

**Average Annual Job Growth (9/84–9/87):** 1.9% (73rd/largest 100)

**Keys to Prosperity:** High-tech, university-related research, government.

**Key Developments:** Austin's real estate speculation suffered a setback in part because Texas taxes are down (oil-related businesses aren't kicking in as much), but the worst seems to be over (oil prices have bounced back partway).

**Key Life-Style Trends:** Austin is still a small, university-government town, a brasher version of Bonn, with an energetic cadre of entrepreneurs ready to bring together state money and university talent. These people have been working at their leisure activities, and the university provides a lot of cultural and athletic diversion.

## WHY OPPORTUNITY KNOCKS IN AUSTIN

Located deep in the heart of central Texas, Austin is the state capital, named for the state's founder-settler, Stephen Austin. The largest corporation headquartered in Austin is Tracor, an electronics manufacturing firm, which exemplifies Austin's manufacturing emphasis. The University of Texas, based in Austin, is at the core of a thriving academic community attractive to electronics

92

and other high-tech firms such as IBM, Texas Instruments and Motorola, all of which have plants in the city.

Unlike Dallas and Houston, whose civic leaders have worked actively to attract high-tech industry, Austin has traditionally been very passive with respect to economic growth, preferring to retain its small-city charm. But industry has flocked to Austin, resulting in a population boom and infrastructural inadequacies. With unemployment at 5.7 percent, below the national average, and a high rate of new business starts and small business growth, Austin represents the current deconcentration of the American economic structure, from low-tech/high-output to high-tech/low-output industry, carried on by new, small and highly adaptable companies, as opposed to sluggish, top-heavy giants. The city's well-educated, professional environment feeds this transformation. In fact, 31 percent of the work force has achieved a college degree or equivalent, making Austin the best-educated of U.S. cities with over 250,000 population. The absence of a large number of big companies means that Austin's small entrepreneurs can get financing that would require more tenacious competition in cities where industrial giants rule.

As the state capital, Austin has a strong governmental presence providing about a quarter of local jobs, so it doesn't have all its economic eggs in one basket. Moreover, government employment is comfortably paid and resistant to business cycles, which serves as a stabilizing force for the area's trade sector during recessions.

---

## QUALITY OF LIFE

**Weather:** Austin has a pleasant climate, which averages 300 sunny days annually. In winter the temperature does not often dip below freezing. The normal daily temperature range in winter is 42 to 62°F; in summer, daily temperatures normally range between 73 and 94°.

**Education:** With its public school system divided into self-taxing and self-regulating local districts, Austin, like Houston and Dallas, spends little on public education. With a dropout rate of 6.7 percent, Austin's high schools send about 59 percent of their graduates to college. Austin's University of Texas flagship campus (with its prestigious Lyndon B. Johnson School of Government) along with one public two-year college and six private four-year colleges and universities have a combined enrollment of 90,000 students.

Bibliophiles can have a rip-roarin' good time with the combined library resources of the city of Austin and its star tenant, the University of Texas, which total around 4,054,000 volumes and 5,000,000 manuscripts.

**Neighborhoods:** Because Austin has grown so quickly in the last decade, it's difficult to pin down formal subdivisions and neighborhoods: What was formerly the north side of the city is now central and considered part of downtown; the south side, once thought wild and woolly, has calmed down to become mainstream residential. In general, Austin's west side, with its hilly terrain, has many of the most desirable residential neighborhoods, and northwest Austin is considered upscale. Old and new designations have been clouded by widespread development in all sections of the city. Residents affirm, however, that pleasant communities exist in almost all portions of the city; Austin's major high-tech concerns have facilities in southeast and northwest parts of the city.

**Politics/Government:** Austin has been swinging every two years between a neighborhood-oriented city-council representation, flying under the colors of the environment and home protection, and a developer-oriented city council advocating growth and progress. Elections are nonpartisan and are held in April, away from partisan elections in November.

**Transportation:** You will need your own car to be independently mobile in Austin and its environs. Still, the city offers municipal busing with service to park-and-ride facilities. The fare is one dollar to fifty cents for students. Austin's downtown area is also served by a twenty-five-cent trolley, known as the 'Dillo. Austin's Robert Mueller Airport offers domestic service by twelve airlines. The city is also served by Amtrak (three days a week), Greyhound and Trailways. The Kerrville Bus Company offers passenger and freight service only within Texas.

**Health Care:** Austin is served by eight hospitals and medical centers. Four of these facilities operate twenty-four-hour emergency rooms.

**Child Care:** The Austin State Department of Human Services (512-835-2350) handles child-care inquiries and maintains lists of licensed care providers.

**Housing:** New homes cost an average of $105,472, but three-bedroom, two-bathroom houses are available for as little as $60,000.

**Public Safety:** With 271 reported 1986 robberies per 100,000 city residents, Austin is among the cities in our study with the lowest crime rates.

**Cultural Attractions:** Austin's cultural menu is greatly enriched by the presence of the university. The Austin Symphony Orchestra is based at the University of Texas Performing Arts Center. The city's Laguna Gloria Art Museum specializes in contemporary exhibits and sponsors concerts, plays and other activities.

**Sports/Recreation:** The city has 160 parks totaling 10,000 acres, and a lovely string of seven lakes, known as Highland Lakes, which starts in the city and spreads some 150 miles into the countryside. Austin presents a unique opportunity to lovers of popular music, since the city is a locus for up-and-coming rock and "new wave" bands, a feature that generates a surprisingly enthusiastic and active nightlife. In the city's downtown, 6th Street, or Old Pecan Street, has twenty-five nightclubs with live music and entertainment. Additionally, the Broken Spoke is a favorite spot for lovers of country-western music.

**Taxes:** Taxes in Austin, as in all of Texas, are low. There is no state income tax (either personal or corporate); residential property is assessed at full market value, but Austinites pay a low $1.8107 per each $100 of assessed value. The sales tax in Austin is 8 percent.

---

## WHERE TO BREAK IN

Individuals with training in the high-tech fields of electrical engineering and computer science may pursue employment in Austin by contacting college alumni organizations or professional associations in the Austin area. We also recommend contacting Austin's major employers directly. Following is a partial list of Austin area major employers (of the Texas state government agencies, only the largest is shown). For more information, call the Austin Chamber of Commerce at 512-478-9383.

| Firm/Organization | Product/Service | No. Employees |
| --- | --- | --- |
| The University of Texas at Austin | education | 16,763 |
| City of Austin | government | 10,262 |
| Bergstrom Air Force Base | military | 7,433 |

| Firm/Organization | Product/Service | No. Employees |
|---|---|---|
| Austin Independent School District | education | 7,300 |
| IBM Corporation/ Communication Products Div. | communications | 7,200 |
| Internal Revenue Service | government | 5,600 |
| Motorola, Inc. | communications | 5,000 |
| Texas Instruments, Inc. | computers | 2,500 |
| Lockheed Austin Div. | aerospace | 2,400 |
| Tracor, Inc. | high-tech electronics R & D | 2,300 |
| Texas Dept. of Human Services | government | 2,050 |
| Advanced Micro Devices | computers | 1,700 |
| State Farm Insurance Co. | insurance | 1,067 |
| AT&T | telecommunications | 1,063 |

## SUMMING UP: OPPORTUNITY FOR WHOM?

One of the reasons high-tech companies have been locating plants in Austin is the city's ample supply of individuals trained in high-tech fields such as electrical engineering and computer science. Nonetheless, Austin is capable of absorbing not only its local people but also scientific personnel from other regions. One reason: Austin's new small businesses, whose advent and growth have been impressive. The Austin area work force of 421,631 is distributed as follows among the basic industrial sectors:

| Industry | Share of Work Force (in %) |
|---|---|
| Government | 26.0 |
| Services/tourism | 23.0 |
| Wholesale and retail trade | 22.6 |
| Manufacturing | 11.0 |
| Finance, insurance and real estate | 7.1 |
| Construction | 6.6 |
| Transportation, communications and utilities | 3.4 |

# Baltimore, Maryland

MSA POPULATION (7/86): 2,280,000 (18th largest)

POPULATION GROWTH 1980–86: 3.7%

COUNTY: None—an independent city

EMPLOYMENT (9/87): 1,070,500

AVERAGE TEMPERATURE: 55°F

YEARLY RAINFALL: 40.46 inches

HUMIDITY: 62% (19th most humid)

COST OF LIVING: 105.5

## KEYS TO THE CITY

**Small Business Growth:** birth rate, growth rate, growth index (rank/86):  3.4  3.9  7.3  (15th)

**Average Annual Job Growth (9/84–9/87):** 2.0% (64th/largest 100)

**Keys to Prosperity:** Skilled services, (defense) manufacturing, tourism, office overflow from D.C., low labor costs.

**Key Developments:** Harborplace, construction of new office buildings.

**Key Life-Style Trends:** As Baltimore shifts from manufacturing to services, the demand for skilled employees will continue to grow and outstrip availability of local talent. The arrival of new talent will gradually enlarge the sophisticated set in Baltimore and change the city's image.

## WHY OPPORTUNITY KNOCKS IN BALTIMORE

Baltimore, Maryland, has always suffered from a Cinderella complex. Growing up in the shadows of her two sophisticated sisters, Washington and Philadelphia, Baltimore was always overlooked. Few ever peered behind her unglamorous factory and freighter smokestacks, and even fewer expected her to undergo a make-over and come out a startling beauty.

Baltimore was particularly hard hit in the 1960s and 1970s,

when manufacturing moved to the nonunion Sunbelt and whites rushed off to the suburbs. But it refused to go down without a fight. The city switched much of its economic base to services and white-collar professions. It also began encouraging tourism and private in-city projects to attract people back downtown. The result has been phenomenal. The city's crown jewel is Harborplace, Baltimore's newly renovated inner harbor, where the U.S.S. *Constellation* docks and where shoppers browse through glittering boutiques. This showcase is the symbol of Baltimore's urban renaissance.

Of course, vestiges of the past remain. Despite the exodus of many manufacturing firms, Baltimore still ranks as one of the largest industrial employers on the East Coast, with more than 2,000 factories. Its per capita income is low compared to that of other major cities, keeping it attractive to employers. Leading industries include the production of radar and electronic equipment, steel, copper and iron. Many Baltimoreans are still employed by Bethlehem Steel, one of the world's largest steel producers, and Westinghouse, manufacturer of appliances and electrical equipment. McCormick and Company, the world's largest producer of spices and seasonings, also employs many of the area's workers. Significant expansion has been enjoyed by the area's defense-related corporations such as Martin Marietta Corp. and Allied Bendix Corp.

However, the greatest growth is reported by the service sector. Ten years ago, more than half of all paychecks went to blue-collar workers, but today white-collar workers outnumber blue-collar workers two to one. From 1980 to 1983, the service sector grew by 11.2 percent, as manufacturing declined 12.5 percent. The mayor's office reports a low area unemployment rate of 5.8 percent, due primarily to this economic reorientation. But city observers are concerned. A 1983 study conducted by the Greater Baltimore Committee reported that though unemployment rates are presently below the national average, the figure might begin to creep up as the area's work force becomes increasingly unable to fill positions requiring higher educational levels. The area lacks skilled professionals and thirsts for fresh talent. This is a good sign for educated workers thinking about moving to Baltimore.

Construction is a really booming segment of the economy. In 1986 twenty-two new buildings went up, representing a $675 million investment. Another $200 million will be spent on future projects, on top of the $825 million already invested in Baltimore's inner harbor. The original inner harbor plan was launched in 1964, calling for 600,000 to 900,000 square feet of office space by 1985; the area's construction fervor, in fact, far surpassed those modest projections. Today, 4.35 million square feet of office space is either recently completed or under construction. Complementing the construction craze is growth in the hotel and tourism industries, both promising significant job growth.

The City of Baltimore's population is 787,000; the metro area's is 2,280,000. Area population is expected to grow at an annual rate of 2.7 percent through the 1990s. Most rapidly growing is the elderly population, which increased by 52 percent in the 1970s. By 1980, the number of people in Baltimore nursing homes surpassed the number in nursery schools. *Advertising Age* magazine recently said that in Baltimore "the quickest way to that growing population's heart is through its stomach. Anything to do with food is a success. The number of eating and drinking establishments has grown 74 percent in the last five years. An average Baltimorean pays $63.50 a week for food compared with $60 nationally."

On the negative side, Baltimore doesn't have a strategic plan. The 1987 report *Baltimore 2000* is merely a collection of local opinions gleaned by a Washington-based writer from some interviews with Baltimoreans. The report's negative view of the city's race relations ("An Uninfluential Black Community") and civic infrastructure ("A Weak Tradition of Civic Action") exemplify the author's gloomy view, which reportedly has influenced several companies against locating in Baltimore.

On the positive side, however, former Baltimore mayor (now Maryland governor) Schaefer was voted the nation's best mayor by *Esquire* magazine, and years earlier Baltimore came out on top of a survey of city responsiveness by the Council on Municipal Performance (merged in 1987 with the National Civic League). Relations between the city and its citizens have not been so bad, and the city's economy is bound to benefit from Washington, D.C., area growth. What the city is missing is a community-wide focus on the future; *Baltimore 2000* doesn't serve this purpose, and a genuine strategic plan is a step the city should and probably will take.

## QUALITY OF LIFE

**Weather:** Even though Baltimore is not very far south, it has mild winters; while the temperature rarely gets down to 0°F, about 100 days are freezing (32°F or lower). Summer in Baltimore is hot and humid, with a month's worth of days in the 90s.

**Education:** Baltimore has 125 public elementary schools and 50 public high schools. It also has 15 combined elementary-secondary schools. About 120,000 students attend Baltimore's public schools. About 18,000 students attend more than 50 Roman Catholic schools, and the city also has about 5,000 students in some 35 non-Catholic private schools. Noted institutions of higher learning include Johns Hopkins and its acclaimed medical center, the University of Maryland and the University of Baltimore. Other schools include Goucher College (formerly a women's college, now coed), Morgan State University (a historically black college) and the Peabody Conservatory of Music.

**Neighborhoods:** Baltimore's downtown area has become a unique mix of retail, office and residential space. One part of it is the loft district, in the upgraded Market Center. Another nearby area is the Otterbein, where not long ago the city sold run-down houses for $1 each to families willing to renovate them; the area's narrow streets and brick sidewalks now have gaslight-style street lamps, and in the wake of the area's rehabilitation new condominium units have been built and have been selling for a lot more than $1 each. Bordering the Otterbein area is Federal Hill, a district of restored older homes exuding a strong sense of deep-rooted community. Nearby is Mount Vernon, long considered the city's most desirable neighborhood, with Baltimore's version of the Washington monument. Mount Vernon recently has seen the addition of some multiunit residences, opening it up to some residents with more modest resources. Other desirable neighborhoods in Baltimore include traditional Roland Park and Carrie Ford; new planned communities include Cross Keys and Coldspring; and cozy, secluded, laidback communities include Hampden, Fells Point and Waverly.

**Transportation:** Baltimore motorists don't face very heavy commuter traffic, so you may actually want to take your car with you if you move to the area. The city also has an excellent municipal bus system and two commuter railroads. The Baltimore–Washington

International Airport is served by twenty-six airlines offering over 200 flights daily. In addition, Amtrak provides thirty-one departures daily.

**Health Care:** The city of Baltimore offers excellent health care to its residents at reasonable cost. Seven noted teaching hospitals include world-famous Johns Hopkins Hospital. The area's two medical schools are Johns Hopkins University School of Medicine and the University of Maryland School of Medicine. About 312 physicians are available for every 100,000 residents. Baltimore also offers a number of cardiac rehabilitation centers and hospices, as well as the Johns Hopkins Oncology Center, which is a comprehensive cancer treatment center.

**Child Care:** The city's Department of Social Services (301-576-5314) is able to refer those interested in child day care to the right place.

**Politics/Government:** Baltimore is an independent city, not a municipality of a county. That is, Baltimore County does not include Baltimore City. The city has a mayor-council form of government, with a strong mayor. The mayor is elected directly by city voters and has veto power over council bills. Of council members, one is elected at large; the others are elected from eighteen wards for four-year terms; the council meets weekly. Former mayor William Donald Schaefer did a remarkable job of maintaining contact with neighborhood groups in a way that challenged them to work together, and has been rewarded by promotion to the governorship of Maryland. He was confronting Baltimore's decline—as a port and manufacturing city in the face of air transportation and the loss of America's competitive advantage in selling manufactured goods—by engaging in public-private partnerships, of which the most famous is Rouse's Harborplace.

**Housing:** The average cost of a single-family detached house in Greater Baltimore is $75,000. A two-bedroom, one-bath apartment costs $300 to $350 a month.

**Public Safety:** Proving that opportunity doesn't knock for everyone, Baltimore has one of the highest robbery rates in our study, registering 1,019 robberies per 100,000 residents in 1986.

**Cultural Attractions:** To enhance life, Baltimore offers many cultural attractions. The Baltimore Opera Company performs in the Lyric Opera House, while the Baltimore Symphony Orchestra performs in the Joseph Meyerhoff Symphony Hall. The Morris A. Mechanic Theatre offers dramas and musicals, and the Center Stage performs plays in its own building. The Baltimore Museum of Art is famous for its collection of modern art, and the Walters Art Gallery features medieval and Chinese art. The Peale Museum specializes in the life and history of Baltimore, and the Maryland Historical Society displays the original manuscript of "The Star-Spangled Banner." The Maryland Science Center includes a science museum, a planetarium and an observatory. It is the home of the Maryland Academy of Sciences.

**Sports/Recreation:** While Baltimore sports fans have their own baseball team (the Baltimore Orioles, American League East), football and basketball fans must root for D.C.'s Redskins and Bullets.

**Taxes:** The Baltimore area state and local tax burden comes to about 4 percent of average annual household income—a relatively high percentage. One reason the percentage is high: Baltimore has a low average income compared to other U.S. cities.

---

## WHERE TO BREAK IN

The area's largest private employers are listed below. For further information, call the Greater Baltimore Economic Development Committee at 301-727-2820.

| Firm | Product/Service | No. Employees | Phone (area code 301) |
|------|-----------------|---------------|-----------------------|
| Baltimore & Ohio Railroad | railroad | 3,500 | 237-2000 |
| AAI Corp. | radio and television | 2,800 | 666-1400 |
| Commercial Credit Co. | short-term business credit | 2,000 | 539-7400 |
| Baltimore Gas & Electric | electric utility | 1,600 | 234-5000 |
| Chesapeake & Potomac Telephone Co. | telephone utility | 1,500 | 539-9900 |
| U.S. Fidelity & Guaranty Co. | insurance | 1,300 | 547-3000 |
| First Maryland Bancorp. | banking | 1,300 | 244-4000 |

## SUMMING UP: OPPORTUNITY FOR WHOM?

Baltimore offers many opportunities to highly educated white-collar workers. It is trying to revamp its image from smoky factory town/port to sophisticated urban center. Yet its residents do not want their city to become a Yuppie haven. What Baltimoreans are aiming for is Old World charm sprinkled with a dash of urban chic.

Baltimoreans are a diverse bunch. One in nine residents is either foreign born or the child of an immigrant who came to this country after 1970. In 1980, blacks constituted 55 percent of the area's population, whites 44 percent. In the 1970s, the area's European-born population fell 8 percent, its Asian-born population quadrupled to 17,128 and its Latin American–born population rose by 65 percent to 22,000. Large ethnic groups that have traditionally lived in Baltimore include Poles, Greeks, Ukrainians and Italians.

Women have been absorbed *en masse* into the work force as the city has adopted a service orientation. More than half the area's women are in the work force, and the number of women in managerial-professional positions has increased 17 percent since 1980.

# Boston, Massachusetts

BOSTON–LAWRENCE–SALEM, MASS. PMSA POPULATION (7/86): 2,824,200 (7th largest PMSA). Part of Boston–Lawrence–Salem CMSA population of 4,055,700 (7th largest).

POPULATION GROWTH 1980–86: 0.7%

COUNTY: Suffolk

EMPLOYMENT (9/87): 1,723,300

AVERAGE TEMPERATURE: 51.3°F

YEARLY RAINFALL: 42.52 inches

HUMIDITY: 65% (10th most humid)

COST OF LIVING: 160.3

## KEYS TO THE CITY

**Small Business Growth:** birth rate, growth rate, growth index (rank/86): 2.8  4.6  7.4  (14th)

**Average Annual Job Growth (9/84–9/87):** 2.1% (62nd/largest 100)

**Keys to Prosperity:** High-tech industry including defense contracting, medical services, professional and business services, universities, tourism.

**Key Developments:** Continuing downtown and harbor renovation.

**Key Life-Style Trends:** Bostonians know how to enjoy their leisure time, with sailing, rowing, running, cycling and country club activities in profusion, not to mention ample cultural activities. A big problem: downtown traffic. Solution: Use the excellent subway, known locally as the "T," or the good commuter rail services (MBTA), or locate business in suburbia and commute from sites such as New Hampshire. Nashua and Manchester, N.H., are developing their communities of residents who work in Boston but prefer the lower cost of living in New Hampshire; they are also seeing some industry sprouting up because of the availability of skilled labor.

## WHY OPPORTUNITY KNOCKS IN BOSTON

Boston has bounced back! In early 1984, Boston's bond rating had fallen to non–investment grade status. The city's most recent master capital plan dated back to 1963, and the consequences of Proposition 2½ were devastating. Now, after four years of good planning and tight spending controls, Boston has emerged from the fiscal quagmire in which it was once floundering. Under Mayor Flynn, with balanced budgets, Boston's bond rating was upgraded by both major rating agencies.

The economic changes during the past few years have been phenomenal. The key to Boston's economic problems was the decline in its manufacturing sector—metal, chemical, paper and textile production. As of 1987 Boston was the center of a surging regional economy based on knowledge industries, high-tech and services. One of every five jobs in the entire state is generated in Boston, and its unemployment rate has dropped to a mere 3.5 percent, from 12 percent in 1975. Of the 697,000 jobs created in the state between 1975 and 1986, 75 percent were generated in Boston.

The "Athens of America," Boston has taken full advantage of the area's cerebral talent. After World War II, a ring of space-age corporations sprang up alongside Route 128, providing a vast number of job opportunities for technologists, computer experts and scientists. Today, high-tech electronic giants such as Polaroid, Wang and Digital draw heavily from the creativity and brainpower that consistently emanate from the prestigious Massachusetts Institute of Technology and Harvard University, not to mention Wellesley, Tufts, Northeastern, Boston College and Boston University. "America's Technological Highway" is the lifeblood feeding Boston's economic upswing.

Behind the growth in the area's high-tech sector has been the success of the local defense industry in gaining Defense Department contracts. Defense-related employment continues to grow throughout Massachusetts, and as the federal budget is cut, attention will have to be paid to converting some of the high-tech employment to nondefense activities.

Just as noteworthy is the significant growth of the service sector, offering white-collar positions in the fields of health care, law, architecture, finance and information. Boston's first-rate medical

schools deserve praise for propelling the city to the foreground in
the medical field by continuously developing medical advance-
ments one step ahead of everyone else, as well as by maintaining
one of the nation's model health-care programs. Boston is second
only to New York as a national financial center. The First National
Bank of Boston, the State Street Bank and various insurance companies controlled an estimated $125 to $150 billion in investment
capital during the early 1980s. The Fidelity Group is a nationally
marketed mutual fund and money market fund manager. Northeastern Mortgage, a financial institution dealing with mortgage
banking, was recently heralded as the twelfth fastest growing small
public company on *Inc.* magazine's list of America's top 100 success stories; between 1982 and 1986 its sales increased nearly 177-
fold and 1,175 employees were added to its original staff of 25.

The standard of living in Boston is very high compared to that of
other American cities. According to an economic report called
*Making the Grade,* developed by the Corporation for Enterprise
Development, Massachusetts residents are the fourth highest earn-
ers in the nation. Only 7.7 percent of Massachusetts residents live
below the poverty level, whereas in Alabama the figure is a high
22.9 percent. The average worker's salary has grown by 30.7 percent in recent years, and despite some racial tension, blacks make
over 86 percent as much as whites—high compared to a state such
as Utah, where blacks earn only 41 percent as much.

Between 1984 and 1985 Boston's nonagricultural employment
soared by 6.5 percent. An average factory worker's income rose by
6 percent, and construction activity leaped up by 11.7 percent.
The national growth rates in these areas respectively were 3.5
percent, 1.4 percent and 6 percent.

---

## QUALITY OF LIFE

**Weather:** A sensitive topic among Bostonians, the weather is varied
and unpredictable. Located in Massachusetts Bay at the mouths of
the Mystic and Charles rivers, Boston is surrounded on three sides
by water. The city's wet and changeable weather is largely determined by the Atlantic's sea breezes. The city receives a great deal of
rain and snow, with an average of 128 days of the year having some
precipitation. Boston is also the second windiest city in America

(after Corpus Christi, Texas—far down the list is the so-called Windy City of Chicago), whipped by winds averaging over twelve miles per hour, which have the benefit of blowing smog somewhere else.

**Education:** The Boston metro area is divided into 109 public school districts, consisting of 775 schools that are responsible for the education of 404,000 pupils. The pupil/teacher ratio is 14.5 to 1, and approximately $2,700 is spent per pupil annually. An additional 76,000 pupils attend the area's 308 private schools. Boston certainly deserves its reputation as a college town, boasting thirty-one private and three public four-year institutions, and thirteen private and six public two-year institutions.

**Neighborhoods:** The population of Boston declined by over 12 percent between 1970 and 1980, but has rebounded since. Most of the loss was from the families of blue-collar workers because many manufacturing plants, along with wholesale/retail businesses, flocked to the suburbs to meet the increasing demands of the shopping-mall generation. Since 1980, Boston has seen a notable influx of Yuppies attracted by jobs and amenities.

Boston is sectioned into many well-defined and picturesque neighborhoods that often retain some of their historically distinctive ethnic flavor. The stately Georgian and Regency mansions of Beacon Hill and Back Bay house many of the city's more affluent residents. South Boston (commonly called "Southie") and Charlestown are predominantly Irish areas. The colorful, aromatic North End, with its winding roads, aromatic restaurants and greengrocers, has an unmistakably Italian presence. Entire sections of the South End, Dudley and Jamaica Plain have a decidedly Hispanic flavor because of the many Latino residents and businesses in those areas, and the city's blacks, who have been a presence in Boston since colonial times and who constituted 23 percent of the population in 1985, live mostly in the Roxbury, Codman Square, Mattapan and Dudley neighborhoods. Immigrants, who continue to arrive and settle in the Boston area, constitute the fastest growing population group. The Flynn administration has made strong and unequivocal commitments to ensuring open access to all neighborhoods for all Boston residents, and the city's police and fair housing and human rights agencies aggressively enforce civil rights laws.

**Transportation:** Boston has excellent mass transportation facilities, consisting of bus, subway, trolley and water shuttle service. The city also has two commuter railroad lines, with connections to subways. The bane of Boston's transportation picture, however, is its frustrating daily expressway bottlenecks. City streets are congested and laid out in a complex meandering pattern, following Boston's historical pathways. Two major public works projects currently in progress, the depression of the Central Artery and the construction of a third harbor tunnel, should significantly improve this picture by the end of the 1990s. Logan International Airport, served by forty-four airlines providing a total of 404 flights daily, is easy to reach by subway and car; a free bus shuttles passengers between the nearby subway station and airline terminals. Boston is also served by Greyhound and Amtrak, with eleven trains daily.

**Health Care:** Boston has high-quality, reasonably priced health care, provided by numerous facilities including sixteen teaching hospitals, twelve cardiac rehabilitation centers, several comprehensive cancer treatment centers and three major hospices. Patients travel from all over the globe for treatment at world-famous institutions such as Massachusetts General Hospital, the Dana Farber Cancer Institute, New England Medical Center, New England Deaconess Hospital and others. The City of Boston, through its Health and Hospitals Department, is both financially and philosophically supportive of a network of twenty-four community-based health centers located throughout its neighborhoods. These centers provide quality primary health care to the city's moderate- and low-income residents. Boston is also one of the American cities that has the most efficaciously and compassionately confronted the nationwide AIDS epidemic, through a coalition of both public and private philanthropic, medical and civic organizations. Its AIDS Action Committee and multiagency AIDS Consortium are models.

**Child Care:** Boston has many child-care options for today's working parents. Although there exists an availability/affordability crunch, with an earnest search one can usually locate a space in one of the 100 child-care centers sponsored by employers. If a private home is preferred, there is the option of sending your child to one of the 800 licensed family day-care provider homes. The

Boston Community Schools supports a variety of child-care programs in fifteen different neighborhoods.

Massachusetts regulates and licenses all child-care centers and providers, thus offering quality-control standards for the consumer. There are many resource and referral agencies that can help the newcomer locate the right day-care facility. Boston recognizes child care as a necessary component to employment and therefore spends more than $1 million annually for such services.

For child-care information, call the Child Care Information and Resource Consortium (617-325-3919).

**Politics/Government:** Perhaps equally as blustery as the city's weather is Boston's local politics. Massachusetts is considered one of the country's most liberal states (it was the only state to vote for Walter Mondale in the 1984 presidential election). Statewide politics is largely controlled by Democrats who have consistently voted their party except during the Eisenhower and Reagan elections. It is from Massachusetts that the Kennedy clan emerged. John F. Kennedy's brother Senator Edward Kennedy (D, Mass.) has fought for liberal immigration laws, airline deregulation, national health-care insurance and nuclear disarmament. The Commonwealth also produced the nation's first black U.S. Senator, Edward Brooke.

Complaints are often heard from Massachusetts business executives about liberal laws and high taxes, but they have benefited from tax concessions and other forms of incentives. Another governmental problem lies in the cumbersome Massachusetts civil service system, which hampers efficiency with complex placement tests and employee dismissal procedures. At press time Massachusetts was further spotlighted by the strong showing in 1988 presidential primaries of Governor Michael Dukakis.

**Housing:** Thorns appear on the Boston rosebush in the form of housing costs. Boston rivals New York in skyrocketing rents and real estate values—a plus if you are already an investor, but a serious drawback if you are a renter or new buyer. Given the growth of service and finance firms in Boston and the strong high-tech and defense industries in the suburbs, it is no surprise that the office real estate market continues to outperform that prevalent in the rest of the nation. At the end of 1987, Boston had a lower vacancy rate than any other major city. Dallas, for example, had a 29 percent vacancy rate; Denver, 30 percent; New York, 11 percent midtown and 15 percent downtown; Boston, 6 percent. Low vacancy rates presage real estate price increases, which put upward pressures on the cost of housing.

**Public Safety:** With 1,084 reported 1986 robberies per 100,000 city residents, Boston is among the cities in our study with a relatively high crime rate. However, under the Flynn administration police services have been raised to the highest priority and Boston's public safety picture has improved a bit. Two of the police stations that had been closed in the wake of Proposition 2½ have been renovated and reopened, and five more are scheduled for restoration. The city invested $5 million in an enhanced 911 computer-aided dispatch system and hired 210 new officers in 1986 to bring its force to the highest number in many years. The bottom line is that robberies dropped from 6,225 in 1986 to 5,408 in 1987, a 13 percent decrease. Major crime overall was down 2 percent. "The city," says a spokesman for the mayor, "is determined to do better."

**Cultural Attractions:** Life in Boston is highlighted by a broad array of historic landmarks, cultural attractions, sports alternatives and entertainment choices. A paradise for culture vultures! Here was the site of the Boston Tea Party, the Boston Massacre, the battles of Lexington and Concord, and Paul Revere's celebrated ride. Visitors are always astonished to discover how close all these historically significant locations are to one another. Known because of its compact size as a "walking city," Boston still manages to hold a wealth of cultural attractions, including the Boston Museum of Fine Arts and the world-renowned Boston Symphony Orchestra. Appealing to a wider audience are the lighter Boston Pops concerts, the Museum of Science featuring the Charles Hayden Planetarium, and the New England Aquarium. Over forty commercial art galleries abound to cater to more selective tastes. If that isn't enough, charming Faneuil Hall, Quincy Market and Cambridge's Harvard Square teem with outdoor performers when the cold winter months clear to usher in the precious months of sunshine.

**Sports/Recreation:** For the area's large number of sports fanatics, Boston is the home of the Red Sox (baseball), the Bruins (ice hockey), the popular Celtics (basketball) and the Patriots (football). Residents participate actively in skating, skiing and sailing.

**Taxes:** Bostonians have historically paid very high taxes, mostly in the form of property taxes. Proposition 2½, adopted in 1980, curbed the state government's ability to hike property taxes higher. The immediate outcome of this was the loss of 40,000 public service jobs and a consequent negative impact on public services.

## WHERE TO BREAK IN

The first step is finding a job. The city's top employers reflect the general economic growth trends toward high-tech and service industries. The following top companies are ranked according to the number employed. For more information, call the Boston Chamber of Commerce at 617-227-4500.

| Firm/Organization | Product/Service | No. Employees | Phone (area code 617) |
|---|---|---|---|
| Digital Equipment Corp. | computers | 85,600 | 897-5111 |
| Sheraton Corp. | hotels | 80,000 | 367-3600 |
| Raytheon Corp. | electronics | 76,100 | 862-6600 |
| Stop & Shop Cos. Inc. | supermarkets | 33,000 | 770-8000 |
| Gillette Co. | personal care products | 31,400 | 421-7000 |
| Howard Johnson Co. | restaurant chain | 30,000 | 847-2000 |
| Wang Laboratories | computers | 30,000 | 459-5000 |
| New England Telephone | communications | 29,600 | 743-9800 |
| John Hancock Mutual Life Insurance Co. | insurance | 20,000 | 421-6000 |
| Liberty Mutual Insurance | insurance | 18,000 | 357-9500 |
| Bank of Boston Corp. | banking | 16,000 | 434-2200 |
| Polaroid Corp. | photography | 13,400 | 577-2000 |
| Kendall Co. Inc. | conglomerate | 12,400 | 574-7000 |
| Pneumo Corp. | aerospace | 9,500 | 262-9300 |
| Purity Supreme Inc. | supermarkets | 8,000 | 667-9511 |

## SUMMING UP: OPPORTUNITIES FOR WHOM?

Boston is one of America's most alluring cities because it combines Old World charm with the upbeat style of contemporary living. Known affectionately as "Beantown" and the "Hub of the Universe," Boston is especially appealing to upwardly mobile young professionals who work hard and play hard. It's a good place to start a career and a home.

If you are a woman, Boston is a good place for you! It follows closely behind Washington, D.C., as a city of opportunity for women, who constitute 45 percent of its work force.

Part of Boston's dynamism stems from integrating a lively youth culture of success-oriented Yuppies, "techies" and collegiate "preppies" into the mainstream society, all before the backdrop of a quaint, historic city rooted in tradition and pride. This is not to give the impression, of course, that Boston is inhabited solely by young, unmarried adults, although they do constitute 39.2 percent of the city's population. Families exist, but they tend to settle along the outskirts of the city in the many suburbs surrounding the metro area.

Boston is a city of opportunity because its knowledge-based businesses are growing rapidly, aided by defense contracts. Women and young people are especially welcomed in the work force, but skills are essential; area universities will provide them. Boston's quality of life has always been good, with ample outlets for leisure time; its schools are more uniformly excellent than they were a decade ago.

# Charlotte, North Carolina

MSA POPULATION (7/86): 1,065,400 (35th largest)

POPULATION GROWTH 1980–86: 9.7%

COUNTY: Mecklenburg

EMPLOYMENT (9/87): 568,200

AVERAGE TEMPERATURE: 60.5°F

YEARLY RAINFALL: 12.48 inches

HUMIDITY: 61% (23rd most humid)

COST OF LIVING: 99.1

## KEYS TO THE CITY

**Small Business Growth:** birth rate, growth rate, growth index (rank/86): 3.3  3.5  6.8  (29th)

**Average Annual Job Growth (9/84–9/87):** 3.6% (25th/largest 100)

**Keys to Prosperity:** Regional financial and control center, manufacturing, health care, high-tech.

**Key Developments:** Arts Center.

**Key Life-Style Trends:** Charlotte is being discovered as a good place to set up local offices of national businesses; this in turn is bringing in people who want more leisure activities. The recent expansion of cultural programs can be expected to continue.

## WHY OPPORTUNITY KNOCKS IN CHARLOTTE

Charlotte, named for the German queen of King George III of England, was the site of North America's first major gold discovery, in 1799. When the interest in Charlotte's gold waned in favor of other mining centers, it had to settle for the profitable but less glamorous textile industry.

Located in the Southern Piedmont region of North Carolina, Charlotte has a population of 353,448; surrounding Mecklenburg County's population is 442,448. The population of the entire Charlotte–Mecklenburg metro area, which includes Gastonia, North Carolina, and Rock Hill, South Carolina, is 1,065,400.

With a well-developed highway system, a central location along the populous East Coast and a pleasant climate shared with its Piedmont neighbors, Charlotte is a magnet for corporate control centers, boasting major presences of 289 Fortune 500 firms. It is within one-hour's flying time from 50 percent of the nation's population.

For a midsize city, Charlotte's economic statistics are impressive. Its 1,000-odd manufacturing firms have a combined employee payroll of over $1 billion. The city's per capita sales are currently the highest in the nation, and Charlotte is the tenth largest wholesale center in the United States; as the location of a branch of the Federal Reserve, and with more than $54 billion worth of deposits in locally headquartered financial institutions, Charlotte is the country's eighth largest financial center. With a well-educated populace, good infrastructure and good educational facilities, Charlotte has attracted 2,025 new firms, representing $1.8 billion worth of capital investment, in the past ten years. New industry is mainly in communications, financial services, and microelectronics research, development and light manufacturing. Other major industries are education, health care, government and transportation.

---

## QUALITY OF LIFE

**Weather:** Charlotte has a moderate climate with long spring and fall seasons, and a summer season with very hot weather conditions (90°F and above) occurring about one-third less often than in southern Florida; the temperature approaches 100°F an average of twice a year. Temperatures fall below freezing on an average of one-half of winter days; snow accumulation infrequently exceeds six inches annually.

**Education:** The Charlotte–Mecklenburg School District has an enrollment of 72,378 pupils in 100 schools. Special educational programs for children with learning disabilities are provided at three separate facilities. Currently, 75 percent of Charlotte's high school graduates go on to attend institutions of higher learning. Four-year colleges and universities in Mecklenburg include the

University of North Carolina at Charlotte, Johnson C. Smith University, Queens College, Sacred Heart College, Barber-Scotia College, Belmont Abbey College, Davidson College, Wingate College and Winthrop College. Two-year institutions include Central Piedmont Community College, Gaston College, King's College and Rutledge College. Combined enrollment of the area's colleges and universities is 43,983 students.

**Neighborhoods:** Five minutes from the city's center is Charlotte's Dilworth section, an older residential neighborhood of mainly upper- and middle-class families. The city's fourth ward section, once a prestigious neighborhood, has been recently revitalized, and features brick sidewalks, granite curbs and Victorian street lamps.

**Politics/Government:** The city of Charlotte is administered by a city council, a city manager and a mayor. Charlotte's new mayor, Sue Myrick, a Republican, defeated former Republican mayor Harvey Gantt over infrastructure improvement issues. Charlotte has a strong, progrowth public-private partnership. City council representation is based on districts, which (thus far) has afforded citizens of Charlotte's various neighborhoods ample voice in economic development issues.

**Transportation:** Although inner-city bus service is available, a car is a necessity in Charlotte. Intercity ground transportation is available from Greyhound, Trailways and Amtrak, which has two scheduled departures each day. The Charlotte–Douglas International Airport is served by nine major airlines, daily operating 85 commuter flights and 267 normal commercial flights.

**Health Care:** Health-care facilities consist of twelve hospitals with a combined capacity of 2,545 beds; five of these hospitals are general medical and surgical facilities. Fully staffed departments offer orthopedic, cardiac rehabilitative, ear-nose-throat, substance abuse and psychiatric care. In addition, there are twelve long-term-care facilities with a total of 1,140 beds, and 554 beds available for immediate convalescence periods.

**Child Care:** Charlotte and surrounding Mecklenburg County have a number of licensed child-care centers and in-home providers. Child Care Resources, Inc., a referral and matching agency that serves Charlotte and Mecklenburg, may be reached at 704-376-6697.

**Housing:** The average three-bedroom, two-bathroom home sells for $87,500 in Mecklenburg County. The median price range for condominium units is $45,000 to $65,000. Rent figures for one-bedroom apartments average between $250 and $450 a month. Housing is mostly apartment and condominium units. Most new residential developments are to the south and southeast of the city, but much new residential construction has occurred recently to the north, near the University of North Carolina technical park.

**Public Safety:** Crime rates in the area are slightly higher than the national average, with 561 violent crimes and 3,155 property crimes reported for 1987 (down from prior years). In 1986 there were 428 reported robberies per 100,000 city residents.

**Cultural Attractions:** Charlotte's cultural life is enriched by the city's Arts Center, in Spirit Square, which sponsors exhibitions, performances, classes in the visual arts and provides offices for area arts organizations. The city's Community School of the Arts enrolls 800 students in the visual arts, music and dance. Charlotte's museum facilities include the Afro-American Cultural and Service Center, which promotes, presents and preserves African and black history and culture; the Discovery Place science museum; and the Mint Museum of Art, which runs exhibitions, lectures, films, tours and classes. Music and theatrical performances are presented by the Charlotte Opera Association, the Charlotte Symphony Orchestra, the Charlotte Community Concert Association, the Charlotte Pops Orchestra and the Charlottetown Players. Other drama companies are the Ace-Charlotte Repertory Theater, the Little Theater of Charlotte and the Playwright's Forum.

**Sports/Recreation:** Baseball fans will have to content themselves with AA minor-league baseball (the Charlotte O's); in participant sports, Charlotte offers boating, swimming, golf and tennis.

**Taxes:** Taxes in the area are low. North Carolina's income tax is 7 percent on earnings over $10,000, and property taxes are levied on the full assessed value of residential property at a rate of $1.3425 per $100. North Carolina's sales tax is 3 percent and Mecklenburg County adds 2 percent; the state sales tax on big-ticket items such as cars, airplanes and boats is 2 percent (Mecklenburg County adds no tax where the rate is less than 3 percent), with a maximum collectible amount per purchase of $300. The area's total local tax bite is 3.38 percent of average annual household income.

## WHERE TO BREAK IN

Individuals interested in seeking employment in the Charlotte–Mecklenburg area should consult personal contacts and college alumni associations, as well as trade and professional organizations. We include a listing of the area's major employers (1,000 or more employees). For more information, call the Charlotte Chamber of Commerce at 704-377-6911.

| Firm/Organization | Product/Service | No. Employees |
|---|---|---|
| Duke Power | electric utility | 10,869 |
| Charlotte–Mecklenburg School District | education | 7,900 |
| IBM Corp./Information Products Div. | computer products | 5,600 |
| State of North Carolina | government | 4,539 |
| Charlotte–Mecklenburg Hospital Authority | hospital administration | 4,182 |
| City of Charlotte | government | 3,965 |
| First Union Corp. | financial services | 3,632 |
| North Carolina National Bank, Inc. | banking | 3,100 |
| Southern Bell | telephone utility | 3,008 |
| U. S. government | government | 2,897 |
| Mecklenburg County | government | 2,707 |
| Presbyterian Hospital | general medical and surgical hospital | 2,241 |
| Belk Brothers | retail sales | 2,100 |
| U.S. Postal Service | government | 1,965 |
| Harris Teeter Supermarkets | supermarkets | 1,957 |
| General Tire and Rubber Co. | auto tires | 1,750 |
| Lance, Inc. | confections | 1,700 |
| Piedmont Airlines | air passenger carrier | 1,450 |
| University of North Carolina at Charlotte | education | 1,300 |

## SUMMING UP: OPPORTUNITY FOR WHOM?

Charlotte's work force of 238,130 enjoys an unemployment rate of 3.5 percent, well below the national average. The healthy diversity of Charlotte's economic structure is illustrated in the following table, which represents the distribution of the area (Mecklenburg County).

| Industry | Share of Work Force (in %) |
| --- | --- |
| Wholesale and retail trade | 28 |
| Manufacturing | 17 |
| General services | 15 |
| Government | 10 |
| Transportation, communications and utilities | 10 |
| Finance, insurance and real estate | 8 |
| Construction | 6 |
| Health-care services | 6 |

As a regional center for health care, Charlotte will continue to generate opportunities for health-care professionals. With a high concentration of both foreign and domestic electronics firms, Charlotte should also continue to absorb electrical engineers, electronics technicians and computer scientists. The healthy financial industry should maintain its demand for bankers, accountants and people with data-processing and communications expertise. In addition, Charlotte's strong trade sector should create more opportunities for retail managers.

# Chicago, Illinois

CHICAGO–GARY–LAKE COUNTY, ILL.–IND.–WIS. CMSA POPULATION (7/86): 8,116,100 (3rd largest), of which Chicago, Ill. PMSA population is 6,118,000 (3rd largest.)

POPULATION GROWTH 1980–86: 2.1%

COUNTY: Cook

EMPLOYMENT (9/87): 2,989,700

AVERAGE TEMPERATURE: 48.9°F

YEARLY RAINFALL: 31.72 inches

HUMIDITY: 63% (16th most humid)

COST OF LIVING: 130.0

## KEYS TO THE CITY

**Small Business Growth:** birth rate, growth rate, growth index (rank/86): 2.4  3.1  5.5  (67th)

**Average Annual Job Growth (9/84–9/87):** 1.7% (75th/largest 100)

**Keys to Prosperity:** Finance, health care, small businesses. Chicago has been suffering through some severe problems in its financial sector (Continental Illinois, First National Bank of Chicago) and other problems related to the downturn in agriculture, and this has left the city pretty subdued. But new small businesses are bubbling up. Chicago will rise again.

**Keys to Development:** Cityfront Center, South Side recycling center.

**Key Life-Style Trends:** It's not a glitzy environment, *Playboy* aside. The middle class is hiding out in suburbia. It will help when the racial confrontation in the city government is resolved.

## WHY OPPORTUNITY KNOCKS IN CHICAGO

Chicago, "City of the Big Shoulders," is one of America's leading industrial and transportation centers. With a 1980 population of 3,005,072, Chicago was the second largest U.S. city following New York; by 1985 it had slipped to third place after Los Angeles. It is the heart of trade and commerce in the Midwest, manufacturing more fabricated metals and food products than any other urban area in the country. The value of goods and services produced yearly in Chicago totals about $154 billion.

But the American economy, once grounded in industry, is steadily shifting toward the service sector. This reorientation has meant exceptionally hard times for Chicagoans. People joke that Chicago is gradually becoming the "City of the Slumping Shoulders." But Chicagoans are not laughing. Since 1970, manufacturing jobs have plunged by 30 percent, representing the biggest loss of industrial jobs in the country. Today, manufacturing accounts for 22 percent of the Illinois work force, down from more than 30 percent during the 1960s and 1970s. Chicago's steelworkers also suffered. Since 1979, more than 13,000 steelworkers have lost jobs due to a general decline in the demand for steel as well as the increasing squeeze of foreign competition. By the end of 1985, Chicago's unemployment rate stayed at a high 8.3 percent while the rest of the United States averaged 6.7 percent. Unemployment in the steel district soared to 25 percent.

Chicago's biggest problem today is luring big businesses to the city and convincing those who are settled to stay. Companies cite many reasons for being unwilling to set up shop. Among the most common are: (1) unfavorable labor relations due to the fact that Chicago doesn't have right-to-work laws; (2) high operating costs; and (3) a poor business climate. Many big businesses are reluctant to locate in Chicago because 41 percent of Illinois's manufacturing employment is unionized, double the national figure of 21 percent. Widely unionized labor, businesses complain, leads to inexorable pressures for high wages and inadequate flexibility for management to compete with nonunionized plants. High utility rates and soaring liability insurance rates also turn businesses away.

So, where are the bright spots in the midst of all this gloom? Chicago does have certain pockets of opportunity. If you are looking to start a small business or are hoping to work for an upstart corporation, you are in luck! According to many economists, big businesses make news, but small businesses create jobs. Dun and Bradstreet recently reported that new business incorporations grew by an impressive 40 percent in Chicago between 1980 and 1985. The national average was only 25 percent, barely half as much. In 1985, Illinois saw the birth of 34,691 new incorporations, becoming the fifth best place in America for fledgling enterprises.

Jobs are also available in the service sector. Chicago is the center for health-related industries and finance in the Midwest. Placing second for best overall health care in the United States, Chicago maintains 226 doctors for every 100,000 residents. The area's six noted medical schools and numerous hospitals and rehabilitation facilities make Chicago one of the world's primary medical research centers.

Chicago has with good reason been hailed as the financial capital of the Midwest. Lining downtown LaSalle Street are six major banks, the Midwest Stock Exchange (the second largest securities exchange in the United States after the New York Stock Exchange), the 7th Federal Reserve Bank and the Chicago Board of Trade. The Chicago Board of Trade was founded in 1848. Today, this institution stands as America's oldest financial exchange as well as the world's largest grain market, accounting for 45 percent of the nation's futures contracts. The Chicago Mercantile Exchange is the busiest market for perishable commodities and accounts for another 25 percent of the nation's futures contracts. Together, the Board of Trade and the Mercantile Exchange make Chicago the world's capital in futures trading.

Chicago's picture is bright if you consider the entire Chicago metro area rather than focus solely on the core city. The U.S. Bureau of Census defines the Chicago PMSA area as consisting of the three Illinois counties of Cook, McHenry and DuPage. Contrary to popular belief, Chicagoans did not flock to the Sunbelt or any other region of the country during their mass exodus from downtown during 1965–85. Most of them moved only a few miles outside of the inner city to surrounding suburbs. Between 1970 and 1980, over 150,000 Chicagoans lost manufacturing jobs. At the same time, some 300,000 people migrated from the city to the suburbs. Today, thirty burgeoning suburbs are the beneficiaries of Chicago's economic decline. Skyscrapers are jutting out of once-residential soil, forming what some call "penturbs"—an intermediary stage between city and suburb.

Of all the suburbs, northwest Cook County has enjoyed the greatest growth. So many shopping centers, restaurants and recreational facilities exist that residents rarely visit downtown Chicago. Today, suburbs account for 60 percent of the metro area's population—as well as 60 percent of the jobs. Big companies have relocated outside of Chicago because they could not resist the suburbs' large expanses of land and low property taxes.

Economic analysts now worry that the suburbs will begin to decline if people continue moving out of the inner city, forcing the rich to retreat even further. The key to combating further degeneration, they insist, is to stimulate growth within the city itself. In 1984, 103 new factories were erected, and both retail sales and employment increased. Today, Alexander Cooper, designer of Donald Trump's sixty-two-acre "Television City," is working on "Cityfront Center" in Chicago. This project will be built on sixty acres of vacant industrial land owned by Equitable Life Insurance Society and Chicago Dock and Canal Trust Co. It will provide 22 million square feet of luxury office space, apartments and hotels, to be built over the next twenty years.

Banker James A. Fitch of Chicago's South Side is also attempting to revitalize business and create jobs by building a waste-recycling center on vacant land in the abandoned steel district of southeast Chicago. The project will not only provide jobs and dispose of waste, it will also generate energy to sell to plants. The plan would preserve existing jobs by helping small machine shops and steel-fabricating plants. As a final step, the plan is to construct a cargo airport in southern Chicago, relieving air traffic congestion at the world's busiest airport, O'Hare, located on the northwest side of Chicago.

---

## QUALITY OF LIFE

**Weather:** Chicago's climate is classified as continental, characterized by hot summers and cold winters. During summer, periods of high heat and humidity may last for several days; the moderating effects of Lake Michigan at times keep the city as much as 10° cooler than outlying areas.

**Education:** Chicago has the third largest public school system, following New York and Los Angeles. The city's 600 schools are responsible for 431,000 students. Institutions of higher learning include publicly funded University of Illinois, Chicago State University and Northeastern Illinois University; private schools include the University of Chicago, Roosevelt University, Loyola University of Chicago, Mundelein College and Northwestern in suburban Evanston. With six medical schools, Chicago is a leader in medical education and research.

**Neighborhoods:** The quality of life in Chicago depends on the area of the city you choose to call home as well as on your social circle. Chicago is divided into four areas.

Downtown Chicago is known for spectacular skyscrapers, huge department stores, fashionable shops and beautiful Grant Park. As many as 575,000 people work in the downtown area. Some 30,000 live in luxurious, modern, high-rise apartments. The main downtown area is circled by elevated trains, hence its nickname, "The Loop." The most impressive downtown building is the 110-story Sears Tower, the tallest building in the world.

The North Side is almost entirely residential. It is home to about 1 million people, of whom 72 percent are white, 18 percent are Hispanic and 6 percent are black. The most famous section in this area is called the "Gold Coast," a luxurious residential area with graceful old apartment buildings, Victorian mansions and expensive skyscraper apartments.

The West Side is the city's chief industrial district. It is plagued with poverty, abandoned and decaying buildings, a high crime rate and intense racial conflicts. Of its 600,000 residents, 50 percent are black, 29 percent are Hispanic and 21 percent are white. Factories, rail yards, truck loading docks and warehouses abound in this area; unemployment is nevertheless high.

The South Side constitutes Chicago's biggest section in area and population. It covers more than one-half of the city's total area. Due to its size, the South Side cannot be characterized by any one trait. It is marked by industrial areas, an international port, parks, pleasant residential communities and poverty-stricken neighborhoods. Of 1,400,000 South Siders, 60 percent are black and the rest are of German, Hispanic, Irish or Polish descent.

**Politics/Government:** One of Chicago's ugliest problems is race relations, exemplified by the strained relations between the late mayor, Harold Washington, and the white-majority city council. Blacks and Hispanics experience extreme levels of poverty. A third of all Chicago black families have an annual income below the nationally accepted poverty line. Half of all black males of working age are unemployed, primarily because they have no marketable skills. Half of all black households in Chicago have no father living at home, and 65 percent of the area's black babies are born to unmarried women.

**Transportation:** With a subway system, numerous city buses, a ferry line and seven commuter railroads, Chicago has excellent public transportation facilities, of which 32 percent of commuters avail themselves daily. Those who choose to drive to work face heavy commuter freeway traffic. The city is also served by Amtrak, which provides twenty-one departures daily. Chicago's O'Hare International Airport is the nation's busiest, handling 42,873,000 passengers annually. The airport is served by forty-two carriers supplying a daily total of 927 flights.

**Health Care:** A leader in health care, Chicago is home to twenty-one teaching hospitals, fifteen cardiac rehabilitation centers and six major hospices.

**Child Care:** In Chicago, call the state's licensing bureau for child-care service—the Department of Children and Family Services at 312-793-8600.

**Housing:** The average monthly rent for a one-bedroom apartment is $325; a three-bedroom, two-bathroom house goes for around $86,000 in Chicago's currently depressed real estate market.

**Public Safety:** With 1,030 reported 1986 robberies per 100,000 city residents, Chicago ranks among the cities in our study with the highest crime rates. People living in black neighborhoods are eleven times more likely to be victims of a violent crime than people who live in white neighborhoods. The Robert Taylor Homes is perhaps the nation's biggest housing project, covering fifteen blocks along South State Street and Dan Ryan Expressway. Its 20,000 residents, almost all black, live in twenty-eight crowded buildings where assaults and robbery are common.

**Cultural Attractions:** If you are looking for cultural attractions, Chicago has them. Five million tourists visit this cultural center yearly to listen to the world-famous Chicago Symphony Orchestra, which performs in Orchestra Hall for thirty-two weeks beginning each September. From late June till the end of August, the Grant Park Symphony Orchestra gives free concerts in Grant Park's outdoor band shell. The Lyric Opera Company has an annual fall and winter season in the Civic Opera House. Chicago's theaters present the more popular Broadway plays.

Chicago is also for museum lovers. The Art Institute of Chicago is world famous for its collection of French Impressionist art. The huge Museum of Science and Industry stands in Jackson Park, and both the Adler Planetarium and the Field Museum of Natural History are located in Grant Park. There is also the Chicago Academy of Sciences and the Chicago Historical Society.

**Sports/Recreation:** Among the city's leading sports attractions are the National Baseball League's Chicago Cubs (Wrigley Field), the American League's Chicago White Sox (Comiskey Park), the NFC's Chicago Bears, the NBA's Chicago Bulls and hockey's Chicago Blackhawks.

**Taxes:** The average annual burden of state and local taxes for Chicago residents is slightly over 3 percent of average annual income, comparatively moderate for such a large city.

---

## WHERE TO BREAK IN

For individuals interested in relocating to Chicago, we include a list of select major area employers. For more information, call the Chicago Chamber of Commerce at 312-786-0111.

| Firm/Organization | Product/Service | No. Employees |
|---|---|---|
| Sears, Roebuck & Co. | retail sales | 450,000 |
| McDonald's Corp. | restaurant mgmt. | 127,000 |
| State of Illinois | government | 110,000 |
| Beatrice Cos., Inc. | food processing | 100,000 |
| Sara Lee Corp. | frozen foods | 90,900 |
| Motorola, Inc. | mobile electronics | 88,800 |
| United Parcel Svc., Inc. | package shipping | 87,100 |
| Borg Warner Corp. | financial services | 82,900 |
| Montgomery Ward & Co., Inc. | retail sales | 78,500 |
| American Info Tech Corp. | data processing | 77,500 |
| Dart & Kraft, Inc. | food | 77,100 |
| City of Chicago | government | 35,535 |
| Cook County | government | 23,000 |

## SUMMING UP: OPPORTUNITY FOR WHOM?

Despite Chicago's declining industrial and manufacturing sectors, the city's economy remains resilient because of its diversity. The city provides many tax breaks and incentives for start-up enterprises, which is why small businesses keep springing up. Opportunities abound for professionals in the fields of law, medicine, education and finance. Those involved with wholesale/retail also have many open doors, but they are advised to walk through suburban doors, because general trends indicate that most Chicagoans spend their money in the huge suburban shopping malls. There are also opportunities extended by big businesses located in the metro area.

Surprisingly, Chicago is not a center for high tech. In the decade 1972–82, the state of Illinois lost 11,000 high-tech jobs while the rest of the nation added 968,000. Nor is Chicago a good place to locate if you are looking for employment in the fields of heavy industry or manufacturing.

# Cincinnati, Ohio

CINCINNATI–HAMILTON, OHIO–KY.–IND. CMSA POPULATION (7/86): 1,690,100 (23rd largest), of which Cincinnati, Ohio–Ky.–Ind. PMSA population is 1,418,600.

POPULATION GROWTH 1980–86: 1.2%

COUNTY: Hamilton

EMPLOYMENT (9/87): 687,900

AVERAGE TEMPERATURE: 54°F

YEARLY RAINFALL: 39.04 inches

HUMIDITY: 64% (13th most humid)

COST OF LIVING: 99.8

## KEYS TO THE CITY

**Small Business Growth:** birth rate, growth rate, growth index (rank/86):   2.7   3.3   6   (48th)

**Average Annual Job Growth (9/84–9/87):** 4.2% (14th/largest 100)

**Keys to Prosperity:** Manufacturing (aircraft, cars, food products, cleaning products), government (postal center), finance, health care.

**Key Developments:** Renovation of convention center, Centennial Plaza, Forest Fair, gradual absorption of overbuilt downtown space.

**Key Life-Style Trends:** Named after the Roman farmer who agreed reluctantly to leave his plow to accept a call to lead his country, Cincinnati was settled by industrious German immigrants and still bears the features of a serious but good-natured town with good business–government relations; it's a good place to bring up a family.

## WHY OPPORTUNITY KNOCKS IN CINCINNATI

Henry Wadsworth Longfellow once called Cincinnati "Queen of the West." And though the "Queen" has been hard hit by foreign competition, she maintains her throne. Greater Cincinnati is blessed with a stable, diverse, mature economy based on numerous

127

recession-resistant industries that rarely boom or bust. Cincinnati ranks thirteenth in the nation in the value of total manufacturing shipments. It is a major center for wholesaling, manufacturing, retailing, insurance, finance, government installations and service industries.

Among its more prominent manufacturing groups are: transportation equipment such as aircraft engines and motor vehicles, food products, metalworking and industrial machinery, chemicals, fabricated metals, printing and publishing, toys, apparel, shoes and housewares.

Cincinnati is the home of several Fortune 500 corporations, including Procter & Gamble, Armco, Cincinnati Milacron, Eagle Pitcher, Palm Beach, Kroger, Federated Department Stores, U.S. Shoe, Western-Southern Life Insurance, American Financial and Ohio Casualty. It is also the location of major federal government installations, including a regional postal service center, a center for environmental research, and an occupational health and safety research center.

International business continues to grow in Cincinnati. Approximately 500 area companies generate sales totalling $2.5 billion abroad each year. These firms export large quantities of jet engines, industrial robots, computer software, paper and consumer goods. About 80 area operations are owned by companies based in Japan, Western Europe and Canada. Japanese auto plants are expected to increase business in the area.

Retail trade is one of Cincinnati's major economic sectors. In 1985, total retail sales in the Cincinnati–Hamilton metro area was estimated to be $9.7 billion. Total retail space downtown is 3 million square feet. A new 1.1-million-square-foot shopping mall called Forest Fair is under way, while a number of other local malls plan to expand.

One of Cincinnati's most attractive features is availability of affordable office space, what realtors call a "soft market." The central business district is overbuilt, forcing Cincinnati developers to offer competitive rental rates that are among the least expensive downtown rental rates in the nation. The Queen City compares well with regional competitors such as Columbus, Cleveland and Indianapolis. Cincinnati has over 12.7 million square feet of office space in the downtown area and 8 million square feet of suburban office buildings and parks. Cincinnati's industrial market is among the largest in the Midwest, with 260 million square feet of total space. Approximately 9 million square feet were available as of September 1986.

Recent construction in the downtown area includes the renovation of the convention center, completed during the summer of 1987; restoration of Cincinnatian Hotel, opened during February 1987; phase two of the Centennial Plaza office building; and Longworth Hall design center and nightclub. Ground-breaking for the Fountain Square West project will be in late 1987, with completion scheduled for 1992. This fifty-one-story building will cost $246 million and will house a Marriott Hotel along with offices and retail stores. Many other projects are taking place both inside and immediately outside the city.

## QUALITY OF LIFE

**Weather:** With a couple of 0°F days, about 100 freezing days (32° and below), and a month's worth of 90° days each year, Cincinnati's climate is quite livable.

**Education:** The Cincinnati metro area is divided into fifty-nine public school districts that provide 394 schools serving 233,481 pupils. The pupil/teacher ratio is about 17 to 1, and an average of $2,456 is spent per student each year. The City of Cincinnati also offers twenty-eight alternative programs, which include specialized enrichment programs such as the School for the Creative and Performing Arts, Reading/Language Arts, Foreign Language, Paideia Critical Thinking School, plus many others.

The University of Cincinnati, with over 35,322 students, is noted for its nationally prominent College of Medicine, School of Engineering and College Conservatory of Music. Other institutions of higher learning include Miami University at Oxford, Xavier University, Northern Kentucky University, Hebrew Union College, Thomas More College, College of Mount St. Joseph and the Cincinnati Art Academy.

**Neighborhoods:** Greater Cincinnati is composed of over 100 communities and municipalities, which were once distinct rural villages when the region's steep hills and deep valleys carved up the geography. Today, many of these expanded villages have become suburban, but Cincinnati's neighborhoods often retain distinct

characteristics relating to the period during which they were settled by waves of German, Irish and Jewish immigrants.

**Transportation:** Although the three interstate highways serving
Cincinnati have heavy commuter traffic, the city's excellent municipal bus system and commuter ferry line make mobility relatively
painless. Amtrak provides two trains daily, and Greyhound and
Trailways service is available. The Greater Cincinnati International
Airport, about fifteen minutes from city center, over the Ohio River
in northern Kentucky, forms a medium-size air travel hub and is
served by thirteen airlines providing a total of 168 flights daily.

**Health Care:** Health care is also a large industry in Cincinnati. The
greater Cincinnati area provides more than thirty hospitals with
over 9,000 beds. At the center of this vast medical community is
the University of Cincinnati Medical Center. The Children's Hospital Medical Center is the largest pediatric facility in the United
States and is recognized throughout the country as one of the
nation's best children's hospitals. It was here that Dr. Albert Sabin
developed the oral polio vaccine and Dr. Leon Goldman established the first laser laboratory. Specialized hospitals treat chroni-
cal illness, psychiatric problems and chemical dependencies.

**Child Care:** Call Child Care Resource and Referral at 513-621-8585.

**Politics/Government:** Cincinnati has a council-manager form of
government with a so-called weak mayor. The mayor is chosen for
a two-year term by the city council from among its membership,
and lacks veto power. All nine of the council's members are elected
at large, serve for two years and meet twice a month. Cincinnati
went 59 percent for Reagan, 36 percent for Carter in 1980.

**Housing:** The average cost in the Cincinnati area of a new three-
bedroom, two-bathroom house is $85,000.

**Public Safety:** According to our bellwether crime standard of robberies per 100,000 residents, Cincinnati emerges as a relatively
safe city, with a comparatively low figure of 328.

**Cultural Attractions:** Cincinnati has much to offer in terms of
cultural attractions. Founded in 1875, the Cincinnati Symphony is
America's second oldest symphony and was the first American
professional symphony to take a world tour. It shares Music Hall
with the Cincinnati Opera, which was founded in 1921. The city
also boasts a ballet company and numerous theater groups. Among
the city's many museums are the Art Museum at Eden Park, the

contemporary Arts Center, the Taft Museum, the Museum of Natural History and Krohn Conservatory.

**Sports/Recreation:** Professional sports include the Reds (baseball), the Bengals (football), the Slammers (basketball), as well as pro golf, tennis and horse racing. The 1987 World Figure Skating Championships were held in Cincinnati. Recreational attractions include the world-famous Cincinnati Zoo and a number of theme parks, which include the 1,600-acre Kings Island Amusement Park, Americana, Coney Island, the Beach, Surf Cincinnati and Fantasy Farm. Old-fashioned fairs such as Oktoberfest Zinzinnati, Summer Fair and Riverfest attract visitors from all over.

**Taxes:** Ohio's sales tax is 5 percent, to which Hamilton County adds an additional 0.5 percent; real estate is assessed at 35 percent of market value, and taxes are levied at a rate of between $33.58 and $67.82 per $1,000, depending on municipality. The city of Cincinnati imposes a 2 percent income tax, and state income tax on taxable earnings between $40,000 and $80,000 is $1,710 plus 6.65 percent of excess over $40,000.

---

## WHERE TO BREAK IN

For people interested in seeking employment in Cincinnati, we supply a list of the area's major employers.

| Firm/Organization | Product/ Services | No. Employees | Phone (area code 513) |
|---|---|---|---|
| General Electric Co.'s Aircraft Business Group | aerospace | 18,000 | 243-2000 |
| Procter & Gamble | household products | 13,000 | 562-1100 |
| University of Cincinnati | education | 10,700 | 475-8000 |
| The Kroger Co. | supermarket | 10,000 | 762-4000 |
| U.S. government | government | 10,000 | 684-2101 |
| U.S. Postal Service | mail/ government | 6,400 | 684-5448 |
| Armco, Inc. | steel products | 6,000 | 425-6541 |
| Cincinnati Public Schools | education | 5,500 | 369-4000 |
| City of Cincinnati | government | 5,500 | 352-3000 |
| Cincinnati Milacron, Inc. | robotics | 5,000 | 841-8100 |
| Hamilton County | government | 4,700 | 632-6500 |

## SUMMING UP: OPPORTUNITY FOR WHOM?

The greater Cincinnati area comprises parts of Ohio, Kentucky and Indiana. Cincinnati is the thirty-second largest city in the nation and the second largest metro area in Ohio. It was ranked among *Saturday Review*'s top five most livable cities and among the *Christian Science Monitor*'s top ten. The city began as a river town settled by German immigrants who established a tradition of industry and innovation. As the city evolved, a close working relationship developed between business and local government, resulting in a congenial business climate. Today, the service sector is also growing. Total commercial banking assets in the Cincinnati metro area for 1986 were $10.8 billion. Major banks in the area include First National, Central Trust, Fifth Third, Provident, Society, AmeriTrust, Bank One, BancOhio and Huntington.

Cincinnati makes the *Cities of Opportunity* list because of its overall hospitable environment for business. It is not a hotbed of entrepreneurship and is traditional in many ways. One survey rates Cincinnati as one of the worst cities for working women. Another rates the city's two largest employers—General Electric and Procter & Gamble—as providing particularly good benefits for women, but says their record of promotion of women has not been outstanding.

# Columbus, Ohio

MSA POPULATION (7/86): 1,299,400 (29th largest)

POPULATION GROWTH 1980–86: 4.5%

COUNTY: Franklin

EMPLOYMENT (9/87): 662,600

AVERAGE TEMPERATURE: 51.5°F

YEARLY RAINFALL: 37.01 inches

HUMIDITY: 63% (16th most humid)

COST OF LIVING: 102.5

---

## KEYS TO THE CITY

**Small Business Growth:** birth rate, growth rate, growth index (rank/86):  2.9  3.8  6.7  (30th)

**Average Annual Job Growth (9/84–9/87):** 4.3% (12th/largest 100)

**Keys to Prosperity:** Five reasons cited by local businesses for Columbus's prosperity: good business environment; quality labor force (productivity, training, work ethic); low cost of operation; availability of research and technology, facilitating enterprise and innovation; and access to markets.

**Key Developments:** In 1986 more than $2 billion in new business construction was completed or begun, starring a $370 million expansion by The Limited, Inc., and including new facilities for Ross Laboratories and a two-block-long downtown mall (Columbus City Center) with more than ninety-five stores anchored by Jacobson's, Marshall Field and Lazarus. A new restaurant and a high-rise condominium fronting on the Scioto River represent a toehold for expected new riverfront development.

**Key Life-Style Trends:** Astonishing volunteerism: nearly 60 percent of all adults in Columbus volunteered more than fifty hours in 1987. Participant sports: miles of bike paths, an abundance of softball teams, numerous golf courses. Growing arts community: opera, ballet, theater, symphony, four professional dance companies, two museums, over twenty galleries—plus the Wexner

Center for the Visual Arts, under construction at Ohio State University.

---

## WHY OPPORTUNITY KNOCKS IN COLUMBUS

Columbus, Ohio, America's nineteenth largest city, faces the future with bright expectations. It is a new metro center, with few of the problems that plague older cities. Columbus's vitality stems from imaginative scientific innovations that have led to substantial upsurges in business activity. Job opportunities abound in the fields of science and technology.

Employment in Columbus since 1979 has grown by 12.9 percent. Unemployment at the end of 1987 was 4.6 percent. The Columbus MSA has added 90,000 jobs in the last four years. In the period 1980–85 Franklin County witnessed a net increase of 4,500 establishments.

Columbus is the third greatest research center in the world, following Washington and Moscow. Major local research and technical centers include: Ohio State University, Battelle Memorial Institute, Industrial Nucleonics Corporation, Ashland Chemical Company, Chemical Abstracts Service (a division of American Chemical Society), Bell Telephone Laboratories, Rockwell International's Columbus Aircraft Division, CompuServe, Inc., Online Computer Library Center, Goal Systems International and Ross Laboratories.

Columbus has also earned a name as headquarters city for such business heavyweights as Borden Inc., Nationwide Insurance Company, American Electric Power, Wendy's International, Inc., and The Limited, Inc., as well as more than sixty insurance companies. Columbus's vitality stems from imaginative scientific innovations that have led to substantial upsurges in business activity. Job opportunities abound in the fields of science and technology. Long-standing local businesses that established the city's initial economic foundation include Jeffrey Mining and Manufacturing (now Dresser Industries, Inc.), Battelle Memorial Institute, F&R Lazarus and Company, Buckeye Steel Castings (a subsidiary of Worthington Industries) and the Dispatch Printing Company.

The availability of research and technology has enabled Columbus businesses to be on the cutting edge of the "Information Age." Battelle Memorial Institute is the world's largest independent research facility, and Ohio State University has more than 4,000 individual faculty members engaged in a wide variety of research, analysis, design testing and consultation. These institutions, along with Chemical Abstracts Service, collected more than $425 million in 1984–87 revenues for contract research and information services. Columbus has one of the highest concentrations of scientists, engineers and information specialists of any city in the world.

This opportunity is supported by a strong network of resources and interaction, for example, through the Technology Alliance of Central Ohio. The Business Technology Center incubator is located near The Ohio State University. The Thomas Alva Edison Welding Institute recently opened at the OSU Research Park.

As a major information-processing center, Columbus is home to insurance companies, several banking and finance centers, and information centers for the Sears Discovery Card, CompuServe's North American network and Online Computer Library Center's international network.

Keeping Columbus's information industries in supplies are more than 120 computer dealers, 100 manufacturers of electronic components and equipment, 70 firms that repair computers and electronic and scientific instruments, and almost 140 companies that offer various types of industrial equipment, machine tools and other specialized forms of equipment. These dynamic industries are the keys to Columbus's future economic growth.

---

## QUALITY OF LIFE

**Weather:** Columbus weather is varied, but subject to cold winters: The area averages about a week of 0°F days, and well over 100 freezing (32°F and less) days each winter; summer, however, is generally comfortable, with about two weeks of 90° days.

**Education:** The Columbus metro area is divided into forty-nine public school districts, consisting of 412 schools responsible for 216,060 pupils. The pupil/teacher ratio in Columbus Public Schools is 18.4 to 1, with $2,822 spent per pupil every year. This emphasis on education is reflected in a dropout rate of less than 3 percent. Sixty-seven percent of the metropolitan area has at least one year of postsecondary education and 18 percent of the adult population holds a bachelor's degree. Forty-three postsecondary and technical training programs are in the Columbus area, with eight degree-granting institutions in Franklin County—the largest of these being the Ohio State University, with 55,000 students.

**Neighborhoods:** Among Columbus's many downtown neighborhoods are German Village, with restored nineteenth-century homes and brick sidewalks as well as restaurants and shops popular among tourists; Victorian Village and Olde Towne East, characterized by large, stately houses, built mostly between the 1880s and the 1920s; and Italian Village, noted for its modest two-story brick-and-frame structures, built during the late nineteenth and early twentieth centuries.

**Politics/Government:** Columbus has a mayor-council form of government. The mayor and seven at-large city-council members oversee more than 7,000 employees and a $473 million operating budget.

**Transportation:** It is easy to get around in Columbus and the surrounding area. More than 1,600 miles of roadway and 210 miles of expressways ensure twenty-minute access to downtown from any point in the county. The Central Ohio Transit Authority provides convenient and affordable public transportation. An extensive state highway and Interstate system makes Columbus less than a twelve-hour drive away from two-thirds of the U.S. population. Port Columbus International Airport, Bolton Field, Don Scott Airport and Rickenbacher Field provide private and commercial aircraft passenger and cargo facilities to reach 80 percent of the population in ninety minutes' air time. Nineteen airlines making 264 daily flights reach all major North American and European markets with direct or one-stop flights.

**Health Care:** Health care in Columbus is of high quality and low cost. The area offers 187 physicians for every 100,000 people. Two teaching hospitals include the Ohio State University Hospitals and Riverside Methodist Hospital. The area's medical school is the Ohio State University College of Medicine. Advances in health-care research and practice are particularly evident in heart care, cancer research and pediatrics.

**Child Care:** Working parents can call Action for Children (614-224-0222) for a variety of child-care services, including information, referral, counseling and emergency care.

**Housing:** A house will run approximately $65,000, while a two-bedroom apartment will cost you about $355 a month.

**Public Safety:** A relatively safe city, Columbus registered 382 robberies per 100,000 city residents in 1986.

**Cultural Attractions:** Columbus's lively arts community has been growing as quickly as the city. The Palace Theater is the home of Opera Columbus, and the restored Ohio Theater is the home of Ballet Met and the Columbus Symphony Orchestra, conducted by Christian Badea. The Columbus Museum of Art and the many Short North area galleries appeal to art lovers. Community theater abounds, and the Center of Science and Industry is a hands-on exposition center. For fair-lovers, Columbus hosts the country's largest state fair. The Ohio State Fairgrounds welcomes 3.5 million visitors each year. The Ohio Historical Society offers displays and demonstrations year-round, including the re-created nineteenth-century Ohio Village. The Columbus Zoo features more than 145 acres of animal habitat, gardens and picnic areas and is world famous for its breeding habitats. In the summer, under the City's "Music in the Air" program, over 150 free concerts are performed in municipal parks.

**Sports/Recreation:** Columbus offers some top-notch spectator sports opportunities, including the PGA Memorial Tournament; the Bank One/Nationwide Marathon; New York Yankee AAA minor-league baseball with the Columbus Clippers; the Little Brown Jug, one leg of the pacing triple crown; football with the Ohio State Buckeyes; and the Columbus 500, a professional car race. The city's gently rolling landscape contributes to an abundance of golf courses (over seventy) and tennis courts. Many of these sports facilities are municipal, making them easily accessible to all Columbus residents. There are over 11,000 acres of metropolitan parks. Bicycling trails (over 110 miles) and public and private swim clubs are close to every neighborhood. Three lighted snow skiing areas are within one hour's drive from the city. For the fisherman and boater, the Olentangy and Scioto Rivers are nearby. Five major downtown riverfront festivals each attract more than 250,000 people yearly.

**Taxes:** The city of Columbus taxes personal income at a flat rate of 2 percent, and some suburban municipalities have income taxes of from 0.5 percent to 2 percent; the State of Ohio has a graduated income tax structure, with a minimum tax rate of 0.743 percent and a maximum rate of 6.9 percent, imposed on incomes of $100,000 or more. Residential property in Columbus is taxed at an effective rate of $41.66 for each $1,000 of assessed valuation. Ohio's state sales and use tax is 5 percent to which Franklin County adds 0.5 percent.

## WHERE TO BREAK IN

Major Columbus employers are listed below.

| Firm/Organization | Product/ Services | No. Employees | Phone (area code 614) |
| --- | --- | --- | --- |
| State of Ohio | government | 19,968 | 466-6511 |
| The Ohio State University | education | 15,200 | 292-6446 |
| Columbus Public Schools | education | 7,639 | 225-2600 |
| AT&T Communications, Inc. | communications | 7,500 | 469-0010 |
| City of Columbus | government | 6,500 | 222-7671 |
| Rockwell International | aerospace | 6,500 | 239-3344 |
| Nationwide Insurance Co. | insurance | 6,000 | 249-7111 |
| Defense Construction Supply Center | military | 5,092 | 238-2224 |
| Franklin County | government | 4,853 | 462-3223 |
| Riverside Methodist Hospital | health care | 4,451 | 261-5221 |
| F&R Lazarus & Co. | dept. stores | 4,200 | 463-2121 |
| Sears, Roebuck & Co. | retailing | 4,200 | 868-7181 |
| Honda of America, Inc. | autos | 4,175 | 864-5250 |
| Big Bear/Hart Stores | auto repair/ supplies | 4,000 | 464-6500 |
| The Kroger Co. | supermarkets | 4,000 | 898-3200 |
| Battelle Memorial Institute | research | 3,711 | 424-6424 |
| The Limited, Inc. | retail clothing | 3,700 | 475-4000 |
| U.S. Postal Service | mail/ government | 3,622 | 469-4276 |
| Bank One of Columbus | banking | 3,592 | 459-1589 |

| Firm/Organization | Product/ Services | No. Employees | Phone (area code 614) |
|---|---|---|---|
| J. C. Penney Co. | dept. stores | 3,564 | 276-9011 |
| BancOhio National Bank | banking | 3,400 | 463-7635 |
| Mt. Carmel Health | health care | 3,200 | 225-1337 |
| Ohio Bell | communications | 3,057 | 223-5123 |
| Catholic Diocese of Columbus | church | 3,000 | 228-2457 |
| Kmart Corp. | discount stores | 3,000 | 459-2150 |

## SUMMING UP: OPPORTUNITY FOR WHOM?

Future employment in the Columbus area will be increasingly dominated by employment in the service-producing sector, which includes transportation, finance, insurance, real estate, wholesale and retail, general services and government. Overall, employment is projected to grow by 80,533, or 12.3 percent, between 1987 and 1995, with approximately 81.3 percent of that growth coming from the services sector. This translates into 3,692 new jobs in transportation and utilities, 19,273 new jobs in wholesale and retail trade, 12,116 new jobs in finance, insurance and real estate, 31,823 new jobs in general services and 6,786 new jobs in government.

The share of manufacturing employment in Columbus, as in the nation, will continue to decline over the next eight years, from 15.7 percent in 1987 to 14.7 percent in 1995. This is the smallest share decline in manufacturing since its employment peak in 1973. However, while the total share of manufacturing employment decreases, the Columbus area is projected to add 5,208 new manufacturing jobs between 1987 and 1995.

The city's turn toward the service sector and high-tech makes Columbus especially attractive to highly educated, white-collar workers. During 1986, total nonfarm employment grew by 26,800, reaching 630,400. The increase was nearly all in nonmanufacturing industries, which added 26,700 jobs. Overall employment increased at 4.4 percent, while nonmanufacturing grew by 5.4 percent.

In nonmanufacturing, the largest job gain was the addition of 9,500 jobs in the service industries. About 2,800 of these were in business services, a segment that grew by 9.5 percent in 1986.

Columbus has approximately 32,200 jobs in advertising, computer and data processing, personnel supply, building cleaning, accounting and auditing, and other services to businesses.

The area's largest service industry is health services, which has been growing at an above-average rate of 5.6 percent. In 1986, the health services sector gained 2,000 jobs, reaching a new annual level of 38,000.

Closely following the service industries is retail employment, which grew by 4.8 percent in 1986. It added 5,700 jobs during 1986, including 1,100 jobs in general merchandise stores.

Strong, steady, stable growth is evident in Columbus, which has doubled in geographic size and population since 1960. Columbus is the only city in the northeastern United States to experience continuous growth since 1970. It has an economy that is nearly recession-proof, with broad-based employment in manufacturing, service industries, research and technology, distribution, government, and wholesale and retail trade. The twenty-first century looks bright for Ohio's largest city.

# Dallas–Fort Worth, Texas

CONSOLIDATED METRO (CMSA) POPULATION 7/86: 3,655,300 (8th largest)

  METRO DALLAS, TEX. (PMSA): 941,700

  METRO FORT WORTH–ARLINGTON, TEX. (PMSA): 446,550

POPULATION GROWTH 1980–86 (CMSA): 24.7%

COUNTIES: Dallas (Dallas), Tarrant (Fort Worth)

EMPLOYMENT (CMSA, 9/87): 1,824,400

  DALLAS (PMSA): 1,306,600

  FORT WORTH–ARLINGTON (PMSA): 517,800

AVERAGE TEMPERATURE: 65.5°F

YEARLY RAINFALL: 32.30 inches

HUMIDITY: 53% (30th most humid)

COST OF LIVING: 108.6 (Dallas), 100.3 (Fort Worth)

---

## KEYS TO THE CITY

**Small Business Growth:** birth rate, growth rate, growth index (rank/86):  5.3  3.9  9.2  (2nd)

**Overall Job Growth (9/84–9/87):**

  Dallas (PMSA): 0.8% (91st/largest 100)

  Fort Worth (PMSA): 2.3% (59th/largest 100)

**Keys to Prosperity:** Dallas–Fort Worth (DFW) recently surpassed Houston in size, primarily because DFW is less affected than Houston by the oil slump. Dallas has some oil and gas headquarters operations, but DFW petroleum industry employment is just a smudge on the chart. Rather, DFW is (1) a financial center (Dallas finances a lot of oil and gas business as well as agriculture, real estate and other things), with one-fifth of its employment in financial services; (2) a distribution and transportation gateway (Fort Worth was a major distribution center even before the arrival of the DFW airport), accounting for nearly one-third of area employment; and (3) a high-tech, aerospace and electronics manufacturing center, accounting for nearly one-fifth of area employment and for two-

141

thirds of all Texas defense dollars. Dallas's aggressive Chamber of Commerce has lured many a company from the Northeast.

**Key Developments:** Dallas's real estate slump was inevitable—buildings were being thrown up at an unsustainable rate. The initial impact of a slowdown was job loss—half of the jobs lost being in the construction industry. Dallas entrepreneurs are aggressively selling their city as a real estate bargain. As oil prices creep back from their $9-per-barrel 1986 low, Dallas will share in the renaissance of real estate prices. Fort Worth was never growing as rapidly as Dallas and has not suffered nearly as much from the slump, though its office vacancy rate is nearly as high.

**Key Life-Style Trends:** Dallas has a requisite number of big musical and performing arts centers, and a football team that has had its proud moments. Smaller Fort Worth is building a name for itself as a major museum center, with an unusually strong art collection. Social life still centers around the backyard barbecue, and talk likely as not will be about business.

---

## WHY OPPORTUNITY KNOCKS IN DFW

The Dallas–Fort Worth area grew rapidly through 1985. As of mid-1986, the consolidated metro statistical area (CMSA) of DFW passed Houston in size to become the eighth largest metro area in the United States and the largest in Texas.

Located in the northeast corner of the state, Dallas is the glitz-and-glamour city of Texas. Dallas covers an area of 378 square miles and shelters a population of 1,957,378. Fort Worth is located in Tarrant County, thirty-five miles west of Dallas. The population of Tarrant County is 1,101,300; Fort Worth's population is 446,550. The consolidated metro area formed by Dallas–Fort Worth had a mid-1986 population of 3,655,300, and its 25 percent growth since 1980 was barely second to Phoenix among metro areas of over 1 million population.

Like other major Texas cities, Dallas proper is physically BIG, covering an area of 378 square miles (still, only two-thirds of the area of Houston proper) and having a density of a low 2,417 persons per square mile, below the national average for big cities. The suburban population increased by 9.8 percent during the boom years 1976–80.

When the first oil strikes were made near Houston, Dallas established itself as the financier of the Texas petroleum industry. After they become rich from the initial wave of Texas oil production, Dallas bankers funded further oil exploration in East Texas (no oil has ever been found in or near Dallas), and financed local diversification into the electronics industry while expanding their banking and finance interests. Dallas is home to three of Texas's largest banks as well as the regional Federal Reserve Bank. In fact, Dallas's enormous 8,000-member Chamber of Commerce has been largely responsible for marketing the city as a center for corporate headquarters, most recently having snagged J. C. Penney from New York City. Unlike Houston, and in spite of the oil glut, Dallas has enjoyed real economic expansion throughout the 1980s, due in part to its more diversified base and in part to the city's aggressive approach to attracting new business. The city is currently base for thirteen of the nation's biggest and richest public corporations: Texas Instruments, LTV Corporation, Diamond Shamrock, Dresser Industries, American Petrofina, National Gypsum, Mitchell Energy and Development, Tyler Corporation, Lafarge, E-Systems, Dr. Pepper, Trinity Industries and Holly. Dallas is also home to 4 of the 100 fastest growing small public companies identified by *Inc.* magazine in 1987. They represent the most innovative and vital growth in the American economy, since they create new jobs in new industries. These four companies are in computer software, oil and gas development, satellite transmissions and development of radiographic systems: Sterling Software, Shanley Oil, Satellite Music Network and Video Science Technology, respectively.

In spite of its rapidly growing population, the DFW area has a weak real estate market, due mainly to earlier speculation and factors external to the area's economy: In the 1970s and early 1980s, heavy speculation in real estate was fed by pension funds. Then, in the early 1980s, federal tax reform reduced the allowable depreciation period from thirty to fifteen years, and the deregulation of savings and loan associations forced borrowers to pay more for their money.

With strong capital resources, good education, the ever-attractive absence of corporate taxation in Texas and a well-trained work force, Fort Worth continues to attract new businesses while already established firms expand their facilities. As with other cities we have selected for our study, job growth and corporate moves have been in high-tech industries such as aerospace and the manufacture of data-processing and telecommunications equipment, plus the proliferation of their support industries, such as software firms, insurance companies and banks, and transportation and shipping companies.

Back in the heyday of Texas steer ranching, Fort Worth was a more important and better-known city than Dallas, which didn't catch up and outshine Fort Worth until the growth of its banking industry. More recently, Fort Worth, with a bit of an identity crisis, has served as a warehousing and distribution center for the northeastern Texas region. Nonetheless, the Fort Worth area's 24.2 percent population growth between 1980 and 1986, accompanied by a 26.9 percent growth in employment over the same period (adding 112,929 new jobs), is well worth noticing.

## QUALITY OF LIFE

**Weather:** The DFW area has a warm, moderately humid climate. The temperature reaches 90°F and above an average of ninety-five days a year, and it dips to 32° or less around forty days a year.

**Education:** The Dallas Independent School District, with 127,584 students enrolled, is the ninth largest in the nation, educating 14.26 students for every 100 residents. Over 19 percent of Dallas's adult population is college educated, and 58 percent of Dallas high school grads go on to higher education. Dallas has 101,784 postsecondary students enrolled at its nine two-year colleges (two private, seven public) and thirteen four-year colleges and universities (ten private, three public); in addition to undergraduate curricula, graduate and professional programs are offered in music, arts, medicine, business and law. The Fort Worth Independent School District consists of sixty-one primary schools, eighteen middle schools and thirteen senior high schools, educating a total of 109,387 pupils. Tarrant County is served by thirty parochial schools (combined enrollment 5,800), two nonreligious private schools offering K–12 (combined enrollment 1,500) and nineteen other private schools, including several with programs for the learning disabled (combined enrollment 1,284). The Fort Worth area has about 62,374 students enrolled full-time in higher educational programs offered by Tarrant County Junior College, Texas Wesleyan College, Southwestern Baptist Theological Seminary, the University of Texas at Arlington, Texas Christian University, Arlington Baptist College and the Texas College of Osteopathic Medicine. Instruction in arts, music, religion, sciences and medicine are offered; the A.A., B.A., B.S., M.A., M.S., Ph.D. and D.O. degrees may be obtained.

**Politics/Government:** As elsewhere in Texas, elections are nonpartisan and are held in April. The city governments of both Dallas and Fort Worth are highly regarded, with well-reputed city councils and a city-manager form of government. Dallas has been described as "the city that works," and Fort Worth has recently won many management awards. Both cities are actively involved in seeking to use the private sector to help provide public services, a sign of taxpayer-oriented innovation in a time of austerity.

**Transportation:** Transportation in and around the Dallas–Fort Worth area will probably be your car. Four major interstate highways pass through Dallas, two of which go on to Fort Worth, but traffic is heavy. Both cities offer municipal busing. The Dallas–Fort Worth International Airport is the biggest in the world, and is served by thirty-seven airlines providing 554 flights a day.

**Health Care:** Health care in the Dallas–Fort Worth area is relatively low-cost, with more than fifty hospitals, including six teaching hospitals, seven cardiac rehabilitation centers and four hospices.

**Child Care:** In the Fort Worth–Tarrant County area, working parents in need of child-care quality/availability information can consult the Day Care Association of Fort Worth–Tarrant County (817-831-0374); in Dallas/Dallas County, consult Child Care Dallas (214-630-7911).

**Housing:** A one-bedroom apartment in Dallas averages $400 a month, and the average house costs $124,600. Folks relocating to the area can get a furnished apartment for $30 a night while they're looking for a job or long-term housing.

**Public Safety:** The crime rates of Dallas and Fort Worth are fairly high, with, respectively, 914 and 780 reported 1986 robberies per 100,000 city residents.

**Cultural Attractions:** Dallas offers impressive cultural and entertainment attractions. The Music Hall in State Fair Park is the home of the Dallas Symphony Orchestra, the Dallas Civic Opera and the Dallas Ballet. The facility also stages musical plays. The Dallas Museum of Art, completed in 1984, has extensive holdings in pre-

Columbian art. There are also a science museum (the Science Place), a Museum of Natural History and a historical museum (Hall of State). Fort Worth offers the Amon Carter Museum of Western Art, the Fort Worth Art Museum and the Tandy Archeological Museum. Fort Worth boasts the Kimball Museum, a major art collection second only to the Getty Museum in its intensity of acquisition. Fort Worth ranks with New York, Los Angeles and Chicago in the art museum field, especially in the post-Impressionist collection. Friends of the performing arts can avail themselves of the Fort Worth Ballet, the Fort Worth Symphony Orchestra, the Fort Worth Opera Association and musicals à la Broadway at the Casa Manana Theater.

**Sports/Recreation:** The Dallas Cowboys (football, NFL) represent the entire CMSA, as do the Texas Rangers (baseball, AL), based in the Fort Worth suburb of Arlington. Dallas is also home of the Mavericks (basketball) and the Sidekicks (soccer).

**Taxes:** Dallasites enjoy very low local taxes, which, including sales, property and auto taxes, amount to only 5.6 percent of average yearly household income. The sales tax in Fort Worth is 5³⁄₈ percent, and local property taxes are about $1.60 per $100 of assessed value. Rent, lighting, food and clothing expenses, however, are fairly high, the fifth highest in the nation after New York, Washington, D.C., Philadelphia and Los Angeles.

---

## WHERE TO BREAK IN

Individuals interested in relocating to the Dallas–Fort Worth area should be aware that a few of the area's major growth industries are aerospace, computer and telecommunications technologies; financial services; trade; and transportation and shipping. We supply a partial listing of major employers. For more information, call the Dallas Chamber of Commerce at 214-954-1111, or the Fort Worth Chamber of Commerce at 817-336-2491.

| Firm/Organization | Product/Service | No. Employees |
|---|---|---|
| General Dynamics— Fort Worth Div. | military aircraft and aerospace | 17,500 |
| City of Dallas | government | 10,000 |

| Firm/Organization | Product/Service | No. Employees |
|---|---|---|
| American Airlines | air passenger carrier | 7,966 |
| Fort Worth Independent School District | education | 7,008 |
| Bell Helicopter Textron | helicopters | 7,000 |
| Tandy Corp./Radio Shack | microcomputers and peripheral equip. | 6,600 |
| City of Fort Worth | government | 6,000 |
| Carswell Air Force Base | military personnel | 5,000 |
| General Motors Corp.—GM Assy. Div. | automotive assy. | 4,000 |
| University of Texas at Arlington | education | 4,000 |
| Arlington Independent School District | education | 3,442 |
| Delta Airlines | air passenger carrier | 3,085 |
| Southwestern Bell | telephone utility | 2,387 |
| Harris Hospital—Methodist | health care | 2,384 |
| Tarrant County | government | 2,006 |
| Gearhart Industries, Inc. | oil well logging equip. | 1,660 |
| Federal Aviation Admin. | government | 1,573 |
| Motorola, Inc. | communications equip. | 1,500 |
| Texas Christian University | education | 1,438 |
| Alcon Laboratories, Inc. | pharmaceuticals | 1,400 |
| Carswell Air Force Base | civilian personnel | 1,400 |
| Lone Star Manufacturing, Inc. | automotive air conditioners | 1,200 |
| Miller Brewing Co. | brewery | 1,100 |

## SUMMING UP: OPPORTUNITY FOR WHOM?

The current unemployment rate of the diversified Dallas work force of 1,482,436 is 5.5 percent; Fort Worth's labor force of 529,400 is currently 4 percent unemployed. The Dallas and Fort Worth work forces have the following distributions for eight basic industrial categories:

Cities of Opportunity

|  | Share of Work Force (in %) | |
|---|---|---|
| Industry | Dallas | Fort Worth |
| Wholesale and retail trade | 26.7 | 29.0 |
| Services | 22.3 | 19.6 |
| Manufacturing | 16.8 | 24.0 |
| Government | 10.6 | 8.7 |
| Finance, insurance and real estate | 10.3 | 5.6 |
| Transportation, communications and utilities | 6.3 | 5.1 |
| Construction | 5.5 | 7.0 |
| Mining | 1.5 | 1.0 |

The current development of the area's economy illustrates the trend in the American economy in general, with a shift from low-skills/high-output manufacturing to high-skills/low-output manufacturing and services. We may predict an increase in the number of members of the area's work force employed in the manufacturing and services categories, with the distinction that the new positions will require training and/or skills in the areas of computer technology and electrical engineering and technology, as well as laboratory skills and training.

Dallas and Fort Worth have few opportunities for people interested in building new office space. Dallas at the end of 1987 had a 29 percent office vacancy rate, Fort Worth a 27 percent vacancy rate. Only Houston at 32 percent and Denver at 30 percent had higher vacancy rates (contrast Boston, with 6 percent, or midtown New York, with 11 percent).

# Denver, Colorado

DENVER–BOULDER CMSA POPULATION (7/86): 1,847,400 (23rd largest), of which the Denver PMSA population is 1,633,100

POPULATION GROWTH 1980–86: 14.1%

COUNTY: Denver

EMPLOYMENT (9/87): 801,400

AVERAGE TEMPERATURE: 50.1°F

YEARLY RAINFALL: 15.51 inches

HUMIDITY: 40% (37th most humid)

COST OF LIVING: 103.8

---

## KEYS TO THE CITY

**Small Business Growth:** birth rate, growth rate, growth index (rank/86): 3.9   3   6.9   (25th)

**Average Annual Job Growth (9/84–9/87):** −0.6% (97th/largest 100)

**Keys to Prosperity:** Natural resource development, high-tech, tourism, regional services, gradual absorption of vacant buildings.

**Key Developments:** A soon-to-be-constructed convention center and international airport will ensure the city remains a regional air travel hub.

**Key Life-Style Trends:** Burgeoning skiing, hiking and backpacking opportunities and growing urban cultural amenities.

---

## WHY OPPORTUNITY KNOCKS IN DENVER

Though the boom of the 1970s seems to have run its course, what made Denver attractive then keeps it attractive now. Throughout the 1970s, scores of energy-related firms relocated to Denver. Since 1978, over twenty new skyscrapers have been built—along with hosts of new hotels, bars and restaurants, and shopping centers—to accommodate the already arrived and the predicted influx of

149

new Denverites. It seems, however, that developers overestimated the eagerness with which firms would flock to Denver, and others were caught in mid-construction by the departure of natural resource company employees after the plummet in oil prices. As a result, at the end of 1987 Denver was the country's second most overbuilt market (after Houston), with a 30.5 percent vacancy rate in office space. But, far from being a ghost town, Denver to many presents a ripening real estate horizon ready for harvesting at rock-bottom prices.

Despite its considerable reliance on the oil industry, Denver has the good fortune to be a petroleum center in a state that is a net importer of oil. This means that lower oil prices have not made Denver as financially strapped as Houston. Greatly diversified, Denver's post–oil boom economy makes a strong showing in its burgeoning service sector as well as in tourism, high-tech, public construction and retail trade. Manufacturing, agriculture and mining have fallen on hard times, but these areas seem to have little effect on Denver's overall economic outlook. Denver ranks ahead of San Francisco, Salt Lake City and Los Angeles in *Inc.* magazine's 1987 list of the fifty fastest growing U.S. metro areas. Growth in jobs for Denver is reported at 9.7 percent for the period 1981 to 1985; business births at 3.7 percent between 1982 and 1986; and high-growth companies at 3.1 percent between 1982 and 1986. Even with now-defunct Frontier Airlines laying off 3,000 employees, job growth is expected to continue rising steadily between 2 and 3 percent and should pick up as ground is broken for the city's new convention center and international airport. The international airport, which is to be completed by 1992–93, is expected to do for Denver what new airports did for Atlanta and Dallas—make the city a hub of international business.

The only persistent economic worry in Denver is overbuilding. Experts predict that the city will take up to five years to absorb the staggeringly high number of office vacancies. Retail centers are also overbuilt and showed a 12.8 percent vacancy rate at the end of 1986. Early in 1987, a local development firm planned the auction of over 200,000 square feet of downtown office space. What rented for $30 to $32 per square foot five to six years ago now brings in only $1 to $4 per square foot. This is an ideal climate for inexpensive business expansion, and another wave of growth seems likely.

## QUALITY OF LIFE

**Weather:** With the front range of the Rocky Mountains forty miles to the west, Denver's skyline includes fabulous scenery—when you can see through the haze. Denver has 300 sunny days a year, more than San Diego or Miami. Relative humidity is low at 40 percent, and average temperature is 50.1°F.

**Education:** The average pupil/teacher ratio in the public schools is a favorable 15.6 to 1, and average expenditure per pupil per annum is $2,965, placing Denver among the top ten American cities in spending on education. Denver's fifteen institutions of higher learning are highlighted by a multi-institutional downtown campus for over 35,000 students.

**Neighborhoods:** Denver offers a variety of residential communities with distinctive life-styles: Cheesman Park, an upper-middle-class district, is characterized by its older homes; popular among young professionals, Capital Hill is mixed ethnically and economically, but large and medium-size renovated structures predominate; the city's Curtis Park neighborhood is also multiracial and has many upgraded older homes. Cherry Creek, also located in incorporated Denver, is a fairly exclusive neighborhood of high-end older homes. Denver's downtown offers a variety of multi-family residential settings. South of Denver lies Cherry Hills, the most upscale and exclusive of the area's suburbs and the location of most of the area's large estates; the average price of a home in Cherry Hills is $400,000. Lakewood is a firmly middle-class suburban town west of Denver where moderately priced ($90,000) homes predominate. To the east, Aurora has an even mix of multi- and single-family dwellings and is accessible to young professional couples starting a family. North of Denver are located the blue-collar and middle, class suburbs of Westminster, Thornton and Northglenn.

**Transportation:** Denver motorists face a nasty commute: The city's freeways are inadequate for the area's traffic volume. Intracity transportation presents a rosier picture, however, because of the city's excellent municipal bus system. For travel to points outside Denver, Amtrak offers six trains daily. Denver's Stapleton International Airport is served by twenty-five airlines offering over 500 flights daily.

**Health Care:** Health care in the Denver area is of high quality and low cost. Area facilities include a number of teaching hospitals, cardiac treatment centers and a center for cancer treatment.

**Child Care:** Mile High Child Care Resource and Referral (303-837-9999) can hook up working parents with licensed day-care providers.

**Housing:** In incorporated Denver the average three-bedroom, two-bathroom home sells for $112,743, while an 800-square-foot apartment rents for around $500 a month.

**Public Safety:** Denver is a relatively safe city, with 405 reported 1986 robberies per 100,000 city residents.

**Cultural Attractions:** Should you wish to involve yourself in an activity that does not require special gear, the city has some great indoor entertainment. The Natural History Museum in City Park is a must-see. The Museum of Western Art is also first-rate and houses a fine collection of Russells and O'Keefes and even a few Rembrandts. Other cultural diversions include the Gates Planetarium, IMAX Theater, Colorado Historical Society, Denver Art Museum and Denver Botanic Gardens. The grand and historic Brown Palace hotel adds yet another dimension to the city's cultural fare. Professional performances are given year-round by the Denver Symphony Orchestra and the Denver Center Theater Company, the University of Denver and the University of Colorado. The opera and ballet companies schedule performances on a less regular basis, and the two major universities and one college in the metro area add to the offerings. In addition, summer concerts are featured in Denver's numerous parks.

**Sports/Recreation:** Professional sports fans can root for any of a number of teams: the Broncos (pro football), the Nuggets (basketball) and the Zephyrs (minor-league baseball).

People in Denver are outdoorsy. Though Denver is not exactly an alpine hamlet, fabulous ski resorts are easily accessible from the city. Vail and Aspen, along with the Keystone/Arapahoe Basin and Copper Mountain clusters, are easy drives from Denver. Snow stays on the slopes until April or May, and the city attracts plenty of powder-loving hearties. Those who take to the slopes in the winter often take to the hills in the summer. Rocky Mountain National

Park, fifty miles to the northwest of the city, offers well-maintained trails and many convenient campsites.

Denver itself, though increasingly congested and cluttered, has made a point of preserving open spaces within the city limits. City Park, Cheesman Park and Washington Park are all great for bicycling, running and general hanging out.

**Taxes:** While the city of Denver levies no tax on personal income, the state of Colorado does, at a flat rate of 5 percent on adjusted federal gross. Residential property in incorporated Denver is assessed at 20 percent of market value and taxed at a rate of 96.711 mills. Colorado's sales and use tax is 3 percent, to which Denver adds 4.6 percent.

---

## WHERE TO BREAK IN

Denver is the business hub of the Rocky Mountain area. Besides being the seat of state government, the mile-high city is the region's major financial center and hosts the state's largest private employers, listed below. For more information, call the Greater Denver Chamber of Commerce at 303-534-3211.

| Firm/Organization | Product/Service | No. Employees |
|---|---|---|
| Coors-Adolph (Golden) | brewery | 8,000 |
| Storage Technology (Louisville) | computing equip. | 7,000 |
| Gates Rubber Co. | rubber and plastic hoses | 5,700 |
| Mountain States Telephone | telephone utility | 4,600 |
| Ideal Basic Industries | cement, hydraulic | 3,500 |
| United Banks of Colorado | state banks | 3,300 |
| Intrawest Financial Corp. | national banks | 1,920 |
| Manville Corp. | mineral wool | 1,450 |
| Cobe Laboratories | medical instruments | 1,200 |
| Public Service of Colorado | electric utility | 1,200 |
| Susquehanna Corp. (Englewood) | plastics | 1,160 |
| Miniscribe Corp. (Longmont) | manufacturing | 1,000 |
| NBI Inc. (Boulder) | electronics | 1,000 |

Denver is also home to a federal mint and the regional offices of many federal agencies. In addition to these large companies, Denver supports a healthy small business community, with over 40 percent of the area's companies employing only one to four persons and 67 percent of companies employing fewer than fifteen people.

The Greater Denver Chamber of Commerce might also prove helpful in a job hunt. The Chamber sells a twenty-five page listing of Colorado employers. This list includes the addresses of the various firms and the number of employees each employer has. To order a list, write for "The Largest Employer List," Greater Denver Chamber of Commerce, Research Department, 1600 Sherman Street, Denver, CO 80203.

---

## SUMMING UP: OPPORTUNITIES FOR WHOM?

Despite Denverites' professed love of the environment, the severity of the city's air pollution is second only to that of Los Angeles. Carbon monoxide gas (CO) is the main pollutant. CO is a byproduct of hydrocarbon reactions, and motor vehicles are its largest single source. Denver is automobile dependent, and to exacerbate the already bad situation, Denver's high altitude causes things to burn less efficiently, thereby creating a greater amount of CO in every combustion reaction. City officials acknowledge the problem, and the EPA has commended Denver for having taken action. In 1986 the city passed an ordinance prohibiting the use of wood-burning stoves. A law requiring the use of highly oxygenated fuel has just been enacted by the state legislature.

The population of the City of Denver has not grown over the last decade as the area has witnessed an increasing trend toward suburbanization. In 1980 the population of Denver was 491,000 and that of the metro area was 1.6 million. Approximately 75 percent of the people in the metro area are white, though 93 percent of the suburban population is white. Hispanics comprise roughly 19 percent of Denver's urban population, blacks comprise around 12 percent and women in the work force represent 43.5 percent of all employed. Though predominantly white, Denver has a broader mix of ethnic and racial groups than its Rocky Mountain counterpart, Salt Lake City, and the many successful blacks and Hispanics in Denver testify to the city's lack of prejudice.

# Detroit, Michigan

DETROIT–ANN ARBOR, MICH. CMSA POPULATION (7/86): 4,600,700 (6th largest), of which Detroit, Mich. PMSA population is 4,334,700 (5th largest).

POPULATION GROWTH 1980–86: −3.4%

COUNTY: Wayne

EMPLOYMENT (9/87): 1,873,500

AVERAGE TEMPERATURE: 49.9°F

YEARLY RAINFALL: 30.96 inches

HUMIDITY: 64% (13th most humid)

COST OF LIVING: 110

---

## KEYS TO THE CITY

**Small Business Growth:** birth rate, growth rate, growth index (rank/86):  2.6   3.2   5.8   (53rd)

**Average Annual Job Growth (9/84–9/87):** 3.1% (34th/largest 100)

**Keys to Prosperity:** Auto industry, high-tech companies, service industries (health care, finance); small businesses are burgeoning in Detroit's northern suburbs.

**Key Developments:** Downtown, the Renaissance Center area is coming more alive. New developments include the Millender Center, new marketplace retailing centers in Greektown, the expansion of the Cobo Hall convention center and a new People Mover elevated rail system that connects them all. The east riverfront is getting a concentration of new residential and office developments (Harbortown, River Place) along with several new parks and a dozen restaurants. Large industrial tracts have been assembled for new automobile manufacturing plants by General Motors and Chrysler Corporation. Suburban office development has been concentrated in the communities of Troy, Southfield and Livonia and along sections of the freeway corridors.

**Key Life-Style Trends:** Suburban orientation, but downtown is coming back in style.

## WHY OPPORTUNITY KNOCKS IN DETROIT

The saying "What's good for General Motors is good for America," when edited a bit to conform more closely to reality ("What's good for America is good for Detroit"), comes closer to explaining (at least in part) why Detroit has experienced a change of fortune in the last few years. After the double whammy of the energy crisis of the 1970s followed by the unforeseen fancy that American motorists took to small, fuel-efficient, imported cars by 1981—when oil prices soared to $38/barrel—the Big Three must have thought they'd died and gone to heaven when Americans began to spend beyond their means to buy American cars again. And big American cars, too, running on cheap oil (in June 1986, oil prices dipped as low as $9/barrel) thanks to OPEC's inability to keep its producer cartel together enough to keep oil prices high.

But bull markets and spendthrift confidence don't last forever, a reality to which Detroit has had to adjust with no small pain. Detroit still is, as it was twenty years ago, a major heavy manufacturing center, but not just of automobiles. At the expense of many downtown low-skills manufacturing jobs, the northern Detroit suburbs have broken into high-technology development and manufacturing, with an emphasis on computers and peripherals, microprocessor-controlled manufacturing and milling equipment, laser systems for a variety of applications, robotics and digital test equipment, and materials engineering. Over the past few years there has been concomitant growth in services employment to support the new high-skills/high-pay/high-tech employment. In addition, 1986 was a banner year for industrial and retail construction. Michigan's deregulation of the health-care industry has resulted in entrepreneurial drive to form new HMOs and other programs in a highly competitive market.

## QUALITY OF LIFE

**Weather:** In spite of its northern location, Detroit's climate is relatively mild, thanks to the moderating effects of the Great Lakes (the city is located on Lake Erie, with access to nearby Lake Huron). Winters are cloudy, with daily highs of 32°F and lows of 17°F. Summers are warm, sunny and fairly humid, with average morning lows of 61° and afternoon highs of 84°. The area gets about forty inches of snow a year.

**Education:** In the wake of high unemployment in the early 1980s, Detroit has made an effort to revamp its school system, with emphasis on marketable occupational skills and the importance of postsecondary education. The city has a wide variety of private and publicly funded colleges and universities offering a full spectrum of programs in fine arts, music, liberal arts, sciences, engineering, medicine, business and law.

**Neighborhoods:** People who like center-city living will be attracted to one of Detroit's high-rise riverfront neighborhoods. The Indian Village neighborhood is historical and exclusive, with high property values, while the city's east side is more typically suburban, with the expected split-level colonial fare. Detroit city has 200 neighborhoods, offering a variety of housing choices and lifestyles. Homes range from simple Cape Cod–style bungalows to Tudor mansions, and there are many areas of older clapboards and duplexes or ranch styles and colonials. Most are much more affordable than similar homes in nearby suburbs. Major new amenities and improvements such as parks, schools, community centers, libraries, fire stations and shopping malls have been added to dozens of city neighborhoods in recent years.

**Politics/Government:** Detroit has a mayor-council form of government in which the mayor is elected at large to a four-year term; the mayor is not a technical member of the city council, and can exercise veto power over council actions. All city council members are elected at large (i.e., nondistricted) to four year, nonoverlapping terms; the city council meets weekly. Mayor Coleman A. Young is in his fourth term.

**Transportation:** Detroit motorists face heavy commuter traffic on the area's seven freeways, including three interstate highways, but may choose to avail themselves of one of the two commuter railroads that serve the city. Intracity mobility is assisted by municipal bus service. For intercity travel, passengers may choose Amtrak, which offers three trains daily, or air travel departing from one of the city's two airports, City Airport and Detroit Metro Airport. Both are being expanded; together, they serve 27,000 passengers and offer over 920 flights daily.

**Health Care:** Over 90 hospitals are located in southeast Michigan; one-third are in the City of Detroit, including Detroit Medical Center, the largest research and practice facility in the world. Five of the largest hospitals are in the Detroit Medical Center, which also has special eye care, oncology, rehabilitation and research centers. The Medical Center has more than 2,000 beds and 14,000 employees, including 2,000 physicians.

**Child Care:** Detroit has one of the nation's model Head Start educational-cultural development programs for youngsters under five, serving 4,000 children at eighty learning centers. There are hundreds of privately operated day-care centers in Detroit and the metro area, licensed through the State Department of Social Services; phone 313-256-2243. Or call the Child Care Coordinating Council at 313-579-2777.

**Housing:** The average price of a 1,600-square-foot, two-bedroom home in the Detroit area is $130,000 (the average price of all homes in Greater Detroit is under $70,000); the average monthly rent for a one-bedroom apartment is about $400. Due to a loss of population in recent years, the real estate market is fairly soft ("affordable") in Detroit; homes in luxury neighborhoods are available at a fraction of their cost elsewhere.

**Public Safety:** With 1,497 reported 1986 robberies per 100,000 city residents, Detroit is the second most "unsafe" city of those in this book after Las Vegas. The figure dropped to 1,258 per 100,000 in 1987. Crime data for suburban communities may be obtained from the state police at 517-373-3700.

**Cultural Attractions:** Aside from the legacy of being Hitsville U.S.A.—the birthplace of Motown and a generation of pop music—the Detroit area possesses a variety of symphonic, operatic, rock, gospel, theatrical and dance attractions throughout the year at over 200 locations. The area has more than twenty-five museums, including the Detroit Institute of Arts, Detroit Historical Museum, Museum of African American History, Henry Ford Museum and Greenfield Village, Cranbrook Institute of Science, and the Detroit Science Center. The local artistic community is supported by annual events such as the Montreux-Detroit International Jazz Festival and the Detroit Festival of Performing Arts, plus a variety of art gallery tours, arts councils, street and park art fairs, and theater and park concerts.

**Sports/Recreation:** Among Detroit's professional sports teams are the Lions (football), the Tigers (baseball), the Pistons (basketball) and the Red Wings (hockey). Other recreational and leisure attractions include two zoos (the Detroit Zoo and Belle Isle Zoo), Belle Isle Park, which at 985 acres is the largest island park in the nation, and a number of riverfront parks offering open space, bicycle trails, fishing, picnic grounds, boating facilities, and cultural exhibitions and performances.

**Taxes:** Local taxes take a 4.5 percent bite from average yearly household income. Residential property is taxed at a rate of $82 per $1,000 of assessed valuation ($31 of which is city taxes and the rest of which is school and county taxes), averaging $1,600 per home. City income taxes are 3 percent for residents and 1.5 percent for commuters. There is also a 5 percent city tax on utilities (phone, gas and electric). The state income tax is 4.6 percent and the sales tax is 4 percent.

---

## WHERE TO BREAK IN

For people considering a move to the Detroit metro area, we provide a selected list of the city's major employers. For more information, call the Detroit Chamber of Commerce at 313-964-4000.

| Firm/Organization | Product/Service | No. Employees |
| --- | --- | --- |
| Chrysler Corp. | automotive mfg. | 9,000 |
| General Motors Corp. | automotive mfg. | 6,000 |
| Ford Motor Co. | automotive mfg. | 3,300 |
| NBD Bancorp | banking | 2,800 |
| Detroit Edison Co. | electric utility | 2,400 |
| Michigan Bell | telephone utility | 2,200 |
| Burroughs Corp. | computer equip. | 1,500 |
| Stroh Companies, Inc. | brewery | 1,400 |
| GMF Robotics | robots and robotics systems | NA |
| Comshare Inc. | financial software | NA |
| Comp-Aire Systems, Inc. | design, const. of clean rooms | NA |
| Midwest Components, Inc. | electroceramic semiconductors | NA |

## SUMMING UP: OPPORTUNITY FOR WHOM?

Detroit continues to be a major manufacturing center, but its new high-tech boom in the northern suburban communities makes its future now less dependent on the mood of the automobile-buying public. Having built up a strong base in the industry of tomorrow, the city has more diversity than in the past and is better able to weather cyclical changes. Other sources of future stability should be the expanding financial, services and health-care sectors.

# El Paso, Texas

MSA POPULATION (7/86): 561,500 (67th largest)
POPULATION GROWTH 1980–86: 17%
COUNTY: El Paso
EMPLOYMENT (9/87): 187,700
AVERAGE TEMPERATURE: 63.4°F
YEARLY RAINFALL: 7.77 inches
HUMIDITY: 27% (40th most humid)
COST OF LIVING: 100.3

---

## KEYS TO THE CITY

**Small Business Growth:** birth rate, growth rate, growth index (rank/86):   5.5   2.7   8.2   (10th)

**Average Annual Job Growth (9/84–9/87):** 2.5% (51st/largest 100)

**Keys to Prosperity:** Aerospace—military contracts are an important component of El Paso's economy—in-bond manufacturing—assembly in Mexico of American-made components—and tourism.

**Key Developments:** U.S. government to locate Free Electron Laser Project at White Sands Missile Base as part of Strategic Defense Initiative program.

**Key Life-Style Trends:** Proximity to U.S.–Mexico border makes for frequent cultural exchange; easy and popular are excursions south of the border to take advantage of the shopping, recreation and entertainment resources of neighboring Ciudad Juarez.

---

## WHY OPPORTUNITY KNOCKS IN EL PASO

El Paso is located in the extreme western part of Texas, near the southern border of New Mexico and just over the border from the Federal Republic of Mexico. When all of what is now the Southwest United States still belonged to Spain, this Texas city was called El Paso del Norte (the Northern Pass), because here, where the Rio Bravo del Norte (the Rio Grande) crosses a low point in the

**161**

Sierra Madre Mountains, was a point of easy penetration into the northern territories. After the Mexican War, El Paso del Norte was partitioned (and its name truncated), and Mexico got the southern, transriver part, Ciudad Juarez.

El Paso's population is 561,500. Juarez is more populous, with nearly 1 million inhabitants. With an area of 240 square miles, El Paso's inner-city population of 500,000 has a density of about 2,100 people per square mile. The suburban population of 55,000 increased at a rate of 22.2 percent in the late 1970s. But this population growth was not due entirely to retirees, as El Paso's median age is less than twenty-eight, well below the national average. El Paso's work force is about 11 percent unemployed, in spite of 6.4 percent annual economic growth from 1979 to 1987. In 1986–87, economic growth was 10 percent.

El Paso's close proximity to the Mexican border city of Juarez has created a unique interdependence. For years El Paso's retail trade industry depended on border Mexicans' buying power. Devaluation of the Mexican peso, from 20 to the dollar in 1976 to the present level of some 1,100 to the dollar, has resulted in a retail slump from which El Paso is only now beginning to recover. To make matters worse, an additional negative influence on the city's downtown retail trade was a strong suburbanization trend throughout the 1970s.

But the fact that things may be looking up for El Paso's long-term future makes it one of our cities of opportunity. Between 1982 and 1986 the local services industry experienced a 22 percent rate of growth; over the same period the insurance, finance and real estate business sectors experienced 19 percent growth. At the same time, however, El Paso's old mainstay, the apparel industry, shrunk by 10 percent, but some 19 percent of the city's work force is still employed in the manufacture of clothing. Employment is currently expanding at a rate of 2.5 percent, and 1986 new construction contracts totaled $385 million—a 10 percent increase over 1985, in a city that doesn't have a vacancy problem.

Which is not to say that manufacturing doesn't look good in El Paso. In-bond manufacturing operations, referred to locally as *maquiladoras* or *maquilas*, take advantage of the low wages in Ciudad Juarez by maintaining two facilities—one in Juarez for the production of component parts or assemblies and another in El Paso for final assembly. The manufacturer can then stamp the finished product "MADE IN U.S.A." when, in fact, only a small portion of the total production process is performed by relatively high-priced U.S. labor.

Many El Paso companies are involved in an in-bond program, and their facilities fill the city's Butterfield Trail industrial park. Butterfield Trail is also a Foreign Trade Zone, where foreign goods may be brought for finishing, assembly or storage, free of United States excise tariffs. The El Paso FTZ has attracted Toshiba to Ciudad Juarez, and many of the Japanese giant's suppliers are locating around Toshiba in Butterfield Trail. These in-bond operations are especially profitable to American firms and foreign firms with a strong U.S. presence because they are, essentially, low-cost, dependent, direct suppliers of semifinished products without the fiscal liability of subsidiaries. Firms on the American side of the *maquila* relationship don't pay for the Mexican workers' benefits and don't have to pay taxes on the Mexican facilities, because they don't belong to them anyway. The relationship between the American firm and the *maquila* is purely contractual.

ECONOMIC IMPACT OF *MAQUILADORA* INDUSTRY

|                                            | **El Paso**      | **Juarez**        |
| ------------------------------------------ | ---------------- | ----------------- |
| Employees                                  | 5,000            | 93,000            |
| Plants                                     | —                | 210               |
| Annual Payroll                             | $60.5 million    | $160.1 million    |
| Lease/mortgage payments for facilities in El Paso | $5.7 million | NA             |
| Cash flow of *maquilas* through El Paso banks | $480.2 million | NA              |
| Taxes paid to El Paso and Texas            | $2.2 million     | NA                |
| Benefit to transportation industry         |                  |                   |
|     Truck              | $38.9 million    | NA                |
|     Air                | $17.1 million    | NA                |
|     Rail               | $3.3 million     | NA                |

The single most valuable industry to El Paso's economy is the government/military employment sector, and the services market it generates is also important. The U.S. Army's Fort Bliss, with 22,000 military personnel, 53,000 dependents, 9,000 civilian employees and a combined payroll of $741 million, is responsible for roughly 28 percent of El Paso's economic activity. The nearby White Sands Missile Test Range and Holloman Air Force Base, both in New Mexico, have payrolls of $384 million and $169.7 million, respectively, and a significant impact on El Paso's economy. Construction and other projects at these bases employ local contractors, and military work forces enhance El Paso's housing and retail markets.

Still "up in the air" is the possible impact of the SDI or "Star Wars" missile defense plan, whose Free Electron Laser Project will be located at the White Sands Missile Range. More than 2,000 workers will be employed there during full-swing construction, and the finished facility will employ about 300 highly trained full-time personnel.

It may seem surprising that, contrary to the popular view of U.S.–Mexico border relations, which assumes antagonism on immigration issues, there is actually a warm cooperation embodied in the highly promoted in-bond program. El Paso business leaders promote the Mexican state of Chihuahua's low labor costs, trainable work force and the region's closeness to U.S. markets, convenient infrastructure, valuable manufacturing facilities, and experienced technical and supervisory personnel. El Paso's city management considers itself internationally oriented, in close partnership with nearby Juarez and the entire nation of Mexico. As they should, El Paso business leaders view their fate as very much linked to the future of Juarez and Mexico.

## QUALITY OF LIFE

**Weather:** The climate of El Paso is typical of dry areas, consisting of abundant sunshine, low humidity and little rainfall; January temperatures average 43.6°F and July temperatures average 82.3°.

**Education:** El Paso's public school system enrolls 60,648 K–12 pupils. The high school dropout rate is 4.5 percent, and 61 percent of high school graduates are college bound. The city has 26,335 students enrolled in postsecondary educational programs at its public junior college, the University of Texas at San Antonio and the Texas Tech University Medical School.

**Politics/Government:** El Paso has a mayor-council form of government in which the mayor is an acting member of the city council.

The mayor is elected at large to a two-year term. Although technically a member of the council, as the body's executive the mayor has veto power. There are six other members of the council, each selected by ward to serve two-year, nonoverlapping terms; the city council meets weekly.

**Transportation:** Public transportation in El Paso is provided by city municipal busing. The city is served by three interstate highways on which commuter traffic tends to be heavy. The El Paso International Airport is a medium hub served by nine airlines offering a total of seventy flights a day.

**Health Care:** Medical care in the El Paso area is provided by thirteen private hospitals and one public hospital. The city's health-care facilities offer extensive outpatient treatment, cardiac rehabilitative care, substance abuse programs, comprehensive cancer treatment, and immediate and long-term accident trauma care. In addition, there are nine nursing homes and eight home nursing services.

**Child Care:** Working parents in search of child care can consult the El Paso chapter of the United Way (915-533-2311). The city has 312 registered family homes, 168 licensed day-care centers and 47 group homes.

**Housing:** A two-bedroom, one-bathroom apartment in the El Paso area may be rented for between $300 and $450 per month; an average 1,600-square-foot home (new) sells for between $75,000 and $90,000.

**Public Safety:** Crime is not particularly problematic, relatively speaking, but El Paso has an incidence of violent crime higher than the national average, while its property crime rate is lower than average for U.S. metro areas. In 1986 El Paso residents reported a low total of 215 robberies per 100,000 city residents.

**Cultural Attractions:** El Paso's leaders claim that their city is not like the rest of Texas, and they're probably right: The city's Latin American orientation saves it from the drab homogeneity that characterizes much of Texas. Sure, the El Paso Symphony performs at the city's Civic Center Theatre from September to April, and Ballet El Paso performs the *Nutcracker* every December, but across the river in Juarez, El Paso inhabitants can sample that most infamous of Hispanic spectacles, a bullfight, at the Plaza Monumental Bullring. Visitors to Juarez can also acquaint themselves with the

Aztec civilization that Hernando Cortes did in during Spain's colonial era, at the Juarez Museum of History and Art, which features pre-Columbian artifacts, and the Juarez Museum of Archaeology, which displays pre-Columbian reproductions and gardens.

**Sports/Recreation:** The Juarez Racetrack offers year-round greyhound racing; if you're a gambler, you'll be pleased to know that winning bets are paid off in U.S. dollars. Back in El Paso, there's an annual Hot Air Balloon Fiesta in May and auto racing from April to October. In addition, the Americana Museum specializes in American art and history, and the Fort Bliss Replica Museum has army and Southwest relics, some dating back to the Civil War. A particularly appropriate attraction for El Paso is its Border Patrol Museum of the Immigration and Naturalization Service; children, however, might prefer Insights, El Paso's science museum, which has many hands-on exhibits. Of course, if you're a Texan at heart, you should visit either the Southwest International Livestock Show and Rodeo, held in February, or the Coors World Finals Rodeo, held at the El Paso Coliseum in November.

**Taxes:** Sales tax in El Paso is 6.25 percent, and state and local taxes amount to a low 0.78 percent of annual average household income. El Paso has one of the lowest urban costs of living in the nation, but also a rock-bottom per capita income, of around $9,000, about 25 to 30 percent below the Texas average.

---

## WHERE TO BREAK IN

After consulting intrafield contacts and organizations, individuals considering relocation to the El Paso area may wish to contact the area's major employers directly. For more information, call the El Paso Chamber of Commerce at 915-544-7880.

| Firm/Organization | Product/Service | No. Employees |
|---|---|---|
| Fort Bliss | U.S. Army | |
| | military | 22,000 |
| | civilian | 9,000 |
| Packard Electric Div. | electronics | 12,000 |
| El Paso Independent School District | education | 5,500 |

| Firm/Organization | Product/Service | No. Employees |
|---|---|---|
| Ysleta Independent School District | education | 5,000 |
| City of El Paso | government | 3,917 |
| El Paso Natural Gas | utility | 3,425 |
| Farah Mfg. | apparel | 2,500 |
| Seven Oaks, Inc. | coupon processing | 2,500 |
| Rockwell International | electronics, telecommunications equip. | 1,750 |
| Allen Bradley | electronic components | 800 |
| LTV Corp. | missile assy. | 500 |
| Honeywell Microswitch | regional headquarters | 200 |

## SUMMING UP: OPPORTUNITY FOR WHOM?

El Paso is one of the few cities in the United States where the manufacturing sector is growing fairly rapidly—faster, in fact, than in any other Texas city. Much of the assembly and manufacturing in the El Paso–Juarez area, however, is low-skilled, assembly-line work. But the fact that much of the electronics manufacturing in the area forms the basis of a complex high-tech network of increasing importance to the national economy should generate a variety of opportunities in a fast-growing services and trade sector that currently occupies over 70 percent of the employed work force. Accountants, computer programmers, retail managers, blue-collar supervisors, clerical workers and individuals interested in finance will encounter employment opportunities in a city with current 5 percent annual manufacturing growth, 2.7 percent finance and trade growth and 12 percent construction growth.

# Greensboro, North Carolina

GREENSBORO–WINSTON-SALEM–HIGH POINT, N.C. MSA POPULATION (7/86): 899,500 (45th largest)
POPULATION GROWTH 1980–86: 5.6%
COUNTY: Guilford
EMPLOYMENT (9/87): 459,600
AVERAGE TEMPERATURE: 58.1°F
YEARLY RAINFALL: 41.36 inches
HUMIDITY: 65% (10th most humid)
COST OF LIVING: 99.2

## KEYS TO THE CITY

**Small Business Growth:** birth rate, growth rate, growth index (rank/86): 3.2   4   7.2   (18th)

**Average Annual Job Growth (9/84–9/87):** 2.5% (51st/100 largest)

**Keys to Prosperity:** Light manufacturing (telecommunications equipment, for example) plants of foreign-based companies, insurance, government; health-care growth not as strong as Raleigh's but better than Charlotte's.

**Key Developments:** In 1986, over fifty companies announced move-in or expansion plans; a big catch was the American Express Travel-Related Services Company offices, employing 1,800 as of late 1987 with 400 more to be added within a year.

**Key Life-Style Trends:** Greensboro is looking for hardworking people under thirty, women (sales, nursing) and construction workers. The implications of this for life-style is that the city will see a growth in recreational facilities, which are currently strong in sailing, golf, bicycling trails, tennis and swimming. Family sports are strong (soccer, softball); this is a family town.

## WHY OPPORTUNITY KNOCKS IN GREENSBORO

Greensboro is North Carolina's third largest city. Located in the central Piedmont region, it lies twenty-six miles from Winston-Salem and less than a hundred miles from Raleigh–Durham. Greensboro is benefiting from the love affair that American business is currently having with the Southeast. The Southeast leads as a destination for service-oriented business, bringing in about 26 percent of the nation's total relocations and expansions. New companies value the city's nearness to markets, availability of skilled labor and low degree of unionization. Existing companies appreciate the availability of trained labor and nearness to markets, but also value the good quality of life for their employees and the low taxes.

Greensboro and other North Carolina cities offer a pleasant climate. Greensboro also has the drawing card of access to good educational facilities. Proof of the city's appeal to business is the fact that area employment grew 12.3 percent between 1984 and 1987 to 181,070.

Traditionally a textiles, tobacco and agricultural center, Greensboro later became an insurance headquarters city. More recently the city has attracted light industry such as the manufacture of telecommunications equipment, as well as the U.S. headquarters and manufacturing facilities for several overseas firms.

In 1986, thirty-six major corporations representing the diverse interests of financial services, construction and electronics manufacturing announced plans to locate new facilities in Greensboro, and fifteen others announced intentions to expand their present facilities there. Private industrial employment is heavily supplemented by extensive federal, state, local and educational employment, as well as considerable health-care employment. The Greensboro trade and construction sectors are also strong, riding the wave of Southeast Mania.

## QUALITY OF LIFE

**Weather:** Greensboro's pleasant, mild, four-seasons climate is partially a result of the city's positioning, blocked from westerly airflows by the Blue Ridge and Brushy mountains. While temperatures do fall to freezing on more than half of all winter days, subzero temperatures are all but unknown to the area.

**Education:** The Guilford County public school system enrolls 21,155 students in forty-four elementary schools, middle schools and senior high schools. The dropout rate in the area's high schools is 5.3 percent, and 70 percent of high school graduates go on to college. The area has twenty-five private schools, most with some religious affiliation.

Greensboro-Guilford has two state universities, three private colleges and one community college. The North Carolina Agricultural and Technical State University is a historically black institution well known for its engineering department. North Carolina Agri-Tech offers six programs and the B.A., B.S., M.A. and M.S. degrees. Students at the University of North Carolina at Greensboro follow academic programs at the baccalaureate, master's and doctoral levels in economics, music, foods/nutrition, textiles, computer science and education. The area's Guilford, Greensboro and Bennett colleges are four-year undergraduate liberal arts schools, and Guilford Technical Community College is a center for vocational, technical and adult continuing education.

**Neighborhoods:** Residential construction in the west and northwest quadrants of the city has been on the increase, and most developments are in the price range of middle- to upper-middle-income families. Closer to downtown are the older, established communities of Irving Park (ritzy) and Fisher Park (upper-middle-income); Sunset Hills is another older community with tree-lined streets, generally in the price range of upper-middle-income families. The southwest quadrant of the city is characterized by retail growth and accessibly priced residential construction. Younger couples just starting out are generally attracted to the northwest and southwest quadrants. The Lake Daniel section of Greensboro is popular among Yuppies with a yen for restoring old houses. Southeastern Greensboro is a firmly working-class neighborhood. Most manufacturing development is in the eastern (tobacco, cigarettes) and southeastern (textiles) parts of the city. While the newer neighborhoods are racially integrated and tension free, de facto segregation continues in older districts.

**Politics/Government:** Greensboro has a council-manager form of government, and the city was one of the first in the nation to convert to that governmental form. When American public school districts were ordered to desegregate, Greensboro accomplished it with relative smoothness, in contrast with other southern metro areas. City council elections are nonpartisan, and representatives are selected by district, assuring minority representation.

**Transportation:** Although municipal bus service is available in Greensboro, most people prefer to avail themselves of private means of transportation: 72 percent of Greensboro's workers drive themselves to work, 19 percent car-pool, 4 percent walk and 3 percent use public transportation. The Regional Airport, a fifteen-minute drive from city center, offers seventy-seven daily departures.

**Health Care:** Health care in Guilford County is of good quality and relatively low cost. Area facilities include one teaching college, one medical school, two cardiac rehabilitation centers, one cancer treatment center and two hospices.

**Child Care:** An estimated 61 percent of Guilford County's mothers of preschool children work outside the home. Accordingly, some 29,550 area children require some degree of day care. The area has 118 licensed day-care centers, with a total capacity of 9,281 clients, and 324 licensed day-care homes, with a combined capacity of 1,620. Day-care costs in 1986 averaged $45 per week.

**Housing:** The average cost of a three-bedroom, two-bathroom house is $83,000, while the average rent for a one-bedroom apartment is between $225 and $300 a month.

**Public Safety:** There were 5,529 serious crimes per 100,000 of population reported for the area in 1985, which is lower than the national average for metro areas, and also lower than in other North Carolina cities. A very low 183 robberies per 100,000 city residents were reported in Greensboro in 1986.

**Cultural Attractions:** A highlight of Greensboro's cultural life is the city's Eastern Music Festival, which consists of free outdoor city-park concerts. Other city arts celebrations are the annual fall arts festival, called City Fest, and the yearly Jazzfest, held in Greensboro's beautifully restored Carolina Theater. During spring the city sponsors a series of downtown lunchtime concerts called Plazazz. Other area attractions are the Greensboro Civic Orchestra, the Greensboro Civic Ballet, the Weatherspoon Art Gallery, the Natural Science Center and the Green Hill Center for North Carolina Art, which provides studio and exhibition space to local artists.

**Sports/Recreation:** Among Greensboro's sports attractions are the Greensboro Hornets (single A minor-league baseball), the annual Kmart Greater Greensboro Open golf tournament and NCAA basketball at the Greensboro Coliseum. In addition, the nearby city of High Point hosts the High Point LPGA golf tournament. Participant sports popular in the area include sailing, fishing, tennis, soccer (numerous youth programs are available for soccer), softball and football. The city has numerous public parks, eight public swimming pools, eighty-eight public tennis courts, two public golf courses, a water theme park, three YMCAs and two YWCAs.

**Taxes:** Residential property is assessed at full value but is taxed at a rate of only $0.625 per $100.

---

## WHERE TO BREAK IN

The following partial listing of Greensboro–Guilford County major employers is illustrative of the area's broad economic base. For more information, call the Greensboro Chamber of Commerce at 919-275-8675.

| Firm/Organization | Product/Service | No. Employees |
|---|---|---|
| Guilford County | government | 4,700 |
| AT&T Technologies, Inc. | computers/ telecommunications equip. | 3,500 |
| Cone Mills Corp. | textiles | 3,500 |
| Lorillard | cigarettes | 2,500 |
| U.S. government | government | 2,500 |
| Guilford County Public Schools | education | 2,200 |
| Greensboro City Schools | education | 2,100 |
| State of North Carolina | government | 2,000 |
| Moses Cone Memorial Hospital | general medical and surgical hospital | 1,900 |
| American Express | regional processing center | 1,800 |
| Gilbarco, Inc. | service station pumps | 1,700 |
| Guilford Mills | textiles | 1,300 |
| Jefferson-Pilot Insurance | insurance carrier | 1,300 |
| AMP, Inc. | electronic components | 1,000 |
| Burlington Industries | textiles | 1,000 |
| Wesley Long Hospital | general medical and surgical hospital | 1,000 |
| University of North Carolina at Greensboro | education | 1,000 |

Two local companies specialize in relocation services: Releguide, 5504 Old Brandt Trace, Greensboro, NC 27405, 919-282-2312; and The Right Connections, 1704 Independence Road, Greensboro, NC 27408, 919-282-6272.

---

## SUMMING UP: OPPORTUNITY FOR WHOM?

The population of Greensboro proper is 190,670, and all of Guilford County is home to 339,000. The area (Guilford County) is currently running a relatively low 4.7 percent unemployment rate. The local economy is diverse, claiming as its major industries textiles and apparel manufacturing, tobacco products manufacturing, electronics and semiconductors manufacturing, education, health care, insurance and financial services. Greensboro's labor force is distributed as follows among ten broad industrial groupings:

| Industry | Share of Work Force (in %) |
|---|---|
| Manufacturing | 30.1 |
| Wholesale and retail trade | 24.4 |
| Services | 17.7 |
| Government | 11.7 |
| Finance, insurance and real estate | 5.6 |
| Transportation, communication and utilities | 5.0 |

Greensboro's growth industries continue to generate employment opportunities for individuals with banking, accounting and clerical skills. Employment in the fields of health care and education should also continue to grow, keeping pace with Greensboro's rapidly growing population. With the city's encouraging level of corporate expansion in the areas of semiconductor, computer and telecommunications technology, we also predict growing opportunities for engineers, computer specialists and electronics technicians. Finally, rapid population growth naturally creates employment opportunities in the financial, real estate and trade sectors.

# Hartford, Connecticut

HARTFORD–NEW BRITAIN–MIDDLETOWN CMSA POPULATION (7/86): 1,043,500, of which Hartford PMSA population is 738,900.

POPULATION GROWTH 1980–86: 3.2%

COUNTY: Connecticut has no county jurisdictions

EMPLOYMENT (9/87): 481,400

AVERAGE TEMPERATURE: 49.1°F

YEARLY RAINFALL: 43 inches

HUMIDITY: 65% (10th most humid)

COST OF LIVING: 119.6

## KEYS TO THE CITY

**Small Business Growth:** birth rate, growth rate, growth index (rank/86): 2.3   2.8   5.1   (72nd)

**Average Annual Job Growth (9/84–9/87):** 3.5% (27th/largest 100)

**Keys to Prosperity:** High-tech, insurance, banking.

**Key Developments:** New office and retail construction.

**Key Life-Style Trends:** Hartford is the archetypical doughnut-and-hole metro configuration. The small downtown area is the home of some smart office buildings but residentially it was abandoned in the 1960s to the area's relatively small minority population. The suburban areas ringing Hartford are thriving residential enclaves, with a growing number of businesses locating outside of the central city.

## WHY OPPORTUNITY KNOCKS IN HARTFORD

Hartford has long been hailed as the insurance capital of the world. With the recent deregulation of insurance and banking, these industries have expanded even more, accounting for the rapid pace of new office construction in the Greater Hartford area.

Hartford is also at the forefront of high-tech development, specializing in aerospace, communications, advanced electronics, energy and control systems, and in the application of micro-

174

processors to manufacturing. Largely due to the demands of its strong service sector, Hartford is a computer capital, with the largest per capita mainframe base in the world.

Hartford has been dubbed the "hottest retail market" by *Adweek* magazine. New malls and shopping centers are currently being built, as the growth of the retail market is expected to flourish for many years more.

Hartford was once called "the Workshop of the Nation." In recent years, the area has experienced a noticeable decline in manufacturing, especially in the production of machinery, instruments and fabricated metals; reorientation of the area's economy toward high-tech and service sectors explains this phenomenon. The manufacturing slump has been offset by new jobs in communications, utilities, finance, insurance, real estate, health services and trade.

Flourishing businesses have called for an unprecedented level of construction in downtown Hartford as well as the city's surrounding area. Over 3 million square feet of office space have been added to the real estate market, tripling the amount built since 1960. Growth is expected to continue at a rate of 500,000 square feet per year. The suburbs have witnessed the addition of over 2 million square feet of office space. Greater Hartford's office market is one of the fastest growing in the world. Over the past few years, many of Hartford's major corporations have built office extensions in the suburbs. Phoenix Mutual Life Insurance Company set up an office in Enfield, while Aetna Life & Casualty branched into Middletown. Simsbury has welcomed satellite offices for Hartford Insurance Group, while Windsor has opened its doors for Konica Business Machines' (formerly Royal Business Machines) new corporate headquarters. To round off the list, American Honda Motor Company recently opened a regional office and distribution center in the suburban community of Windsor Locks.

Hartford's retail center is both diversified and convenient. The core is composed of the Civic Center Shops, connected to the Richardson Mall and the G. Fox and Sage-Allen department stores by the traditional shopping district of Pearl, Asylum and Pratt streets. The once fashionable Pratt Street is undergoing a major revitalization effort that is scheduled for completion in 1989. The new Pratt Street will feature unique retail shops and stunning office space. The newest addition to the retail scene is the Pavilion at State House Square, which opened in May of 1987 and has added numerous shops and eateries to the downtown market. In the evening, residents and visitors alike may enjoy concerts, sporting events, plays, symphonies and shows, as well as an array of excellent restaurants and nightclubs.

Hartford provides many business incentives for corporations. Among the most important are:

1. No state or general income tax.
2. No county tax.
3. No state personal property tax.
4. No local sales tax.
5. No corporate net worth tax.

The state of Connecticut also offers the following from a long list of business development assistance programs:

1. Low-cost industrial development financing through the Connecticut Development Authority.
2. Low-cost, ready-to-build sites in state-subsidized industrial parks.
3. Job creation and powerful investment incentives, including business and property tax reductions, new job grants, and low-interest industrial financing for manufacturing and research-and-development activities in "Urban-Job" municipalities.
4. Venture capital grants and low-cost loans through the Connecticut Product Development Corporation.
5. Nationally acclaimed assistance for small business and women-and-minority-owned firms, including technical, marketing and managerial counseling, business generation programs and low-cost financing.
6. Benefits for commercial and retail businesses through the Urban Enterprise Zone Program, which targets six state-designated municipalities.

## QUALITY OF LIFE

**Weather:** The region enjoys a moderate New England climate, with few extremes of cold or heat. During the summer months there is a balance between hot, humid weather and dry, more comfortable days. The warmest month is July, when the average temperature is 75°F. Hartford receives between 3.2 and 3.8 inches of rain in the summer, although there can be weeks of dry weather. Greater Hartford winters are generally moderate. There are some stretches of very cold weather, when temperatures stay in the teens or low twenties during the day and drop into the single digits at night. This usually occurs in January or February, when the average temperature is 29°. These can be very snowy months, with an average of 11.6 inches in February. By the end of March, there is a trend toward warmer weather, although winter can still be present. March snowfall is not at all uncommon, with an average of 9.5 inches. Snowfalls of 12 inches or more occur upon occasion.

**Education:** Through the thirty-three-town Hartford region, public education is provided by 151 elementary schools, 44 junior high schools and 39 senior high schools, with per-pupil expenditures far exceeding the national average. Except for neighborhood schools in Hartford and other heavily populated areas, transportation to school is provided by each of the towns. In addition, the Hartford area is served by 42 private schools; several specialized institutions serve the needs of pupils with learning disabilities.

Greater Hartford is home to six two-year colleges and nine four-year colleges and universities. These institutions include community colleges, branches of the state university, and private colleges and universities. Among these institutions are Central Connecticut State College, St. Joseph College, Trinity College and the University of Connecticut. Greater Hartford is also the location of three vocational-technical high schools, offering programs in forty basic skills: A. I. Prince Regional High School, Howell Cheney High School and Goodwin Technical High School.

**Neighborhoods:** Among Hartford's many communities are the towns of East Hartford and West Hartford, originally sections of Hartford itself but now separately incorporated. East Hartford is both residential and industrial, which makes for a pleasant and prosperous mix. West Hartford has an excellent public school system, several private secondary schools and three colleges; the volume of industrial activity generates ample local revenues to support high-quality municipal services. Housing in East Hartford is mainly rental apartments, condos and attached multifamily houses; the housing form of choice in West Hartford is unattached single-family houses, but rental apartments, condominiums and multifamily houses are available. Windsor is the oldest English settlement in Connecticut. Mainly residential, with a growing business community, the town maintains its old New England appearance. Windsor Locks, formerly agricultural, now has a thriving business community, especially since the building of Bradley International Airport. Simsbury, located north of Hartford, is noted for its fine residences, good municipal and commercial services, and peaceful natural surroundings.

**Politics/Government:** Hartford has a council-manager form of government, with a directly elected mayor.

**Transportation:** Although Hartford motorists tolerate heavy commuter traffic, significant improvements in the capital area's highway system may soon bring relief. Intracity movement is facilitated by a good municipal bus system. Hartford's Bradley International Airport is served by eighteen airlines providing a total of 120 flights daily. Intercity travel may also be achieved with Amtrak, which provides twelve daily departures.

**Health Care:** The thirty-three-town metro area has thirteen hospitals, of which six are general and seven are specialized. The Hartford Hospital is one of the largest hospitals in the United States, with 1,025 beds. The University of Connecticut Health Center comprises a 200-bed teaching-and-research hospital, a medical school and a dentistry school. The Institute of Living is an internationally acclaimed mental health institution. The area also provides 100 nursing and convalescent homes.

**Housing:** A "typical house" (2,000 square feet, three bedrooms, two baths, dining area, family room, two-car garage and basement) in an above-average-to-prime neighborhood costs $93,600, while the same house averaged $211,000 in New York's suburbs, $149,000 in Boston and $86,000 in Providence, Rhode Island.

**Public Safety:** With 1,221 robberies per 100,000 city residents reported in 1986, Hartford ranks 5th among the cities in our study with the highest crime rates. However, the crime rate is for the small central city. The suburban areas outside the downtown area have lower crime rates.

**Cultural Attractions:** When it comes to the arts, Hartford cannot compare with cultural centers such as New York, Boston or Chicago, but for a city of its size, it fares well. The Hartford Stage Company is one of the nation's leading regional theaters, while the Hartford Symphony and the Wadsworth Atheneum rank among the top twenty symphonies and art museums in the country. The Hartford Ballet tours extensively around the country. And Bushnell Memorial Hall, home base for the symphony, the ballet and the Connecticut Opera Association, brings in visiting artists and performers from all over the world. Quaint New England attractions such as the homes of Mark Twain and Harriet Beecher Stowe are nearby.

Many of Hartford's art programs are supported by the business community, which contributed more than $7 million during the past ten years to the Greater Hartford Arts Council. Among forty-five major U.S. cities, Hartford ranks first in corporate contributions per capita to the arts.

**Sports/Recreation:** Greater Hartford is within easy driving distance of both ski resorts and beaches. Connecticut, two-thirds undeveloped, has more than 100 state parks and forests that offer outdoor recreational facilities such as fishing, hunting, snowmobiling, ice skating, cross-country skiing and camping.

Since the reopening of the newly renovated 16,000-seat Coliseum in the Hartford Civic Center, professional sports are growing in opportunity. The Hartford Whalers (hockey) are perhaps the most prominent team.

**Taxes:** The number of households in 1986 was 371,849, up by 91,500 since 1980; their 1986 regional median income was approximately $33,695. In 1982, per capita personal income was $13,918 in Hartford County, versus the national average of $11,100. The area's tax burden amounts to around 1.25 percent of average yearly household income.

The area's relatively high income is accompanied by a correspondingly high cost of living; with a cost-of-living index of 119.6, Hartford is the third most expensive metro to live in the United States, following New York and Newark. Broken down into components, Hartford measured 112.6 for groceries, 119.6 for housing, 144 for utilities, 108 for transportation, 88.9 for health care and 110.5 for miscellaneous goods and services.

## WHERE TO BREAK IN

For individuals interested in relocating to Hartford, we include a listing of select area major employers.

| Firm/Organization | Product/Service | No. Employees | Phone (area code 203) |
|---|---|---|---|
| State of Connecticut | government | 19,800 | 566-4200 |
| Pratt & Whitney Aircraft | aerospace | 16,890 | 565-4321 |
| Aetna Life & Casualty | insurance | 14,200 | 273-0123 |
| Travelers Insurance Co. | insurance | 11,000 | 277-0111 |
| Hartford Insurance Group | insurance | 8,280 | 547-5000 |
| CIGNA Corp. | insurance | 6,500 | 726-6000 |
| Connecticut Bank & Trust Co. | banking | 5,454 | 244-5000 |
| Hartford Hospital | health care | 5,000 | 524-2115 |
| Combustion Engineering Power Systems Group | aerospace | 4,500 | 688-1911 |
| Simon Konover & Associates | real estate development | 1,700 | 232-4545 |
| Heublein, Inc. | alcohol and food products | 960 | 678-6500 |

In order to qualify for incentives under the Urban Jobs Program or the Urban Enterprise Program, companies should contact the Connecticut Department of Economic Development.

*Urban Jobs Program:* Leo Tetreault, Program Manager, 203-566-8267

*Urban Enterprise:* Carol Johnson, Enterprise Zone Coordinator, City of Hartford Development Commission, 203-722-6434; or Beverly Dawes, Enterprise Zone Manager, 203-722-8008

## SUMMING UP: OPPORTUNITY FOR WHOM?

At the core of Hartford's newfound sophistication is still a strong sense of New England's Yankee heritage. The city is a quaint blend of Early American architecture standing side by side with modern skyscrapers.

Demographics also reflects a largely white "Yankee" population, relatively undiversified for an urban area. Greater Hartford's population is 86 percent white, 8 percent black, 5 percent Hispanic and 1 percent other, with the minority population disproportionately concentrated in the central city.

Like Cincinnati, Hartford is a city of opportunity because it continues to make a go of its major businesses—insurance and aerospace. It is not a hotbed of small business formation and growth. Opportunities are greatest for those who come to Hartford with a specific niche in mind, especially if that niche relates to the city's technical traditions.

# Houston, Texas

HOUSTON–GALVESTON–BRAZORIA, TEX. CMSA POPULATION (7/86): 3,634,300 (9th largest), of which Houston PMSA population is 3,230,700.

POPULATION GROWTH 1980–86: 18.1%

COUNTY: Harris

EMPLOYMENT (9/87): 1,376,600

AVERAGE TEMPERATURE: 68.9°F

YEARLY RAINFALL: 48.19 inches

HUMIDITY: 67% (6th most humid)

COST OF LIVING: 100.3

---

## KEYS TO THE CITY

**Small Business Growth:** birth rate, growth rate, growth index (rank/86): 4.2  2.8  7  (21st)

**Average Annual Growth (9/84–9/87):** −2.5% (100th/largest 100)

**Keys to Prosperity:** High-tech (space, defense, computers), oil, finance, real estate, health care.

**Key Developments:** Recent overbuilding has left entire buildings unoccupied, but if oil prices creep back up in 1988 business should rebound; meanwhile, Houston's laid-off ex–oil employees have been busy putting their technical talents to work on entrepreneurial activities. Look for more international trade involvement. Private space initiatives should bear fruit soon. Houston continues to expand its nationally prestigious health-care facilities. A new diversification coup: a 1.1-million-square-foot facility calculated to boost Houston's yearly convention revenues from around $75 million to as much as $200 million.

**Key Life-Style Trends:** More subdued than a few years ago, Houstonians are in touch with their cowboy past through rodeos and other sports, but are developing a respectable cadre of artists and cultural attractions and patrons. The typical Houstonian is a dyed-in-the-wool suburbanite, tied to a community miles from downtown—and subjected to a congested auto commute that is unlikely to ease up soon. Despite its enormous area, Houston (unlike Minneapolis or Kansas City) is a hard-to-drive-in city because it is still centralized around downtown.

## WHY OPPORTUNITY KNOCKS IN HOUSTON

Although its economy has been severely damaged by the world oil glut, Houston has the infrastructure, the kind of population and the potential for economic diversity necessary for significant redevelopment.

The collapse of petroleum prices in the early 1980s, though a godsend for Northeasterners, was a nightmare for Texans—especially in Houston, which grew up and grew rich on oil, without the economic diversity, relatively speaking, of Dallas. But petrobusiness, like any other well-run industry, had attracted a large number of talented management, financial and technical personnel to Houston, and in the mid-1980s they found themselves confronted with several options: they could (1) find a job, (2) get out of town, (3) remain unemployed in Houston or (4) start their own businesses. Many Houston specialists selected this fourth option, as did down-and-out northeastern professionals in response to the manufacturing crisis that hit their region in the late 1970s. In recent years Houston entrepreneurs have applied the skills they cultivated in the petroleum industry to found medical labs, testing facilities, financial software companies and consulting firms. Between 1982 and 1985 Houston had the fourth largest number of new companies founded, placing after Los Angeles, New York and Chicago.

These types of businesses, attractive to financial and technical specialists, are more resistant to cyclic influences than manufacturing firms, and within the next five to six years could inspire a whole new economic upswing for Houston along highly diversified lines. If this economic expansion takes place, the currently overbuilt and underrented Houston metro area (its 31.8 percent office vacancy rate at the end of 1987 is the hightest of any major U.S. city) can look forward to new tenants.

The present or future prosperity of Houston depends entirely on the advent and growth of the above-mentioned small companies. Houston is the home to ten of the United States' largest and most profitable public corporations: Shell Oil, Tenneco, Coastal, Pennzoil, Cooper Industries, Superior Oil, Anderson-Clayton, Hughes Tool, Cameron Iron Works and Big Three Industries. It is also the home of Exxon (U.S.A.), the operating U.S. subsidiary of the Exxon Corporation. Their diversified interests, and the fact that oil and oil-derivate prices are again on the rise, may portend a brighter not-so-distant future for Houston.

With a barrel of crude oil again selling for as high as $18 in the fall of 1987, the rate of oil drilling is picking up in the Houston area. Even so, Houstonians aren't complacently pulling the spurs off their boots. The oil slump has forced Houston's leaders to get aggressively bullish on their city, as they actively court corporations contemplating investment or relocation.

They emphasize Houston's nonoil attractions, such as the fact that the port of Houston is the busiest in the nation in foreign volume, making it the Sunbelt's leader in international trade and finance. In 1985, about 88 million tons of cargo passed through the port of Houston, and the value of customs collections exceeded $434.7 million. Though the trade emphasis is still on petroleum products, it could easily be shifted to the importation and exportation of other commodities. Houston's multisite Foreign Trade Zone is the biggest in the country, and in 1985 handled about $84.9 million worth of imports. Houston's port is regularly serviced by some 200 steamship lines, and Texas's intercoastal waterway system facilitates barge service to the Mississippi River. Houston's distribution capabilities are rounded out by five major railroads operating on fourteen sets of main-line track, thirty-eight common carrier trucking firms and a highly developed oil-and-gas pipeline system.

A marketing campaign is also under way for Houston's Lyndon B. Johnson Space Center, targeting high-tech companies anxious to experiment in, and develop production processes unique to, the weightless environment of space. Among the projects in this direction are the University of Houston's Center for Commercial Development of Space, financed in part by a $5.5 million grant from NASA, and Grumman Aerospace's advanced materials and semiconductors research project, embodied in the firm's Space Systems Division, which has been moved to Houston to take advantage of the facilities at the Johnson Space Center. In addition, Space Industries, Inc., and Westinghouse have entered into partnership to develop an orbital laboratory/workshop at the Space Center. The University of Houston–Clearlake, Texas A&M University, Rice University, the Lunar and Planetary Institute and about 120 commercial firms have also established operations at the Johnson Space Center. Houston is also taking advantage of its world-class medical facilities to attract new capital. Fueled by $125 million in annual federal funding, Baylor College of Medicine, the University of Texas Health Science Center and the University of Texas Medical Branch have combined talents to engage in advanced medical research.

## QUALITY OF LIFE

**Weather:** Although Houston does have a humid climate, its location on the Gulf Coast results in moderate temperatures. On the average, Houston experiences temperatures of 32°F or less for twenty-three days a year, and temperatures of 90° or above for ninety-two days a year. The average high in winter is 65°, and the average daily high in summer is 92°.

**Education:** Houston has the seventh largest school district in the nation, with about 194,000 students enrolled, roughly 12 students per 100 residents. In Houston, as in Dallas and Austin, the various communities within the city form independent school districts that tax and administer themselves, allowing the city government to assign less than 0.01 percent of its total public expenditures to education. Houston has a very low high school dropout rate (3 percent, compared to over 40 percent for New York); about 62 percent of high school graduates go on to college, and 20 percent of Houston adults (persons over twenty-five) are college educated. Houston also has a high enrollment rate in postsecondary occupational programs. A possible measure of the success of the city's public education is the fact that less than 5 percent of its high school students attend private high schools, though this datum should also be viewed in terms of Houston religious affiliations (the city is less than 14 percent Catholic). In addition to undergraduate colleges, Houston has graduate and professional schools in business, law, medicine, music and the arts, with 119,000 enrolled postsecondary students, distributed among five public two-year colleges and thirteen four-year colleges and universities—seven public, six private.

**Politics/Government:** Houston has a mayor-council form of government. Elected directly by the city voters, the mayor serves a two-year term; he acts as member of the city council and lacks veto power over council bills. The city council is composed of fifteen members, six elected at large and nine by ward; all members serve two years. Houston went 59 percent for Reagan (seventeenth highest of the eighty-six largest metro areas), 38 percent for Carter in 1980; Anderson got a low 3 percent of the vote.

**Transportation:** Mobility in and around Houston is enhanced by the city's METRO municipal bus service, consisting of 108 intracity routes plus 85 park-and-ride routes with express service from suburban parking lots to the inner city. The city also offers an overnight, computerized car-pool coordination service. Municipal busing for the handicapped, METROlift, is available upon request for approved users. Intercity bus service is provided by four bus lines, including Greyhound and Trailways. The Houston Intercontinental Airport is served by thirteen international carriers and twelve domestic carriers.

**Health Care:** The fifteen-county area including and surrounding Houston has ninety-eight hospitals with a total of 21,692 beds. Houston's Harris County has sixty-five hospitals and 17,507 beds; of these, fully forty-nine hospitals, corresponding to 14,731 beds, are within Houston's city limits. These facilities include four teaching hospitals serving two area medical schools, six cardiac rehabilitation centers, one cancer treatment center and a hospice for cancer patients. Health-care costs in the Greater Houston area, however, are rather high.

**Child Care:** Working parents in need of child-care information and referral should call one or more of the following agencies: Child Care Council of Greater Houston (713-526-2761), United Way Information (713-527-0222), Texas State Department of Human Resources (713-229-9195) or Neighborhood Centers, Inc. (713-529-3931).

**Housing:** The average cost of a three-bedroom, two-bathroom house in the Houston area is currently around $81,000.

**Public Safety:** Houston has a fairly high crime rate, registering 793 violent crimes and 7,055 property crimes for 1984 (violent crimes include murder, rape, robbery and aggravated assault; property crimes include burglary, larceny and auto theft). In 1986 there were a total of 614 robberies reported per 100,000 city residents.

**Cultural Attractions:** Texas's biggest city is also a very "complete" city in that it provides a well-rounded cultural life. Houston's Jones Hall is the base for the Houston Symphony Orchestra and the Houston Grand Opera. During the summer, the Miller Outdoor Theater stages free performances by these groups, in addition to an annual summer Shakespeare festival. Houstonians also have access to year-round Broadway-style plays and nightly comedy shows. For the howdy-and-y'all crowd, there are evening rodeo performances all year, which ensures that this sophisticated and cosmopolitan southwestern city does not lose touch with its rough-and-ready cowboy past. For the more sedate but no less fun-loving, the Houston Museum of Fine Arts offers an extensive collection of Impressionist and post-Impressionist pieces.

**Sports/Recreation:** Sports fans are likely to know that Houston's colossal Astrodome is the home of the Astros (baseball) and the Oilers (football); if basketball is your sport, Houston also has the Rockets.

**Taxes:** Neither the state of Texas nor the city of Houston imposes either a personal or corporate income tax. There is a 6.125 percent sales tax currently in effect in the city, which includes the state sales tax of 4.125 percent plus an additional 1 percent each for the city itself and the city's Transit Authority. Property taxes are assessed on 100 percent of market value. Harris County takes $.450 per $100 of valuation; Houston, $.495; and the Houston Independent School District takes an additional $.7045.

---

## WHERE TO BREAK IN

People wishing to relocate in Houston should be aware that professional skills and specialization in high-tech will be very much in demand. In the case of graduates with influential college affiliations, we suggest contacting alumni associations or clubs. Following is a listing of selected local professional organizations.

*Texas Society of Certified Public Accountants*
PRESIDENT: Donald M. Clanton
             1700 W. Loop S., Suite 750
             Houston, TX 77027

*Houston Advertising Federation*
CONTACT PERSON: Leta Baldwin
　　　　　　　P.O. Box 66056
　　　　　　　Houston, TX 77266

*American Institute of Aeronautics and Astronautics*
PRESIDENT: Carl Huss
　　　　　MDTSCO
　　　　　16055 Space Center Blvd.
　　　　　Houston, TX 77062

*American Institute of Architects, Houston Chapter*
PRESIDENT: Peter H. Brown, AIA
　　　　　c/o Philips & Brown
　　　　　2603 Augusta Dr., Suite 122
　　　　　Houston, TX 77057

*Cultural Arts Council of Houston*
CONTACT PERSON: Mary Anne Piacentini
　　　　　　　1950 West Gray, Suite 6
　　　　　　　Houston, TX 77019

*Bank Marketing Association, Texas Gulf Coast Chapter*
PRESIDENT: Dorann Valka
　　　　　c/o Bellfort National Bank
　　　　　P.O. Box 31699
　　　　　Houston, TX 77231

*Houston Venture Capital Association*
PRESIDENT: Philip A. Tuttle
　　　　　910 Louisiana, 3rd Floor
　　　　　One Shell Plaza
　　　　　Houston, TX 77002

*Executive Women International*
PRESIDENT: Becky Wade
　　　　　Quanex Corporation
　　　　　1900 W. Loop S., Suite 1500
　　　　　Houston, TX 77027

*Houston Business Council*
CONTACT PERSON: Richard A. Huebner
　　　　　　　6161 Savoy Dr., Suite 1030
　　　　　　　Houston, TX 77036

*Houston Association of Radio Broadcasters*
PRESIDENT: John Cravens
　　　　　1020 Holcombe, Suite 1201
　　　　　Houston, TX 77030

*International Television Association, Houston Chapter*
PRESIDENT: Philip C. Booth
c/o University of Houston–University Park
Library Bldg., Room 56
Houston, TX 77004

*Press Club of Houston*
PRESIDENT: Sue Davis
c/o KTRH Radio
P.O. Box 1520
Houston, TX 77251

*American Society of Civil Engineers*
PRESIDENT: Wayne Klotz
c/o Klotz/Haile Inc.
1155 Dairy Ashford, Suite 705
Houston, TX 77079

*Houston Engineering and Scientifc Society*
PRESIDENT: Terry A. Anderson
2615 Fannin
Houston, TX 77002

*Society of Women Engineers*
PRESIDENT: Vivienne L. McKitrick
9247 Theyson
Houston, TX 77080

*Texas Society of Professional Engineers, San Jacinto Chapter*
PRESIDENT: David W. Peters, P.E.
ERT/REI
3000 Richmond
Houston, TX 77098

*Association of Information Systems Professionals, Houston Chapter*
PRESIDENT: Susan Coon
c/o DISC, Inc.
1820 Heights Blvd.
Houston, TX 77008

*Independent Insurance Agents of Houston*
PRESIDENT: Thomas J. Baker III
5606 Richmond
Houston, TX 77057

*Houston Bar Association*
PRESIDENT: Raymond C. Kerr
707 Travis, Suite 1300
Houston, TX 77002

*Institute of Management Consultants*
PRESIDENT: Brad W. Robbins
c/o Price Waterhouse
1200 Milam, Suite 2900
Houston, TX 77002

*American Marketing Association*
PRESIDENT: Judith Jones
c/o Sisters of Charity
6400 Lawndale
Houston, TX 77023

*Harris County Medical Society*
PRESIDENT: Max C. Butler, M.D.
400 Jesse H. Jones Library Bldg.
Houston, TX 77030

*Houston District Dental Society*
PRESIDENT: Dr. Donald Morgan
One Greenway Plaza, Suite 110
Houston, TX 77046

*Houston Organization of Nurse Executives*
PRESIDENT: Margo Snider
c/o Veterans Administration Hospital
2002 Holcombe Blvd.
Houston, TX 77211

*Retail Merchants Association of Houston, Inc.*
PRESIDENT: Rex Givan
4201 Fannin
Houston, TX 77004

*Houston Board of Realtors*
PRESIDENT: B. Kelley Parker III
3693 Southwest Freeway
Houston, TX 77027

*Professional Secretaries International, Houston Chapter*
PRESIDENT: Rachel Golden, CPS
5718 Westheimer, Suite 2200
Houston, TX 77057

*Houston Area Transportation Safety Association*
EXECUTIVE DIRECTOR: Paul L. Broussard
501 Crawford, Suite 401
Houston, TX 77002

Elsewhere in our city profiles we have stressed the importance of new, growing, small companies to the economic health of a city. A new small company, however, is more in the domain of an entrepreneur than that of an individual seeking employment. Hence, we provide a listing of the area's major employers of over 1,000 people.

The number of employees for each firm is included to suggest the firm's relative importance and impact on the local economy.

| Company | Product/Service | No. Employees | Phone (area code 713) |
|---|---|---|---|
| Browning Ferris Industries | refuse systems | 15,500 | 870-8100 |
| Hughes Tool Co. | oil machinery and equip. | 12,700 | 222-0686 |
| Shell Oil | crude oil and gas | 5,800 | 241-6161 |
| Schlumberger Technology Corp. | oil and gas services | 4,400 | 928-4000 |
| Enron Corp. | gas transmission/ distribution | 3,100 | 654-6161 |
| Texas Commerce Bancshares | national bank | 3,050 | 236-4865 |
| Cameron Iron Works | oil machinery and equip. | 3,000 | 939-2211 |
| Tenneco Inc. | construction machinery | 2,500 | 757-2131 |
| Bechtel Petroleum | engineering and architecture | 2,500 | 235-2000 |
| CRS Sirrine, Inc. | engineering and architecture | 2,500 | 552-2000 |
| First National City Bank | national bank | 2,400 | 658-6011 |
| United Gas Pipeline Co. | gas transmission | 2,200 | 229-4123 |
| Texas Eastern Corp. | gas transmission/ distribution | 2,000 | 759-3131 |
| Houston Industries | electric utility | 2,000 | 228-2474 |
| American General | insurance | 1,900 | 522-1111 |
| Associated Bldg. Services | cleaning and maintenance | 1,600 | 227-1261 |
| Compaq Computer Corp. | computers | 1,600 | 370-0670 |
| Transco Energy Co. | gas transmission/ distribution | 1,500 | 439-2000 |
| United Energy Resources | gas transmission/ distribution | 1,300 | 229-4123 |
| Keystone International | valves and pipe fittings | 1,200 | 937-5346 |
| Coastal Corp. | deep-sea foreign shipping | 1,000 | 977-1400 |

## SUMMING UP: OPPORTUNITY FOR WHOM?

With a view to predicting the composition of Houston's work force some five to six years hence, it is helpful to examine its current makeup. The Houston work force of 1,488,400 added 17,900 jobs in the past year, and the city's unemployment rate currently stands at around 9 percent. We provide the distribution of the Houston work force among eleven basic industrial categories:

| Industry | Share of Work Force (in %) |
|---|---|
| Retail trade | 17.7 |
| Government | 13.9 |
| Medical and professional services | 13.3 |
| Business and personal services | 11.3 |
| Manufacturing | 10.7 |
| Wholesale trade | 7.7 |
| Finance, insurance and real estate | 7.3 |
| Transportation, communications and utilities | 6.8 |
| Construction | 6.1 |
| Mining | 4.7 |
| Agricultural services | 0.5 |

Given Houston's current high-tech services and manufacturing push, we project a future demand for highly trained personnel, such as lab technicians, computer programmers and electrical engineers. But the detailed work that high-technology manufacturing requires will also demand wire wrappers and assemblers, as well as packagers and inspectors. Companies specializing in computer services need clerical and other office personnel in addition to the more specialized people with computer training. Paralleling the diversification of Houston's economy will be an estimated 27.7 percent increase in managerial employment and a 21.2 percent increase in clerical employment between 1982 and 1990. We expect, therefore, expansion in the services and manufacturing portions of the Houston work force, as the city experiences the shift in business emphasis from a few large companies to a number of smaller, more specialized companies.

# Indianapolis, Indiana

MSA POPULATION (7/86): 1,212,600 (32nd largest)
POPULATION GROWTH 1980–86: 3.9%
COUNTY: Consolidated with Marion County
EMPLOYMENT (9/87): 609,700
AVERAGE TEMPERATURE: 52.3°F
YEARLY RAINFALL: 38.74 inches
HUMIDITY: 66% (7th most humid)
COST OF LIVING: 97.6

## KEYS TO THE CITY

**Small Business Growth:** birth rate, growth rate, growth index (rank/86):   3   3.6   6.6   (33rd)

**Average Annual Job Growth (9/84–9/87):** 3.8% (20th/largest 100)

**Keys to Prosperity:** Motor vehicles, drugs, consumer electronics, health care, efficient government, low living costs.

**Key Developments:** Hoosier Dome, Indianapolis Center for Advanced Research, Japanese investments, successful wooing of athletic team (Colts), research center (Hudson Institute), sports headquarters.

**Key Life-Style Trends:** With emergence of Indianapolis as a sports center (Pan Am Games in 1987), athletes as well as car racers are in.

## WHY OPPORTUNITY KNOCKS IN INDIANAPOLIS

There is a lot more to Indianapolis than turbocharged race cars circling the Motor Speedway. In fact, faster than the city's famous race cars is the pace of the city's growth. In mid-1986, 576,000 people were employed in Greater Indianapolis, a gain of 16,000 over the previous year. The city's unemployment rate in mid-1986 was 5.2 percent, a full two points below the national average and the lowest of the larger metropolitan areas in the Great Lakes states.

Indianapolis is a center for commerce and industry. Although the city's economy is reorienting toward the service sector, industrial development continues. More than 130,000 people work in 1,500 manufacturing firms, producing 1,200 different products. Prominent corporations headquartered in the area include the pharmaceutical giant Eli Lilly and Company, RCA Consumer Electronics, General Motors' Detroit Diesel Allison, Chrysler, Ford Motor Company and the Kroger Company.

Second only to Hartford, Indianapolis is a major center for the insurance industry. The city is home to thirty-five life companies and thirty-six casualty companies. American United Life, the largest, is forty-eighth among all U.S. life insurance companies.

During 1984–86, over 1,100 new businesses were formed in Indianapolis. Restaurants and hotels are opening at a rate of one per month. In June 1985, the service sector showed an 8.3 percent growth in employment over the 1984 average.

Many companies find the Indianapolis business environment inviting. Known as the "Crossroads of America," Indianapolis is the most centrally located of the nation's 100 largest cities. It is served by more segments of interstate freeways than any other metro area. Between 1982 and 1986, first-rate office space grew by 1.7 million square feet. Another 2 million square feet were to be added by the end of 1988. In addition, Indianapolis enjoys the lowest electric bills of any city in the country served by a privately owned utility.

Over $1.1 billion has been invested in public and private developments within the central business district in the decade 1976–86, and another $800 million is in the works, aiming for completion by 1990. Monument Circle and new downtown buildings have just had a face-lift. Convention Center has been renovated, and the $80 million Hoosier Dome has just been completed. Indiana University–Purdue University at Indianapolis (IUPUI) has just built a $35 million sports complex. By 1990, the new $200 million White River State Park will be completed close to downtown. The 250-acre park will feature a world-class zoo, entertainment centers and exhibit areas.

Indianapolis has established several specialized resource centers that serve the needs of business and industry, universities and governmental agencies. The Indianapolis Center for Advanced Research (ICFAR or I-See-Far) uses electronics, software, engineering, environmental research, medical instrumentation developments and technology transfers to find practical, economical solutions to problems.

The prestigious Hudson Institute "think tank" examines issues of public interest primarily in the areas of national security, economics, education, international affairs, labor force, and social and cultural trends. The institute was designed to be a research bridge between governmental agencies and private corporations.

The Environmental Research Service interprets environmental regulations for compliance in Marion County and develops the technical rationale for sound environmental policy affecting central Indiana.

The Aerospace Research Applications Center was organized in 1963 to provide assistance to U.S. industry on technical problems and is now the most experienced research application center in the NASA network.

To enhance its position as a transportation hub in the Midwest, the city has established the Greater Indianapolis Foreign Trade Zone Inc. at the Indianapolis International Airport. Here manufactured goods from foreign countries can be stored, assembled and packaged without incurring customs duties before the goods leave the zone.

In 1986 retail sales were up 15 percent over 1983 figures. Automotive sales increased by 66 percent, while department store sales increased by 13.5 percent. Shopping facilities in the Indianapolis area are unparalleled. Downtown Indianapolis has been described as an urban planner's masterpiece. Some $850 million is being spent or committed to downtown development projects. In addition, the area has six enormous malls among the forty-nine shopping centers with 50,000 square feet of selling space.

The Consolidated City of Indianapolis had the greatest increase in population of all midwestern cities between 1980 and 1984. Among major metro areas, Indianapolis at 2.4 percent is only one of two in the Midwest region to show a population growth greater than 1 percent. Indianapolis MSA has a population of 1,212,600; Marion County, 774,800; and the city of Indianapolis, 710,280.

Since 1970, Indianapolis and Marion County have enjoyed the benefits of a unified government called Unigov. The county-city merger has reduced bureaucratic red tape and opened the door to city growth from within. Unlike many other major cities that cannot extend their boundaries, Indianapolis now has ample room within for expansion of residential, industrial and commercial areas. Unigov has been a major contributor to business growth potential through:

1. Broadening the tax base.
2. Streamlining business access to government services.
3. Allowing development without further annexation.
4. Providing atmosphere and institutions for public–private cooperation.

---

## QUALITY OF LIFE

**Weather:** Indianapolis's temperate climate is characterized by very warm summers and no dry season. The temperature hits 90°F or more on a total of 17 days each year, while it dips to 32° or less on about 120 days yearly; temps fall to 0° about 9 days a year. Indianapolis is a cloudy city, experiencing sunny, clear weather on about one-quarter of the days of the year, while the rest of the year is cloudy or partly cloudy. On the average, thunderstorms occur on about 44 days each year.

**Education:** Improving public education has become a top priority for civic leaders. Indianapolis has thirty-six high schools, of which fifteen are private. The Japanese Language School is one of twenty-seven in the nation founded to help Japanese students maintain an accredited curriculum while living in the United States.

Indianapolis is considered a college town because it is home to nineteen institutions of higher learning. Most famous is Indiana University–Purdue University in Indianapolis, with 22,500 students. Other schools include Butler University, Indiana Vocational Technical and Aristotle College.

**Neighborhoods:** The city has a variety of residential neighborhoods, including the downtown historical districts of Lockerbie Square, Chatham Arch, the Old Northside, Woodruff Place and Herron-Morton Place. Consisting mainly of upscale and expensive homes, the Meridan-Kessler neighborhood has maintained its high standards and good reputation in the face of a protracted suburbanization trend. Devout suburbanites can make their homes in

Carmel or Noblesville to the north of downtown, or in Greenwood to the south of the city. Although Indianapolis is landlocked, waterfront property on the area's natural reservoirs is available.

**Politics/Government:** In 1970, to avoid wasteful duplication of effort, the governments of Indianapolis and Marion County, with the exception of a few municipalities, were merged according to the Unigov principle. Structurally, the consolidated government consists of the mayor of Indianapolis and an active city-county council: The mayor has veto power over council acts, and the council can investigate the activities of municipal departments (parks and recreation, metropolitan development, public works, transportation and public safety). The city is well run.

**Transportation:** Indianapolis commuters fight heavy rush-hour traffic on the four interstate highways that serve the city. Intracity public transportation is available in the form of trolley cars and municipal buses. Travel to points outside Indianapolis may be accomplished with Greyhound, Trailways or Amtrak, which runs one daily departure from the city. The Indianapolis International Airport is served by fourteen air carriers supplying a total of 138 departures daily.

**Health Care:** With the world's largest university medical center and the second largest medical school in the nation, Indianapolis provides excellent medical care for its residents as well as out-of-staters who go there for treatment. The Indiana University Medical Center comprises three hospitals, including University Hospital, Long Hospital and James Whitcomb Riley Hospital for Children. University Hospital is known for its treatment of testicular cancer, while the Children's Hospital gives special care to seriously ill children. St. Vincent's Hospital and Health Care Center specializes in heart surgery and microvascular hand surgery. Winona Memorial Hospital has a Sleep Disorder Clinic. Several hospitals in the area treat psychiatric illness, alcoholism and drug abuse. With its intense interest in athletics, Indianapolis is also becoming a leader in sports medicine. The existence of twenty-four area hospitals, providing 7,500 beds, makes health care a vital industry in Indianapolis.

**Housing:** The ratio of new housing units to population has been greater in the Indianapolis MSA than in all of the major midwestern cities since 1980. The median sale price of houses is $55,700. Median resale price of homes rose 9.75 percent from June 1985 to June 1986. Apartment rates vary from $250 to over $650 per month. Condominiums will cost from $48,000 to $250,000.

**Public Safety:** With 334 reported 1986 robberies per 100,000 city residents, the crime rate in Indianapolis is about average for the metro areas in our study.

**Cultural Attractions:** Cultural and recreational attractions include the Indianapolis Symphony Orchestra, Opera Company, Museum of Art, Ballet Theatre, the world's largest children's museum, Indiana Repertory Theatre, Indianapolis Zoo and Corner Pioneer Settlement.

**Sports/Recreation:** Sports are a way of life in Indianapolis. The famed Indianapolis 500 is eagerly awaited by auto racing enthusiasts each year. This Memorial Day classic is the largest single-day sporting event in the world.

Indianapolis is also known as an international center for amateur athletics such as diving, gymnastics, rowing and synchronized swimming. The city was host to the U.S. Olympic Committee's 1982 National Sports Festival and the Pan American Games in 1987.

The area's professional teams include the Colts (football), Pacers (NBA basketball), Indians (ABA basketball) and Checkers (hockey).

**Taxes:** Indianapolis's cost of living is consistently near the national average or below. According to the American Chamber of Commerce Research Association, the cost of living in Indianapolis is 97.6, a little below the base figure of 100. Broken down, groceries measured 100; housing, 97; utilities, 87.8; transportation, 107.7; health care, 98.5; and miscellaneous goods and services, 95.8. The average local property tax bill is around $1,000, and the average tax bite amouts to 3.25 percent of average yearly household income.

---

## WHERE TO BREAK IN

Indianapolis residents can take advantage of a host of state and local business incentive programs. You can call the Indianapolis Chamber of Commerce at 317-635-4747 or the Indianapolis Economic Development Corporation at 317-236-6262 for more information concerning the following programs:

1. Industrial Revenue Bonds.
2. Real Property Tax Abatement.
3. Personal Property Tax Abatement.
4. Industrial Development Loan Program.
5. Investment Incentive Program.
6. Indiana Corporation for Science and Technology (R&D grants).
7. Corporation for Innovation Development (venture capital).
8. State Loan Guarantee.

For individuals interested in seeking employment in the Indianapolis area, we provide a list of selected major employers. For more information, call the Indianapolis Chamber of Commerce at 317-267-2925.

| Firm/Organization | Product/Service | No. Employees |
|---|---|---|
| Eli Lilly & Co. | pharmaceuticals | 7,305 |
| GE/RCA Consumer Electronics | high-tech electronics | 7,100 |
| Allison Gas Turbine Division, GMC | military truck transmissions | 7,000 |
| Detroit Diesel Allison Division, GMC | military truck transmissions | 5,900 |
| Methodist Hospital of Indiana | health care | 4,796 |
| Indiana Bell | telephone utility | 4,468 |
| Fort Benjamine Harrison | military | 4,200 |
| Truck & Bus Division, GMC | military mfg. | 3,500 |
| St. Vincent's Hospital | health care | 3,225 |
| Naval Avionics Center | military | 3,125 |
| Community Hospital, Indianapolis | health care | 3,120 |
| Ford Motor Co. | automotive mfg. | 3,000 |

## SUMMING UP: OPPORTUNITY FOR WHOM?

The diverse Indianapolis work force is distributed as follows among the basic industrial sectors:

| Industry | Share of Work Force (in %) |
|---|---|
| Wholesale and retail trade | 25.5 |
| Manufacturing | 20.8 |
| Services | 20.6 |
| Government | 15.6 |
| Finance, insurance and real estate | 7.4 |
| Transportation, communication and utilities | 5.8 |
| Construction | 4.2 |

The growing Indianapolis population should in the future generate employment opportunities for health-care professionals and educators. The large and expanding services and finance and insurance sectors should maintain a healthy demand for bankers, communications and data-processing specialists, and people with office skills, while the continued strength of high-tech avionics and consumer electronics industries will require an influx of design and production engineers, as well as electronics and research technicians.

# Jacksonville, Florida

MSA Population (7/86): 852,700 (47th largest)
Population Growth 1980–86: 18.1%
County: Consolidated with Duval County
Employment (9/87): 392,600
Average Temperature: 68.4°F
Yearly Rainfall: 54.47 inches
Humidity: 73% (the most humid city)
Cost of Living: 102.3

## Keys to the City

**Small Business Growth:** birth rate, growth rate, growth index (rank/86): 3.6  3.4  7  (21st)

**Average Annual Job Growth (9/84–9/87):** 4.7% (8th/largest 100)

**Keys to Prosperity:** Distribution, communication, transportation hub, finance, health care.

**Key Developments:** Creation of research park near University of North Florida campus, and a branch of Mayo Clinic. Jacksonville is earning the title of "Florida's Business City"; its Chamber of Commerce is aggressively pursuing high-tech companies.

**Key Life-Style Trends:** The city has some notable cultural attractions, but has some catching up to do (and is doing it) in strengthening its higher education facilities.

## Why Opportunity Knocks in Jacksonville

Although Jacksonville has traditionally called itself "Florida's First Coast City," it has more recently dubbed itself "Florida's Business City." The new moniker fits. With employment up 16 percent since 1979, and buying income up 10 percent, Jacksonville residents are reaping the benefits of the 100-odd companies—including AT&T, American Transtech and Allied Bendix Corporation—that have chosen to locate major facilities in the city.

With its large, busy, deep-water port and its developed railroad
and trucking capabilities, Jacksonville has the attraction of a shipping and distribution hub. The most expansive city in the con-
tiguous forty-eight states, Jacksonville offers 830 square miles of
largely undeveloped territory ripe for the establishment of clean,
light industry and high-tech research facilities.

Having a slightly cooler climate, Jacksonville doesn't attract as
many tourists as South Florida, and has traditionally had to promote and develop industries largely independent of the hordes of
beach lemmings and retirees who constitute the mainstay of the
South Florida economy.

One result is that Jacksonville is a new major insurance and
finance center, with over 9 percent of its 436,126-person work
force employed in the finance, insurance and real estate industries.
Blue Cross/Blue Shield, Prudential, Gate Petroleum Real Estate,
Gulf Life, Independent Life & Accident, State Farm, Peninsula Life
and numerous banks are among the area's major nonmanufacturing
employers.

Local manufacturing is concentrated in the food-processing,
clothing, packaging, shipping-related and printing industries; but
the city's aggressive Chamber of Commerce, with three high-tech
development committees, is tenaciously committed to attracting
high-tech research-and-development corporations. The three committees, with their separate emphases on defense, information
services and biomedical technologies, are taking a sophisticated
approach to attracting business, involving the location of a
research park near Jacksonville's University of North Florida
campus.

To improve the quality of technical instruction in the area, the
university has instituted an electrical engineering program under
the auspices of the University of Florida's well-established engineering department, and has recently entered into agreement with
the Georgia Institute of Technology to offer a joint degree program
in physics and mechanical engineering.

The city may be viewed as a wide-open market for development,
since it currently is not overbuilt, has a low 5.8 percent unemployment rate and possesses a developed computer technology base,
thanks to its prosperous banking and finance resources. Jacksonville also has top-notch medical facilities, including a recently
opened branch of the Mayo Clinic, the famous facility's first such

non-Minnesota location. With amenities such as pleasant, moderate climate, improving technical education, low taxes and low living expenses, Jacksonville is confident that more new business will move in and that a First Coast Technical Park will be under construction within a year.

---

## QUALITY OF LIFE

**Weather:** Located on the St. John's River on the northeast coast of Florida, Jacksonville has a humid, subtropical climate characterized by mild winters and hot, stormy summers. The temperature never hits 0°F, there are about ten freezing (32°) days a year and about eighty days in the 90s.

**Education:** Typical of Southern cities, Jacksonville uses a parish system of organization for public education. The city's 189 elementary schools, middle schools and senior high schools are distributed among four districts; total enrollment is 130,710. Jacksonville's high school dropout rate is 2.6 percent, and 48 percent of area high school graduates go on to college. The Jacksonville area has 72 private and parochial schools, enrolling a total of 18,607 pupils. Jacksonville has one public junior college, located at four campuses throughout Duval County; the area's four-year colleges and universities include Jacksonville University (private), the University of North Florida (public), Jones College of Business (private), Edward Waters College (private, Methodist), the University of Florida at Jacksonville (public) and Flagler College (private).

**Neighborhoods:** Although Jacksonville is quite an old city, most of its housing is new and spread throughout Duval County. The detached single-family house is the form of choice, though a substantial number of multifamily rental and condominium units is available. Close to downtown are the neighborhoods of Independent Square and North Bank. Farther out, the most desirable areas include Atlantic Beach, Jacksonville Beach, Mayport, Neptune and St. Augustine.

**Politics/Government:** Jacksonville has a mayor-council form of government. All council members are elected by district or ward; only the mayor is elected at large. The governments of Jacksonville and Duval County were consolidated by referendum in 1968, a tribute to the efficiency-mindedness and collaborative spirit of the area. Jacksonville was fairly evenly split between Reagan (53 percent) and Carter (45 percent) in 1980, and was one of the fifteen metro areas with the smallest percentage of votes (2.6 percent) for Anderson.

**Transportation:** Travel in and around the city is facilitated by municipal busing and two interstate highways; rush-hour commuter traffic is heavy. Amtrak provides four departures daily, and the Jacksonville International Airport, a medium-size air travel hub, is served by eleven airlines, supplying ninety-three flights a day.

**Health Care:** Health care in the Jacksonville area is low-cost and consists of fourteen hospitals, including one teaching hospital and two cardiac rehabilitation centers. The area also has sixteen nursing homes and three hospices.

**Child Care:** As of early 1987, Duval County had 326 licensed child-care centers, with a total capacity of nearly 23,300 children. Several area centers receive either public or private financial assistance, which should improve the relationship between quality and cost. In addition to formally licensed centers, the county has day-care facilities in over 200 homes, with a capacity of over 1,000 children. As in most metro areas, the total capacity is less than 50 percent of estimated need. The Jacksonville Community Council has completed an in-depth study of child-care facilities in Jacksonville–Duval County and is a prime source of up-to-date information. Call 904-396-3052.

**Housing:** A single-family house (three-bedroom, two-bathroom) costs $85,000. A two-bedroom, one-bathroom apartment costs $250 to $350 a month.

**Public Safety:** With 484 reported 1986 robberies per 100,000 city residents, Jacksonville is among the cities in our study with an average crime rate.

**Cultural Attractions:** Cultural attractions in Jacksonville include the restored Florida theater, a Mediterranean-style building that houses the city's Florida Ballet, considered the best in the state. The landmark edifice also hosts concerts, visiting dance troupes, theater groups and musical comedy shows. The city's Theater Jacksonville is the nation's oldest continuously operating theater. Circulating museum collections may be viewed at Jacksonville's Prime F. Osborn Convention Center, which recently hosted the

Ramses II exhibit. Finally, Jacksonville's annual Free Summer Jazz Festival is renowned as one of the finest in the nation.

**Sports/Recreation:** Professional sports attractions include the Jacksonville Expos, of baseball's AA minor league, as well as pro golf and tennis. College sports include the Gator Bowl (football) and Jacksonville University baseball and basketball.

**Taxes:** Neither the state of Florida nor the city of Jacksonville imposes an income tax; real property is assessed at full market value and is taxed at a rate of $19.1657 per $1,000. The state sales tax is 5 percent. There is a 10 percent utilities tax on electric, water, gas and local telephone service, and other "taxes" come in the form of professional licensing fees.

---

## WHERE TO BREAK IN

For individuals interested in relocating to Jacksonville, we include a listing of major area employers. For more information, call 904-353-0300.

| Firm/Organization | Product/Service | No. Employees |
|---|---|---|
| Southern Bell | telephone utility | 3,793 |
| CSX Transportation | shipping/transportation | 3,500 |
| Blue Cross/Blue Shield | health insurance | 3,000 |
| Prudential Insurance Co. of America | insurance | 2,800 |
| Baptist Medical Center | health care | 2,300 |
| St. Vincent's Medical Center | health care | 2,200 |
| Gate Petroleum | petroleum products/ real estate | 2,000 |
| University Hospital | health care | 2,000 |
| Memorial Medical Center | health care | 1,800 |
| Gulf Life Insurance | insurance | 1,295 |
| AT&T American Transtech | shareowners services | 1,223 |
| Independent Life & Accident Co. | insurance | 1,154 |
| Methodist Hospital Inc. | health care | 1,035 |

## SUMMING UP: OPPORTUNITY FOR WHOM?

Jacksonville's labor force of 436,126 is currently 5.8 percent unemployed. The First Coast area's economy is diversified, and major industries are wholesale and retail trade, insurance, information management, telecommunications, shipping and health care. Agriculture is also very important to the Jacksonville area, with agricultural occupations claiming almost 8 percent of the local work force. We include a distribution of Jacksonville's work force among eight basic industrial categories.

| Industry | Share of Work Force (in %) |
|---|---|
| Wholesale and retail trade | 27.9 |
| Services | 23.4 |
| Government | 14.6 |
| Manufacturing | 10.0 |
| Finance, insurance and real estate | 9.0 |
| Transportation, communication and utilities | 7.5 |
| Construction | 7.4 |

Jacksonville's strong services, financial and health-care sectors are growing and should continue to create new jobs for bankers, clerical and data-processing personnel, and health-care professionals. Anticipated growth in high-tech manufacturing and research should generate opportunities for engineers and electronics and electrical technicians.

# Kansas City, Kansas–Missouri

MSA POPULATION (7/86): 1,517,800 (25th largest)

POPULATION GROWTH 1980–86: 5.9%

COUNTIES: Wyandotte (Kansas), Jackson (Missouri)

EMPLOYMENT (9/87): 718,400

AVERAGE TEMPERATURE: 53.7°F

YEARLY RAINFALL: 37 inches

HUMIDITY: 59% (28th most humid)

COST OF LIVING: 98.4

## KEYS TO THE CITY

**Small Business Growth:** birth rate, growth rate, growth index (rank/86): 3.2  3.1  6.3  (41st)

**Average Annual Job Growth (9/84–9/87):** 1.3% (95th/highest 100).

**Keys to Prosperity:** High-tech, autos, agribusiness, printing.

**Key Developments:** Continued growth of Crown Center and similar clusters of retail and other facilities such as the Plaza (America's original shopping mall, trendier than ever).

**Key Life-Style Trends:** New York's Yuppies might not recognize their midwestern counterparts, but Kansas City is growing an honest-to-goodness Yuppie population with all that implies—a thriving nightlife and gourmet shopping. It is reported that the first place where Godiva chocolates were available between New York and San Francisco was the Plaza. Like Minneapolis, Kansas City is easy to get around in a car (don't leave home without it).

## WHY OPPORTUNITY KNOCKS IN KANSAS CITY

As the large Sunbelt cities for one reason or another lose some of their magnetism, many companies looking to relocate or expand are setting their sights on what experts call second-tier cities. One of the hottest is Kansas City, the most centrally located of any major U.S. city. Second-tier cities represent the fourth wave of corporate locations, following the big industrial cities, the suburbs and the Sunbelt. They are attractive because they offer lower living costs, cheaper labor, construction activity and office space.

Big opportunities have opened up for entrepreneurs servicing the larger companies moving into the second-tier cities. During the early 1980s, construction and real estate started booming. Now, retail trade is also growing at a fast pace. Opportunities abound for printers, caterers and others who can serve the needs of arriving corporate giants. Kansas City has already attracted General Motors, Burlington Northern, and the first and only U.S. office of the Japan Chamber of Commerce and Industry.

Kansas City's chief strength is its economic diversity. The Kansas City metro area ranks second only to Detroit in the production of automobiles. In 1984, employment in the auto industry grew by 16.6 percent, representing almost 2,000 additional workers. A new 2.3-million-square-foot General Motors auto assembly plant is under construction in Kansas City, Kansas, reflecting expectations of continued growth in the auto industry.

Agribusiness is big business in Kansas City. The industry deals with the cultivation, shipment, storage and processing of crops; the production of chemicals and pharmaceuticals; the manufacture of farm supplies; and related finance and trading services. Agribusiness employs nearly 90,000 persons (or 14 percent of the work force) and produces over $5 billion in products and services. Major employers in this industry include Farmland Industries, Butler Manufacturing Company, Mobay Chemical Corporation, Pfizer, Inc., Bayvet Division of Miles Laboratories, Coopers Animal Health and Kansas City Board of Trade.

The printing and publishing industry flourishes in Kansas City. The area serves as the international headquarters of Hallmark Cards as well as twenty-six other substantial printing firms. Kansas City ranks first in the nation for greeting-card publishing.

Fast becoming the area's leading employers are AT&T Communications, H&R Block, DST (a major data-transfer corporation), Blue Cross and Blue Shield of Kansas and Missouri, and a number of noted Kansas City–based insurance companies.

Economists predict that Kansas City will be turning more and more to high-tech in the future. The Midwest Research Institute concluded that more than 180 high-tech firms are already operating in the Kansas City area. Among the high-tech heavyweights are United Telecom, Allied Bendix and Wilcox Electronic. Smaller enterprises include Kansas Crystals Filtronetics and Innovative Software.

The goal of Kansas City, however, is not to radically reorient its economy toward high-tech. What the city aims to do is use high tech to enhance the area's existing economic strengths. Three major goals are to attract new industry, retain and expand existing industry, and form new businesses. Opportunities will exist in three fields where high-tech will be targeted: agribusiness/high technology, specialized fields/high technology and international business. Many of the high tech industries that promise future growth are linked to agribusiness areas such as the production of herbicides, fungicides and soil fumigants, as well as to commodity services. Companies growing in these areas include Mobay Chemical Corporation, Farmland Industries, Agrigenetics, Bayvet, Burst Agri Tech and CEVA Laboratories.

Firms involved with high-tech special fields also have great growth potential. Prominent are fields that synthetically grow quartz crystals and produce quartz electronic components. Kansas City has a large concentration of quartz crystal firms, and is second only to Erie, Pennsylvania. They include American Crystal Co., Electro Dynamics, Kansas Crystal Inc. and Oscillatek.

The third area of opportunity in high-tech expansion is international business. Agribusiness has given Kansas City a strong international image. Today, about thirty firms from abroad have branches in the area. The largest include Sony Corp., Toyota, Airco Industrial Gases, Parmalee Products and AOC International. Manufacturing increasingly demands the use of high tech to develop sophisticated methods of production.

Kansas City has numerous assets that contribute to its prosperous business climate. Among these are:

1. Excellent transportation access by rail and highway.
2. A productive labor force.
3. Relatively low labor costs.
4. Comparatively low natural gas costs.
5. Good quality of life.
6. An attractive tax climate.

What the city lacks are enough highly skilled professionals, especially engineers and computer scientists. It also lacks venture capitalists willing to finance new operations.

As Kansas City attracts more business, its population will grow by leaps and bounds. Between 1970 and 1980, the metropolitan area experienced 4.25 percent population growth, an addition of 54,000 people. The Mid-America Regional Council projects that population will grow by 12.9 percent from 1980 to 1990. By the year 2000 the population of Kansas City is expected to reach over 1,600,000 (up from 1,380,000 in 1980).

---

## QUALITY OF LIFE

**Weather:** The Kansas City climate is characterized by a long autumn, an occasionally hot summer with cool nights of low humidity and a winter of about 100 freezing days. The average January temperature is 25.9°F, and the average July temperature is 78.5°. Spring is characterized by capricious weather fluctuations.

**Education:** Kansas City is divided into thirty-seven public school districts, comprising 284 schools. They have an enrollment of 151,946 pupils. The pupil/teacher ratio is 14.95 to 1, and approximately $2,459 is spent on each pupil annually. The area also offers 83 private schools, which have an enrollment of an additional 21,581 pupils. Institutions of higher learning include ten private four-year, one public four-year, one private two-year and four public two-year institutions.

**Neighborhoods:** With an inner-city population of 161,072, Kansas City, Kansas, is distinguished by its strong ethnic communities, which have sprouted roots and remained on the Kansas side of the city. The result is a concentration of cultural diversity unique to the metro area. Kansas City, Missouri, located in Jackson County, is the center of population of the Kansas City metro area. Quality Hill is known for its downtown lofts and renovated apartment buildings, while the Westport, Hyde Park and Plaza areas are noted for historic homes and condo conversions; a variety of elegant old homes stands near the Nelson Atkins Museum and along Ward Parkway. Brookside and Near Northeast are convenient to the Kansas City Museum and are popular among young families that desire older homes in a stable community setting.

**Politics/Government:** Kansas City, Kansas, has a mayor-council-administrator form of government with six council seats and a mayor. Kansas City, Missouri, has a council-manager form of government with a twelve-member city council and a mayor. As the center of population of the Kansas City metroplex, Kansas City, Missouri, tends to have more of the uniquely inner-city problems than does the Kansas side; under federal court order to desegregate its public school district, the Missouri side has imposed a higher school tax to cover the costs of capital improvements needed to comply with the order—the result has been, among some, a resentment of the civil rights issue with a highly pecuniary dimension.

**Transportation:** Kansas City motorists must face heavy commuter traffic daily on the three interstate highways that serve the area. Intracity movement is facilitated by municipal buses. Travel to points outside the metro area may be accomplished with Amtrak, which offers three trains daily, or by flying—the Kansas City International Airport and the Kansas City Downtown Airport form a large air travel hub, served by a total of twenty-six airlines supplying over 200 daily flights.

**Health Care:** In an effort to raise the level of job performance via improved physical health, corporations in Kansas City are cooperating with area hospitals to devise health-care programs for employees. Foremost are programs that help employees combat drug addiction problems. Many hospitals provide diabetes education classes, seminars for families of chemically dependent people, stop-smoking classes, stress- and pain-management clinics, and exercise groups. The Mid-American Coalition on Health Care was formed by fifty corporations to control the cost of health care, while the Kansas City Area Health Planning Council provides information regarding changes within the health-care field.

Kansas City supports 159 doctors per 100,000 residents. The medical schools in the area are the University of Kansas Medical Center, the University of Missouri–Kansas City and the University of Health Science, an osteopathic school.

**Child Care:** Quality licensed day care is available in the metropolitan area, but parents are advised to inspect each facility for health and safety regulations. A list of approved facilities can be acquired from the Licensing Division for Wyandotte County by calling 913-321-4803, or for Johnson County at 913-791-5841. The

Day Care Connection can be reached at 913-648-0424 to suggest licensed day-care homes, or at 913-262-2273 to suggest licensed day-care centers or preschools.

**Housing:** The average cost of a new three-bedroom, two-bathroom home in Kansas City, Kansas, is $91,000 (Johnson County) and $80,500 (Wyandotte County); a comparable home costs $90,000 in Kansas City, Missouri.

**Public Safety:** Crime rates in Kansas City range from average to high: In 1986 there were 385 reported robberies per 100,000 city residents on the Kansas side, while the figure for the Missouri side was 768.

**Cultural Attractions:** Long known as the city where jazz was made great by the contributions of immortals Count Basie and Charlie Parker, Kansas City also extends its cultural commitment to other types of music, art and theater. The Kansas City Symphony recently completed a $10 million endowment campaign, while the Lyric Opera of Kansas City has performed more than 100 different productions since its origin. The Nelson Atkins Museum of Art, pride and joy of Kansas City's art enthusiasts, boasts a priceless Oriental collection. The region's historical, scientific and industrial development is preserved by the Kansas City Museum, which houses a quarter of a million artifacts and also features a planetarium.

The Missouri Repertory Theatre, a professional equity company, is known for its acclaimed productions of classics such as *Nicholas Nickleby* and *A Christmas Carol*, but it also often experiments with more offbeat work. Starlight Theatre brings traveling Broadway musicals to Swope Park each summer, and other summer theater has been provided by the Johnson County Park and Recreation District. A six-block district downtown boasts five legitimate theaters and two dinner theaters (Tiffany's Attic and the Waldorf Astoria).

No cultural center is complete without a ballet company. The Kansas City Ballet has earned recognition both regionally and nationally for its progressivism as well as for its strong ties with New York City's late George Balanchine and Alvin Ailey's ballet company.

Jazz continues to be the city's cultural gem. The city plans to build an International Jazz Hall of Fame, to hold annual jazz festivals and to sponsor summer concerts in the park.

**Sports/Recreation:** Area spectator sports include baseball's Kansas City Royals, the NFL's Chiefs and the Comets of pro indoor soccer.

**Taxes:** Residential property is assessed at 19 percent of true market value and taxed at a rate of between $3.55 and $5.76 per $100 of evaluation, depending on location within the city. Both Missouri and Kansas impose a graduated income tax, and the city of Kansas City imposes an income tax of 1.0 percent on salaries, wages and tips earned by people who live or work there. The Missouri state sales and use tax is 4.225 percent, and Kansas City, Missouri, adds an additional 2 percent.

## WHERE TO BREAK IN

For individuals interested in seeking employment in Kansas City, we supply a listing of major employers. For more information, contact the Kansas City Area Development Council at 816-221-2121 (services both sides of the Kansas–Missouri border).

| Firm/Organization | Product/Service | No. Employees | Phone |
|---|---|---|---|
| U.S. government | government | 22,000 | (816) 374-5156 |
| State of Kansas | government | 7,197 | (913) 296-3581 |
| State of Missouri | government | 6,114 | (314) 751-4165 |
| City of Kansas City, Missouri | government | 4,535 | (816) 274-1628 |
| City of Kansas City, Kansas | government | 1,700 | (913) 573-5660 |

SELECTED MAJOR EMPLOYERS OF 500 OR MORE

| Firm/Organization | Product/Service |
|---|---|
| Allied Bendix Corp. | aerospace/engineering |
| General Motors Assembly Div., Fairfax Plant | auto assy. |
| Hallmark Cards, Inc. | cards/gifts |
| Trans World Airlines, Inc. | air carrier |
| University of Kansas Medical Center | health care |
| AT&T Communications, Inc. | telecommunications |
| AT&T Technologies, Inc. | telecommunications R&D |

SELECTED MAJOR EMPLOYERS OF 500 OR MORE (continued)

| Firm/Organization | Product/Service |
|---|---|
| Ford Motor Co. Kansas City, Assembly Plant | auto assy. |
| General Motors Assembly Div., Leeds Plant | auto assy. |
| Macy's | retail sales |
| Sears, Roebuck & Co. | retail sales |
| Southwestern Bell | telephone utility |
| St. Luke's Hospital | health care |

## SUMMING UP: OPPORTUNITY FOR WHOM?

Kansas City's diverse economy provides opportunities for people from all walks of life, but is especially attractive for skilled engineers, computer specialists and financial experts. Between 1983 and 1984, employment grew by 17,868 jobs, with all major sectors showing improvement. The construction industry showed the greatest growth, increasing activity by 13.9 percent, while manufacturing increased by 6.2 percent. Both fields are expected to experience continual growth. Real estate, finance and insurance are also expected to expand. Kansas City will especially need high-tech specialists in many different capacities.

# Las Vegas, Nevada

MSA POPULATION (7/86): 569,500 (66th largest)
POPULATION GROWTH 1980–86: 23.0%
COUNTY: Clark
EMPLOYMENT (9/87): 288,900
AVERAGE TEMPERATURE: 80°F
YEARLY RAINFALL: 1.27 inches
HUMIDITY: 20% (the least humid city)
COST OF LIVING: 103.2

## KEYS TO THE CITY

**Small Business Growth:** birth rate, growth rate, growth index (rank/86): 4.1 2.9 7 (21st)

**Average Annual Job Growth (9/84–9/87):** 6.0% (4th/largest 100)

**Keys to Prosperity:** Climate, services industry (primarily tourism), low taxes (retirement).

**Key Developments:** Construction of several retirement communities. The biggest yet will be the Las Vegas version of Phoenix's Sun City (Delwebb).

**Key Life-Style Trends:** Ski area (one hour away), water sports (Lake Mead National Park, thirty minutes away), golf. Local residents attend major entertainment events such as concerts.

## WHY OPPORTUNITY KNOCKS IN LAS VEGAS

Las Vegas's 30 percent population growth in the 1970s has continued into the 1980s, making the city sixty-sixth in size. Fueled by the continued popularity of gambling and entertainment, as well as by the arrival of high-technology research and manufacturing, the city's employment growth has been outstanding. The growth in employment opportunities has been met by the ready availability of affordable housing and retail space and by the welcome absence of congestion. The city's location in southern Nevada, which makes it attractive to tourists, is equally appealing to prospective residents looking for a mild climate with few extremes in either temperature or precipitation. The city's air quality is good, although occasional inversions can make it smoggy.

While the nearby Nellis Air Force Base provides revenue to Las Vegas, the money-generating champion continues to be the city's gambling casinos, in spite of the strong showing by the retail and manufacturing sectors. And gambling revenue has been put to good use; the city has financed capital projects such as road construction, upgrading of the city jail and annex, and the construction of numerous parks.

---

## QUALITY OF LIFE

**Weather:** Las Vegas's climate is typical of desert areas—characterized by low humidity, sparse precipitation, warm sunshine, hot days and cool nights. During summer, daytime highs frequently reach into the 100s, while nighttime lows drop back to the 70s. Winters are mild, with daytime temperatures averaging in the 60s; Las Vegas residents are strangers to 0°F days. Snow is rare, but in January of 1949 the city received a seventeen-inch dusting (the yearly average works out to one and a half inches).

**Education:** The Clark County School District is the twenty-first largest in the nation, with 116 schools, 95,000 students and pupil/teacher ratios of 23 to 1 (secondary schools) and 26.8 to 1 (elementary schools). An advantage of the fact that Clark County has one large school district is that area schools are equally well funded. The University of Nevada at Las Vegas (UNLV), with a total enrollment of 13,000 students, boasts a faculty of 400 and facilities occupying 335 acres. The Las Vegas–Clark County Library District has 600,000 volumes distributed among eight branch locations.

**Neighborhoods:** Las Vegas residents don't have the sense of "neighborhoods" that an easterner or other big-city dweller might. After all, the area is so spread out that a neighborhood-size population takes up the area of a whole city. In fact, Las Vegas has several cities in its metro area beside Las Vegas itself: North Las Vegas, Henderson and Boulder City. Certain areas are considered chic, such as Rancho Circle, where the entertainers live; Quail Park, home of the corporate executives from the hotels; and Spanish

Trails, a planned community with golf courses and pool facilities built in.

**Politics/Government:** Power resides in Clark County rather than the city, because all of the high revenue–producing hotels on the Strip are in the unincorporated part of the county. The county (which is the size of New Jersey) also runs the airport. Of the seven members of the board of county commissioners, one is a well-regarded black ophthalmologist from the West Side in North Las Vegas, one represents the large Latino community and two are women (that is to say, there is a majority of minorities).

**Transportation:** The municipal bus system that serves the area is jointly owned by Clark County and the city of Las Vegas, but is privately maintained and operated by the Las Vegas Transit System. McCarran International Airport serves the area with some 300 daily flights offered by twenty-six air carriers. The city is also served by Amtrak.

**Health Care:** The Las Vegas area has eight hospitals with 1,986 beds. The largest facility is Humana Hospital–Sunrise. The next largest is the county hospital, University Medical Center of Southern Nevada, which has a special burn-care unit. Nevada has been made famous for having licensed bordellos, but these are not in Clark County; rather, they are in neighboring Nye and other rural counties.

**Child Care:** Private day-care facilities are available. These services are licensed and growing. The fire safety codes are being revised to reconcile safety needs with the need for more day care.

**Public Safety:** Our bellwether public safety test of robberies per 100,000 city residents (1,683) is the highest of the cities in this book. Of course, a large proportion of easily identified potential victims in the city at any given time are out-of-towners.

**Cultural Attractions:** Cultural attractions in Las Vegas include Nevada Dance Theater, the Las Vegas Chamber Symphony Orchestra and the Las Vegas Civic Symphony. Of course, if you like your culture well lit, all of the city's major casinos offer nightly shows, the best of which are at the Lido de Paris, the Stardust and the Tropicana (Les Folies Bergere).

**Sports/Recreation:** In Las Vegas, an appreciation for professional spectator sports is best indulged with a television set. A local favorite is college basketball, especially since UNLV has been doing very well. For those capable of recovering from the city's nightlife, daytime recreational opportunities include nearby Wet and Wild Water Park and visits to Nevada's numerous ghost towns.

**Taxes:** When tax time comes around, Nevada residents get off light, due mainly to heavy revenues from the dependable gambling industry. Las Vegasites are no exception, with local taxes amounting to just over 1.0 percent of average annual household income.

---

## WHERE TO BREAK IN

For individuals interested in relocating to Las Vegas–Clark County, here is a select listing of the area's major employers. For more information, contact the Las Vegas Chamber of Commerce at 702-457-4664.

| Firm/Organization | Product/Service | No. Employees |
|---|---|---|
| Nellis Air Force Base | military | 13,000 |
| Reynolds Electrical & Engineering | R&D/mfg. | 4,800 |
| Clark County School District | education | 4,600 |
| EG&G Engineering | R&D/engineering | 1,800 |
| Nevada Power | power utility | 1,300 |
| Central Telegraph | telecommunications | 1,000 |

Smaller companies in the gambling and entertainment business account for over half of all employment.

---

## SUMMING UP: OPPORTUNITY FOR WHOM?

A metro area with population and employment growth like Las Vegas's simply can't be ignored as a relocation prospect. Typically pooh-poohed as a tacky, classy-trashy tourist trap/vice town/sin city, Vegas is attracting a swelling core of permanent residents eager to take advantage of the clean air, sunshine and employment opportunities in the services, entertainment, education, health-care and high-tech R&D/manufacturing industries.

# Los Angeles, California

L.A.–LONG BEACH, CALIF. PMSA POPULATION (7/86): 8,295,900 (2nd largest), part of the Los Angeles–Anaheim–Riverside, Calif. CMSA population (7/86) of 13,074,800 (2nd largest).

POPULATION GROWTH 1980–86: 10.9%

COUNTY: Los Angeles

EMPLOYMENT (9/87): 4,089,700

AVERAGE TEMPERATURE: 64.8°F

YEARLY RAINFALL: 14.05 inches

HUMIDITY: 53% (30th most humid)

COST OF LIVING: 107.3

---

## KEYS TO THE CITY

**Small Business Growth:** birth rate, growth rate, growth index (rank/86):   3.5   3.4   6.9 (25th)

**Average Annual Job Growth (9/84–9/87):** 2.5% (51st/largest 100)

**Keys to Prosperity:** Los Angeles has benefited from a diversified economy, strong in both the rapidly growing services area and the surprisingly hardy (for a large city) manufacturing area. New construction, to accommodate a population increase, has helped fuel growth, but has created problems of congestion and housing cost that bring the city close to the limits of its enormous freeway network and public endurance, with people driving in to the city every day from as far away as seventy miles.

**Key Developments:** Growth has spilled out beyond neighboring Orange County (Anaheim) to Riverside. Public transportation, used by only a small fraction of the population since trolleys were eliminated decades ago, is virtually nonexistent and is finally getting some attention, with the construction of a subway and two light-rail lines.

**Key Life-Style Trends:** The L.A. area will become increasingly international day by day, with Hispanics and Asians accounting for three-fourths of its population increase through 1995. Its high growth ensures it will continue to have a youthful outlook.

219

## WHY OPPORTUNITY KNOCKS IN LOS ANGELES

L.A. has matured in spite of the city's popular image—as a backdrop for a segment of "Lifestyles of the Rich and Famous." The tinsel town of movie stars, mansions and musicians has seemingly overnight developed into the financial, commercial, industrial and perhaps even cultural capital of the West Coast.

As the growth of key East Coast cities (for example, Boston or New York) was linked to their coastal locations and proximity to Europe, so has L.A. benefited from the economic vitality of the Pacific Rim. The emergence of Japan, Taiwan and Korea as major financial and manufacturing powers places West Coast cities with developed infrastructures and skilled populations—such as L.A.—in a perfect position to prosper.

And prosper, or at least grow, it has. Between 1980 and 1986, the Los Angeles–Long Beach PMSA experienced a 10.9 percent increase in population, gaining 818,700 residents. Between 1983 and 1985, the area gained 267,900 jobs; the city is currently the location of 1.3 million jobs.

And this expansion does not show signs of abating soon. The county of Los Angeles is expected, by Census estimates, to lead U.S. counties in employment and population growth through the end of the century. Between 1987 and 1995, over half of California's population growth is expected to take place in the five-county L.A. metro area, due mainly to Asian and Hispanic immigrants, who will contribute 75 percent of that population increase.

Key to the growth of the Los Angeles metro area has been the healthy diversification of its economy. Although recent employment growth has been mainly in the services sector, the manufacturing sector continues to thrive, aided by a rebound in high tech. While high tech accounts for only 11 percent of employment in L.A. County, compared to one-third in the Silicon Valley, that 11 percent amounts to one and a half times the number of jobs in the valley. Overall, manufacturing accounts for 23.8 percent of the area's nonagricultural employment.

Trade is another strength of the local economy. The combined taxable retail sales of the L.A.–Long Beach area exceed $18 billion, making it the largest retail market in the United States. The wholesale and retail trade sectors together employ another 22.8 percent of the area's work force. The city's large and growing population places high demands on government; consequently, the public sector employs roughly 15 percent of L.A.'s workers. The city's entertainment industry employs 80,000 workers who produce 90 percent of the world's recorded entertainment, with a gross sales value of $7 billion annually. The market demand of the large Southern California population makes the transportation and distribution industries highly profitable. L.A.'s port has the highest income of any American port facility, and 60 percent of imports are consumed locally. Also strong and thriving is the city's finance, real estate and insurance sector.

Though home to a number of corporate giants (for example, Atlantic Richfield Co., Occidental Petroleum, Lockheed, Carnation, Teledyne and Northrop), Los Angeles, unlike other big U.S. cities, continues to provide a healthy climate for small business, outperforming both New York and Chicago in new small business starts and successes. In their scramble to either attract or retain large corporate citizens, cities often forget that it is the small businesses that generate the vast majority of employment growth in the United States.

## QUALITY OF LIFE

**Weather:** The Los Angeles area generally enjoys a two-season (summer-winter) climate. Summer is characterized by morning lows of 61° and afternoon highs of 81°; the average winter morning low is 47°, but the temperature usually rises to about 67° by afternoon. Dry weather is the rule, with relative humidity averaging slightly more than 50 percent yearly. The area average yearly rainfall of fourteen inches occurs during the cooler season (November–April). Snow is a rarity, except in the outlying mountains and elevated desert regions.

**Education:** The Greater Los Angeles metro area is served by over 100 private and parochial schools, 157 four-year colleges and universities, and 31 two-year community colleges. A measure of the area's high-tech capacity: L.A. boasts the largest concentration of engineers, technicians, science specialists and mathematicians in the nation. Spearheading the West Coast's science and technology research facilities are the California Institute of Technology and the Jet Propulsion Laboratory. The University of California at Los

Angeles is one of the finest public research universities in the United States, and its library system of some 5 million volumes places it among the top 5 U.S. universities. The university has an international student body and offers a number of programs for both full-time and nonmatriculated students, including the largest on-campus extension program in the world. Other area colleges and universities include the University of Southern California, the California Institute of the Arts, Occidental College, Pepperdine University, the Claremont Colleges and Loyola. The full gamut of professional programs is available, with particularly strong medical education facilities, consisting of four medical schools, two dental schools and a number of teaching hospitals throughout metropolitan Los Angeles. Overall, the area's population is well educated, with 19.8 percent of adults twenty-five years of age and older having four or more years of college.

California's public primary and secondary education is of high quality and is likely to enjoy more uniform funding in the future. In past years, the state's education budget has been subject to discretionary and sometimes substantial reductions. In response, a broad-based coalition of educators, parents and citizens has been rapidly organized and effectively mobilized. Known as the California Movement for Education Reform (CMER), the group is expected to secure restoration of the state education budget, with assurances that it won't be cut in the future.

**Politics/Government:** How much growth is too much? Political careers in Los Angeles—including that of the city's most successful mayor, Tom Bradley—could turn on how that question is answered. San Francisco's decision to limit high-rise construction downtown is likely to detrimentally affect that city's future development, and may have done so already, allowing L.A. to emerge as California's number-one financial and commercial center—Los Angelenos may be unwilling to make the same mistake. But what was largely an aesthetic decision in Frisco is more a question of necessity in Los Angeles: For forty years Los Angeles has been growing outward, but empty space is now scarce and population density similar to that of other U.S. urban centers has been achieved. With few viable mass transportation options, L.A. motorists face the heaviest commuter traffic in the nation, some of them beginning their morning journeys from seventy miles east of downtown—at the edge of the Mojave Desert. Antigrowth activists have begun to win seats on the city council, and may well give Bradley a run for his money if he chooses to seek a fifth term in office. Contrary to the popular image of Southern California, Los Angeles may have to adjust itself to the urban reality of a compact life-style.

**Neighborhoods:** In the case of L.A. County, which covers some 4,000 square miles, it is difficult to speak of neighborhoods, and the metro area is more illustratively defined in terms of regions. Those who prefer a quiet, suburban life-style tend to settle in the San Fernando Valley, which is a relatively close twenty minutes from downtown and fairly accessible financially. Upscale and more expensive are the communities of Burbank, Toluca Lake, Van Nuys, North Hollywood and Sherman Oaks, which are popular among entertainers and well-off professionals. Chatsworth, Northridge, Granada Hills and Bell Canyon are situated north of downtown. Residential development is newer to these communities, and the rural past of Southern California has not yet given way entirely to condos and tract houses.

**Transportation:** L.A.'s 562 miles of freeways constitute the most advanced, modern and extensive highway network in the world. Nonetheless, it is woefully inadequate for the immense commuter volume it must carry during weekday rush hours. The frustration of L.A. motorists has recently surged to infamy, coming to a head in a frightening series of highway shootings, with mobile gunmen taking potshots at commuting colleagues. Since most of the sprawling region's commuters are either unable or unwilling to avail themselves of L.A.'s commuter rail system, ferry line and municipal buses (for most, these are not viable transportation alternatives), there is little relief in sight.

A bright spot in the Los Angeles transportation picture is the newly renovated and ultramodern Los Angeles International Airport (LAX). The expanded facility sports new terminals, landscaping and extra parking. In addition, roadway access has been improved, along with hotel capacity, passenger amenities and cargo-processing facilities. The airport's new Tom Bradley Terminal can accommodate thirty-five international carriers and a yearly volume of 7 million passengers; the airport serves about 40 million air travelers and handles 930,000 tons of cargo annually.

**Health Care:** The quality, accessibility and variety of health care in the L.A. metro area is large, but costs are high. Well-staffed departments exist for virtually every medical specialty, including cancer treatment, cardiac rehabilitation, psychiatry and substance abuse. Los Angeles is among the U.S. cities that took an early role in constructively confronting the AIDS epidemic. The downside of the L.A. health picture is the city's notorious smog and low air quality.

**Child Care:** Of the L.A. metro area's 444,000 working women, 46 percent have children under six years of age. To assist working parents in locating a quality day-care facility, a local network of ten state-funded child-care resource centers serves as a clearinghouse for information on licensed child-care providers (Pasadena: 818-796-4341; Santa Monica: 213-395-3605; San Fernando Valley: 818-781-7099; San Gabriel Valley: 818-289-9484).

**Housing:** A measure of the extent to which L.A. and Southern California have grown up is the relatively high cost of housing. The average market value of a typical house in the seven-county L.A. metro area is now about $160,000. The average monthly rent for a one-bedroom apartment is between $300 and $450.

**Public Safety:** Los Angeles registered 918 robberies per 100,000 city residents in 1986, placing the city among the least safe metro areas in our study. Nonetheless, our bellwether reference identifies L.A. as substantially safer than several other of the cities of opportunity.

**Cultural Attractions:** Long considered a cultural desert (except for the prodigious output of Hollywood's cinema and TV studios), L.A. now holds its own with the likes of New York, Boston and San Francisco, with a variety of galleries, museums (J. Paul Getty Art Museum, Los Angeles County Art Museum, Museum of Contemporary Art, Aerospace Museum, Natural History Museum, Museum of Science and Technology, and the Black History Museum), live theater, stage productions, orchestras, dance companies and concerts.

**Sports/Recreation:** Spectator sports are well represented in Los Angeles, home of the Raiders (football), the Dodgers (baseball), the Kings (hockey), the Lazers (soccer), and the Lakers and Clippers (basketball). Participants have access to a number of municipal golf courses, tennis courts and swimming pools, as well as ski slopes and miles of beach for a variety of water sports.

**Taxes:** California has a graduated income tax structured like the federal income tax. Residential property taxes in the L.A. area average 1 percent of market value, and the sales tax is 6.3 percent.

---

## WHERE TO BREAK IN

For individuals interested in relocating to the L.A. metro area, we include a listing of selected major employers (some are headquarters of national organizations). For more information, contact the Los Angeles Chamber of Commerce at 213-629-0602. It offers various publications for sale.

| Firm/Organization | Product/Service | No. Employees |
|---|---|---|
| Hughes Aircraft Co. | aircraft manufacturers | 15,000 |
| MCA, Inc. | records | 7,900 |
| Western Air Lines, Inc. | passenger airline | 6,000 |
| Specialty Restaurants Corp. | restaurants | 4,000 |
| Atlantic Richfield Co. | oil/gas | 2,200 |
| Automobile Club of Southern California | motor vehicles | 2,000 |
| Flying Tiger Line, Inc. | cargo shipping | 2,000 |
| Pacific Lighting Corp. | holding company | 2,000 |
| Unocal Corp. | chemicals | 1,800 |
| Garrett Corp. | aerospace | 1,600 |
| Southern California Gas Co. | gas distribution | 1,600 |
| Farmers Group, Inc. | insurance | 1,260 |
| Quotron Systems, Inc. | computer mfg. | 1,000 |
| Thrifty Corp. | pharmaceuticals | 700 |
| Virco Mfg. | furniture mfg. | 735 |
| National Medical Enterprises | health care | 500 |
| Litton Industries, Inc. | military navigational guidance | 350 |
| Occidental Petroleum Corp. | oil | 250 |
| Northrop Corp. | aircraft and electronics | 200 |

## SUMMING UP: OPPORTUNITY FOR WHOM?

It is an American civic reality that where economic opportunity is great, construction, commerce and population will grow, no matter how strong the opposition. Antigrowth activism in Los Angeles may well prove to be more a political tactic than a realistic agenda, especially in an area where expansion pressure is strong and destined to remain so for years to come.

With well-established high-tech computer, aerospace and electronics industries, the L.A. metro area is strong in the kind of manufacturing and R&D in which the U.S. is currently, and likely to remain, a world leader. With a large, generally affluent, and growing population, the area's strong services and trade industries should continue to expand and prosper. Finally, the area's strategic West Coast location will continue to be a valuable asset as the nations of the Pacific Rim emerge as world economic powers.

Still a youthful city with progressive values and tastes, Los Angeles is an excellent job market for women, young people and minorities with the right education and training for the financial, technical and skilled services occupations needed to sustain the city's growth into the coming century. Los Angeles will sustain its demand for health-care professionals, educators, accountants, data-processing specialists, engineers, technicians, research scientists, sales specialists, and white-collar, blue-collar and retail managers.

# Memphis, Tennessee

MSA POPULATION: 959,500 (41st largest)
POPULATION GROWTH 1980–86: 5%
COUNTY: Shelby
AVERAGE TEMPERATURE: 61.6°F
YEARLY RAINFALL: 49.1 inches
HUMIDITY: 60% (27th most humid)

---

## KEYS TO MEMPHIS

**Small Business Growth:** birth rate, growth rate, growth index (rank/86): 3.2   3.8   7   (21st)

**Average Annual Job Growth:** 2.8% (42nd/largest 100)

**Keys to Prosperity:** Distribution, telecommunications, health care, defense, tourism.

**Key Developments:** Starting with the Memphis Jobs Conference in 1979, Memphis has been headed toward a bright future. The poorest large city in the 1980 Census, it is now a headquarters city for the likes of Federal Express, Holiday Corporation, International Paper Company, Schering-Plough and Litton Industries. In addition, the Memphis International Airport has become a major regional hub. In August 1987, *Fortune* cited Memphis as one of six "booming" U.S. cities.

**Key Life-Style Trends:** With a new look and a revitalized business community, incomes in Memphis are heading upward, and downtown is being spruced up. Most important, Memphis has found citizens who care about its future. According to Neal Peirce, Memphis hit the comeback trail when—and only when—it moved to heal its racial divisions, when a strong business-government partnership was formed." He cites Republican Governor Lamar Alexander's Memphis Jobs Conference, initiated in 1979, as a decisive element in the city's turnaround. The Jobs Conference is credited with supplying Memphis with a direction and program for development at a time when the city had a desperate reputation as the poorest big city in America.

227

## WHY OPPORTUNITY KNOCKS IN MEMPHIS

The historical and present economic growth of Memphis is directly related to the city's central location on the Mississippi River, at a convergence of river, air, highway and rail transportation systems. It has become one of the nation's top ten distribution centers—Federal Express, the overnight letter and package courier, is the city's largest private employer. Memphis business leaders boast that because of the city's south-central location, 60 percent of the U.S. population is within overnight truck delivery range.

The first major commodities to flow through the port of Memphis were cotton and hardwoods, and the city remains the world's largest processor of soybeans, and the nation's third largest processor of foods in general.

Memphis has also become a major telecommunications center, principally because of large capital investments by Federal Express, the Holiday Corporation and South Central Bell. Memphis-based RCA Data Transmission Services is part of RCA's Global Communications Division, offering satellite transmission of computer-generated business information. Because of the history of telecommunications pioneering in Memphis, in the next four years South Central Bell will invest $45–50 million above its yearly annual investment of $150 million. This commitment puts Memphis on the leading edge of telecommunications technology; as a result, Memphis will be the first city in the United States to have System 7 signaling. In addition, Memphis's Christian Brothers College has instituted a telecommunications curriculum intended to train students in telecommunications equipment use as well as telecommunications engineering and development methodology. Memphis's communications significance is rounded out by its headquartering of the U.S. Postal Service's Southern Region, with an automated mail-processing facility serving nine states and 5,878 post offices.

With nineteen major hospitals in the metro area, employing some 37,000 people and generating about $2 billion annually for the local economy, Memphis is also a health-care center, with over 7,600 hospital beds and a broad range of facilities. Currently under consideration is a downtown redevelopment plan that would establish a biomedical research zone in the city, combining the research capacities of several of the area's hospitals as well as accessible medical school resources.

Distribution, communications and health care are not as sensitive to business cycles as manufacturing, a clear benefit to the city's services- and retail-oriented economy. In addition, the large proportion of government employment, including a naval air station, enhances the buffering effect of the city's other major industries.

---

## QUALITY OF LIFE

**Weather:** Indirectly affected by opposing airflows from both Canada and the Gulf of Mexico, Memphis has a climate characterized by capricious storms. While 0°F temperatures are all but unknown, the temperature does drop to freezing or below on about sixty days out of every year. On the other end of the spectrum, Memphians experience about the same number of 90° or above days each year.

**Education:** The K–12 enrollment of the Memphis public school system is 114,520 pupils. All schools offer special educational programs for the learning impaired. There are seventy-one private and parochial schools in the area, with a total enrollment of 19,932. Memphis has a diverse menu of higher educational institutions from which to choose. The University of Tennessee at Memphis offers health-careers programs in general medicine, dentistry, nursing, pharmacology and allied health. Memphis State University offers programs of study toward the B.A., B.S., M.A., M.S., Ph.D. and J.D. degrees. Memphis's Rhodes College, listed among the nation's "most prestigious" colleges and universities, offers the B.A. and B.S. degrees, as do Christian Brothers College and LeMoyne-Owen College, a historically black institution. The State Technical Institute at Memphis is a two-year technical college offering the associate degree in business, engineering and computer science. The Memphis College of Art offers the B.F.A. degree. Additional institutions in the area are Shelby State Community College, The University of Tennessee College of Social Work and Tusculum College, an adult continuing education college offering master's degrees in management and education.

**Politics/Government:** Memphis is distinguished by the fact that it is one of the few cities in the country with strong city and county mayors; the City of Memphis has a mayor-council form of government, while Shelby County has a mayor-commissioner form of government.

**Transportation:** Intracity transportation in the Memphis area is provided by municipal busing. The city is served by two major interstate highways; heavy traffic is common. Amtrak provides two departures a day, and the Memphis International Airport, now one of the nation's twenty-five "large hubs," is served by thirteen carriers providing 318 daily flights.

**Health Care:** Health care in Memphis is big business, and area hospitals have a combined capacity of 7,600 beds. Specialized facilities exist for cardiovascular, cancer, eye, ear, and nose and throat research, as well as childhood cancer treatment, liver and kidney transplant, spinal cord injury, stroke, head trauma, substance-abuse rehabilitation and psychiatry.

**Child Care:** Day care in the Memphis area is available through 385 licensed providers, with total capacity of 19,324 children. Care is available in group, family or formal center settings. Crittendon Services provides child-care information and referral services. The State of Tennessee child-care program can be reached at 901-373-2500.

**Housing:** The cost of a new, 1,800-square-foot home in the Memphis area is $90,000; the average monthly rent for a two-bedroom, one-bathroom apartment is $360. The area's average utility bill (electricity, gas and water) amounts to $95.

**Public Safety:** With 881 reported 1986 robberies per 100,000 city residents, Memphis is among the cities in our study with the highest crime rates.

**Cultural Attractions:** Memphis has a variety of cultural and recreational attractions from which to choose. Beale Street (birthplace of the blues) and Elvis Presley's Graceland are major tourist attractions. The Memphis Brooks Museum of Art specializes in Renaissance and Baroque painting, American portraiture and photography; the Dixon Gallery and Gardens features French and American Impressionist works; and the Memphis State University Art Gallery has a collection of Ancient Egyptian art and artifacts. Friends of the performing arts will be anxious to sample the Memphis Symphony Orchestra, Opera Memphis, the Tennessee Ballet and Roscoe's Surprise Orchestra. Theater Memphis and Playhouse on the Square offer schmaltzy Broadway-style musicals, while the

Circuit Playhouse runs *au courant* off-Broadway-caliber shows and experiments with new scripts by local playwrights. Memphis's Orpheum Theater is a magnificently restored nineteenth-century theater that runs dramatic plays, musical performances and opera.

**Sports/Recreation:** Sports fans enjoy the Annual Liberty Bowl, the Federal Express–St. Jude Classic TPD Golf Tournament, the U.S. National Indoor Tennis Championships, and minor-league baseball and soccer.

**Taxes:** With no state income tax, a city sales tax of 7.75 percent and local property taxes of $7.09 per $100 of assessed valuation, the Memphis tax burden amounts to about 1.1 percent of average annual household income. Per capita income in the Memphis area is currently around $11,575.

---

## WHERE TO BREAK IN

We have stressed the importance of new, growing, small companies to the economic health of the city. A new small company, however, is more in the domain of an entrepreneur than that of an individual seeking employment. Hence, we provide a listing of the area's major employers of over 1,000 people. The number of employees for each firm is included to suggest the firm's relative importance, and impact on the local economy. For more information, contact the aggressive Memphis Chamber of Commerce at 901-523-2322.

| Firm/Company | Product/Service | No. Employees |
|---|---|---|
| Naval Air Station, Memphis | government | 16,835 |
| U.S. government | government | 15,036 |
| Memphis City Board of Education | education | 14,552 |
| Federal Express | air courier | 14,000 |
| Malone & Hyde, Inc. | foods distributor | 6,250 |
| Baptist Memorial Hospital | general medical and surgical hospital | 6,035 |
| Memphis City | government | 5,940 |
| First Tennessee Bank | national commercial bank | 4,000 |
| The Kroger Co. | grocery stores/bakery | 4,000 |
| State of Tennessee | government | 3,190 |

| Firm/Company | Product/Service | No. Employees |
|---|---|---|
| Holiday Corp. | hotels/motels/ telecommunications | 3,100 |
| University of Tennessee at Memphis | education | 3,000 |
| Memphis Gas, Light, and Water Div. | utility | 2,892 |
| Goldsmith Div., Inc. | department stores | 2,800 |
| Defense Logistic Agency | government | 2,573 |
| Northwest Airlines | air passenger carrier | 2,500 |
| Memphis State University | education | 2,250 |
| McDonald's/Century Management | restaurants | 2,200 |
| Schering-Plough Consumer Operations | pharmaceutical, cosmetic and foot-care prods. | 2,200 |
| Defense Depot | government | 2,198 |
| Cleo Wrap | wrapping paper mfg. | 1,700 |
| South Central Bell | telephone utility | 1,501 |
| Commercial Appeal/ Memphis Publishing Co. | newspaper publishing/ printing | 1,300 |

## SUMMING UP: OPPORTUNITY FOR WHOM?

Memphis is located in the southwest corner of Tennessee, wedged between Arkansas and Mississippi. Inhabiting an area of 290 square miles, Memphis's population of 652,640 has a density of 2250.5 persons per square mile.

The diversified Memphis economy employs a work force of 449,800, which is currently 5.4 percent unemployed. Memphis's nonagricultural work force is distributed as follows among eight basic industrial categories:

| Industry | Share of Work Force (in %) |
|---|---|
| Services | 24 |
| Retail trade | 19 |
| Government | 16 |
| Manufacturing | 13 |

| Industry | Share of Work Force (in %) |
|---|---|
| Transportation, communications and utilities | 9 |
| Wholesale trade | 9 |
| Finance, insurance and real estate | 6 |
| Construction | 4 |

As we have already pointed out, Memphis's major industries are the storage and distribution of agricultural and other products, food processing, transportation, communications, health care and related sciences, and education. We predict opportunities for persons with training in data processing, accounting, electrical engineering, biological and biotechnical sciences, and medicine, as well as retail trade, blue-collar work and office management.

# Miami, Florida

MIAMI–FORT LAUDERDALE, FLA. CMSA POPULATION (7/86): 2,912,000 (11th largest), of which the Miami–Hialeah population is 1,769,500.
POPULATION GROWTH 1980–86: 8.9%
COUNTY: Dade
EMPLOYMENT (9/87): 814,800
AVERAGE TEMPERATURE: 75.5°F
YEARLY RAINFALL: 59.8 inches
HUMIDITY: 71% (2nd most humid)
COST OF LIVING: 110.9

---

## KEYS TO THE CITY

**Small Business Growth:** birth rate, growth rate, growth index (rank/86): 3.8  2.8  6.6  (33rd)
**Average Annual Job Growth:** 1.9% (73rd/largest 100)
**Keys to Prosperity:** Tourism, transportation, finance and real estate, publishing, utilities, fashion.
**Key Developments:** Miami Design Plaza and plans to found a Biomedical Research and Innovation Center to develop high-tech medical devices and equipment.
**Key Life-Style Trends:** Continued immigration of Cubans to Miami has left them in a dominant position; the city remains a window on Latin America and a doorway to the United States for Latinos. If you want to work here, learn Spanish—and be careful. A loophole in Florida's handgun law for a brief period made it legal for people to carry a six-shooter on their hip. The loophole has since been closed. But Miami cab drivers, for example, are still allowed with a permit to keep a pistol or two on the seat beside them (for self-protection). So for heaven's sake, don't argue about the fare.

---

## WHY OPPORTUNITY KNOCKS IN MIAMI

Opportunity, like beauty, is in the eye of the beholder. The city that was born and built along a long expanse of white sand and surf near the southern tip of Florida as a snowbird's Art Deco vacation paradise has more recently suffered the effects of illegal immigra-

234

tion, drug trafficking, violent crime, economic depression and race rioting.

But opportunity, like hope, also springs eternal. The Latin business community built by Cubans settling in Miami after Castro's seizure of that Caribbean island in 1959 was by the 1970s catering to Latin American business. South American executives anxious to do business in the United States found in nearby Miami a "user friendly" metropolis whose bilingual bankers and businessmen were the perfect intermediaries. South American visitors, mainly from Brazil and then oil-rich Venezuela, pumped millions of dollars into Miami's retail, medical, services and tourist industries. When oil prices dropped in 1985, oil-poor Venezuelans pulled out, along with the ever-cautious *hombres de negocios* from other debt-ridden South American republics.

To make matters worse, a new wave of Cuban immigrants, a steady flow of Haitan refugees and an increasing number of Nicaraguan refugees lent such an aura of "foreignness" to the city that American companies contemplating relocation, already antsy over the high drug-related crime rate (vividly portrayed in the "Miami Vice" television series), were afraid to come near. The fact that Miami blacks—largely excluded from the success and growth spurred by the Cuban community—have rioted has only exacerbated the situation.

But even if Anglo big business was cold on Miami, the Cubans who had invested years of work in building up the city's business community weren't about to abandon it, and European, Middle Eastern and Asian clients, zealously recruited by these go-getters, have largely replaced the fleeing Latin Americans. Moreover, the race riots were five years ago. While law enforcement efforts have hardly made a dent in drug traffic volume, the city's drug-related crime rate has subsided. Unemployment is also down from its high point in the early 1980s.

Miami has the nation's third largest number of Hispanics enrolled in higher educational programs, and these young Cuban-Americans appear to be less extreme than their fanatically conservative, anti-Communist parents (over 70 percent of Cuban-Americans registered to vote are Republicans). So, as the city's Cuban community becomes increasingly a North American establishment, Miami will begin to attract more of the domestic companies it needs to sustain economic growth in more resilient sectors.

## QUALITY OF LIFE

**Weather:** Miami's subtropical climate has essentially no seasons, except that during summer months it rains a lot, and during the winter it's dry. The temperature almost never goes down to freezing, and there's about a month's worth of 90° days each year.

**Education:** Miami's public education system consists of one district and 279 schools, with a K–12 enrollment of 227,000 students. There are 210 private and parochial schools in the Miami area, with a combined enrollment of 56,915 students. Miami has 250,000 students enrolled in college, university and advanced vocational programs. Among the city's institutions of higher learning are Miami–Dade Community College, the University of Miami, Florida International University, Barry Universtiy and St. Thomas University. A full range of professional, technical, business, medical and liberal arts programs is available.

**Neighborhoods:** The greater Miami area consists of twenty-seven cities covering some 2,000 square miles. Each operates its own government, and is responsible for administrative and services delivery functions within its boundaries. Among these communities are Biscayne Park, Miami Shores, Miami Beach and West Miami, all residential areas; Coral Gables, characterized by exclusive residential living and headquarters for a number of multinational firms; Indian Creek Village, an ultra-exclusive island of Mediterranean villas; Hialeah, known for its greyhound racetrack; Hialeah Gardens, an attractive residential area; and North Bay, a community of mainly high-rise, waterfront apartment buildings. The city of Opa Locka is notable for its classically moorish architecture, inspired by *The Thousand and One Nights*. Bal Harbor is famous for its exclusive shops and boutiques. Those preferring a quieter, small-town residential setting would be attracted to South Miami and Surfside.

**Politics/Government:** Miami's government is a weak-mayor, council-manager form. A city commission, elected at large and including the mayor, appoints a professional city manager. City commissioners serve overlapping four-year terms and meet twice a month. City government in Miami is highly representative of the large, successful and influential Cuban community (the incumbent mayor is from the Cuban community), but also includes representation from the city's black and Anglo communities. The established Cuban community is politically conservative and staunchly anti-Communist, although the 1980 citywide vote pattern doesn't show this conservatism so clearly because the other votes tend to be Democratic (former Mayor Maurice Ferre was a Carter ally until the end). Dade County serves greater Miami well.

**Transportation:** Private passenger car transportation in the Miami area is supplemented by municipal busing, a light-rail system (Metrorail) and the elevated Metromover. Amtrak provides four departures a day, and the Miami International Airport is served by sixty-one airlines supplying 381 daily departures.

**Health Care:** Health care in the Miami area is good but expensive. With more than 12,000 total hospital beds, the area boasts thirty-seven licensed hospitals, including three teaching hospitals, seven cardiac rehabilitation centers and one cancer treatment center. The city's Jackson Memorial Medical Center was ranked sixteenth among the nation's top twenty-five hospitals and is second in the nation in total admissions.

**Child Care:** Working parents interested in the availability of child day-care services should call the United Way of Miami–Dade County at 305-579-2200.

**Housing:** Miami is not an inexpensive housing market. In the southwest section of the city, a three-bedroom, two-bathroom house sells for approximately $100,000, and a two-bedroom, one-bathroom apartment rents for about $650 a month; naturally, many homes sell for much more, and luxury apartments in the most exclusive parts of town can have monthly rents in the thousands.

**Public Safety:** The main strike against Miami, its crime rate, remains very high, with 1,455 reported 1986 robberies per 100,000 city residents. Miami is the fourth "most unsafe" of the forty-two metro areas in this book. Those wary of going to Miami—because they watch too much television—should be aware that the cost of producing a single episode of the "Miami Vice" TV series exceeds the 1987 budget of the Miami police department's vice unit by $400,000.

**Cultural Attractions:** Miami's cultural life features the Central Miami Youth Symphony, the Miami Beach Symphony Orchestra, the Miami Chamber Symphony and the Greater Miami Opera Association. Local museums include the Cuban Musuem of Arts and Sciences, the Historical Museum of Florida and the Metro Dade Center for the Fine Arts, which offers traveling exhibitions. The city's Art Deco Weekend, celebrated each year in January, recognizes the architecture of Miami's glamour days.

**Sports/Recreation:** Sports attractions include both greyhound and horse racing, jai alai and the NFL's Miami Dolphins. And then there's the beach—admission: free.

**Taxes:** Neither Florida nor the city of Miami imposes an income tax, and the local tax bill is a low 1.03 percent of average annual household income. Living costs, however, are high—the twenty-fifth highest in the nation—while per capita income is the nation's fifth lowest. The city's low per capita income, however, is attributable to Miami's whopping immigration problem, which severely overstresses Dade County's welfare resources.

---

## WHERE TO BREAK IN

For individuals interested in relocating to Miami, we include a listing of major area employers. For more information, contact the Miami Chamber of Commerce at 305-350-7700.

| Firm | Product/Service | No. Employees |
|---|---|---|
| Knight Ridder Newspapers | newspaper publishing | 22,000 |
| Eastern Airlines | air passenger carrier | 13,200 |
| Florida Power & Light Co. | electric utility | 2,100 |
| Wilson Brothers Inc. | apparel retail | 1,350 |
| Avatar Holdings Inc. | land development | 1,200 |
| General Telephone Co. of Florida | telephone utility | 1,200 |
| Southeast Bank NA | financial services | 1,200 |
| Southeast Banking Corp. | financial services | 1,200 |
| Ryder Systems Inc. | truck rental | 1,000 |

---

## SUMMING UP: OPPORTUNITY FOR WHOM?

Unlike other cities in our study, some of which have grown up seemingly overnight with the coming of high-tech research and development, Miami is no new kid on the block. Tourism put the city on the map, but a smaller proportion of Miami's work force falls under the telltale services/miscellaneous category than other cities blessed with sand and surf. Still, the tourism factor is undeniable: the city is a world leader in the passenger cruise industry, and the Miami Seaport had 1985 revenues of $17.5 million.

The Miami Design Plaza symbolizes one of the city's other major industries: interior design. With some 250 tenants representing 2,000 manufacturers, the Design Plaza attracted $250 million worth of business in 1985. Miami's garment district, severely harmed by the loss of Latin American business, has rebounded recently, and the combined annual revenues of the Miami Children's Wear Manufacturers Guild's thirty members is $75 million.

Miami's other major industries are health care, biomedical and related technologies (Miami is one of the nation's top ten manufacturing centers of medical instruments, treatment devices and electronic diagnostic equipment), printing, filmmaking and shipping. With a good manufacturing sector, a thriving retail sector (taxable retail sales in Dade County amounted to $3.3 billion in 1985) and a growing financial sector, Miami is a good bet for relocation. When more people come around to this fact, the real estate and construction industries, presently in a slight slump because of the city's bad reputation, should boom.

Miami's work force of 731,900, currently under 6 percent unemployed, is expected to add 132,500 jobs by the year 2000. We provide a distribution of the area work force among six major industrial categories:

| Industry | Share of Work Force (in %) |
| --- | --- |
| Retail trade | 17.95 |
| Manufacturing | 14.91 |
| Services/tourism | 13.55 |
| Finance, insurance and real estate | 8.27 |
| Wholesale trade | 5.74 |
| State government | 2.20 |

# Minneapolis–Saint Paul, Minnesota

MSA POPULATION (7/86): 2,295,200 (16th largest)

POPULATION GROWTH 1980–86: 7.4%

COUNTY: Hennepin (Minneapolis), Ramsey (Saint Paul). The MSA includes a slice of Wisconsin

EMPLOYMENT (9/87): 1,274,000

AVERAGE TEMPERATURE: 44.1°F

YEARLY RAINFALL: 25.94 inches

HUMIDITY: 60% (26th most humid)

COST OF LIVING: 104.5

## KEYS TO THE CITY

**Small Business Growth:** birth rate, growth rate, growth index (rank/86): 3.5  3.4  6.9  (25th)

**Average Annual Job Growth (9/84–9/87):** 2.1% (58th/largest 100)

**Keys to Prosperity:** As in other cities of opportunity, the "city" is really at least two cities, Minneapolis and Saint Paul. In fact, the Twin Cities area is polycentric, because the retailing/office centers in the southern and western suburbs have become significant competitors to Minneapolis and Saint Paul. The Twin Cities area specializes in running things, in management and marketing—business services. It isn't so much into manufacturing computers as into using them. Its expertise is evident in the way people in the area apply their minds to running human services (they are the best in the country). Agribusiness and food processing continue to be local employment mainstays. The Twin Cities metro area is second only to the Boston metro area in the number of company head offices per capita.

**Key Developments:** New outlets of national retail store chains such as Saks and Bloomingdale's are giving Dayton's some competition and local residents more choice. The scary thing for downtown merchants is the specter of a megamall with hundreds of stores opposite the airport on the old stadium site, in a suburban community called Bloomington, which in the 1950s was largely meadowland and is now the third largest city in Minnesota.

**Key Life-Style Trends:** Minneapolis and Saint Paul are open towns. Class distinctions are minimal, and business or professional people go for other communities to the south. People support the arts, especially music, and get involved. It's a "red wine town," meaning people know their wine (and brandy) and aren't chasing after a passing vogue for white wine. The people are entrepreneurial and mobile (you can drive almost anywhere in the area at an average speed of fifty miles per hour).

---

## WHY OPPORTUNITY KNOCKS IN MINNEAPOLIS–SAINT PAUL

Minneapolis–Saint Paul is a hotbed of opportunity frozen in an ice cube. The attractions are strong for those who can brave the city's Nordic blasts. The region from the Bear Paw Mountains in Montana to the Porcupine Mountains in Michigan's Upper Peninsula, and from the Skunk River in Iowa to the Rainy River on the Canadian border, contains one-tenth of the land area of the country. It is a region as large as Texas, with half the number of people, and the Twin Cities area is its capital.

Minneapolis started as a grain town and is headquarters for the world's four largest grain-milling companies. Saint Paul has traditionally been a hub of transportation and a warehousing center for the entire Upper Midwest. Today it is a government town (home to the state capitol, state offices, related associations and many lobbyists) and a college town (with Hamline University, Macalester, St. Thomas, St. Catherine and Concordia colleges all within the city limits, and the University of Minnesota's "St. Paul" campus right across the street, technically in Falcon Heights). Saint Paul also specializes in nonprofit business; generally it is the headquarters of Minnesota Public Radio, KTCA Public Television and the Wilder Foundation, among others.

In recent years, the "Twin Cities" area has enjoyed sustained economic growth because venture capitalists have targeted it as a key place to invest sizable amounts of capital. The burgeoning of big companies has done wonders for the region's economy, resulting in increased output and decreased unemployment. Today, over thirty billion-dollar corporations operate in the area.

A turn away from the stagnating farm and mining industries

toward the lucrative high-tech field accounts for the region's growth spurt. Today, a quarter of the work force is engaged in either a professional career or an occupation related to electronics and computers. Studies report that over 1,200 firms in the area are involved in intensive technology. Other major industries that have made this area one of the nation's fastest growing and most economically stable markets include machinery, food products and processing, dairy products, medical products, textiles and apparel, printing, and graphic arts.

The Twin Cities area has one of the lowest unemployment rates in the nation. Businesses are attracted to the region because of its stable, productive and skilled labor force of nearly 1 million persons, with low absenteeism and low turnover. Major corporations based in the Minneapolis–Saint Paul region include 3M Company, Honeywell, General Mills, Control Data, Pillsbury, Bemis, International Multifoods, Cargill Carlson Companies, Dayton-Hudson and Northwest Airlines.

Some locals are distressed that the area's largest employer, 3M Company, has chosen to locate an R&D facility in Austin and has purchased a site in Sacramento. In the 1960s, Honeywell, then the area's largest employer, facing an impulse to spread its operations, decided to develop its computer business, mainly in Massachusetts. In the 1980s, when Honeywell sold out to Bull and NEC, the Boston area, rather than the Twin Cities area, experienced the greatest cutback in jobs.

An economic study called "Making the Grade," conducted by the Corporation for Enterprise Development, rated Minnesota fourth in economic performance out of fifty states surveyed. In 1987, employment grew by 5.4 percent as the unemployment rate hovered around 6 percent. Personal income grew by 14.3 percent, with per capita income $11,682. Only 12.2 percent of the area's population lived below the poverty level. The black population remains small in the Twin Cities (around 5 percent), and the area provides many opportunities for blacks. A measure of equity shows that Minnesotan blacks earn 85.3 percent of what whites earn. This is the sixth highest figure in the United States, surpassing New York by a large margin.

In terms of financial resources, Minnesota is ranked seventh in the country. It is the twelfth largest financial center in the nation, with that industry employing 7.6 percent of the total work force.

Residents have a high savings rate, and banks are willing to extend themselves with local loans. Minneapolis–Saint Paul has also been blessed with the confidence of venture capitalists, who have injected large sums of capital into the local economy.

---

## QUALITY OF LIFE

**Weather:** If you hate cold weather, stay far away from Minneapolis–Saint Paul. Ranked second coldest in the United States, the area reports an average of thirty-five days when the mercury doesn't even rise up to the 0°F mark. However, note that the city itself is well designed to cope with the cold, with many "skyways" (second-floor enclosed pedestrian bridges) to connect buildings. Average temperature for the Twin Cities is 44°. In the 1986–87 winter, no snow fell at all, and locals argue heatedly that it's easier to cope with clear minus 0 weather than with the mushy, slushy 30s characteristic of more southerly winters. The rain is mainly in the spring. The summers are best described as cool and dry. The Twin Cities can have days where the temperature climbs over 100°, but also whole summers when it does not get past 90°.

**Education:** Minneapolis and Saint Paul both place a premium on public education, and a measure of their effectiveness is the fact that 77 percent of area high school graduates go on to some form of higher education. The Twin Cities is the location of the main campus of the University of Minnesota, a major research institution with a long tradition of community and public service. Programs are offered in humanities, fine arts, natural sciences, engineering, law, medicine and health sciences, agriculture, forestry and business. In addition to the University of Minnesota's Continuing Education and Extension Division, Metropolitan State University serves working adults in the Twin Cities by offering something unusual—a competency-based route to a degree. Private four-year colleges in the area include Augsburg College, Bethel College, Concordia College, Minneapolis College of Art/Design and the School of Associated Arts. In addition, the area is served by six community colleges and three major vocational/technical schools.

**Politics/Government:** Both Minneapolis and Saint Paul have a mayor-council form of government; in practice, Saint Paul's mayor is stronger vis-à-vis the council than is Minneapolis's mayor. Both cities have independently elected (as opposed to appointed) school boards. In Minneapolis and Saint Paul, generally speaking, most things are accomplished by consensus rather than by conflict. The area has a long history of public–private cooperation and partnership on a variety of efforts, such as Minneapolis's main downtown shopping thoroughfare—opened twenty years ago, it consists of twelve blocks restricted to pedestrian traffic with the exception of buses and taxis. Even its current renovation reflects the city's tradition of citizen involvement and local government participation, formally through advisory commissions and informally through neighborhood coalitions.

**Transportation:** The Twin Cities does possess a mass transit system, comprising of 1,012 city buses. Traffic on the freeways is usually moderate. Locals think some freeways are congested. Visitors from other cities would not. There is a large network of individual small freeways. Access is metered to control traffic flow. Amtrak provides three trains a day. The Minneapolis–Saint Paul International Airport is served by about twenty airlines, which provide 304 flights daily; however, since Northwest made the airport its hub, it has four-fifths of the gates, reducing competition.

**Health Care:** Hay fever sufferers beware! The area has a pollen count of 99, while an index of 10 means a lot of discomfort. High pollen counts, combined with extreme weather fluctuations, increase the chances of becoming ill. Health care in the area is excellent, and prices are reasonable. Facilities include five teaching hospitals, twelve cardiac rehabilitation centers and thirteen hospices. The Twin Cities area has the highest proportion population enrolled in prepaid medical plans of any area in the United States.

**Child Care:** The Greater Minneapolis Day Care Association (612-823-7243) connects working parents with licensed day-care providers.

**Housing:** A one-family house averages $80,600, while an apartment will cost you $330 a month.

**Public Safety:** According to our bellwether crime reference of robberies per 100,000 city residents, the two cities receive a mixed review, with 772 for Minneapolis and 295 for Saint Paul.

**Cultural Attractions:** Within Minneapolis–Saint Paul is a great store of cultural attractions that appeal equally to art connoisseurs, music enthusiasts and theater lovers. Museums include the Minneapolis Institute of Art, which features works from many time periods as well as a wide range of cultures; the American Swedish Institute, which emphasizes Swedish-American art pieces and ethnic exhibits; and Walker Art Center, which houses contemporary art works.

The Twin Cities' major arts facilities have recently been renovated. A nationally renowned repertory company performs in the glass-walled Gutherie Theater, which adjoins the Walker Art Center. The Children's Theater Company, which is the largest young people's theater in the United States, is located in the Minneapolis Institute of Art. Orchestra Hall is home to the Minnesota Orchestra. The Ordway Music Theater features the Saint Paul Chamber Orchestra, the Minnesota Opera Company and two festivals—the Twin Cities Jazz Festival and the International Flute Festival.

**Sports/Recreation:** Many of the area's tourist attractions focus on outdoor sights. The Lake of Isles sits in the midst of stately mansions, while bikers, joggers and skaters circle Lakes Calhoun and Harriet. Windsurfers and sailors abound in the summers. Across the southern suburbs there is a "belt" of entertainment that includes the Minnesota Zoo, restored Old Fort Snelling, the Canterbury Downs racetrack and the Valleyfair rides/amusement complex. Spectator sports attractions include the Minnesota Vikings (football), the Minnesota Twins (baseball), the Northstars (hockey) and the Timberwolves (basketball, coming in 1989).

**Taxes:** Minnesota's high quality of life costs money. State and local taxes take a huge bite out of household incomes, drawing over 5 percent of salaries; Twin Cities area residents shoulder the fourth highest tax burden in the United States. Income and property taxes are progressively scaled. The sales tax base is narrow, exempting food, clothing and many services.

---

## WHERE TO BREAK IN

For individuals interested in relocating to the Twin Cities, we include a list of the area's largest employers. For more information, contact the Chamber of Commerce of Minneapolis at 612-370-9132 or Saint Paul at 612-223-5000.

| Firm/Organization | Product/Service | No. Employees |
|---|---|---|
| Dayton-Hudson Corp. | retail | 100,000 |
| Honeywell Inc. | computers | 94,200 |
| 3M Co. | food processing | 85,700 |
| General Mills Inc. | food processing | 80,300 |
| The Pillsbury Co. | food processing | 79,400 |
| Control Data Corp. | computers | 54,100 |
| Honeywell Information Systems | computers | 25,000 |
| Carlson Cos. Inc. | hotels/inns | 24,000 |
| Norwest Corp. | banking | 17,700 |
| Northwest Airlines | airlines | 15,100 |
| Bemis Co. Inc. | packaging | 8,110 |
| Land O'Lakes, Inc. | food processing | 8,000 |
| International Multifoods Corp. | food processing | 7,900 |

## SUMMING UP: OPPORTUNITY FOR WHOM?

Business vitality is strong, but so far focused mostly around middle-to-large-size companies with white male owners. In 1987, minorities owned only 6.3 percent of the area's businesses, while women owned only 9.4 percent, even though women constituted 45 percent of the area's total work force, putting Minneapolis–Saint Paul in fifth place as a city of opportunity for working women.

The Minneapolis–Saint Paul area is an excellent place to operate a business that depends on human resources. In this area Minnesota places twelfth out of the fifty states. Nearly 91 percent of the population graduates from high school, and nearly 17 percent go on to college (Colorado has the highest percentage of college graduates, 23 percent of the state's population). Minnesota spends about $3,100 per student annually, an average amount for American public schools, and it maintains a pupil/teacher ratio of 17 to 1. The Twin Cities area holds special appeal for urbanites who opt to "return to nature" on the weekends. The nearby rural areas and the northern woods in Minnesota and western Wisconsin are used year-round for hunting, fishing, boating, canoeing and skiing. Minnesota was hailed as the most environmentally conscious state by the Washington-based Conservation Foundation. No wonder thousands of tourists and campers flock to the area each summer to enjoy the great outdoors.

The Minneapolis–Saint Paul area is a great place for those with a pioneering spirit . . . both to face the elements and to take advantage of business opportunities. The area has a well diversified economic sector, with a can-do spirit and a liberal, tolerant social atmosphere that should be especially attractive to blacks, women and those with a technological bent. The Twin Cities has experienced a boom in recent years and can look forward to increasing growth in the future.

# Nashville, Tennessee

MSA POPULATION (7/86): 930,700 (43rd largest)
POPULATION GROWTH 1980–86: 9.4%
COUNTY: Consolidated with Davidson County
EMPLOYMENT (9/87): 464,500
AVERAGE TEMPERATURE: 59.4°F
YEARLY RAINFALL: 46 inches
HUMIDITY: 62% (19th most humid)
COST OF LIVING: 102.7

## KEYS TO THE CITY

**Small Business Growth:** birth rate, growth rate, growth index (rank/86): 4.2 4.2 8.4 (8th)

**Average Annual Job Growth (9/84–9/87):** 3.6% (25th/largest 100)

**Keys to Prosperity:** Transportation, manufacturing (cars, high-tech), music/recording, tourism, low taxes and living costs.

**Key Developments:** New GM Saturn Plant.

**Key Life-Style Trends:** Suburbs are growing, but country music still rules and keeps downtown lively at night.

## WHY OPPORTUNITY KNOCKS IN NASHVILLE

The capital city of Tennessee is the fifth most expansive city in the continental United States, with an area of 533 square miles. With all that space, however, Nashville's central city population is only 477,811, making for a relatively low population density of 855 persons per square mile. However, Nashville's suburban population grew at a rate of 84 percent between 1976 and 1980 to 394,854.

Nashville has come to prominence for much the same reason as Memphis: Nashville's south-central U.S. location, 200 miles south of the center of U.S. population, makes the city an ideal distribution center. Six major branches of the interstate highway system, as well as nine federal highways, pass through and radiate from

248

Nashville, facilitating access for the 100 or so trucking lines that serve the city. Freight arriving via the Seaboard System Railroad or the Cumberland River, which has access to the Ohio and Mississippi rivers and thence to the Gulf of Mexico, is conveniently transferred to highway carriers for distribution throughout the United States. Nashville is within overnight delivery of about 75 percent of the U.S. population, making it a good location for industry.

General Motors located its $3.5 billion Saturn automotive manufacturing plant in Nashville precisely to take advantage of the city's highly developed transportation system, as well as its inexpensive and strike-free labor—less than 16 percent of Tennessee is unionized, versus the national average of 21 percent.

Nashville is also famous as the "holy land" of country music, being the home of the Grand Ole Opry, which means that the city not only benefits from its increasingly profitable recording industry but also from the tourism dollars generated by the yearly pilgrimage of hordes of country music's faithful to visit the city's Opryland U.S.A. theme park. Tourism is worth about $2 million annually to Nashville.

Nashville's other major industries are textiles and clothing; retail trade ($3 billion annually); health care; education; finance, insurance and real estate; and, as the state capital, government.

---

## QUALITY OF LIFE

**Weather:** In Nashville it's cloudy and it rains often, but extremes in temperature seldom occur. There are about seventy days a year with temperatures of 32°F or below, and only thirty days with temperatures of 90° or above. The temperature hits 0° about once a year.

**Education:** The public school system in Nashville is administered by the city's Metropolitan Board of Public Education and enrolls 73,831 pupils. The city appropriates about 38 percent of its budget to public education. Public school facilities consist of eighty-nine elementary schools, seventeen middle schools and sixteen high schools; special educational programs are administered at six separate facilities. There are fifty private and parochial schools in the Nashville metro area. Total postsecondary enrollment is 31,588, distributed among five two-year colleges (four private, one public) and eleven four-year colleges and universities (ten private, one public). Higher educational institutions include Meharry Medical School, Vanderbilt University Medical School, YMCA Law School and Nashville State Technical Institute.

**Politics/Government:** Nashville is one of the nation's relatively few metro areas with consolidated city-county government. The move to consolidation was made to simplify and streamline administrative structure while saving on the costs of government and municipal services delivery by eliminating wasteful duplications of effort. In the 1980 presidential election, Nashville–Davidson's voting pattern was strongly democratic, with nearly 60 percent of all votes cast going to Carter.

**Transportation:** Although Nashville has a municipal bus service, a car is necessary. The three area freeways used primarily by commuters are plagued by heavy traffic. The Nashville Metropolitan Airport is serviced by thirteen carriers and offers 115 departures daily.

**Health Care:** Nashville has a strong commitment to health care, which is relatively low-cost. There are eighteen hospitals serving the greater Nashville area, supplying a total of 5,974 beds. Four of these hospitals are teaching facilities; two offer cardiac rehabilitative programs and one is a psychiatric facility.

**Child Care:** Among Nashville's day-care providers are the South Street Community Center (615-256-5108) and Saint Mary Villa Child Department (615-356-6336). Many centers in the area will provide care on an ability-to-pay basis, charging according to a sliding scale based on income. The Nashville area chapter of the United Way can provide information on the area's child-care providers (615-255-8501).

**Housing:** Living costs overall are well below the national average, and a one-bedroom apartment rents for about $320 a month.

**Public Safety:** In our bellwether crime-evaluation category, there were 415 reported 1986 robberies per 100,000 city residents, placing Nashville among those cities in our study with average crime rates.

**Cultural Attractions:** As the home of the Grand Ole Opry, it shouldn't be surprising that entertainment and nightlife are built around Nashville's country music industry. The Grand Ole Opry, which originally occupied Ryman Auditorium, was moved in 1976 to Opryland U.S.A., a theme park that combines Hollywood tackiness with country homeyness. The famous Opry show is held every Friday and Saturday night, but the theme park offers continuous country music performances daily, in addition to various amusement park rides and attractions.

For the more urbane, the Tennessee Performing Arts Center is the home of the Nashville Symphony. Nashville's nightlife is fun, with a number of downtown bars and cafés featuring country music performed by locals struggling to break into the city's up-and-coming recording industry. Of historical significance are the Hermitage, Andrew Jackson's residence, and Belle Meade Mansion, which showcases the life-style of the Old South's landed aristocracy.

**Sports/Recreation:** Nashville sports fans have to content themselves with AAA minor-league pro baseball. Participant sports include boating, swimming, golf and tennis.

**Taxes:** Tennessee has no state income tax, and Nashville residential property is taxed at a rate of $3.92 per $100 of assessed value; residential property is assessed at 25 percent of real value. Tennessee sales tax is $5^{1}/_{2}$ percent, but Nashville adds $2^{1}/_{4}$ percent, bringing the local total to $7^{3}/_{4}$ percent. The total local tax burden amounts to a low 1.2 percent of average annual household income.

---

## WHERE TO BREAK IN

The following list of Nashville's major employers illustrates the diversity of the area economy, distributed relatively evenly among manufacturing, services and retail firms. For more information, call the Nashville Chamber of Commerce at 615-259-3900.

| Firm/Organization | Product/Service | No. Employees |
|---|---|---|
| Tennessee State | government | 17,865 |
| Metropolitan Nashville and Davidson County | government | 9,395 |
| U.S. Government | government | 9,005 |
| Metropolitan Nashville and Davidson Public Schools | education | 8,220 |

| Vanderbilt University Medical Center | teaching hospital | 8,185 |
|---|---|---|
| Avco Aerostructures Textron | aircraft wing mfg. | 6,805 |
| Opryland U.S.A. | theme park | 6,030 |
| HCA, the Health Care Company | integrated health care | 4,985 |
| South Central Bell | telephone utility | 3,500 |
| St. Thomas Hospital | general medical and surgical hospital | 2,810 |
| Newspaper Printing Co. | printing/publishing | 1,930 |
| AT&T and AT&T Technologies, Inc. | computer and telecommunications equip. | 1,700 |
| Commerce Union Bank | financial services | 1,620 |
| American General Life & Accident Insurance | insurance | 1,610 |
| E.I. du Pont de Nemours & Co. | synthetic fibers | 1,560 |
| General Electric | industrial and appliance motors | 1,500 |
| Northern Telecom | telecommunications equip. | 1,500 |
| Genesco, Inc. | shoe and apparel mfg. | 1,415 |

## SUMMING UP: OPPORTUNITIES FOR WHOM?

Nashville's manufacturing economy is so broad-based that the city managed to weather the 1981–82 recession very well. But today, manufacturing is high paying and increasingly high tech, with several companies representing aerospace, semiconductor, computer, chemical and telecommunications technologies. Satellite industries are also proliferating, and Nashville has a high level of new business starts and small business growth. The Nashville work force of 261,990 is currently only 3.9 percent unemployed.

As an established insurance center and a growing financial center, Nashville should continue to generate opportunities for people with accounting and data-processing skills. The city's thriving retail sector, cushioned by a high concentration of public employment and a generally diversified manufacturing sector, should continue to absorb retail management personnel. As a regional health-care and educational center with a growing population, Nashville should also be a strong seller's market for nurses, physicians, medical technicians and teachers. Finally, the city's expanding high-tech industries should create jobs for engineers, technicians and individuals with computer-related training.

# New York, New York

PMSA POPULATION (7/86): 8,473,400 (largest), part of New York–Northern N.J.–L.I., N.Y.–N.J.–Conn. CMSA population (7/86) of 17,967,800 (largest.)

POPULATION GROWTH 1980–86: 2.4%

COUNTY: New York City is unique in the United States for consisting of more than one county. It has five, called "boroughs": Manhattan, Brooklyn, Bronx, Queens and Staten Island.

EMPLOYMENT (9/87): 4,115,500

AVERAGE TEMPERATURE: 54.5°F

YEARLY RAINFALL: 40.19 inches

HUMIDITY: 61% (23rd most humid)

COST OF LIVING: 140.2

---

## KEYS TO THE CITY

**Small Business Growth:** birth rate, growth rate, growth index (rank/86): 2.6  3.1  5.7  (56th)

**Average Annual Job Growth (9/84–9/87):** 1.5% (78th/largest 100)

**Keys to Prosperity:** Financial sector, travel and tourism, professional services, fashion, communications, entertainment.

**Key Developments:** New Javits Convention Center opened, downscaled West Side Highway to be built, major renovation of subway system in process, office-building boom ending, luxury-residential-building boom still under way.

**Key Life-Style Trends:** Hardworking New Yorkers have had to cut corners. One way is by putting off marriage—or at least putting off having children until the last minute (i.e., mid- or late thirties). Another way is by cutting down on personal entertaining. The city's social problems are never out of sight because of the omnipresence of homeless people in public places. They are a reminder of a large underclass seemingly locked into poverty, in part because many children are not being educated well enough to take on tomorrow's highly skilled jobs (though New York City schools also consistently produce many nationally recognized graduates.)

254

## WHY OPPORTUNITY KNOCKS IN NEW YORK CITY

New York City is good for two kinds of people: first, those who are the best at something, or think they can be, and want to hone their skills and be rewarded for them; second, those who don't aspire to ultimate excellence for themselves, but want to learn from or be near such superachievers.

For many, New York City is the ultimate destination. It is the "big time," where Herbert Spencer's "survival of the fittest" is understood as the primary axiom of life. The Big Apple is fast, sexy, modern ... and will leave you in the dust if you don't keep up. Nowhere else do people work harder and smarter. Nowhere else do they have to work so hard at using their leisure time. Competition, guts and originality are key to all aspects of life, and the city's intrinsic sense of excitement and challenge is its chief allure.

For others, the temptations of New York are easy to resist. Like the sailors around Odysseus, they have sealed off their ears to the sound of the Sirens (not a bad idea when a fire truck blasts down Ninth Avenue at 4 A.M.).

For those who are seduced, New York's racy, maximum-intensity life can become an addiction. Nowhere else can you experience such soaring highs and such plummeting lows. Nowhere else are more dreams fulfilled and more hearts broken. But in this city of extremes and uncertainties, one thing is for sure—you never have to be bored, and you will always know that you are dealing with stark reality. By comparison, "everywhere else is out of town."

New York City is the largest city in the United States and the ninth largest city in the world. It has earned a worldwide reputation of being the place to "make it big," whether you are an actor or a businessman, a painter or a chef. It is an international center for trade, industry, finance, communications, fashion, art, politics and entertainment.

The city's economy in recent years has been booming. Retail stores, 50,000 of them selling anything imaginable, have been opening everywhere. Of the city's 14,000 restaurants, Manhattan alone claims 7,500, or one for every 200 residents. Wall Street's precrash prosperity overflowed its immediate borders to nurture auxiliary services that catered to the huge finance, real estate and insurance firms in the area. Only time can tell what the October 19,

1987, crash will mean to the retail and services businesses that got fat during the "roaring eighties."

By the year 2000, New York City's economy was projected (pre-crash) to grow by 300,000 new jobs; the region's supply of labor will grow only three-fourths as fast. In the best-case scenario, this means that as older people retire and fewer young people are available to replace them, the city will be able to offer more career opportunities to job seekers. However, the kind of jobs available will be quite different from those lost in the 1970s and before. They will call for a higher degree of education and more sophisticated skills.

Most new jobs will be in the service sector, but fewer than formerly expected precrash in the fields of finance, real estate and insurance. Traditional manufacturing has been declining in New York since 1950 at nearly four times the national rate: Between 1984 and 1987, the city lost about 50,000 manufacturing jobs. Manufacturing's decline hits the city's blacks and Latinos particularly hard because they fill almost half of the city's manufacturing jobs, which used to provide entry-level jobs for the unskilled. Older people without the necessary skills to compete in the new job market have also felt the pinch.

Some people will benefit from New York's economic reorientation—highly skilled workers who can take advantage of the gap that exists between the job openings and the inadequate number of qualified people to fill them.

Until the crash, New York's tremendous economic engine was fueled by the ever-expanding services sector. More of the world's largest and most prominent financial institutions have their headquarters in New York City than in any other U.S. city, and the only competitor that comes close worldwide is London. In 1972, approximately 40 foreign banks had substantial operations in New York. A decade and a half later, more than 300 such firms had established a base there. Financial institutions and related professional organizations hired more than 242,000 clerks and managers between 1977 and 1987. As of October 1987 New York City financial institutions (banks, brokerage houses, insurance companies, real estate firms, stock exchanges) employed about 495,000 people (the PMSA employed 578,000).

Before the crash, the booming financial sector more than compensated for the decline in other areas of the city's economy, although admittedly financial expansion was also responsible to some extent for the departure of jobs in the city's other industries, because it meant the eviction of some businesses and the driving up of real estate rentals in some low-rent areas.

The most famous financial institution in New York City is the New York Stock Exchange, at the corner of Broad and Wall streets in the heart of the Financial District. It is the largest stock exchange in the world. The American Stock Exchange, created for trading in the stocks of smaller companies, is also one of the nation's largest exchanges and is nearby.

Growth of the service sector has meant rapid absorption of new office space; since 1981, 52 million square feet of office space have been built in the city. The steady supply of new office space has helped to keep average rental rates stable. The average asking rate between 1981 and 1986 remained at $40 a square foot in midtown Manhattan; between 1978 and 1981 it had jumped from $15 to $40.

Despite a general decline in manufacturing employment, New York City still ranks third, after Los Angeles–Long Beach and Chicago, as a leading manufacturing center in the United States. It is home to 17,000 industrial plants employing approximately 430,000 workers. With the softness in the job market resulting from postcrash financial sector layoffs, these manufacturing industries might take up some slack for those with transferrable skills if the dollar stays weak. Tourism will also grow.

The city's two largest industries are printing/publishing and clothing production. New York has more printing plants than any other U.S. city and is responsible for one-sixth of the nation's printing and publishing. About a third of the books published in the United States are published in New York; the industry employs approximately 93,000 people.

New York's clothing industry is centered in Manhattan's famous Garment District around Seventh Avenue southwest of Times Square. Although the industry is declining because of rising business costs and low-wage foreign competition, it still employs about 119,000 people. New York is regarded as a fashion capital of the world; what appears first as an oddity on Manhattan streets may become a hot new trend copied by people around the world.

Other important New York industries include the production of chemicals, food, furniture, machinery, metal, paper and textiles. Flexible manufacturing firms specializing in high-quality goods tied to the service sector are prospering. For example, printing companies that cater to the daily needs of financial, retail and services firms are doing very well. So are companies that manufacture sophisticated computer software. Costume making for theater, dance and opera is flourishing along with the growth in high fashion. The general trends indicate that any enterprise that latches on to what is new and chic—or at least different—has a chance of prospering in New York.

The city's image has been damaged and its revenues and employment dented by the departures of Mobil Corporation (which employed 3,500 in New York City) and J. C. Penney (which employed 5,000). Mobil has moved to Fairfax, Virginia, and Penney to Plano, a Dallas suburb. Mobil and Penney cited as reasons for their departures high business costs, housing shortages, long commutes and a troubled public school system. An additional factor is the very success of New York City, making the Penney building, for example, worth a full year's profits.

Business costs include high taxes—New York City's corporate taxes are the highest in the country. While these taxes may irk large corporations, they can be deadly for small businesses, which remain the dominant form of business in New York (98 percent of the city's companies are small). Over the past few years, the state and city have reduced personal and corporate tax burdens, and Mayor Koch has introduced tax abatements for businesses.

The other overwhelming problem is education. Although the services sector will open up some unskilled jobs, 90 percent of new jobs will require a high school diploma. However, 40 percent of the city's adult workers lack such a diploma, and one-third of high school students drop out before graduation. Clearly, New York City's public school system has not as a whole been providing a future generation of workers with the necessary skills to compete in the city's highly demanding job market. Fortunately, this problem has been widely recognized and a strong new administrator has been recruited from Minneapolis to overhaul the city's public school system. The city's elite public and private schools continue to produce an impressive annual crop of award-winners, including one-third of the National Merit Scholars.

Added to outright departures of head offices are partial relocations to New Jersey by firms such as AT&T and Merrill Lynch, though they still retain their New York bases. (The "Where to Break

In" section shows what a small percentage of their jobs some firms, nominally headquartered in New York, actually retain in the city.)

New York has lost thousands of jobs and a sizable chunk of tax dollars from the Mobil and Penney moves (both these firms were among the city's top twenty-five corporate taxpayers.) In addition, the 3 million square feet of office space dumped on the market has contributed to cancellations of several planned office buildings and the loss of construction jobs. The expected West Side resurgence could be delayed for years, while some fear that a possible glut of office space could scare foreign real estate investors away.

Are we seeing a repetition of the 1970s, when the flight of numerous large corporations helped drive the city toward bankruptcy? No. New York City is still corporate America's most likely place to set up shop—in an April 1987 survey of 403 chief executive officers, almost 100 said they planned to acquire office space in the Big Apple during the following twelve months.

William H. Whyte has endorsed New York's value for business in a study of the performance of companies that fled New York to relocate in the suburbs (see Chapter 6). He found that thirty-nine companies that remained in New York enjoyed substantially higher profits than forty-one comparable corporations that left ten years before. Whyte suggests that firms choosing to stay in the "Big City" perform better than those that relocate to the suburbs because employees are kept on their toes by day-to-day exposure to new ideas, new people and fierce competition. On the other hand, relocation to the suburbs, he says, tends to reduce stimulation and dull aggressiveness.

Meanwhile, city officials are not sitting idly by as their economy is threatened by corporate evacuation. In an attempt to lure more firms to New York City and keep the established ones happy, Mayor Koch has introduced some business incentives. He offers relocating companies energy costs equal to those in New Jersey, real estate taxes at least as low as those in New Jersey and business taxes that in "most instances" would be no higher than those in New Jersey.

To qualify for the proposed program, companies must move either to a new or to a substantially rehabilitated office or manufacturing space in northern Manhattan, the Bronx, Queens, Brooklyn or Staten Island. A credit on city business taxes of $500 a year for each employee is offered for twelve years; an exemption from the commercial rent tax is also offered for twelve years. At stake are millions of square feet and thousands of jobs.

The bottom line is that New York's economy is currently ranked as one of the healthiest in the world, and at the moment, for every company that leaves, dozens are ready to start up or move in to its place.

## QUALITY OF LIFE

**Weather:** With about eighty days a year on which the temperature dips to freezing or below, and only about two weeks a year of 90°F temperatures, New York's climate is fairly mild. Proximity to the Atlantic Ocean, however, makes Gotham vulnerable to capricious storms during winter, summer and fall; hurricanes and whopper snowfalls are not unknown, but are taken in stride.

**Education:** The city's public schools are widely criticized for having fallen short in their mission to educate the city's 930,000 students. Many elite public schools do well, and the city has an abundance of world-class private schools. The higher education picture is much brighter. New York has about 150 colleges and universities, with an institution for virtually every specialization. The City University system, with its open admissions policy and a broad range of colleges, accounts for many of these. Among the more prestigious of the Big Apple's (private) colleges and universities are Columbia, New York University, Fordham University, the New School for Social Research and Pace University. Programs are offered in every imaginable area. A number of fine adult, continuing and extension curricula are offered by colleges and universities in New York, including the specialized fashion and design institutions. New York also boasts the largest public library system in the nation, with over 7.2 million volumes; many branches include specialized lending libraries such as those for children, literature or business. (Much of the research for this book, for example, was done using the magnificent resources of the Mid-Manhattan Library's business reference section.) The listing of business libraries in *The Harvard Guide to Careers* shows more in the New York area than anywhere else in the country; the Brooklyn Public Library's collection is particularly strong.

**Neighborhoods:** The first question facing people considering a move to New York is whether or not they wish to live in Manhattan itself. The key Manhattan neighborhoods range from SoHo (artsy, lofts) in the south, through Greenwich Village (once avant-garde, now settled ... if still a bit offbeat), up to Chelsea (being gentrified), east to the old stronghold of Gramercy Park, and finally to the Upper West Side and Upper East Side, where most New York professionals live. (The West Side is older, more progressive, the home of writers, artists and struggling young professionals; the East Side is newer, more conservative, and home to Wall Streeters who haven't bought suburban homes).

In the Bronx, the best area is Riverdale; it's a longer commute than from a Manhattan residence, but Liberty Lines express buses and Metro North get up there in well under an hour, and it's great for raising a family because nearby schools have more sports space. In Brooklyn, Brooklyn Heights or Park Slope are convenient to Wall Street. Many areas in Queens also offer gracious homes.

For those prepared to commute to suburbia, the options are one of innumerable fine communities in North Jersey, places like Fort Lee, Montclair, Teaneck, Short Hills (via bus from 42nd Street, PATH train or good New Jersey Transit trains from Penn Station); Westchester County, towns like Scarsdale, Dobbs Ferry, Hastings-on-Hudson (bus or comfortable Metro North commuter trains from Grand Central Station); or Long Island, places like Valley Stream, Massapequa, Manhasset, Glen Cove (warning: the Long Island Railroad is a crush and the Penn Station end is hot and unpleasant; the Long Island Expressway is jammed at rush hours). None of the options is ideal.

When we talk about "neighborhoods" within New York's gigantic Consolidated Metropolitan Statistical Area of 18 million residents, we should note that besides the core Primary MSA of New York City (which includes Westchester County as well as the five boroughs, for a total of 8.5 million residents) the suburban areas make up eleven more PMSAs. These other PMSAs are Nassau–Suffolk, N.Y. (i.e., Long Island, pleasant living for 2.6 million residents); Newark, N.J. (1.9 million); Bergen–Passaic, N.J. (1.3 million); Middlesex–Hunterdon, N.J. (950,000); Monmouth–Ocean (the "Jersey Shore," 935,000); Jersey City, N.J. (553,000); Bridgeport–Milford, Conn. (444,000); Orange County, N.Y. (282,000); Stamford, Conn. (195,000); Danbury, Conn. (186,000); and Norwalk, Conn. (128,000). All of the four Connecticut communities are pleasant and expensive.

New York City is surely the hardest city in America to move to for a job if you have a family, because of the high costs of living in town and the commuting time to the suburbs. It's easier to accept—for both grown-ups and children—if you haven't become used to a cheaper or easier life-style!

**Politics/Government:** New York has a mayor-council form of government onto which has been grafted a unique entity, the so-called Board of Estimate, which unilaterally alters and ratifies budget plans and decides on franchises, contracts and land use. Representation on the Board of Estimate is not in proportion to population, giving lopsided power to the less populous boroughs; this is a source of no small controversy as the city, under a court order, prepares to revise its charter. New York's mayor has traditionally had a strong image vis-à-vis the council. Council representation is by district, roughly proportional to population. Recently rocking New York's politics has been evidence of widespread corruption in several branches of city government, at a wide range of administrative levels. Another is seemingly relentless development of Manhattan, frequently displacing low-income families (some into the streets), favoring expensive high-rise condominium and cooperative units. Another controversy is the city's attempt to reinstitutionalize homeless mental patients.

**Transportation:** New York motorists put up with unacceptably heavy rush-hour traffic, but commuter traffic is much worse in other areas, such as Los Angeles. If you get started early enough to beat the worst of rush-hour traffic, you'll have less trouble finding a place to park. But if you're one of the pack, you'll have to hunt hard for a place to park or opt for an overpriced parking garage (many do this anyway, for security). Only a small number of the city's apartment buildings have underground parking garages, and most motorists are forced to park on the street regardless of which borough they live in. Alternate-side-of-the-street parking rules have motorists up with the roosters on staggered days to move their cars across the street to make way for street sweepers. For peace of mind, don't assume you can commute by car. On the bright side, however, New York's public transportation facilities, in their vastness and convenience, are second to none in the country. Only in New York do more than half of all commuters choose to avail themselves of public transportation rather than their automobiles. The current $16 billion subway renovation has been called the costliest public works project in history. The highly developed subway and municipal bus systems carry five million riders per day. Several ferry systems, a tramway and three busy commuter railroads give Big Apple commuters an unparalleled choice of public transit options. Amtrak runs twenty-seven inter-city trains a day through Grand Central and Pennsylvania stations. New York's John F. Kennedy International and LaGuardia (domestic) airports are served by some eighty-seven airlines, providing over 800 flights daily, and the booming Newark airport is closer to downtown Manhattan than is Kennedy.

**Health Care:** New York's mix of health-care facilities is unmatched anywhere in the world. The city government spends approximately $4 billion on health care—far more than any other city in the world. The New York health sector accounts for more than 13 percent (over $16 billion) of the city's gross product and just over 9 percent of total employment in the city.

The city has long adhered to a compassionate but costly policy of providing medical care to all who need it, regardless of their ability to pay. The federal, state and city governments combined pay more than 55 percent of the costs of the city's voluntary hospitals and cover nearly 90 percent of costs in over a dozen municipal hospitals. In addition to supporting the hospital system, the city contributes 23 percent of all Medicaid services for low-income people—a very high share, unmatched by any city or county outside of New York State. New York City's Medicaid costs in 1986 totalled $1.2 billion. The quality of health care in New York is broadly considered the highest in the nation, but, unfortunately, is also the nation's most expensive.

The biggest threat to New York City's public health care system is the AIDS epidemic. By May of 1987, nearly 10,000 AIDS cases had been reported to the Department of Health. Over 5,700, or 58 percent, of these patients have died. By the year 1991, the department predicts that the number of AIDS cases in the city will total 110,000. AIDS is already the leading cause of death among New Yorkers under forty. The pressure that AIDS is putting on hospital facilities is serious and growing, in part because of the need for private rooms and special procedures.

**Child Care:** Gotham's child-care resources, like those available in nearly all cities, are inadequate. High prices and long waiting lists are the rule, and here, as elsewhere, many working mothers are forced to quit their jobs or take extended leaves of absence—often without pay—in order to "bring up baby." The city has a number of nonprofit and for-profit information and referral services: Child Care Inc. (212-929-7604), Child Care Information Resources (212-929-4999), and the Child Care Network (212-736-2510) are a few. Nursery school and pre-kindergarten facilities are growing throughout the area.

**Housing:** New York City suffers from an inadequate supply and a high cost of housing. Hardest hit are low- and moderate-income households, many of whom spend well over one-third of their income on shelter. In Manhattan, apartments cost $600 a room even in less desirable areas. Purchase prices for coops or condos usually exceed $75,000 a room. Prices in the four other boroughs run substantially lower, but they are still almost double those of cities outside the region. The city is constructing 10,000 to 20,000 units a year. The need is three to five times that. Manhattan has more than enough luxury housing; the need is for less costly housing, and the problem is that such housing is expensive to build. The Nehemiah housing project offers a model for construction of such housing, having produced 3,000 Brooklyn and Bronx homes.

Housing in New York City differs in structure from that in most other American cities. In other cities, most people live in one or two-family houses, which they own. In New York about 70 percent rent, with about 65 percent of New York families living in apartment buildings or hotels. About half of housing in New York City was built before 1940, and many of the older buildings are poorly maintained.

New York City built many public housing projects, back in the days when federal and state subsidy for such projects was more available. About 170,000 low-income families live in city-owned public housing. Steadily rising construction costs and the lack of open land make further development difficult, but Mayor Koch has been seeking to rehabilitate or build 250,000 more dwelling units for lower- and middle-income residents. The most likely areas of significant new construction are the Upper West Side along the Hudson River, the South Bronx, or Brooklyn .

In an effort to stem the rising number of homeless families in New York City, some welfare recipients will be offered extra benefits ranging from furniture allowances to baby-sitters. The project, called "Housing Alert," is intended to shore up unstable living situations and help families find new apartments before they are forced to seek emergency housing from the city. It is the first time the city has offered such a broad range of services to try to stop homelessness before it occurs. Under the experimental project, the city will focus on two neighborhoods, contacting about 3,000 welfare families who exhibit certain characteristics. Officials say the two-year project, which will cost the city at least $2 million, will ultimately save millions.

Up to now Mayor Koch has been trying to house the homeless in hotels and group shelters, especially in winter. The city spends some $80 million a year, mostly federal funds, for this purpose. More than 4,800 families were sheltered in 1987, and the city expects to house 5,400 families in 1988.

**Public Safety:** Sure, Fun City has a lot of crime—more in absolute numbers than any other city in the nation. But relative to population it's not the worst. Also, most crime in New York is concentrated in certain areas, and at certain times of the day, that are well known to residents. With 1,126 robberies reported in 1986 per each 100,000 city residents, New York is actually exceeded in "unsafeness" by six other cities in this book.

**Cultural Attractions:** Each of New York City's museums has a unique personality, style and purpose. The American Museum of Natural History is the largest science museum in the world. A forty-five-foot-long tyrannosaurus inspires both fear and fascination in the Hall of Dinosaurs, while J. P. Morgan's Indian emeralds dazzle spectators in the Hall of Minerals and Gems. The museum also houses the Hayden Planetarium, which offers celestial light shows and "Laser Rock" on Friday and Saturday nights.

The Metropolitan Museum of Art houses a superb collection of works from almost every period through the Impressionists. Particularly strong are its collection of Egyptian and non-Western sculpture and its collection of European painting. Blockbuster exhibits that tour the world never fail to stop at the Met.

The Museum of Modern Art houses the most extensive post-

Impressionist collection in the world. It was started in the 1930s to counter the Met's reluctance to embrace contemporary art.

When one thinks of the Guggenheim Museum, one immediately pictures a round building with a long, spiraling ramp. Midwesterner Frank Lloyd Wright was responsible for the museum's controversial architecture. Works of different artists are displayed along the ramp every few months, while permanent collections remain in flanking galleries.

Other major attractions are the Brooklyn Museum, which features folk art; the Cloisters, which concentrates on medieval art; the Frick collection, which is a private collection donated to the city by robber baron Henry Clay Frick; and the Whitney Museum of American Art.

The city's many independent galleries allow glimpses of contemporary works and provide more intimate atmospheres for appreciating the creative energies now brewing in the city's artistic communities.

Musical organizations in New York City cluster at Lincoln Center for the Performing Arts, the fulcrum of New York culture. The New York Philharmonic, one of the world's greatest symphony orchestras, and the Metropolitan Opera Association, a world-renowned opera company, both perform at Lincoln Center. The recently restored Carnegie Hall, considered one of the world's acoustically superior auditoriums, is the forum for a variety of musical performance forms, including opera, jazz, chorale singing, instrumental solos and symphony orchestras. The Metropolitan Museum of Art's Cloisters museum periodically hosts performances of medieval music.

For concerts, dancing and general nightlife, New York offers clubs and cafés too numerous to mention. Nightclubs go in and out of vogue; these days, our young friends say Nell's is number one. Like other nightclubs of its kind, it is noted for its capricious admittance policies. For loud and mobbed concerts, Madison Square Garden is the place. Located above Pennsylvania Station, the Garden is the place where Bowie, Madonna, Jagger, Sinatra and the rest of the biggest (and most commercial) pop music artists perform. Radio City Music Hall still draws crowds.

For dance, the late great George Balanchine's New York City Ballet and the Juilliard School of Music both make their homes at Lincoln Center. Other notable dance companies are American Ballet Theater (at the Met), the Joffrey Ballet (City Center), Alvyn Ailey's American Dance Theater (the Met), Martha Graham, Merce Cunningham and the Dana Theatre of Harlem. For theater, the costly musicals and proven dramas are performed "on Broadway," which means in the twenty or so theaters in midtown between 44th and 50th streets (only a few of which are actually on Broadway). Often worthwhile and much less expensive are the many nonmainstream performances given in off-Broadway theaters all over the city. The city sponsors a popular annual Summer New York Shakespeare Festival at the open-air Delacorte Theater in Central Park.

In addition, a fine variety of arts programs can be found at the New York City Center of Music and Drama on West 55th Street.

**Sports/Recreation:** New York City is great for sports fans. Baseball features the Yankees and the Mets; football, the Jets and the Giants (though the latter now play in New Jersey); hockey, the Islanders and the Rangers; and basketball, the Knicks. No other city has so many high-quality teams. With scores of parks—Central Park, Fort Tryon Park, Battery Park, and the Bronx, Brooklyn and Queens botanical gardens are some of the more famous—New York has 38.5 square miles of parkland—half again the size of Manhattan, with plenty of open space for relaxing, playing ball, swimming, boating and golf. In addition to the world-class Bronx Zoo and the Staten Island Zoo, Central Park has a children's zoo and a soon-to-be-reopened general zoo, and an acclaimed aquarium may be found at Coney Island in Brooklyn. Astroland, also at Coney Island, is the home of the famous Cyclone roller coaster—neither the tallest nor the longest, but a real thriller. New Yorkers also have access to the state parks on Long Island, and upstate; they offer excellent beaches, horseback riding, golf and camping. On vacations, New Yorkers who have the resources take off to their country homes in Vermont, Connecticut, upstate New York or "the Hamptons" at the East End of Long Island.

**Taxes:** This is not your tax haven. New York City and State both have income taxes. Commuters who work in New York City also have to pay an income tax. The city and state have a combined sales tax of 8.25 percent. Property taxes are very low for single-family homes; renters (still more than half of all residents) have the property taxes included in their rent. In addition, the city has imposed a variety of special taxes and fees that add up to a lot of nuisance for certain kinds of activities. On the bright side, in the same year (1987) that Texas imposed the largest state tax *increase* in U.S. history, New York State introduced the largest state tax *cut* in U.S. history. By 1990, the maximum personal income tax rate in the state will be half what it was in 1980.

## WHERE TO BREAK IN

Of the area's enormous number of large employers, we have selected N.Y. headquarters companies, since these are the most likely to lure those who don't already live in New York City into making the move. We show below the largest companies (based on total employment; all firms over 40,000) headquartered in New York; included, for contrast, is the number of people actually employed in the head office. The prize for the leanest headquarters company goes to TW Services, parent of the Canteen Corporation, with only forty employees. For Northern New Jersey companies, call the Newark Chamber of Commerce at 201-242-6237. For Southwest Connecticut companies, call the SW Area Chamber in Stamford at 203-359-3220.

| Firm/Organization | Product/ Service | No. Employees | | Phone |
|---|---|---|---|---|
| | | Total | Head- quarters | |
| IBM (Armonk, N.Y.) | computers | 405,000 | 1,200 | 914-765-1900 |
| AT&T | communications | 365,000 | 3,000 | 212-605-6278 |
| ITT Corp. | communications | 232,000 | 789 | 212-752-6000 |
| Exxon Corp. | petroleum prods. | 140,000 | 700 | 212-333-1000 |
| PepsiCo (Purchase, N.Y.) | soft drinks, snacks | 133,000 | 1,500 | 914-253-2000 |
| F. W. Woolworth Co. | retailing | 118,000 | 1,400 | 212-553-2000 |
| Philip Morris Cos. | tobacco, beer, etc. | 114,000 | 1,400 | 212-880-5000 |
| NYNEX Corp. (White Plains, N.Y.) | communications | 90,000 | 130 | 212-370-7400 |
| W. R. Grace & Co. | chemicals | 89,000 | 900 | 212-819-5500 |
| TW Services | food and vending services | 85,000 | 40 | 212-972-4700 |
| Citicorp | banking | 81,300 | 2,000 | 212-559-1000 |

| Firm/Organization | Product/ Service | No. Employees | | Phone |
|---|---|---|---|---|
| | | **Total** | **Head- quarters** | |
| American Brands, Inc. | foods | 76,500 | 250 | 212-883-1025 |
| American Express Co. | financial services | 74,500 | 8,000 | 212-640-2000 |
| Melville Corp. (Harrison, N.Y.) | retailing | 73,000 | 100 | 914-253-8000 |
| Schlumberger Ltd. | oil drilling equip. | 73,000 | 120 | 212-350-9400 |
| Sperry Corp. | electronics/defense | 70,000 | 400 | 212-484-4444 |
| Allied Stores | retailing | 65,000 | 800 | 212-764-2000 |
| Associated Dry Goods Corp. | retailing | 59,000 | 250 | 212-679-8700 |
| Dun & Bradstreet | publishing, credit | 58,300 | NA | 212-593-6800 |
| Rapid-American | conglomerate | 56,500 | 150 | 212-621-4500 |
| Texaco | petroleum prods. | 54,400 | 1,500 | 914-253-4000 |
| R. H. Macy & Co. | retailing | 54,000 | 6,000 | 212-560-3600 |
| North American Philips Corp. | consumer electronics | 51,800 | 250 | 212-697-3600 |
| American Standard | plumbing equip. | 50,400 | 200 | 212-703-5100 |
| American Home Products Corp. | household prods., drugs, food | 47,200 | 1,500 | 212-878-5000 |
| Chase Manhattan Corp. | banking | 46,500 | 4,700 | 212-552-2222 |
| Merrill Lynch & Co. | securities | 44,000 | 7,500 | 212-637-7455 |
| Pfizer, Inc. | pharmaceuticals | 40,700 | 2,000 | 212-573-2323 |
| Colgate-Palmolive | personal care, household prods. | 40,600 | 1,200 | 212-310-2000 |
| Union Pacific Corp. | transportation | 40,300 | 156 | 212-418-7800 |
| United Brands Co. | fruit importers | 40,000 | 200 | 212-307-2000 |

## SUMMING UP: OPPORTUNITY FOR WHOM?

"Give me your tired, your poor, your huddled masses yearning to breathe free . . ." New York has traditionally been the gateway to opportunity for millions of immigrants seeking a new life. By the year 2000, the Big Apple will still have the world's most hetero-geneous population and the most ethnically diverse neighbor-hoods (one-quarter of New York's population is foreign born). The Dutch who originally settled the area in 1625 were followed by millions of other European immigrants during the 1800s and early

1900s; New York was sometimes just a first stop, and after a few months or years the immigrants continued their journey westward. New immigrants are still pouring in—since World War II including large numbers of Haitians, Dominicans, West Indians, Koreans and Chinese. A large migration of people is expected from Hong Kong between now and 1997, when the British Crown Colony is scheduled to be returned to the People's Republic of China. People from politically turbulent areas of the world may also decide to settle in New York.

By the year 2000, nonwhites and Hispanics will constitute 60 percent of the city's population, an increase from 48 percent in 1980. The number of blacks, Hispanics and Asians will increase along with the number of old people, especially those over eighty-five.

Economics and demographics will combine to create many future job openings, but the positions will call for a high degree of education. One of the city's major problems will lie in the inadequate skills possessed by the majority of the city's population. Unemployment rates for black and Hispanic males are twice those of white and Asian males. Also on the rise are single-parent families, which make up 12 percent of the city's households today. By the year 2000 these domestic situations will grow to about 15 percent. Almost 90 percent of single-parent homes are headed by women whose earnings total only one-quarter of those made by average two-parent families.

Five major ethnic groups—black, Irish, Italian, Jewish and Puerto Rican—constitute 75 percent of New York City's people. Blacks are the largest ethnic group in the city, making up 25 percent of the city's population. New York has about 1,784,000 blacks, more than any other city in the United States. A large number of New York City's blacks live in poor neighborhoods, but more and more are joining the ranks of the middle class.

Jews make up about 20 percent of New York City's population. Many of them live in Jewish neighborhoods and own their own businesses. As a group they are well represented in the garment industry, the financial community, and the legal, medical and teaching professions.

Italians, who constitute 14 percent of the city's people, are concentrated in the areas of construction, restaurant operation and food wholesale/retail. They are also heavily represented in civil service jobs in the city's parks, public works, sanitation, police and fire departments. Most Italian-Americans are Roman Catholic.

About 12 percent of New York City's people are Puerto Rican, many of whom immigrated to the Big Apple in the 1950s. At first nearly all Puerto Ricans lived in East Harlem in Manhattan, but today Puerto Rican neighborhoods are scattered throughout the five boroughs. Many Puerto Rican immigrants found jobs as unskilled workers in hospitals, hotels and restaurants. The city has provided many programs to help Puerto Ricans learn English and become better assimilated into mainstream society.

The percentage of Irish New Yorkers has declined from 30 percent in 1870 to 9 percent today. They have lost much of the political power they once wielded, in part because they are largely assimilated into the business world; still, they remain the largest single group in the city's police and fire departments, and account for many leaders in the city's Roman Catholic Church.

Growing ethnic groups include Koreans, who are concentrated in Flushing, Queens. They have made remarkable inroads into the retail fruit-and-vegetable business throughout the city by keeping their small stores open twenty-four hours a day and maintaining superior quality standards; they are now entering other areas of business.

Overall, New York City continues to provide opportunities for people without family wealth to work their way to financial success. It is still, for all its social and living problems, a city of opportunity without equal.

# Orlando, Florida

MSA POPULATION (7/86): 898,400 (46th largest)
POPULATION GROWTH 1980–86: 28.4%
COUNTY: Orange
EMPLOYMENT (9/87): 477,500
AVERAGE TEMPERATURE: 71.8°F
YEARLY RAINFALL: 51 inches
HUMIDITY: 71% (2nd most humid)
COST OF LIVING: 107.4

## KEYS TO THE CITY

**Small Business Growth:** birth rate, growth rate, growth index (rank/86):  4.9  4  8.9  (5th)

**Average Annual Job Growth (9/84–9/87):** 6.9% (2nd/largest 100)

**Keys to Prosperity:** Tourism (Disney World), finance, publishing trade and agriculture.

**Key Developments:** Airport traffic growth, new cultural attractions.

**Key Life-Style Trends:** From a small population base rooted in agriculture, Orlando has seen tourism multiply local jobs; high-tech manufacturing is now a third-phase development, bringing a new class of worker and resident. The boom town seems to have space and sunshine enough to go around.

## WHY OPPORTUNITY KNOCKS IN ORLANDO

As the second home of Disney World's Mickey Mouse and Donald Duck since 1971, Orlando has grown tremendously as a result of tourism alone, which is worth around $2 billion annually to the local economy. But this Sunbelt boom town, which boasts of itself that it is the best new job market and the fastest growing city in America, is making a name for itself in clean, high-tech manu-facturing. R&D corporations include AT&T, Westinghouse, Martin Marietta Aerospace, Harcourt Brace Jovanovich, Paulucci Enter-

272

prises, General Mills Restaurant Group and Sears, Roebuck & Company.

Orlando's employment growth of 38.5 percent between 1970 and 1982 reflects the new manufacturing, financial, real estate and services growth trends. Orlando's traditionally important agricultural and related industries have continued to thrive alongside the advent of tourists and manufacturing.

The area's high population growth of 54.4 percent between 1970 and 1980 continues to be reflected in the $14 billion worth of new commercial and residential construction projects slated for completion by 1990. With such phenomenal population growth, and with the number of tourists (and tourist attractions) increasing yearly, the need for more and better services in all sectors should increase accordingly, creating opportunities for entrepreneurs and professionals anxious to settle down in an area with low taxes and yearly average temperatures of around 72 degrees.

## QUALITY OF LIFE

**Weather:** Orlando has a hot, humid, rainy climate; freezing temperatures are a rarity, but the mercury hits the 90s on at least 100 days annually.

**Education:** With K–12 enrollment of 123,920 pupils, the Orlando public school system consists of three districts and 163 school facilities. There are 60 private and parochial schools in the area, enrolling a total of 16,018 students. Orlando is served by two public junior colleges and four universities and four-year colleges (three private, one public).

**Politics/Government:** Orlando has a mayor-council form of government. It is also the Orange County seat. The mayor is elected at large for a four-year term, serves as a member of the city council and lacks veto power. The council consists of seven members, one (the mayor) elected at large and six by ward. All serve overlapping four-year terms and meet weekly.

**Transportation:** As in the rest of Florida, a car is a must in Orlando, and commuter traffic is heavy; intracity transportation is assisted by bus municipal service. Travel to points outside Orlando is provided by Amtrak, which offers six departures daily, and the Orlando International Airport, a medium-size air transportation hub. Orlando is served by twenty-two major airlines offering 185 flights daily.

**Health Care:** Health care in Orlando is affordable, and facilities include a cardiac rehabilitation center and a hospice.

**Child Care:** For information, call Common Coordinated Child Care for Central Florida at 305-425-0509.

**Housing:** A single-family house (three bedrooms, two bathrooms) costs $80,000 to $85,000. A two-bedroom, one-bathroom house costs $250 to $300 a month to rent.

**Public Safety:** With 842 reported 1986 robberies per 100,000 city residents, Orlando has a fairly high crime rate, probably due to the steady influx of vacationers, who are ever vulnerable to crime.

**Cultural Attractions:** For those who tire of Mickey and Donald, the rockets at NASA and the killer whales at Sea World, Orlando offers a number of music and dance attractions, including the Florida Symphony Orchestra, the Orlando Opera Company and the Southern Ballet Theater. Other performing companies include the Florida Symphony Youth Orchestra, the University of Central Florida Symphony and Orlando's Ballet Royal.

**Sports/Recreation:** Professional sports fans must content themselves with the Orlando Twins, a AA minor-league baseball team, and spring training for several major-league teams. Participants, however, can work off nervous energy with tennis, golf, swimming and boating.

**Taxes:** With no state or city income tax and low property taxes, the Orlando area's tax burden amounts to around 1 percent of average annual household income. The state sales tax is 5 percent.

---

## WHERE TO BREAK IN

For individuals interested in relocating to the Orlando area, we include a partial listing of major employers in addition to Disney World. For more information, call the Orlando Chamber of Commerce at 305-424-1234.

| Firm/Organization | Product/Service | No. Employees |
|---|---|---|
| Sun Banks, Inc. | financial services | 800 |
| Sea World of Florida, Inc. | amusement park | 500 |

| Firm/Organization | Product/Service | No. Employees |
|---|---|---|
| Harcourt Brace Jovanovich, Inc. | book publishing | 300 |
| South Fruit Distribution | canning/preserving | 240 |
| Attorney's Title Insurance Fund | title insurance | 200 |
| Orlando Holding Inc. | beer/ale | 179 |
| Sun Flooring, Inc. | home furnishings | 170 |
| Allen Company | pharmaceutical retail | 130 |
| Acoustical Engineering | construction contractor | 125 |

## SUMMING UP: OPPORTUNITY FOR WHOM?

With a work force of about 330,000 and an unemployment rate of less than 5 percent, Orlando's service-based and increasingly high-tech economy is likely to continue generating employment opportunities for health-care professionals, engineers, educators, and people with banking, finance, office and clerical backgrounds. We provide a distribution of Orlando's economy among eight basic industrial categories.

| Industry | Share of Work Force (in %) |
|---|---|
| Services | 33 |
| Wholesale and retail trade | 25 |
| Manufacturing | 10 |
| Finance, insurance and real estate | 9 |
| Construction | 8 |
| Transportation, communication and utilities | 7 |
| Farming | 4 |
| Government | 4 |

# Philadelphia, Pennsylvania

PHILADELPHIA–WILMINGTON–TRENTON, PENN.–N.J.–DEL.–MD. CMSA
POPULATION (7/86): 5,832,600 (5th largest), of which Philadelphia,
PENN.–N.J. PMSA population is 4,825,700 (4th largest)
POPULATION GROWTH 1980–86: 2.3%
COUNTY: Consolidated with Philadelphia County
EMPLOYMENT (9/87): 2,162,100
AVERAGE TEMPERATURE: 54.6°F
YEARLY RAINFALL: 39.93 inches
HUMIDITY: 63% (16th most humid)
COST OF LIVING: 120.5

---

## KEYS TO THE CITY

**Small Business Growth:** birth rate, growth rate, growth index
(rank/86):   2.5   3.8   6.3   (41st)
**Average Annual Job Growth (9/84–9/87):** 2.7% (45th/largest 100)
**Keys to Prosperity:** High-tech start-ups (Route 202), manufacturing (pharmaceuticals, food processing, printing, etc.).
**Key Developments:** Real estate market has picked up dramatically in recent years.
**Key Life-Style Trends:** Philadelphia is home to some people who commute to New York City. Good housing is one reason. Heavily suburban, but downtown is being rediscovered (gentrified).

---

## WHY OPPORTUNITY KNOCKS IN PHILADELPHIA

After years of manufacturing decline and urban population loss, Philadelphia is experiencing strong economic and employment growth, at about parity with the national rates, due mainly to the strength of the city's nonmanufacturing sector.

In the 1940s, about 40 percent of Philadelphia's workers were employed in the manufacturing sector. Today that figure is 20 percent, but the transformation was by no means smooth and painless. Because of the shift of manufacturing and assembly work to Asia and South America in the 1960s and 1970s, and two recessions (in the late 1970s and early 1980s), Philadelphia experienced high unemployment and population loss, giving it a "dying city mentality," exemplified by the city's fatalistic recognition that Houston had exceeded it in population in 1975.

But the city appears to have readjusted to a changing national economy, as evidenced by favorable statistics in a number of areas. Although manufacturing employment dipped by 2.0 percent between 1986 and 1987, total employment in the area grew by 1.4 percent, buoyed by nonmanufacturing employment growth of 4.2 percent. Over the same period, the number of unemployed fell by nearly one-fifth.

In the area of high-tech growth, the Philadelphia area has had less difficulty than other cities in attracting firms engaged in advanced manufacturing and R&D, evidenced by its thriving high tech corridor, Route 202. The region has many characteristics, such as nationally recognized universities and highly educated workers, that are attractive to high-technology firms. Montgomery County has the highest concentration of high-tech employment in the Philadelphia area and is likely to remain the locus for most of the area's high-tech growth.

But Philadelphia's upswing has not been entirely due to high tech. The area continues to enjoy growth in a number of manufacturing industries, including pharmaceuticals, medical products, food processing, printing and publishing, fabricated metals, chemicals, apparel, plastics and electronics.

Philadelphia also doesn't have the downtown commercial/office vacancy problems of many other urban centers. With 3.6 million square feet of commercial space currently leased, and another 2.4 million square feet under construction, the citywide commercial occupancy rate is 92 percent. Other favorable indicators are $3.2 billion of retail sales in the PMSA in 1986 (up 9 percent from 1985) and improvements in commuter and other transit facilities, including the connection and unification of two commuter railroad systems and the completion of a high-speed rail line from downtown to the airport, allowing connection from commuter railroads and Amtrak.

## QUALITY OF LIFE

**Weather:** Philadelphia's climate benefits from the moderating influence of its location between the Appalachian Mountains and the Atlantic Ocean. Philadelphia's climate is fairly mild, with few or no 0°F days, about three months of freezing days (32° or less) and roughly twenty uncomfortably hot days (90° or higher) each year. The city's humidity runs high, however, which can increase the discomfort of warm summer days.

**Education:** The eleven-county Philadelphia region has eighty-nine colleges and universities, including the University of Pennsylvania, Drexel, Temple, Swarthmore, Haverford, Bryn Mawr, Villanova, St. Joseph's, LaSalle, Princeton and Rutgers. The area's higher educational facilities offer a full range of professional training, as well as specialized curricula in the visual and performing arts. Philadelphia also has a long tradition of excellence in elementary and secondary education. The city's public school system is divided into 170 districts and enrolls nearly 700,000 pupils. The region has some 650 private schools, with a total enrollment of over 130,000 pupils. Philadelphia has the second largest Catholic school system in the nation, as well as a number of nationally recognized Quaker schools. Private schools in the region include Chestnut Hill Academy, Episcopal Academy, Germantown Academy, Haverford School, the Baldwin School, the Shipley School and the Agnes Irvin School.

**Neighborhoods:** Of the older American metro areas, Philadelphia has been especially active in maintaining and restoring its historic neighborhoods. The city's eighteenth-century Society Hill district was one of the first urban residential areas in the country to be restored. Since the rejuvenation of Society Hill, several other of Philadelphia's older neighborhoods have been similarly renovated, including the Art Museum area and the Northern Liberties section, as well as the converted Old City districts surrounding Christ Church and Betsy Ross House. The city is filled with residential neighborhoods of distinction and charm, ranging from South Philadelphia and Germantown to Center City and Chestnut Hill. Philadelphia's suburbs also offer many historic communities. Philadelphians are famous for their tendency to feel and express a strong attachment to and identification with their individual communities. Among the most famous are those that fall along the wooded Main Line.

**Politics/Government:** The city is committed to constantly improving the quality of life. There is a strong commitment to both social services and economic growth. W. Wilson Goode has recently begun his second and final term as mayor with a commitment to see through to completion the projects he has started—including the city's economic revitalization. Both elective components of city government—mayor and council—are strong; local issues generate interest and excitement and attract a high level of citizen participation.

**Transportation:** Commuters in and to Philadelphia experience a relatively short trip to work. Although traffic has been recently heavy, due to improvements—construction of additional access ramps to highways and a new crosstown expressway—the completion of these projects should speed commuter traffic. Philadelphia gets good marks in mass transportation. With intracity rapid rail service, commuter railroad service to area suburbs, trolley service and a good supply of municipal buses, Philadelphia residents and commuters have many transit options. For intercity travel, the city is served by two airports, North Philadelphia and Philadelphia International, with some thirty airlines providing roughly 600 daily departures, with direct service to over 100 cities. In addition, a new $75 million terminal is currently under construction, which should facilitate greater service volume. Amtrak offers forty-two daily departures, with service to New York, Boston, Montreal, Baltimore, Washington, D.C., Florida and the West.

**Child Care:** Philadelphians have been active and innovative in the development of day-care options for working parents. Among local organizations are the Delaware Valley Child Care Council (a regional coalition of parents, care providers, government and employers) and Child Care Choices (a nonprofit referral service). Additionally, there are projects designed to assist in the creation of family day-care homes, and many local businesses either run day-care facilities or subsidize day-care costs to their employees.

**Health Care:** To complement its strong medical, educational and industrial resources (six medical schools, two dental schools, two pharmacy schools, ten universities offering advanced degrees in biological sciences, twenty-nine pharmaceutical firms, sixty biomedical research firms, and seventy-seven manufacturers of medical, surgical and dental instruments and supplies), Philadelphia has top-notch health-care services and facilities. The Philadelphia area has 137 hospitals, with a total capacity of 24,421 staffed and set-up beds. Among the area's better known health-care facilities are the Scheie Eye Institute, Will Eye Hospital and Children's Hospital; in addition, the area has a number of university-related (for example, the hospital of the University of Pennsylvania) and teaching hospitals.

Health care is not only a specialty of the city, it's also a growing sector of the local economy. Examples are an $80 million children's center extension being added to St. Christopher's Hospital, a $300 million facility being installed in a recently closed hospital and the Veteran Administration's decision to build a facility in the city.

**Housing:** The Philadelphia metro area has one of the nation's most affordable housing markets—less expensive than New York, Chicago, Boston, St. Louis, Denver–Boulder and Los Angeles–Long Beach. Comparably sized and located suburban homes cost 28 percent less in Philadelphia than in New York. Rental units are also significantly less expensive, with the average two-bedroom, one-bathroom apartment renting for approximately $400.

**Public Safety:** With only 641 reported robberies per 100,000 city residents, Philadelphia is a relatively secure megacity.

**Cultural Attractions:** Philadelphia is the home of the nation's most historic square mile, including Independence Hall, the Liberty Bell and Betsy Ross's House. The city has always maintained a strong commitment to its historical and cultural traditions. Among the city's well-known cultural attractions are the Philadelphia Orchestra, the Pennsylvania Ballet, the Opera Company of Philadelphia, the University Museum (Egyptology, archaeology), the Barnes Foundation Museum (French Impressionist painting) and the Pennsylvania Academy of Fine Arts (American art). The city's Benjamin Franklin Parkway (called "America's Champs-Elysées") is the location of the Rodin Museum, the world-renowned Philadelphia Museum of Art and the Franklin Institute Science Museum. Nearby are many eighteenth-century mansions. The city also has scores of galleries and several artists' colonies in nearby suburbs. Philadelphia is also famous for its culinary attractions, with first-class restaurants for virtually every international cuisine. Among the city's celebrations and festivals are the New Year's Day Mummers Parade, the July Fourth Freedom Festival, the Thanksgiving Day Parade, the Philadelphia Folk Festival, the Philadelphia Flower Show, and the American Music and Theater Festival.

**Sports/Recreation:** Philadelphia also offers a full menu of professional sports: the NFL's Eagles, ice hockey's Flyers, basketball's 76ers, and National League baseball's Phillies. In addition, there is Big Five college basketball and both flat and harness racing. The city also hosts the U.S. Indoor Tennis Championship, the Army-Navy Game, the Core States Bicycle Championship, PGA golf events and the nation's most prestigious Half Marathon.

Recreational possibilities abound, with scores of public parks, including Fairmont Park, the largest landscaped garden in the world. The city, in fact, has more public gardens than any other city in the world, and is particularly proud of Longwood Gardens for its scenic beauty. There are also a number of private facilities for golf, tennis, swimming, boating, etc. The seashore, which includes Atlantic City, is only an hour's drive away, and mountains with skiing facilities are within ninety minutes.

**Taxes:** Pennsylvania has no progressive tax on income.

---

## WHERE TO BREAK IN

For individuals interested in relocating to Philadelphia, we include a listing of the area's top fifteen employers:

| Firm/Organization | Product/Service | No. Employees | Phone |
|---|---|---|---|
| City of Philadelphia | government | 30,000 | (215) 686-1776 |
| Philadelphia School District | education | 25,000 | (215) 299-7000 |
| U.S. Dept. of the Navy | military | 17,500 | (202) 545-6700 |
| University of Pennsylvania | education/research | 13,000 | (215) 888-5000 |
| U.S. Postal Service | government | 9,000 | (202) 245-4000 |
| Southeast Penn. Transportation Authority | transportation | 8,500 | (215) 456-4000 |
| Bell Atlantic | communications | 7,700 | (215) 963-6000 |
| Philadelphia Electric Co. | electric utility | 7,500 | (215) 841-4000 |

| Firm/Organization | Product/Service | No. Employees | Phone |
|---|---|---|---|
| U.S. Dept. of Defense | military | 7,400 | (202) 545-6700 |
| Temple University | education | 7,250 | (215) 787-7000 |
| Commonwealth of Pennsylvania | government | 6,000 | (215) 787-2121 |
| Conrail | transportation | 6,000 | (215) 977-4000 |
| Thomas Jefferson University Hospital | health care | 5,500 | (215) 928-6000 |
| Philadelphia Newspapers | printing/publishing | 4,400 | (215) 854-2000 |
| Amtrak | transportation | 4,000 | (202) 383-3000 |

## SUMMING UP: OPPORTUNITY FOR WHOM?

People attracted to an established, East Coast, thriving cultural and business center with historic significance will enjoy Philadelphia. Philadelphia's current high-tech manufacturing and non-manufacturing (especially skilled and professional services) boom should continue to generate employment opportunities for trained office personnel, health professionals, finance specialists, educators, research technicians, biomedical engineers, electrical engineers, data-processing specialists, electricians, electronics technicians and technical writers.

# Phoenix, Arizona

MSA POPULATION (7/86): 1,900,200 (21st largest)

POPULATION GROWTH 1980–86: 25.9%

COUNTY: Maricopa

EMPLOYMENT (9/87): 902,400

AVERAGE TEMPERATURE: 70.3°F

YEARLY RAINFALL: 7.05 inches

HUMIDITY: 40% (37th most humid)

COST OF LIVING: 106.8

## KEYS TO THE CITY

**Small Business Growth:** birth rate, growth rate, growth index (rank/86): 5   4.2   9.2   (2nd)

**Average Annual Job Growth (9/84–9/87):** 4.9% (7th/largest 100)

**Keys to Prosperity:** High-technology companies, financial services, tourism, branch offices, retirees, business climate.

**Key Developments:** Construction of area-wide freeway system, community partnership efforts for planning, education.

**Key Life-Style Trends:** Phoenix has gone way beyond being a sunny home for retirees. Younger people, who initially came for jobs, are now beginning to stir up some citizen activism in support of better air, better schools and other quality-of-life issues of importance to Phoenicians.

## WHY OPPORTUNITY KNOCKS IN PHOENIX

Metro Phoenix—or, as the locals refer to it, "the Valley of the Sun"—includes the city of Phoenix plus the outlying areas of Scottsdale, Tempe, Mesa, Glendale, Chandler, Sun City and a host of smaller communities. The Phoenix Metropolitan Statistical Area (MSA) ranks twenty-first in population, and its impressive 24.2 percent growth rate between 1980 and 1987 puts it at the top of the growth rate list for MSAs of over 1 million people. Major industries of the region are agriculture, manufacturing of high-technology products, financial services, tourism and travel. Phoenix is a hub of commerce as well, offering fast, easy and direct access to key markets in the Sunbelt, all areas of the United States and the world. The wholesale and retail trade sector is the largest nonfarm employer in the metro area, and the service sector is a close second.

From 1984 to 1986, the Phoenix economy was responsible for 70 percent of the new jobs generated statewide, during a period that saw Arizona ranked first nationwide, among states, in the rate of job creation. Moreover, seven out of every ten new businesses formed in the state were started in the Phoenix metro area, and sixty-six cents of every dollar increase in state personal income occurred in the Phoenix Metro area.

With Phoenix as the center of government for the state of Arizona, over 10 percent of those employed in the area work in the government sector. Government, however, has historically worked to facilitate, not stand in the way of, private opportunity.

Development has been the name of the game in Phoenix for the last fifteen years and literally paved the way for fantastic growth rates throughout the booming 1970s and 1980s. Between 1975 and 1985, the population grew by 51 percent, from 1.2 million to 1.8 million; retail sales grew by 187 percent; and bank deposits grew by 253 percent. Personal income increased by an incredible 230 percent. No other state can boast such high growth rates. It's no surprise that Arizona received the number-one rating in *Inc.* magazine's 1986–87 survey of states' performance in stimulating entrepreneurial growth. Population in the Valley (Metro Phoenix) is expected to continue growing and reach 2.1 million by 1990, with job opportunities and markets expanding accordingly.

A number of factors may be seen as responsible for the phenomenal growth rates realized in Phoenix. Projects at all levels of government, as well as from the private sector, appear to have ensured the availability of energy and water to the Valley area. The city's recent commitment to improving transportation facilities has diminished the perception of Phoenix as isolated. Moreover, the availability of land, relatively low building costs and the absence of a strong trade union presence have made the Valley attractive to regional and national businesses as well as to local entrepreneurs. The strength of the high-tech industry has also benefited Phoenix. High-tech employment is up sharply statewide; the Valley's thriving economy is fed by its high-tech base and nourished by the resort business and the growing service economy.

Many of the Valley's industries, however, are smaller parts of larger operations. This gives rise to what is called the branch-town syndrome—the potential for serious staff cutbacks in response to national economic conditions. Branch offices make the Valley's economy more fragile than one where more of the control centers are head offices. An abundance of branch offices also means fewer ultimate decision makers and may have impeded business– community cohesion. However, despite the greater prevalence of branch offices, the Phoenix metro area is head office to over forty-five corporations, including America West Airlines, Circle K Corporation, U-Haul International and Ramada Inns, Inc. Thus, Phoenix has seen, and is likely to continue to see, high rates of population and growth up to and beyond the twenty-first century.

---

## QUALITY OF LIFE

**Weather:** The weather is generally mild and sunny year-round, with low annual rainfall and low humidity. Winter days are fairly warm, with temperatures in the 60s and 70s, while the temperature only rarely drops below freezing during winter nights. Light snow falls once every six or seven years, but immediately melts on the ground. Summers are very hot, but bearable, according to residents, because of the area's low humidity. Despite the desert surroundings, the landscape is far from desolate. One or more mountain ranges can be seen from almost any point in Phoenix. The famed Superstition Mountains lie to the east.

**Education:** Higher educational programs are innovative and comprehensive, geared to meet the needs of a diverse economy. Nearby Arizona State University, a strong community college system and many specialized schools contribute to an education level that exceeds the national average. Arizona State University is noted for its excellence in engineering and computer technology. This special competence complements local high-tech industries.

Primary- and secondary-level education in Arizona has come in for criticism. Now, the community has begun to exert pressure for changes. Numerous partnerships and cooperative efforts, such as the mayor's Task Force on Excellence in Education, the Committee on Excellence in Education, the Youth Commission and the Hispanic-Jewish Coalition, have emerged to deal with pressing issues such as school curriculum and standards, chemical dependency, dropout prevention and teenage sexuality. The city of Phoenix regularly meets with school officials to plan for new school facilities necessary to keep pace with growth and has recently included education as a top priority in its new corporate plan. Additionally, plans are being developed in Phoenix for the implementation of the "Cities in Schools" program, a national partnership effort of cities, community leaders and businesses. Thus, private and public leaders alike are taking a proactive stance in dealing with the special educational problems caused by rapid growth and a diversified educational system.

**Neighborhoods:** Neighborhoods in Phoenix consist of housing stock that includes "as-is, fix-up" properties, affordable housing for first-time home buyers, previously owned up-scaled housing for middle-class families and expensive, luxurious dwellings. The availability of suburban neighborhoods is increasing because of the area's expanding new housing construction industry. These neighborhoods are distinctive because of their desert valley setting; the consistently dry climate lends itself to outdoor activities and neighborhood functions.

Phoenix has a small minority population, but does not have the traditional ethnic neighborhoods found in many major cities. Despite some concentrations of blacks and Hispanics in a few sections of the metro area, Phoenix is an open city and dwellings are available without regard to race, religion or national origin.

Both the public and private sectors have a growing pride in the preservation of Phoenix neighborhoods. Many are part of a valleywide movement organized under the Greater Phoenix Neighborhood Coalition. Additionally, Phoenix voters, in October 1987, approved the enactment of a property maintenance ordinance that established minimum standards of maintenance for all building exteriors, premises and vacant land.

**Politics/Government:** Phoenix has a council-manager form of government, with a mayor and an eight-member district council; the mayor is elected by the city at large, while council members are selected by district. Political dynamics in Phoenix center on the preservation of the few real established neighborhoods the city has. When it became obvious that Phoenix was developing into a sprawling, *ad hoc* web of residential and commercial districts, an "urban village" plan was implemented to impose neighborhood character upon localities within the city. But Phoenix has the lowest number of freeway miles per capita of any major American metro area, and much-needed infrastructure improvements are likely to impinge on the hard-won efforts at "community" of years past.

**Transportation:** Transportation costs can be considerable. Because Phoenix is generally comprised of single-family homes on large lots, a car is a must. However, voters recently authorized the creation of a Regional Transportation Planning Authority that is developing long-range transit plans for the region. For air travel, Phoenix is served by Phoenix Sky Harbor International Airport (twenty-two airlines, 420 flights daily), located near downtown Phoenix. It is also served by a few Amtrak trains and two major interstate freeways. Moreover, in conjunction with valley cities, the Arizona Department of Transportation is constructing over 200 miles of new freeways throughout the metropolitan area.

**Health Care:** The city has excellent health care. Phoenix has 184 physicians per 100,000 residents, three teaching hospitals—the Good Samaritan Hospital, Maricopa County General Hospital, and St. Joseph's Hospital and Medical Center—six cardiac rehabilitation centers and four hospices. Because Phoenix is a competitive health-care environment and is in the forefront of state-of-the-art medical technology, top health-care professionals are easily attracted to the area.

**Child Care:** Phoenix's Association for Supportive Child Care (602-829-0500) certifies home-care providers and assists working parents in locating licensed day-care centers. The service also provides training for staffers of child-care centers and family day homes.

**Housing:** Since 1980, Phoenix has doubled the number of new housing permits issued. In 1986, the single-family sector accounted for 47 percent of all residential permits in the metropolitan area, exceeding multifamily activity. Vacancy rates in 1986 ranged from 1 percent for single-family homes to 11 percent for the multifamily sector. Housing prices in the valley compare favorably to other Sunbelt cities and generally remain lower than in areas such as Las Vegas, Austin, Los Angeles and San Diego. The median price of a new home in the Phoenix area is approximately $90,000.

**Public Safety:** Phoenix has fairly high rates of property crime, ranking fifth in 1986 among the twenty largest cities, but rather low rates of violent crime, ranking seventeenth among the same twenty cities. Moreover, comparing the first half of 1987 with the same period in 1986 shows that Phoenix has experienced the largest decrease in violent crimes (−12.5 percent) and total crimes (−7.5 percent) among the country's ten largest cities. The reduction in property crime (−6.9 percent) is not far behind, ranking second among the same cities. Projections indicate these reductions will continue. The Phoenix Police Department has been recognized nationally for its effectiveness and innovation. Generally, theft can be a problem but personal safety is greater than in other large cities. The 1986 robbery rate was a low 321 per 100,000 population.

**Cultural Attractions:** Cultural attractions include the Heard Museum (an outstanding museum of Native American artifacts), the Phoenix Art Museum, the Phoenix Symphony, the Phoenix Little Theatre, the Phoenix Children's Theatre and the Metropolitan Ballet. The Arizona State University is located in Tempe and offers the usual college fare—sports, theater and other performing arts events—to area residents.

**Sports/Recreation:** The city's mountain parks, including South Mountain Park, the world's largest municipal park, offer outdoor enthusiasts ample opportunities for hiking, picnicking and enjoying breathtaking views of the Valley of the Sun. Much of this land has been designated mountain preserve, protecting it from substantial development. Additionally, the nearby Tonto National Forest provides preserved nature for its lovers. The Salt River lakes offer water sports enthusiasts plenty of room for action. Other recreational diversions might include a trip to the Phoenix Zoo, to the Phoenix Suns (NBA basketball) or to AAA Phoenix Firebirds baseball games—or to the horse, dog or auto racing tracks. Phoenix has just bagged the (St. Louis) Cardinals, a coup for this city eager to be "major league." Seven major-league baseball teams are welcomed for spring training in the Valley. The Valley of the Sun offers year-round play on nearly 100 major golf courses and 1,000 tennis courts.

**Taxes:** There is a state sales tax of 5 percent, an additional city tax of 1.2 percent and a county transportation tax of 0.5 percent. Food and prescription drugs are exempt. Personal state income tax ranges from 2 percent on the first $1,000 earned to 8 percent on income over $6,000. Property taxes vary with school districts, and the average combined property tax rate is slightly under $10 per $100 assessed valuation. The portion of property value taxed is as follows:

| | |
|---|---|
| Homes | 10% |
| Utilities | 30% |
| Commercial/industrial | 25% |
| Mines/airline flight property | 30% |
| Railroads | 27% |
| Agricultural/vacant land | 16% |
| Rental/residential | 16% |

The annual property tax bill on a $90,000 house averages about $834.

The cost of living in the Valley is higher than the national average but is in line with other major urban centers and is less expensive than the nearby cities of L.A. and San Diego as well as other Sunbelt cities such as Dallas and San Jose, California. Grocery prices are relatively low and bring the all-items index below 106.8 (national average 100).

## WHERE TO BREAK IN

The greatest number of people in Phoenix are employed in the service, retail trade, construction and manufacturing sectors. Major employers, defined for our purposes as firms employing over 1,000 persons, in the Phoenix metro area include the following. For more information, call the Phoenix Chamber of Commerce at 602-254-5521.

| Firm/Organization | Product/Service | No. Employees |
|---|---|---|
| State of Arizona | government | 40,000 |
| Motorola, Inc. | manufacturing | 21,000 |
| City of Phoenix | government | 10,000 |
| Arizona Public Service | public utility | 8,500 |
| Mountain Bell | telephone utility | 7,100 |
| Valley National Bank of Arizona | national bank | 7,000 |

Small businesses (one to four employees) in the greater Phoenix area number 19,880, or 38 percent of total businesses, and businesses with fewer than fifteen employees number 32,308, or 62 percent of the total. Though the relatively low percentage of small companies suggests a slowing down of entrepreneurial activity, Phoenix has many strong mid-size companies that more than take up the slack. In comparison with other western cities, Phoenix also has few very large employers, thus making the city's economy less susceptible to swings in a single sector.

The following relocation services may prove helpful in providing information about short- or long-term accommodations.

*Apartment Hunters*
1333 W. Camelback, #111
Phoenix, AZ 85013
602-241-9988

*Arizona Insights Relocation Center*
3610 N. 44th Street
Phoenix, AZ 85018
602-952-2177

*Arizona Newcomer Center*
4300 N. Miller Road, #147
Scottsdale, AZ 85251
602-941-8339

*Century 21 Relocation Center*
P.O. Box 7149
Phoenix, AZ 85011
602-265-0333

## SUMMING UP: OPPORTUNITY FOR WHOM?

Laissez-faire local government is often credited with ushering in this period of spectacular growth. Unfortunately, the age of do-as-you-please left some spectacular problems, well documented in the Neal Peirce Report (see *The Arizona Republic*, February 8, 1987). Historically, one of these problems has been poor communication between local businesses and government and the resultant lack of effective city planning. Although strong single-family residential areas exist, leapfrog development has helped create a sprawling landscape that includes office buildings, condominiums and strip malls.

Currently a high priority for change is the city's lack of a strong downtown business core. Zoning seems not to have been considered in a planning context until recently. In 1985 the Phoenix City Council adopted a new general plan, based upon an urban village concept, to designate certain areas for residential, commercial and industrial growth. The plan calls for village cores to serve as job and retail centers and be surrounded by residential development. Any project that proposes to depart from the general plan must be brought before the planning commission and city council and be the subject of public hearings. Additionally, planners from the metro area cities have begun meeting on a regular basis to discuss issues facing the area.

Business-government cooperation has been weak in devising long-term projects that would be mutually beneficial to the business community and general public. Although changing significantly, education has also been cited by both sides as an area that has suffered from lack of community dialogue. Where most states and municipalities initiated educational reforms in the early 1980s and are now moving on to a second wave of change, Arizona has only begun to implement some basic reforms. Defensive Arizonans claim that the schools are in good shape already, but a private commission designed to study the state of the valley's educational system reports that this is sadly not the case. The same commission points out that the city's education establishment is so entrenched that only a strong local business–local government partnership would be effective in righting more than a decade of wrongs. Recent cooperative efforts are an encouraging step in this direction.

Long-term economic and environmental issues, such as targets for future growth and air quality, also could be the focus of such a partnership. Although in the past there has been little central economic planning for the Phoenix region, efforts are being made to correct this. The Maricopa County Association recently restructured a standing committee to focus on aiding large employers who are looking at the valley as a relocation site. The Metrogroup, an affiliate of the Phoenix Metropolitan Chamber of Commerce, has been established to promote regional economic development. Additionally, the city of Phoenix, in a unique, joint public-private venture called the Phoenix Economic Growth Corporation, is involved in similar activities and strives to ensure that economic growth adheres to the city's general plan.

The valley's chambers of commerce also strive for solutions to quality-of-life issues, such as cleaner air and improved schools. Air quality is being addressed in other regional forums. A recent clean air campaign, spearheaded by the Phoenix Metropolitan Chamber of Commerce, the Regional Public Transportation Authority and the Arizona Energy Office, emphasizes the participation of area local governments as well as area businesses. Moreover, both pollution levels and numbers of violations have been declining, although very slowly. Fortunately, the alarms raised by the Pierce Report appear to have been heard, and metro area citizen activism is on the upsurge, as evidenced by regional conferences and study groups.

Most residents seem to enjoy the upbeat economy and the can-do spirit still alive in this part of the West, and many are prepared to fight for this way of life.

# Providence, Rhode Island

PROVIDENCE–PAWTUCKET–FALL RIVER, R.I.–MASS. (7/86) CMSA POP-
ULATION: 1,108,500 (34th largest), of which Providence, R.I. PMSA
population is 633,900.

POPULATION GROWTH 1980–86: 2.5%

COUNTY: Rhode Island has no county jurisdictions.

AVERAGE TEMPERATURE: 50°F

YEARLY RAINFALL: 42.75 inches

HUMIDITY: 66% (7th most humid)

COST OF LIVING: 117

## KEYS TO THE CITY

**Small Business Growth:** birth rate, growth rate, growth index
(rank/86): 1.9  3  4.9  (73rd)

**Average Annual Job Growth (9/84–9/87):** 2.3% (59th/largest 100)

**Keys to Prosperity:** High-tech manufacturing (robotics, high-
precision products, electronics), health care, education, marine
products, low energy costs, low property prices/rentals, low degree
of unionization.

**Key Developments:** A new railroad station, diversion of local river
through the city to open up prime real estate, new financing agencies for business; legislature has made key moves to encourage
business location.

**Key Life-Style Trends:** Providence is easy to reach from nearby
residential communities and offers extraordinary access to water
sports. It has a strong Roman Catholic community. As a relatively
undiscovered (as yet) mini-Boston, it offers cultural activities
through its institutions of higher education. Brown has been as
popular among college applicants as Harvard.

## WHY OPPORTUNITY KNOCKS IN PROVIDENCE

Providence is the capital of Rhode Island, and the venerable state
capitol looks down protectively on the city. Although Rhode Island
is America's smallest state, it is big on development and Providence

293

is its heart and soul. More than 65 percent of the population of New England lives within seventy-five miles of Providence. *The New York Times* has referred to Providence as "a vibrant, charming city, one of the most attractive medium-sized cities in the country, rich in history and culture."

This city of approximately 160,000 people is only forty-five minutes from Boston and three and one-half hours from New York City by automobile, bus or train. This gives Providence proximity to industrial customers and suppliers in electronics, machinery, metalworking and plastics. Rhode Island is a well-known center for advanced research and development, so it is a good choice for businesses engaged in robotics, pharmaceuticals, health care and ocean-science or marine-related electronics. Providence has prime industrial-park space, available financing, an attractive tax structure, and a well-trained and skilled labor force.

Providence is a prime area for service industries, financial institutions, light and medium manufacturing, and retail outlets. Providence used to be known for its traditional industries, but is diversifying and adjusting itself to new ones—a growing number of insurance companies, high-tech companies, high-precision product suppliers, commercial fishing and processing plants, boat building firms and foreign-based companies.

Providence is in a fortunate position regarding high-tech because it is only thirty minutes away from Boston's Route 128. Rhode Island and Providence work together in helping the state capital's economy prosper. On February 23, 1987, *Forbes* credited the state for having over the past few years: (1) reduced personal income taxes; (2) built state aid for local education to alleviate property taxes; (3) begun a phaseout of the state estate tax; (4) repealed or reduced special business taxes, such as those on petroleum and telephone companies; (5) streamlined worker's compensation procedures; (6) restructured the state's unemployment compensation system to the benefit of steady employees, which saved business $10 million in 1986; (7) repealed a unique striker's benefit law (strikers were entitled to worker's compensation) and replaced it with a much more probusiness law; (8) reduced the size of state government and restructured key operations within it; (9) appointed a business executive as director of Rhode Island's Department of Economic Development (an unprecedented move);

(10) created a local coordinating council to foster cooperation in development; (11) created a Business Action Center with the Department of Economic Development to provide one-step information for small business; and (12) started an innovative state Business Investment Fund, which uses state pension funds to make low-interest, fixed-rate loans.

Other reasons companies have chosen, and will continue to choose, Providence: (1) an average industrial energy cost 20 to 50 percent less than in New York, Connecticut or Massachusetts; (2) an average industrial space cost as much as $3 less per square foot than in New York, Hartford or Boston; (3) a median home cost far below that of nearby metro areas ($84,400 in Providence, $156,200 in Boston, $127,600 in Hartford, $160,000 in New York); and, finally, (4) a low percentage of private-sector unionized workers— 12 percent.

In 1985, Governor Edward DiPrete and the Rhode Island Port Authority established the Rhode Island Partnership for Science and Technology, a program that will link business and university projects. The area universities had been attracting more than $60 million a year for research programs.

Rhode Island imposes no local property tax on manufacturers' machinery and equipment; no manufacturers' inventory tax; no sales tax on manufacturers' machinery, equipment and replacement parts. A taxpayer may elect to write off expenditures paid or incurred during taxable years with respect to research-and-development facilities depreciable under the Internal Revenue Code and located within the state. Corporations operating multi-state businesses can still save with the state's tax structure as long as the goods are destined for a state location. Rhode Island has a state and local per capita tax burden of only $1,479, compared to $2,334 in New York, $1,816 in Connecticut, $1,749 in New Jersey, and $1,715 in Massachusetts. Rhode Island's tax burden is also lower than that in the states of California, Maryland, Michigan and Delaware.

Rhode Island has one-step financing offered by the state's Department of Economic Development, which assists enterprises in all phases of economic development, including financing of real estate, improvements, machinery and equipment. They do this using Tax-Exempt Industrial Revenue Bonds, Insured Conventional Mortgage Financing, Small Business Association Financing and Recreational Building Authority Insured Mortgage Loans. The Rhode Island Industrial Facilities Corporation and the Rhode Island Port Authority and Economic Development Corporation are empowered to issue industrial revenue bonds of up to $10 million. Interest on these bonds is exempt from federal and state income tax.

Rhode Island's Industrial Building Authority (IBA) guarantees manufacturing and industrial mortgages and gives up to $5 million in credit. Under IBA programs, the business has to provide 10 percent of the project costs for real estate and 20 percent of the machinery and equipment costs.

The Ocean State Business Development Authority is a private, nonprofit organization that can provide up to 90 percent financing on loan requests from $200,000 to $1 million at low interest rates. The Rhode Island Building Investment Fund (RIBIF) can make loans ranging from $25,000 to $50,000. The Small Business Revolving Loan Fund program will provide funds for fixed assets ($25,000 to $150,000) and working-capital loans (up to $30,000) with terms lasting up to fifteen years. The Rhode Island Municipal Development Fund will provide matching funds to communities to complete an infrastructure financing package necessary to support industrial activity at a specific site.

Providence offers its own one-stop financing. The Providence Industrial Development Corporation is another excellent example of public–private cooperation. PIDC has been instrumental in creating some $18 million in investments and 1,600 jobs through new industrial activity. The Business Development Company of Rhode Island was established in 1953, and it helps the state's business and industry grow by bridging the gap between conventional and venture-capital lending sources as a supplemental lender.

Other development groups in Providence are the Johnston Chamber of Commerce, the Providence Office on Economic Development, the Providence Redevelopment Agency, the Providence Industrial Development Corporation and, of course, the Greater Providence Chamber of Commerce. Providence has twenty-one banks and ten credit unions (total assets, over $162,215,752).

All of these institutions have helped construction companies build $93,082,000 worth of new projects over the period from

1980 to 1986. Industrial construction totalled $7,320,000 and public works construction projects $82,600,000 over those six years.

## QUALITY OF LIFE

**Weather:** Because of its location on the Atlantic coast, Providence is subject to capricious weather patterns, characterized by sudden storms. The average January temperature is 29.9°F, while July averages 72.8°F.

**Education:** As of 1980, 53.4 percent of the residents of Providence twenty-five years of age and over had completed high school and 15.7 percent had completed college. The median school year completed for residents of Providence twenty-five years of age and over in 1980 was 12.1 years. In that same year, approximately 19,055 students were enrolled in kindergarten through grade 12, with 17.2 pupils to every teacher. In the fall of 1985, 4,102 were enrolled in parochial schools and 1,645 were enrolled at other private schools.

Providence has six colleges and universities: Brown University, with an enrollment of 7,200; the Rhode Island School of Design, with 1,800 students; Providence College, with 3,600 undergraduates and 500 graduate students; Rhode Island College, with more than 7,600 undergraduates and 1,400 graduate students; Johnson and Wales College, with 4,700 students dispersed among its various locations; and the New England Institute of Technology, which has 2,300 students. Providence has a nine-branch library system, and the city has fifteen other private libraries.

**Neighborhoods:** Close in to Providence, a notably desirable residential area is the East Side, with its elegant, spacious, historic homes. Greater Providence's more desirable suburban communities include Barrington, East Greenwich and Lincoln. More affordable, and offering ethnic variety, are Bristol-Warren, Cranston, East Providence, North Providence and Warwick.

**Politics/Government:** Providence has a mayor-council form of government. The mayor is elected directly to a four-year term, is not a member of the city council and has veto power over council bills. The council consists of fifteen members elected by ward to four-year nonoverlapping terms. Thanks to a constructive public-private partnership and satellite growth from booming Boston, Providence has recently reversed the population decline that was taking place in the 1960s and 1970s. Local political controversy is, however, common, revolving around a history of corruption-related service delivery failure.

**Transportation:** Providence's motorists do not face particularly problematic commuter traffic. Intracity mobility is assisted by an adequate municipal bus system. Intercity travel options are Amtrak, which offers eleven trains a day, or a flight out of the city's Theodore Francis Green State Airport, served by nine carriers offering about fifty daily departures; many air travelers avail themselves of Boston's Logan International Airport.

**Health Care:** Seven hospitals are located in Providence, with a combined bed capacity of 2,142. Providence is served by the Metropolitan Nursing and Health Services Association of Rhode Island. There are also seventeen nursing homes, with a combined bed capacity of 1,400. The Rhode Island Group Health Association, one of the first health-maintenance organizations in the country, is located in Providence.

**Child Care:** Call Child Care Resource and Referral, 401-272-7520.

**Housing:** The average cost of a three-bedroom, two-bathroom house in greater Providence is $104,528.

**Public Safety:** With 550 reported 1986 robberies per 100,000 city residents, Providence has a slightly higher than average crime rate.

**Cultural Attractions:** The city's twelve theaters include the recently renovated Ocean State Center for the Performing Arts, the 2,200-seat Veterans Memorial Auditorium and the Trinity Square Repertory Theater. Providence has a nine-branch library system, and the city has fifteen other private libraries.

**Sports/Recreation:** The city's 104 parks, playgrounds, playfields and playlots have a combined area of 1,000 acres and they include eight outdoor swimming pools, thirteen recreation centers and a public golf course. The city is also home to several yacht clubs. The Providence Civic Center can house 10,000 for hockey games and up to 13,000 for other events.

**Taxes:** Rhode Island imposes an income tax of 14.65 percent of the federal income tax liability on Rhode Island earnings. The state sales tax is 6 percent. Property taxes in Providence range from

$9.20 to $81.00 for each $1,000 of assessed value, depending on location within the city.

---

## WHERE TO BREAK IN

For individuals interested in relocating to Providence, we provide a listing of selected area employers. For more information, call the Rhode Island Department of Economic Development at 401-277-2601.

| Firm/Organization | Product/Service | No. Employees |
|---|---|---|
| Rhode Island Hospital | general medical and surgical hospital | 5,000 |
| Brown University | education | 3,400 |
| Fleet National Bank | banking | 2,150 |
| Blue Cross/Blue Shield of Rhode Island | health insurance | 1,900 |
| New England Telephone | telephone utility | 1,900 |
| Trust National Bank | banking | 1,800 |
| Providence College | education | 1,500 |
| Providence Journal Co. | publishing, broadcasting | 1,500 |
| Miriam Hospital | health care | 1,300 |
| Old Stone Bank | banking | 1,200 |
| Women and Infants Hospital | health care | 1,050 |
| Amica Mutual Insurance Co. | insurance | 1,044 |
| Citizens Savings Bank Co. | banking | 1,000 |
| Narragansett Electric Co. | electric utility | 900 |

The Providence metro area has many large employers, such as General Dynamics Corp., which employs 5,700 and is the state's largest private employer, and Hasbro, which employs 2,200; both are located in Pawtucket. A total of eighty-two companies in Rhode Island employ over 500.

---

## SUMMING UP: OPPORTUNITY FOR WHOM?

Providence currently has a population of roughly 160,000. Of these, 36.9 percent live in owner-occupied housing, while 63.1

percent rent their residences. The largest private-industry employer is the service sector, which accounted for 38.3 percent of total private employment in 1985. This was followed by manufacturing at 26.4 percent; retail/wholesale trade, 16.7 percent; finance, insurance and real estate, 11.7 percent; transportation and public utilities, 4.9 percent; construction, 1.88 percent; and agriculture, forestry and fishing, which employed less than 1 percent.

# Raleigh–Durham, North Carolina

MSA POPULATION (7/86): 650,600 (56th largest)

POPULATION GROWTH 1980–86: 16%

COUNTIES: Wake and Durham, respectively

EMPLOYMENT (9/87): 380,700

AVERAGE TEMPERATURE: 59.1°F

YEARLY RAINFALL: 43 inches

HUMIDITY: 64% (13th most humid)

COST OF LIVING: 101.5 (Raleigh), 100.6 (Durham)

---

## KEYS TO THE CITY

**Small Business Growth:** birth rate, growth rate, growth index (rank/86): 4.6  4.5  9.1  (4th)

**Average Annual Job Growth (9/84–9/87):** 4.5% (11th/largest 100)

**Keys to Prosperity:** Research (high-tech manufacturing, biomedical, fiber optics, computers, telecommunications), health care, state government.

**Key Developments:** Continued growth of Research Triangle Park and the new Treyburn mixed-use development.

**Key Life-Style Trends:** Durham continues to offer cultural diversity through its many arts attractions and its university connection; larger Raleigh, a state capital, has in recent years developed its own diverse program of visual and performing arts.

---

## WHY OPPORTUNITY KNOCKS IN RALEIGH–DURHAM

Located in the central Piedmont region of North Carolina are the cities of Raleigh and Durham. Raleigh, with a total area of 84 square miles and a population of over 214,000 as of 1987, is the capital of North Carolina. With 125,000 current residents and an area of 66 square miles, Durham is somewhat smaller. Both are growing rapidly.

There can be little doubt that Raleigh–Durham owes its present prosperity to the three major universities in the area: Duke University in Durham, North Carolina State University in Raleigh and the University of North Carolina in Chapel Hill. In the late 1950s, aware of the technical resources concentrated in the area by its institutions of higher learning, a group of "Triangle" area business leaders planned the famous Research Triangle Park, targeting as tenants major high-technology corporations in need of access to university people and facilities.

Today, the Research Triangle Park is the largest facility of its kind in the nation, and it has attracted, and continues to attract, a great number and variety of high-tech firms specializing in computer technology, telecommunications, fiber optics, biomedical technology and data processing. The Park straddles the Durham–Wake county line and is adjacent to the city of Durham as well as Raleigh–Durham Airport. Even beyond the boundaries of Research Triangle Park are many high-tech industries that have located in the region. Activity in the Park is limited to research and development with some light manufacturing.

In the new 5,000-acre Treyburn development north of Durham, research-related manufacturing is integrated with residential, commercial, professional and recreational uses. Treyburn was conceived of as a forward-looking successor to the twenty-five year-old Research Triangle Park. Its industrial park component is designed to focus on high-tech activities such as light manufacturing and research. Treyburn's main attraction is the labor pool; it is located two miles from Durham's concentration of Ph.D. scientists and engineers (ranked number one in the nation relative to population). Another strong point is quality of life. Treyburn will include a range of housing and supporting services, and the metro area consistently ranks well in quality-of-life surveys.

In addition to the region's booming high-tech industries, the traditional tobacco, textile and lumber industries continue to provide substantial employment, but little or no growth.

Corporations seem anxious to locate in the Raleigh–Durham area primarily because of its research orientation (of which the Park is an expression), the quality of life, and the abundance of educated and skilled workers, as well as for the mild, pleasant, four-seasons climate. Highly attractive to pharmaceutical and biotechnical research firms is Durham's Duke University Medical Center (Duke University is the area's single largest employer). In addition, the area's central location along the populous East Coast ensures proximity to major markets. Employers in need of stable, productive workers find that the Triangle area offers a favorable formula of reasonable housing costs, low taxes and crime rates, and little crowding. Following is a select list of firms with newly installed facilities in the Raleigh–Durham area.

| Firm/Organization | Product/Service |
| --- | --- |
| Mitsubishi Semiconductor | semiconductor chips |
| Glaxo, Inc. | research and manufacture of pharmaceutical products |
| Organon Technika, Inc. | medical supplies and test materials |
| Du Pont Electronics | electronics research |
| BASF Wyandotte | agricultural chemicals |
| Wandel & Goltermann, Inc. | telecommunications equip. |
| American Sterilizer Co. | medical industry sterilizing equip. |
| Federal Pacific Railroad | electrical products mfg. |
| Imperial Clevite | high-performance mechanical seals, gas turbines, air compressors, refrigeration equip., turbo pumps, aerospace, missile mfg. |
| Underwriters Laboratories | testing facility for electrical, marine, heating, air-conditioning, refrigeration, fire-fighting and chemical equip. |
| Union Carbide Corp. | paints, sealants, adhesives and coatings |
| Charles River Breeding Laboratories, Inc. | research animals |
| Flexline Industries | specialized industrial hoses |
| Teletec Corp. | telecommunications systems R&D |
| Kaiser-Permanente | the nation's largest, most successful prepaid medical-care system |
| Dynamit Nobel Grace Silicon | silicon wafer mfg. |
| A.P. Parts, Inc. | auto exhaust system mfg. |
| American Airlines | has chosen Raleigh–Durham Airport as its north-south East Coast hub |
| Datalogic Optic Electronics, Inc. | bar code reading equip. |
| Bell Northern Research, Inc. | telecommunications R&D |

Exceptionally low unemployment rates in the Raleigh–Durham metro area, as well as the continuing trend of high-tech relocation to the Research Triangle Park, suggest a strong future of growth and prosperity for the region, especially since the industrial shift is toward the cutting-edge technology in which the United States continues to be strong. The fact that Raleigh is North Carolina's capital city means a local concentration of stable, high-paying government employment to cushion the area's thriving retail trade industry from the effects of an occasional high-tech downturn.

---

## QUALITY OF LIFE

**Weather:** Overall, Raleigh-Durham's climate is mild, but the summers are humid. Even so, while the area averages eighty freezing days (32°F and below) during winter, the summer is characterized by only about three weeks worth of 90° days.

**Education:** The Wake County Public School System consists of seventy-eight K–12 facilities, with a total enrollment of over 59,000 pupils. There are fifty-three private and parochial schools in Wake County, educating about 5,000 pupils. The Durham City and Durham County public schools systems include the North Carolina School of Science and Mathematics, a public, coeducational residential junior and senior high school that is nationally recognized. About 66 percent of students graduating from the area's inner-city high schools attend college, while the average is better for the suburbs, at 75 percent. Durham city schools require computer training for all students, and Durham county schools maintain test score averages among the highest in the state.

Postsecondary institutions in Durham include Duke University, North Carolina Central University, Durham Technical Community College and Rutledge College. Located in Raleigh are North Carolina State University at Raleigh, Hardbarger Business College and Rutledge Business College. Other Wake County colleges are Meredith (all-women), Shaw University and Saint Augustine's College (both historically black), and Southeastern Baptist Theological Seminary. Saint Mary's College is a women's college whose program consists of the second two years of high school and the first two years of college; Peace College is a two-year women's college. The combined enrollment of North Carolina State University at Raleigh, Duke University and the University of North Carolina–Chapel Hill is 55,000.

**Neighborhoods:** Raleigh and Durham have a great variety of neighborhood living opportunities, ranging from converted historic tobacco warehouses and textile factories adjacent to downtown to large, award-winning planned unit developments near Research Triangle Park. Durham's neighborhoods, offering great diversity in history, architecture, amenities and price, can be found close to job centers in almost any area of the city. Neighborhoods are also located in close proximity to Raleigh and Durham regional malls, specialty centers and attractive new neighborhood shopping centers.

**Politics/Government:** Both cities operate under a council-manager form of government. City council and mayoral seats are elected on a nonpartisan basis, by ward, while selection of the mayor is citywide. Area neighborhoods have a strong voice in local government affairs, and the cities strive to involve citizens in citywide planning efforts.

**Transportation:** Transportation in and around the cities of Raleigh and Durham is difficult without a car, and traffic on the two interstate highways serving the cities is heavy. Municipal bus service is available. Travel to points outside the area is provided by Greyhound and Amtrak. The Raleigh-Durham Airport is served by about 100 flights daily.

**Health Care:** The area's excellent, low-cost medical-care facilities include four teaching hospitals, two medical schools (Duke and Chapel Hill), two comprehensive cancer treatment centers (Duke and Chapel Hill) and three hospices. Raleigh has six hospitals, while Durham has five; Durham likes to call itself the "City of Medicine," which is not unjustified in view of the reputation and quality of research and care at the Duke University Medical Center and because of the multimillion-dollar biomedical research and development industry that has grown up at the nearby Research Park.

**Child Care:** A variety of child-care options is available in the area, ranging from home care, to parochial and private providers, to day care arranged by some employers, even to some publically supported programs.

**Housing:** There are a variety of housing types and price ranges available in the Raleigh-Durham area. Prices for housing in the area are in many instances less than those in other major metropolitan areas on the East and West Coasts. Within the Triangle area, the average cost in 1987 of a new single-family house was $109,056 in Durham and $126,236 in Raleigh–Wake County. Average prices for townhouses and condominiums in the area are significantly less

than single-family home costs, with Durham's prices again somewhat lower than those in Raleigh. New construction and rehabilitation activity has been very high over the last few years in both
Raleigh and Durham.

**Public Safety:** Neither Raleigh nor Durham has a high crime rate.
Reported 1986 robberies per 100,000 city residents amounted to
268 (Raleigh) and 195 (Durham).

**Cultural Attractions:** Durham's rich cultural life revolves around
four major institutions: the Durham Arts Council, the American
Dance Festival, Duke University and North Carolina Central University. The Arts Council has led downtown revitalization efforts
with the construction of a $15 million Arts Center that includes
galleries, theaters, studios, classrooms, rehearsal halls and cin-
emas. These facilities house fifteen affiliated arts agencies, which
range in scope from a modern dance troupe to an opera company.

Durham is a city of festivals. Each spring the Arts Council presents an outdoor opera festival that places opera literally in the
streets of downtown. The summer marks the beginning of the internationally acclaimed American Dance Festival (ADF). ADF presents a six-week festival of the world's best modern dance
companies. The Dance Festival includes a complete school for
aspiring young dancers, dance critics, choreographers, composers
and media specialists. Concurrently, the Duke University Office of
Cultural Affairs presents a Summer Artsfare of cultural programs.
A major July Fourth celebration is held each year in Durham. Thousands of citizens flock to the Folklife Festival on the Eno River.

The fall begins with the Arts Council's CenterFest, a street arts
celebration of downtown Durham. During the winter months, the
Duke University Institute of the Arts presents a WinterFest of
Contemporary Arts, focusing on modern painting and sculpture.

Spearheading Raleigh's cultural attractions is the "Artsplosure"
festival, held each April, which consists of free exhibitions and
performances by area painters, mimes, dancers, puppeteers and
musicians. The festival also features performances by artists of
national fame. Raleigh's Memorial Auditorium is the home of the
North Carolina Symphony Orchestra and the North Carolina Theater, a professional company that performs both musical and dramatic plays.

Among other Raleigh musical and dramatic attractions are Theater in the Park, the Raleigh Oratorio Society, the Raleigh Symphony Orchestra, the Raleigh Civic Symphony, the Capital Community Chorus, Ballet Theater Company and the Raleigh Little Theater, a community group that produces five to seven shows a year. Raleigh's North Carolina Museum of Art, the first state-owned art museum in the country, specializes in works by European Renaissance masters. Raleigh is also the home of the North Carolina Museums of History and Natural History. Recently completed are a City Art Gallery, which displays the works of area artists, and "Artsplace," which also supplies low-cost studio space to qualified local artists.

**Sports/Recreation:** Football and especially basketball fans have plenty of local college sports to watch: Duke, North Carolina State University and the University of North Carolina at Chapel Hill all have teams that are regular national contenders. If you like baseball, watch it on television, play it yourself, send your kids to Little League or go to Durham Athletic Park to watch the Durham Bulls, a minor-league baseball team with a strong local following. Raleigh, not to be outdone, has recently approved funds for a $3.5 million baseball stadium and is seeking a minor-league team to fill it.

**Taxes:** The North Carolina State income tax ranges from 3 to 7 percent of North Carolina earnings, on a graduated scale; annual incomes over $10,000 are taxed at 7 percent. The state sales tax is 3 percent, but many area municipalities add to it. Residential property in Wake County is assessed at full market value and taxed at a rate of fifty-nine cents for the county and sixty-six cents for the city for each $100 of valuation; Durham area property taxes are comparable.

## WHERE TO BREAK IN

For skilled people interested in relocating in the Raleigh–Durham area, we include a partial list of major employers. The diversification of the local economy, including strong educational and health-care presences, should be very encouraging. For more information, call the Raleigh Chamber of Commerce at 919-833-3005 or the Durham Chamber of Commerce at 619-682-2133.

| Firm/Organization | Product/Service | No. Employees |
|---|---|---|
| Duke University (including Medical Center) | education (including 11,000 at its teaching and research hospital) | 17,000 |
| State of North Carolina | government | 16,000 |
| IBM | computer technology | 9,500 |
| North Carolina State University | education | 6,500 |
| Wake County Public School System | education | 5,350 |
| Northern Telecom, Inc. | digital telephone and switching equip. | 5,200 |
| Carolina Power and Light | electric utility | 3,500 |
| City of Raleigh | government | 2,400 |
| General Telephone Co. of the South | telephone utility | 2,200 |
| Wake County Medical Center | general medical and surgical hospital | 2,200 |
| ITT Telecom | telecommunications equip. | 1,850 |
| Durham County General Hospital | general medical and surgical hospital | 1,800 |
| Durham County Schools | education | 1,700 |
| Liggett & Myers Tobacco Company, Inc. | cigarettes | 1,650 |
| Veterans Administration Medical Center | health care | 1,500 |
| Wake County | government | 1,460 |
| Burroughs Wellcome | pharmaceuticals | 1,450 |
| Blue Cross/Blue Shield of North Carolina | insurance | 1,400 |
| City of Durham | government | 1,370 |
| Rex Hospital | health care | 1,370 |
| Dorothea Dix Hospital | health care | 1,300 |
| Westinghouse Electric Corp. | electric components | 1,300 |
| U.S. Environmental Protection Agency | government | 1,200 |
| Research Triangle Institute | headquarters | 1,100 |

| Firm/Organization | Product/Service | No. Employees |
|---|---|---|
| Durham County | government | 1,000 |
| Telex Computer Products, Inc. | computers | 1,000 |

## SUMMING UP: OPPORTUNITY FOR WHOM?

The combined work force of Wake and Durham counties is 284,520. Unemployment in the area is currently very low, between 3 and 4 percent. The area work force is distributed among eight basic industrial categories.

| Industry | Share of Work Force (in %) |
|---|---|
| Wholesale and retail trade | 23.5 |
| Government | 21.8 |
| Services/miscellaneous | 20.5 |
| Manufacturing | 13.8 |
| Construction | 8.9 |
| Finance, insurance and real estate | 5.8 |
| Transportation, communications and utilities | 5.7 |

While area business leaders don't expect growth in the traditional tobacco and textile industries, they do expect the current education, health, telecommunications, electronics, biomedical and computer science research industries growth trends to continue well into the 1990s. To better illustrate opportunity expectations in these fields, we include a table with employment projections to 1990 for eleven professional and occupational categories.

PROJECTED PROFESSIONAL, TECHNICAL AND KINDRED JOB GROWTH
FOR THE RALEIGH-DURHAM AREA

| Occupation | Employment 1981 | 1990 | Annual Increase Average (in %) |
|---|---|---|---|
| Engineers | 4,050 | 7,940 | 10.7 |
| Physical scientists | 910 | 1,350 | 5.4 |

| Occupation | Employment | | Annual Increase |
| | 1981 | 1990 | Average (in %) |
| --- | --- | --- | --- |
| Engineering, science technicians | 4,280 | 7,700 | 8.9 |
| Medical workers, excluding technicians | 5,330 | 9,150 | 8.0 |
| Other health technologists and technicians | 4,230 | 6,830 | 6.8 |
| Computer specialists | 2,350 | 5,490 | 14.9 |
| Social scientists | 800 | 1,240 | 6.1 |
| Teachers, college and university | 6,220 | 8,810 | 4.6 |
| Teachers, elementary and high school | 8,020 | 12,670 | 6.4 |
| Writers, artists, entertainers | 1,900 | 3,170 | 7.4 |
| Other professional and technical | 12,770 | 19,860 | 6.2 |
| Other Kindred | 8,320 | 12,080 | 5.0 |
| TOTALS | 59,180 | 96,290 | 7.0 |

The projected growth in most of the occupations listed above reflects the general trend toward high-tech R&D in the Raleigh–Durham area. Some of the other occupations included in the listing, such as entertainers, are also significant in that they reflect the economic diversification that a strong, growing economy can support, regardless of its specific emphasis.

All in all, Raleigh–Durham is a city of the future.

# Sacramento, California

MSA POPULATION: 1,291,400 (30th largest)
POPULATION GROWTH 1980–86: 17.4%
COUNTY: Sacramento
EMPLOYMENT (9/87): 551,200
AVERAGE TEMPERATURE: 60.3°F
YEARLY RAINFALL: 17.22 inches
HUMIDITY: 46% (35th most humid)
COST OF LIVING: 106.2

## KEYS TO THE CITY

**Small Business Growth:** birth rate, growth rate, growth index (rank/86): 2.8  2.9  5.7  (56th)

**Average Annual Job Growth (9/84–9/87):** 5.0% (6th/largest 100)

**Keys to Prosperity:** Defense (air force bases), health care.

**Key Developments:** New sports arena, research village.

**Key Life-Style Trends:** Sacramento is close enough to San Francisco to share in the latter's cultural life, which is just as well since Sacramento doesn't have a lot of its own. Its residents have an agricultural, small-town outlook, and the area has not been as affected by the downturn in agriculture as most other areas in California because Sacramento has a strong governmental (state capitol, air force bases) and increasingly important private industrial and commercial employment base.

## WHY OPPORTUNITY KNOCKS IN SACRAMENTO

The capital of the state of California is located east of San Francisco, in the Great Central Valley, at the confluence of the Sacramento and the American rivers. It has long been a transportation center because of the rivers and, most important, because it is where the Southern and Western Pacific railways converge. One of the world's most productive agricultural regions, the Sacramento area is blessed with a very mild climate, with few cold or hot days

**311**

in the year. Despite this, the area offers both winter and summer attractions.

Metro Sacramento includes four counties: El Dorado, Placer, Sacramento and Yolo. Sacramento residents are relatively well educated and affluent. Homeowners make up 63 percent of all residents, renters 37 percent. Owning a home is relatively easy. A Bank of America report says that homes are more affordable in the Sacramento MSA than in the other growing metro areas.

Sacramento has grown, largely due to a movement of people away from crowded coastal metro areas to inland areas, and from agricultural jobs to those in manufacturing and wholesale and retail trade. According to a 1985 study by the Bureau of Economic Analysis of the Department of Commerce, the Sacramento metro area is one of the ten fastest growing areas, with a 37 percent population increase to the year 2000. Most population growth comes through migration. A June 1986 Wharton Econometrics report also estimates that Sacramento will have the fastest growth of any metro area with a population of 1 million or more.

The Bank of America's *Economic Forecast 1986* says Greater Sacramento is experiencing rapid growth and economic diversity and its economy has become more recession-resistant. It predicts little chance for a local economic downturn in the foreseeable future. In 1986 Sacramento ranked sixth nationally in economic growth. Sacramento will do better than California in employment percentage change, total personal income change, home sales and permit change, taxable sale change and population change.

The big shift in employment in Sacramento's economy is a decrease in government employment and a commensurate increase in the service sector. In six years government employment fell 13.5 percent, while the service sector grew 10 percent. Health care, part of the service sector, provided the most new jobs in 1985. Between 1980 and 1986, government jobs as a percent of total employment dropped from 35.4 percent to 30.5 percent; service was up to 21.2 percent; retail trade was up from 18.9 percent to 20.3 percent; manufacturing was up from 6.9 percent to 7.4 percent.

While government employment has not been growing as fast as the service sector, it has helped drive the area's economic growth. For example, between 1970 and 1980, the Mather and McClellan air force bases made government the top employer during a period when state and local government increased only 4.5 percent.

McClellan AFB has been called "a city within a city." It employs approximately 15,000 civilians, while maintaining a base population of over 19,500. McClellan itself is the area's third largest state employer, behind the state of California and the Sacramento County Office of Education. It is the home of the Air Logistics Center and is one of the air force's busiest bases. Its total expenditures for 1986 will be over $1.6 billion. The total impact of these expenditures on the economy will be approximately $2.2 billion, creating with it 26,700 more jobs. Mather AFB, a place where 3,000 students annually learn to fly, adds approximately $540 million to the economy and is also a stable employer.

Both air force bases helped the service sector become the fastest growing sector in the region. It is growing so quickly that by 1990 it will be the area's largest employer. Service firms have found it easy to establish themselves in Sacramento because of the low rents. This, along with improvements in new telecommunications technology, has enabled service industries to be headquartered away from where actual business transactions are taking place. Even more services are expected to relocate to Sacramento, especially since it is so close to San Francisco and yet offers much less costly space.

Trade is the second largest employer, providing over 25 percent of nonagricultural jobs. Sales from trade (retail, wholesale) are expected to reach $10.4 billion in 1986, according to the Bank of America forecast.

Manufacturing jobs will account for 7.4 percent of the work force. Recently, food canning and processing industries have grown rapidly. Growth has also occurred in durable goods production. Many electronics firms such as Intel, a subsidiary of IBM, Hewlett-Packard, NEC Electronics and Avantek are planning expansion in the area.

Agriculture has suffered serious losses all over Northern California, but Sacramento has not felt the full impact because of its economic diversification. Although the "port" of Sacramento (the city is on the Sacramento River) does not profit from farm export growth, the Sacramento region contains the focal point of the state's high-tech farm economy. Biotechnology applied to agriculture is expected to be a multibillion-dollar business by the 1990s.

A nonprofit economic development organization, the Sacramento Area Commerce and Trade Organization (SACTO), was founded in 1975, and its major goal has been the recruitment of the best companies to the area. SACTO has been doing this by screening the various economic sectors to see which would promote the greatest economic benefit to the region.

Sacramento is blessed with: (1) plenty of inexpensive land and space in all sections of the MSA; (2) a stable and growing economy; (3) an expanding industrial base, well balanced between high-technology and conventional enterprise; and (4) an excellent transportation system providing easy access to the major markets of the San Francisco Bay area and the center of the electronics industry in Santa Clara County. As mentioned previously, improvements in telecommunications technology have enabled businesses to have offices in Sacramento while doing business elsewhere. Sacramento is also graced with ample and inexpensive water and energy and a large, well-educated labor supply.

Unfortunately, the area may be impeded by its modest infrastructure and amenities, as well as by public sentiments questioning unbridled growth (since Sacramento has always been very agriculturally based, its residents have had a small-town feeling). Funding for infrastructure has been difficult to obtain now that it is to be provided more by the public and less by developers. Long-range planning is necessary for the Sacramento MSA. The highway will easily become congested. Funds for light-rail systems and more highways are needed.

The North Natomas community is planning $55 million in infrastructure improvements ranging from utility sources to major roads. A 3,500-acre high-tech research village in Placer County is sure to attract more high-tech companies. Other parks are also planned. Regional transit is to be developed so that Sacramento will have more than its Yolo County–based Yolobus.

Communities that are growing are the Natomas, Roseville, Folsom and Rancho Cordova areas.

---

## QUALITY OF LIFE

**Weather:** With low humidity, mild winters and hot but not uncomfortable summers, Sacramento has a very pleasant climate. It almost never snows, and freezing days (32°F and less) number about fourteen a year; on the other extreme, Sacramento has only about a month and a half of days in the 90s each year.

**Education:** In such a young and well-educated community (55 percent of the population has had some college, while 25 percent has had at least four years), educational institutions are central. The University of California at Davis (UCD) has 20,000 students. UCD has helped the area's biotechnology and genetic engineering firms both by providing employees for them and by carrying on some of the research on its campus. The School of Engineering at UCD, which includes computer sciences and electronic engineering as well as civil and mechanical engineering, is also an aid to the electronics industry. In the Sacramento area, there are also the McGeorge School of Law, the Lincoln School of Law, Golden Gate University, Chapman College (with Mather and McClellan AFB facilities) and National University. Community colleges are distributed among the counties. American River Community College is the primary center for electronics programs, and Sierra College has its educational programs supported by Hewlett-Packard. In addition, the Sacramento area has seventy-five trade schools.

**Neighborhoods:** In the heart of Sacramento is the restored Old Sacramento District. Not far from here is the largest concentration of multifamily residences, along with the city's commercial areas, spaced out by thirteen municipal parks, and the state and federal offices; this area includes the city's best restaurants. Also within Sacramento proper is the very desirable neighborhood of Land Park, with well-landscaped streets and good-size older single-family homes. One of Land Park's best features is that for which it is named, the 600-acre William Land Park, which contains the fifteen-acre Sacramento Zoo. Sacramento's East Area consists of McKinley Park (shaded streets, older homes), Oak Park (blue collar, affordable), Tahoe Park (modest, established, affordable) and Campus Commons (large homes, condos, townhouses—all expensive). Among the most exclusive suburban areas in Greater Sacramento are Cameron Park and El Dorado Hills (both developed in the 1960s) and Folsom Lake and Rancho Murieta. Older communities include American River Drive and Carmichael (the nice homes are along parts of Fair Oaks Drive).

**Politics/Government:** Sacramento has a council-manager form of government. The mayor is elected directly for a four-year term. He serves on the council and lacks veto power over council bills. The other eight council members are elected by district to overlapping four-year terms; the council meets weekly. Sacramento went 49 percent for Reagan in 1980, versus 41 percent for Carter.

**Transportation:** Sacramento's motorists are slowed down by heavy commuter traffic. Intracity movement is assisted by municipal bus service. Amtrak runs six trains through Sacramento every day, and Sacramento Metropolitan Airport is served by thirteen carriers providing eighty flights daily.

**Health Care:** Sacramento has a relatively small number of hospital beds, under 6 per 1,000 residents, reflective of its youthful population. The number of doctors per 1,000 population averages at 2.1. The area has had the highest suicide rate in the nation, over 30 per 100,000 residents, reflective of the large number of people who move to the area and their high expectations (in general, the younger California cities have three or four times the suicide rates of older, more traditional East Coast cities).

**Child Care:** Call California Children's Services at 916-440-5551.

**Housing:** The average cost of a three-bedroom, two-bathroom house in metro Sacramento is $90,000, but prices go as high as $200,000 or more. An average monthly rent for a one-bedroom apartment is $369.

**Public Safety:** With 691 reported 1986 robberies for each 100,000 city residents, Sacramento has a higher than average incidence of crime.

**Cultural Events:** Sacramento has ballet, opera and a symphony. The biggest cultural event is the annual Sacramento Dixieland Jubilee, held over Memorial Day Weekend, crowds at which exceed 20,000.

**Sports/Recreation:** Sports attractions include the Sacramento Kings (basketball), who opened their maiden season in 1987, selling out all their season tickets. Current development includes a new sports arena for the Kings that will also be used for other sports events. The new arena is expected to attract other professional sports franchises.

**Taxes:** California income taxes are the seventeenth highest in the nation; local property taxes amount to about 1.2 percent of assessed valuation. Effective sales and use tax amounts to between 6 and 6.5 percent, depending on locality.

## WHERE TO BREAK IN

For individuals interested in seeking employment in Sacramento, we include a listing of the area's major employers. For more information, contact the Sacramento Chamber of Commerce at 916-443-3771.

| Firm/Organization | Product/Service | No. Employees |
|---|---|---|
| Pacific Bell | telephone utility | 5,000 |
| Aerojet General | rocket mfg. | 4,300 |
| Sutter Health System | health care | 4,100 |
| Mercy Health Care | health care | 2,640 |
| California Almond Growers Exchange | food suppliers/ manufacturers | 2,500 |
| Campbell Soup Company | food processing | 2,500 |
| Kaiser Permanente | health insurance | 2,400 |
| Hewlett-Packard | computers/electronics | 1,680 |
| A. Teichert & Son | construction | 1,200 |
| McClatchy Newspapers | printing/publishing | 1,100 |
| Pacific Gas & Electric | electric utility | 1,040 |
| AT&T | telecommunications | 1,000 |
| Intel Corp. | electronics | 1,000 |

## SUMMING UP: OPPORTUNITY FOR WHOM?

Sacramento's adult population is 52 percent male; 61 percent of the population is between eighteen and forty-four years of age; 500,000 are married; 181,800 are single; 30 percent earn $35,000 or more; 63 percent own their own homes, while 37 percent rent. Half the population are managers, white-collar workers and craftsworkers; unemployment in 1985 was only 5 percent.

The city's growing population and economy should continue to generate employment opportunities for educators, health-care professionals, engineers, technicians, managers, computer experts and people with clerical and other office skills.

# Salt Lake City, Utah

MSA POPULATION: 1,041,400 (37th largest)
POPULATION GROWTH 1980–86: 14.4%
COUNTY: Salt Lake
EMPLOYMENT (9/87): 453,600
AVERAGE TEMPERATURE: 51.0°F
YEARLY RAINFALL: 15.17 inches
HUMIDITY: 42% (36th most humid)
COST OF LIVING: 98.9

---

## KEYS TO THE CITY

**Small Business Growth:** birth rate, growth rate, growth index (rank/86): 3.2  2.9  6.1  (43rd)
**Average Annual Job Growth (9/84–9/87):** 2.4% (56th/largest 100)
**Keys to Prosperity:** Biomedical companies, computers, work ethic, high birthrate, Mormon influence and low cost of living.
**Key Developments:** Drainage of Salt Lake to Bonneville Salt Flats will raise values of adjacent properties that are now threatened by floods.
**Key Life-Style Trends:** Salt Lake City has developed some after-hours clubs for drinkers.

---

## WHY OPPORTUNITY KNOCKS IN SALT LAKE CITY

Salt Lake City presents widely expanding employment opportunities in a greatly diversified industrial sector. The manufacturing, trade and service sectors are expanding statewide, while agriculture, mining and government services industries are holding steady or slowly declining. Growth for six of seven standard occupational categories is predicted to lie between 16 and 19 percent over the five-year period 1986–91. The six high-growth fields are (1) managerial and administrative; (2) professional, paraprofessional and technical; (3) sales and related; (4) clerical and administrative support; (5) service; and (6) production, operating

318

and maintenance. Only agriculture, forestry and fishing show a declining employment outlook. Plants and animals just can't keep up with the rapid growth of businesses in Utah.

In financial terms, Salt Lake City has been called a "Cinderella City"—one that is to lead its region in economic growth. Not only does the city lay claim to a wide variety of large corporations, it also has a booming small-business community. Two Salt Lake firms are in *Inc.* magazine's list of America's 100 fastest growing, small, publicly traded companies. Bonneville Pacific, which develops power facilities, ranks as seventh, and Symbion, which manufactures artificial organs, ranks thirtieth.

Extensive commitment to high-tech artificial organ research and manufacture has led locals to call Salt Lake the "Bionic Valley." Spare parts made in the area include the well-known Jarvik artificial hearts, as well as arms, ears, bladders, blood vessels and sphincters. Supported by the University of Utah, fledgling biomedical companies enjoy financial backing and access to the university's resources, and the university in turn takes initial equity positions in order to reap proceeds from future sales and licensing fees. To be biotechnical, the companies and the university enjoy a symbiotic relationship that has *Business Week* magazine calling Salt Lake City's organ concern the "hottest growth industry for years to come."

Salt Lake City's population is ever increasing from internal growth (Mormons, even more than Catholics, favor large families). Utah has the second highest birthrate in the United States and, despite a sizable out-migration from oil-dependent areas over the last year, the state's population rose 1.3 percent for the year 1985–86. The U.S. national average was only 0.9 percent for the same period. Most of Utah's population growth occurred in the four Wasatch Front counties—Davis, Salt Lake, Utah and Weber. Considered together, this area's population increased by 19,000, accounting for 90 percent of total growth. In 1980 Salt Lake City proper had a population of roughly 163,000, Salt Lake County had 625,000 residents and the Greater Salt Lake–Ogden Metropolitan Statistical Area had 941,000. Of all the people living in the Salt Lake–Ogden MSA, an overwhelming 91.3 percent are white, and the largest minority group, the Hispanic population, makes up only 5 percent of the total.

An increasing population does not necessarily lead to an increasing cost of living. In fact, the American Chamber of Commerce Researchers Association reports that the prices of groceries, housing, utilities and transportation in Salt Lake City are all below the national average. Though health-care costs are slightly above the national average, the all-items index remains below it. The horizon becomes even brighter when one considers that median family income rose 58 percent from 1985 to 1986, making Salt Lake City's level the sixth highest in the country with the fastest rate of growth in the nation.

## QUALITY OF LIFE

**Weather:** Salt Lake City's climate has its extremes: hot summers and cold winters with lots of snow. Each year there are several 0° days, over 100 freezing (32°F and below) days and about a month and a half of days in the 90s.

**Education:** Institutions of higher learning in the Salt Lake area include the University of Utah, Westminster College, Salt Lake Community College, Utah State University (Logan), Weber State College (Ogden) and Brigham Young University (Provo). A full complement of professional, business and occupational programs is offered, as well as programs in arts and sciences, music and religion.

**Neighborhoods:** Single-family detached homes are the living arrangement of choice, although recently developers have begun to construct multifamily apartment houses or condominiums in response to higher land prices and a demand for low-upkeep units, and have integrated shopping amenities and recreational facilities into attractive complexes. The abundance of mountain scenery makes Salt Lake residents even more view conscious than the average home-proud American—whether the Salt Laker lives on the valley floor and looks up, or lives in the elevated "benches" of the valley rim. Old and new residential districts tend to blend into one another, and neighborhoods reflect a variety of architectural styles and periods, from restored wood-frame Victorian mansions to more contemporary stone, brick, wood and glass structures.

**Politics/Government:** Salt Lake City has a nonpartisan mayor-council form of government. The mayor is elected directly, while all the council members are elected from districts. The mayor has veto power over council bills. Salt Lake County, of which the city is a part, administers unincorporated portions of the county directly and coordinates municipal services delivery with constituent towns. It is headed by a three-person board of commissioners elected at large, two members for a four-year term and one member for a two-year term.

**Transportation:** Salt Lake City has heavy commuter traffic, but a good municipal bus system. Amtrak offers four trains a day, and Salt Lake International Airport is served by thirteen carriers offering a total of 200 flights daily.

**Health Care:** Health care in the Salt Lake area is of high quality and low cost. There are thirteen general hospitals, five emergency-care centers and two cardiac-care units.

**Child Care:** Call Child Care Resource and Referral at 801-537-1044.

**Housing:** The average cost in 1986 of a single-family home with 1,800 square feet and three bedrooms was estimated at $80,524. Average rent in Salt Lake County for a one-bedroom, 605-square-foot apartment is $332. For a two-bedroom, 901-square-foot apartment, expect to pay an average of $409. Salt Lake City has virtually no slum areas.

**Public Safety:** Salt Lake City has a fairly low crime rate for a city its size. In 1986 there were 304 reported robberies per 100,000 city residents.

**Cultural Attractions:** Culture vultures will enjoy the state's internationally known Utah Symphony Orchestra, the resident opera and ballet companies, along with numerous theater companies. The Mormon-run genealogical library is the world's finest, and the Mormon Tabernacle Choir is the star of the nation's longest running live radio show.

**Sports/Recreation:** In addition to its strong economy and relatively-low-to-average cost of living, Salt Lake City has great scenic beauty and enough cultural diversions to be ranked as one of America's "Most Livable Places." The city and environs are a sports paradise. Though unparalleled in its proximity to powder-covered ski slopes in the winter, Salt Lake also is home to hikers who might venture into any of the area's eight canyons during the summer. Salt Lake *does* have a long, snowy winter, but there is more than enough summer for residents to visit the zoo and aviary and to make use of the city's twenty-six golf courses. For the watchers rather than the doers (though the categories are by no means mutually exclusive), Salt Lake has three professional sports teams: the Jazz (basketball), the Golden Eagles (hockey) and the Trappers (Pioneer League baseball).

Nightlife is more active than the heavy conservative influence might seem to predict. Though Mormons do not drink alcoholic beverages and the state has laws prohibiting privately owned package stores and liquor by the drink, drinking does go on in members-only clubs, which are easily joined. The state's stringent liquor laws may have little effect inasmuch as Salt Lake seems to attract the healthy and health conscious.

**Taxes:** Residential property is assessed at 15 percent of market value and taxed at a rate of $72.55 for each $1,000. Sales taxes vary between $5^3/_8$ and $5^3/_4$ percent depending on municipality. The state personal income tax on Utah earnings over $7,500 is 7.75 percent, whether filing individually or jointly. Average utilities bills amount to $100 a month: electricity will run you about $46, gas about $47, with sewer and water rates varying by municipality.

---

## WHERE TO BREAK IN

The Mormon Church is an easy way into Salt Lake City; it is an integral part of the community, with each parish serving as both spiritual and social center for its neighborhood. In addition, the Church proper and its LDS Hospital are large employers in the Salt Lake area.

Nevertheless, job opportunities are many and varied. The largest employers in the Salt Lake area contract for defense, provide financial services, furnish utilities, retail merchandise and manufacture high-technology products. Listed below are the eleven private companies whose employees number over 2,000. For more information, contact the Salt Lake City Chamber of Commerce at 801-364-3631.

| Firm/Organization | Product/Service | No. Employees |
|---|---|---|
| Morton Thiokol | rocket boosters | 6,000 |
| First Security | banking | 5,000 |

| Firm/Organization | Product/Service | No. Employees |
|---|---|---|
| Hercules Aerospace | rocket engines/missiles | 5,000 |
| Utah Power & Light | utility | 4,500+ |
| UNISYS (formerly Burroughs) | computers | 3,500+ |
| American Express | worldwide processing center | 3,000+ |
| ZCMI | department store | 3,000+ |
| LDS Hospital | health care | 2,500+ |
| Mountain Bell | telephone utility | 2,500+ |
| Mountain Fuel | fuel supplier | 2,500+ |
| Delta Airlines | regional hub | 2,000+ |

Large public employers in the area include Hill Air Force Base (21,000 employees), IRS Service Center/Regional Office (5,000+), Jordan School District (4,500+), Toole Army Depot (4,000–4,999), Salt Lake County Government (3,000+) and Salt Lake City Government (2,000+).

---

## SUMMING UP: OPPORTUNITY FOR WHOM?

All this might suggest that Salt Lake City is a great place to be. But the city is over 90 percent white, and blacks on the average make in salaries and wages only 40 percent of what whites do. Women comprise less than 30 percent of the city's work force, a very low figure. Above all, the city is 70 percent Mormon, which, for those used to a more varied urban mix, gives the city the feeling of a small town. Utah's state legislature is even more dominated by socially conservative Mormons than Salt Lake City. Unlike the Catholics, who established their own parochial schools, the Mormons rely on public schools for the education of their children— don't be surprised to find dedicated Mormons in the classroom and principal's office! How you feel about all this will affect your ability to adjust to the city.

A more general problem with Salt Lake City is the Salt Lake itself. The lake is now at its highest level in recorded history, and rising waters have caused over $200 million in damage in the mid-1980s. City planners have given the go-ahead to an ambitious project to lower the level of the lake by four feet in 1987–90. The lake is to be drained onto the Bonneville Salt Flats, and though it will cover roughly 500 square miles, the new lake will only be two and a half feet deep. The operative principle here is that greater surface area will hasten evaporation, yet at the same time the new lake, called West Pond, may well generate billowing banks of fog, causing traffic tie-ups and airport delays.

---

### THE PROMISED LAND

Salt Lake City has more than its share of mountains and Mormons. Mormons have faith, and faith moves mountains, which explains the grand array of mountains ringing the city.

Joseph Smith was the founder and first president of the Mormon Church, also known as the Church of Latter-Day Saints. A religious dissenter living in Palmyra, New York, Smith planned as early as 1833 for a city sympathetic to and centered around the Church, what he called a "City of Zion." The Midwest seemed to offer such a site, but Smith and his followers met with continual persecution as they attempted settlement (people didn't always take kindly to the Mormons' proselytizing and polygamist practices). A religious dispute with local townspeople landed Smith in a Carthage, Illinois, jail. An enraged mob reportedly stormed his cell, and though he was armed with smuggled weapons, Smith was killed in the ensuing shoot-out.

Leadership of the Church then fell to Brigham Young, who initiated the Mormons' final move in 1846. "If there is a place on this earth that nobody else wants," Young is reported as having said, "that is the place I am hunting for." That place was to be Salt Lake City. Just west of the Rocky Mountains and cradled in the valley, the unpopulated area allowed the Mormons to practice their controversial religion free from outside influence and interference.

Though in 1847 the initial band of settlers numbered only 148, the population swelled to 11,380 by 1850. Thereafter, the mass Mormon resettlement in the West produced a fourfold increase in the permanent dwellers. By 1890, Salt Lake City was home to more than 100,000 Mormons. Today, Mormons constitute nearly three-fourths of Greater Salt Lake's population. Mormons are very family oriented, as shown in their varied community activities, their large families and their interest in genealogy. (Mormons believe descendents can retroactively ensure the salvation of their ancestors.)

# San Antonio, Texas

MSA POPULATION (7/86): 1,276,400 (31st largest)
POPULATION CHANGE 1980–86: 19.1%
COUNTY: Bexar (pronounced "Bear")
EMPLOYMENT (9/87): 496,000
AVERAGE TEMPERATURE: 68.8°F
YEARLY RAINFALL: 27.54 inches
HUMIDITY: 52% (34th most humid)
COST OF LIVING: 98.4

## KEYS TO THE CITY

**Small Business Growth:** birth rate, growth rate, growth index (rank/86): 4.2  3.6  7.8  (12th)

**Average Annual Job Growth (9/84–9/87):** 2.1% (58th/largest 100)

**Keys to Prosperity:** Military bases, tourism, growing high-tech sector.

**Key Developments:** Historic preservation in downtown area (Riverwalk, etc.).

**Key Life-Style Trends:** Increasing downtown entertainment opportunities.

## WHY OPPORTUNITY KNOCKS IN SAN ANTONIO

Like other frontier towns such as Phoenix and Tucson, San Antonio may well owe its current level of development and prosperity to the fact that big corporations such as Datapoint and Fairchild located plants there years ago, attracted by mild climate and low-cost real estate. To be sure, though, two major high-tech manufacturing facilities don't make or break a city's economy. San Antonio also banks on its five local military bases; with a total military employment of 43,739 and a related civilian employment of 34,598, these bases were worth $2.5 billion to San Antonio in 1985. Factor in San Antonio's thriving tourist trade based on its beautiful café-lined Riverwalk (Paseo del Río), the Alamo and four

325

other Spanish missions, and it's clear that San Antonio either domiciles or attracts enough people to support its developed retail sector. Because military employment and tourism are less affected by economic cycles, the city's retail/services sector is well cushioned.

When another major high-tech firm intending to locate a manufacturing-and-development plant in Texas turned down San Antonio for Austin, claiming that San Antonio was weak in high-tech educational facilities, the San Antonio Economic Development Foundation searched for a field the city was strong in: medical and biological research. San Antonio's Southwest Research Center is a nonprofit foundation consisting of two branches, the Foundation for Biomedical Research and the Southwest Research Institute. Together they employ 2,334, including over 500 research technicians, engineers and scientists, engaged in medical-related and applied research on a grant basis. Recently, the University of Texas selected San Antonio as the location for its Institute of Biotechnology, which will include the Center for Molecular Targeting to conduct advanced research on human cells.

---

## QUALITY OF LIFE

**Weather:** In summer, a lot of rain falls in a short period, but in wintertime the rain tends to be light, a drizzle. Thunderstorms occur in all seasons. Measurable snow accumulation occurs once every three or four years, with snowfalls of two to four inches occurring once every decade. San Antonio's location, only 140 miles from the Gulf of Mexico, makes the city vulnerable to occasional tropical storms, characterized by high winds (the highest ever recorded from such a storm is 74 miles per hour) and heavy rains. The first incidence of freezing temperatures is in late November and the last is in early March.

**Education:** The San Antonio public school system has a total enrollment of 66,597 students. With a relatively low dropout rate of 1.6 percent, San Antonio high schools manage to send 51 percent of their graduates to college. The city kicks 1.43 percent of its yearly budget into public education, with individual neighborhoods picking up the majority of the bill. Economic inequality among San Antonio districts forces poorer neighborhoods to tax themselves at a higher rate on their smaller tax bases in an attempt to provide as good an education as the wealthier districts can supply with less fiscal hardship. San Antonio has eleven colleges and universities, with a total enrollment of 55,000 students. Degree programs are available in criminal justice, business, medicine, nursing, dentistry, arts and sciences, engineering and divinity.

**Neighborhoods:** The housing form of choice in San Antonio is the detached single-family house. The citywide apartment occupancy rate is a low 82 percent, indicating wide availability of rental apartment housing. Condominiums are scattered throughout the city but are concentrated on the North Side. Among the most exclusive of the city's communities is the Dominion, where homes may be priced at $1 million or more. More accessibly priced suburban communities include Alamo Heights, Balcones Heights, Leon Valley, Olmos Park and Terrell Hills.

**Politics/Government:** The city government of San Antonio is run by a mayor elected at large and ten council members elected by districts. Council members serve two-year terms. The council sets the policies of the city and hires a professional chief administrative officer to serve as city manager. San Antonio's incumbent mayor, Henry Cisneros, is one of only three Hispanic mayors of major U.S. cities (the other two being the mayors of Miami and Denver), and is the one with the longest incumbency; as such, and in view of the tremendous underrepresentation of Hispanics in American political life, he is a statewide and even national political figure. Bexar County is governed by a four-person county commission presided over by a county judge. The county area includes twenty-two suburban cities and special districts (created for water and sewer service and flood control). The San Antonio metro area went 53 percent for Reagan in 1980.

**Transportation:** Transportation in and around San Antonio is difficult due to heavy traffic on its three interstate highways. Municipal bus service within the city and Greyhound and Trailways service to points outside the city are available. The San Antonio International Airport, which forms a medium-size air travel hub, is serviced by fourteen airline carriers, providing 106 flights daily.

**Health Care:** Health care in San Antonio is of high quality and is relatively reasonably priced. Area health-care facilities include three teaching hospitals, a medical school (University of Texas

Medical School at San Antonio), a cardiac rehabilitation center and a hospice.

**Child Care:** Working parents in need of information about child-care availability or referrals should call the local chapter of United Way at 512-224-5000.

**Housing:** A new single-family home costs $45,000 to $1 million; the average price is $81,900. Apartments cost $200 to $500 a month.

**Public Safety:** Crime rates in Dallas and Houston are rather high in relation to population. San Antonio's robbery rate is half as high, with only 371 reported 1986 robberies per 100,000 city residents.

**Cultural Attractions:** The quality of life in San Antonio is enriched by the sense of history evoked by the city's five missions, notable for their Spanish Colonial architecture, as well as by the San Antonio Museum of Art, with its pre-Columbian, Native American, Spanish Colonial and Mexican folk collections, and the McNay Art Institute, which specializes in European post-Impressionist pieces. Music lovers in search of entertainment, however, had better like country-western music; if they don't, they'd do well to move: San Antonio may have a strong Hispanic presence, but it's still in Texas!

**Sports/Recreation:** Professional sports attractions include AA minor-league baseball (San Antonio Dodgers) and basketball (San Antonio Spurs); participants will enjoy the city's golf, tennis and swimming facilities.

**Taxes:** Residential property in San Antonio and Bexar County is assessed at full market value and taxed at a rate of $1.38 for each $100 of assessed value (not including school district tax, which varies as described above). The sales tax effective in San Antonio is 6.75 percent (5.25 percent state, 1 percent city, 0.5 percent Metro-politan Transit Authority). There is no city or state income tax.

---

## WHERE TO BREAK IN

People with biological, medical and bioengineering back-grounds should refer themselves to colleagues and other intrafield contacts in order to secure placement in the San Antonio area. We include a number of the metro area's largest employers. For more information, contact the San Antonio Chamber of Commerce at 512-229-2100.

| Firm/Organization | Product/Service | No. Employees |
|---|---|---|
| Datapoint Corp. | data-processing systems | 1,500 |
| Fairchild | aircraft mfg. | 1,100 |
| Advanced Micro Devices | microprocessors | 550 |

The following companies are in the process of locating facilities in San Antonio:

| Firm/Organization | Product/Service | No. Employees |
|---|---|---|
| VLSI Technology, Inc. | semicustom semiconductors | 750 |
| Sprague Electric Co. | electronic components | 550 |
| Harcourt Brace Jovanovich, Inc./The Psychological Corp. | educational materials, R&D, corporate headquarters | 400 |
| Isotronics, Inc. | microelectronic packages | 200 |

## SUMMING UP: OPPORTUNITY FOR WHOM?

With a population of 898,000 and a total area of 263.6 square miles, San Antonio has a population density of about 3,000 persons per square mile. The metro area suburbs grew at a rate of 42.1 percent from 1976 to 1980. San Antonio's work force grew at a rate of 2.5 percent between 1980 and 1985, and experienced in 1985 an unemployment rate of 6.5 percent. San Antonio's work force is distributed among eight broad industrial groupings as follows:

| Industry | Share of Work Force (in %) |
|---|---|
| Wholesale and retail trade | 27 |
| Government | 21 |
| Services/tourism | 21 |
| Manufacturing | 10 |
| Construction | 8 |
| Finance, insurance and real estate | 8 |
| Transportation, communications and utilities | 4 |
| Mining | 1 |

We offer up this Texan city, once again, as a city of opportunity
for people with technical training, especially in biochemistry, bioengineering, biomedical engineering, genetics, medical technology
and medicine. San Antonio's infant but promising biomedical
research industry is also destined to create opportunities for entrepreneurs in service-oriented industries such as computer software
and computer maintenance and repair, as well as in the supply,
maintenance and repair of research equipment.

# San Diego, California

MSA POPULATION (7/86): 2,201,300 (19th largest)
POPULATION GROWTH 1980–86: 18.2%
COUNTY: San Diego
EMPLOYMENT (9/87): 868,900
AVERAGE TEMPERATURE: 62.9°F
YEARLY RAINFALL: 9.45 inches
HUMIDITY: 61% (23rd most humid)
COST OF LIVING: 120

---

## KEYS TO THE CITY

**Small Business Growth:** birth rate, growth rate, growth index
(rank/86):   4.1   4.3   8.4   (8th)

**Average Annual Job Growth (9/84–9/87):** 5.3% (5th/largest 100)

**Keys to Prosperity:** Defense spending, biomedical and technical
research, and financial sector.

**Key Developments:** Waterfront Convention Center.

**Key Life-Style Trends:** Winning the America's Cup will focus
world attention on the city's leisure sailing; land-based recreational and cultural opportunities are also growing.

---

## WHY OPPORTUNITY KNOCKS IN SAN DIEGO

Years ago when San Diego was the only rival deep-water port in
the West, San Francisco railroad magnates decided to thwart San
Diego's desire to become the terminal for the second East–West
railroad route, by selecting Los Angeles instead. At the time, Los
Angeles couldn't take large ships. Alas for both San Diego and San
Francisco, Los Angeles arranged for federal support to deepen its
harbor. However, San Diego has prospered nonetheless, becoming
a major navy port.

With San Diego's high employment, steady population growth,
and a broad base of high-tech, service, education, research, defense
and tourism industries, the area's economy today is solid. Rapid

**331**

growth of biomedical and biotechnical fields in San Diego proper and in the traditional high-tech outposts of Sorrento Valley and Mira Mesa are gradually eclipsing the city's current image as a parochial navy town. California's second largest city has more going for it than a renowned zoo, year-round mild weather and its nabbing of "the jug" (the America's Cup) from New York City via Australia.

Though office vacancy is high (10 to 15 percent), absorption rates of vacant offices are up, and hotel, apartment and retail real estate markets remain strong. In addition, the city's new Waterfront Convention Center is rightly seen as a catalyst for further down-town development. By the year 2000, the metro area's population is expected to top 2.8 million, up considerably from 1980's 1.9 million, with an additional half a million people in nearby Tijuana. In line with this population growth, Wharton Econometrics places San Diego's employment growth rate in the nation's top ten and predicts a 3.3 percent annual increase through 1990.

One reason for higher growth is that 70 percent of San Diego's manufacturing employment is in defense-related industries— machinery, instruments and transportation equipment. Another is that employment in the finance industry grew at an annual rate of 5.5 percent in the county from 1980 to 1985, and local economists say the trend is expected to continue through the 1990s as San Diego expands its financial services sector. Gross regional product is growing faster than California's as a whole, and home values are rising faster as well. Growth from tourism is expected to continue; San Diego hosted the Superbowl in 1988 and will host the America's Cup in 1991.

---

## QUALITY OF LIFE

**Weather:** San Diego's southern location lands it plenty of sunshine. Its coastal location provides surf and one of the most mild, even climates in the country. Freezing temperatures are unknown, and there are only a handful of 90°F days. Summer in San Diego is warm and dry, while spring is cooler and rainy; there are, essentially, only two "seasons."

**Education:** The San Diego Unified School District enrolls 115,461 K–12 pupils, and special education is available for learning-impaired as well as advanced children. Among the city's higher educational facilities are San Diego State University, the University of California at La Jolla, the California Western School of Law and the University of San Diego; curricula are offered in humanities, psychology, law, engineering, business, religion and music.

**Neighborhoods:** Downtown San Diego offers a mix of pricey and affordable studio apartments, one- and two-bedroom apartments, condos and townhouses. In addition to panoramic views of San Diego Bay, downtown offers proximity to good restaurants, shopping and theaters. Among the city's most exclusive neighborhoods is Point Lome. More accessibly priced, and still close to downtown, are the communities of City Heights, East San Diego, Golden Hill (Victorian houses, some needing work), Sherman Heights, South Park (pink sidewalks and a gala mix of architectural styles) and Southeast San Diego.

**Politics/Government:** The city of San Diego is governed by a council-manager form of government with an appointed city manager. It serves as the county seat. San Diego County is governed by five elected supervisors and an administrative officer appointed by the Board of Supervisors of the sixteen incorporated cities in the county. The area went 62 percent for Reagan in 1980, the eighth highest percentage vote of the eighty-six metro areas.

**Transportation:** The city also has excellent transportation services. For car owners/drivers/commuters, three interstate highways serve the metro area. But with a wide and efficient network of city buses, a car is not essential. In addition, Amtrak serves the San Diego area, as do the San Diego International and Lindbergh Field airports.

**Health Care:** It helps that the city has excellent health-care facilities—216 physicians per 100,000 residents, with an impressive array of teaching hospitals, cardiac rehabilitation centers and hospices, the University of California at San Diego Medical School and the UCSD comprehensive cancer treatment center.

**Child Care:** Call Child Care Resources at 619-275-4800.

**Housing:** A home in San Diego may be safe and sound, but it's not cheap. Rent averages $410 a month, and a house on average costs $124,000; property taxes run roughly $1,300, bringing the annual cost of mortgage and taxes to $13,000. Add $1,500 for utilities and you're shelling out $14,500, quite a bit more than the national average.

**Public Safety:** With 394 reported 1986 robberies per 100,000 city residents, San Diego's crime rate is about average.

**Cultural Attractions:** The city has a lot to see and do. Museums include the Natural History Museum, the San Diego Museum of Art and the San Diego Museum of Man. The Old Globe Theatre features Shakespeare and classics, the La Jolla Playhouse presents avant-garde works and the San Diego Repertory offers a smattering of this and that. The city is also home to a Class A symphony orchestra, a seasonal opera company and at least six professional dance troupes.

**Sports/Recreation:** Professional sports teams—the Padres (baseball) and the Chargers (football)—pull in the sports fans, while the much-famed zoo and Sea World seem to have broad-based appeal. With Cleveland National Forest and Tijuana Slough National Wildlife Refuge nearby, in a day one can retreat to nature and return home safe and sound.

**Taxes:** The sales tax in effect in San Diego is 6 percent (5 percent state, 1 percent city). California has a graduated income tax similar in structure to the federal income tax; a family of four with an income of $30,000 will pay, after personal exemptions, about $660. Residential property in San Diego County is assessed at full market value and taxed at an average rate of 1.1 percent; some residents may apply for a $7,000 property value exemption.

---

## WHERE TO BREAK IN

For individuals interested in seeking employment in San Diego, we provide a partial listing of the area's major employers. For more information, contact the San Diego Chamber of Commerce at 619-232-0124.

| Firm/Organization | Product/Service | No. Employees |
|---|---|---|
| Rohr Industries Inc. | aircraft parts | 5,000 |
| PSA Inc. (Pacific Southwest Airlines) | air carrier | 3,700 |
| Kyocera International Inc. | nonclay refractory | 1,850 |
| Cubic Corp. | engineering/scientific instruments | 1,600 |

| Firm/Organization | Product/Service | No. Employees |
|---|---|---|
| Imperial Savings Association | state savings and loan | 1,500 |
| San Diego Gas and Electric | electric utility | 1,210 |
| Home Federal Savings and Loan | state savings and loan | 1,200 |
| Atlas Hotels | hotels | 1,000 |
| Sea World Inc. | amusement park | 1,000 |

San Diego's business community is filled with not-so-large organizations as well. Small businesses with four or fewer employees constitute 49 percent of the area establishments, and those with fewer than fifteen employees make up 76 percent of the area's total businesses (these small businesses are doing better than large ones nationwide, and are a more reliable source of future jobs). One San Diego concern, Beeba's Creations—an importer of women's garments—made *Business Week*'s list of small high-growth companies of 1987.

---

## SUMMING UP: OPPORTUNITY FOR WHOM?

San Diego's population is growing by approximately 50,000 residents each year. As of 1980, 76 percent of the city's residents were white, 15 percent were Hispanic, 9 percent were black and 6.5 percent were Asian. As with most other cities, the suburbs of San Diego are 86 percent white. The number of women in the work force compares favorably to other large metro areas, with females making up 44 percent of all employed.

With its impressive population and high-tech industrial growth, the San Diego area should continue to generate employment opportunities for people with scientific, technical and engineering backgrounds, as well as health professionals, educators, people with office and clerical training, and skilled tradesmen. The service sector will also continue to experience growth, creating jobs for individuals with various levels of skill, education and training.

# San Francisco, California

SAN FRANCISCO–OAKLAND–SAN JOSE, CALIF. CMSA POPULATION (7/86): 5,877,800 (4th largest), of which San Francisco PMSA population is 1,588,000.

POPULATION GROWTH 1980–86: 6.7%

COUNTY: San Francisco

EMPLOYMENT (9/87): 939,000

AVERAGE TEMPERATURE: 56.7°F

YEARLY RAINFALL: 20.66 inches

HUMIDITY: 66% (7th most humid)

COST OF LIVING: 120.7

## KEYS TO THE CITY

**Small Business Growth:** birth rate, growth rate, growth index (rank/86): 2.8  3.9  6.7  (30th)

**Average Annual Job Growth (9/84–9/87):** 1.1% (89th/largest 100)

**Keys to Prosperity:** The city attracts creative people and tourists. They in turn attract high-technology companies (nearby in Silicon Valley) and life-style-oriented businesses, offsetting a decline in the financial services sector. Trade with the Pacific Rim countries also promises continued growth.

**Key Developments:** San Franciscans have opted to rein in development, sacrificing short-term growth for long-term livability. Growth opportunities within and outside the city are ample enough for business and for recreation.

**Key Life-Style Trends:** Growing use of the renovated dockside areas.

## WHY OPPORTUNITY KNOCKS IN SAN FRANCISCO

Long the West Coast's banking headquarters, anchored by the once formidable Bank of America, San Francisco has now been edged out by rival Los Angeles as the western economic heavy. Though some major local banks have lost their former influence or have moved out of the city, other sectors are strong.

In her October 1986 State of the City Address, Mayor Dianne Feinstein acknowledged that 20,000 to 30,000 jobs had been lost during the previous year because large financial institutions and other businesses moved out of the city to avoid taxes and high rents. But, she pointed out, the city's employment continued to grow because the number of very small businesses (employing four or fewer people) rose an impressive 20 percent over that same year.

Upscale retail stores in downtown and residential areas make up a hefty chunk of these new business start-ups, and tourism and conventions remain the city's consistent money-makers to support these fledgling establishments. In general, Mayor Feinstein reported that the city's work force is becoming more white-collar, office-based and small business oriented.

This sits well with image-conscious San Franciscans. According to a 1987 life-style poll in the Chronicle, San Francisco residents prefer by a three-to-one margin a life with fewer material possessions to economic growth in their city. And in an attempt to stem the tide of what is disparaged as the Manhattanization of the city, Bay Area residents passed Proposition M in late 1986 to limit most new commercial development in the city to 475,000 square feet per year. This proposition allows only one to two medium-size office buildings to be built in the city each year and serves to protect each neighborhood from excessive change. Big real estate projects cannot now get final building permits unless approved by public hearings. Ross Turner, the president of the San Francisco Chamber of Commerce, thinks that this measure "will drastically affect the job prospects and economic well-being of thousands of San Francisco residents and will substantially reduce the city's potential tax revenue."

Yet this may be overstated. Though no office building over 50,000 square feet has been approved since September of 1985, in early 1987 a glut of new office space kept a lid on rents and encouraged businesses and offices to move back into the city. The economy seems to be on a growth path acceptable to San Franciscans, continuing its brisk trade with the Pacific Rim countries and realizing the long-term promise of the high-tech sector concentrated in the Silicon Valley, southwest of the central city. The city's large Asian population has forged strong ties with the prosperous Far East, exemplified by Toyota's joint project with General Motors.

Overall, the city enjoys a jobless rate of only 4.2 percent (lower than the 7 percent national average), and San Francisco is projected to have the highest personal income in the nation by the year 2000.

The city's Old Guard seems to fear that, with the decline of the Montgomery Street financial sector, San Francisco is becoming no more than a crazy quilt of hotels, restaurants, boutiques and tourists. But the New Guard is quick to point out that the city is home to more Fortune 500 companies than it was ten years ago and has logged an increase of 900,000 jobs over the same period. Though big (and ugly) development projects have been discouraged or halted, development in general is by no means reined in. It has simply been redirected in an effort to retain some of the original architectural character and beauty of the area. Los Angeles may have replaced San Francisco as the dominant city on the Pacific Coast, but San Franciscans are content to let this happen. Baghdad-by-the-Sea has little desire to follow what it views as La La Land's unbridled plunge into growth.

---

## QUALITY OF LIFE

**Weather:** The Bay Area has a pleasant, mild, two-season climate, free of uncomfortably hot weather as well as freezing temperatures.

**Education:** To complement the city's strong commitment to its 170,000 K–12 pupils, the Bay Area is served by fifty-four colleges, universities and professional schools, among them some of the finest in the nation (Stanford, the University of California at Berkeley). Top-notch curricula are offered in medicine, engineering, biomedical engineering, law and business administration. Local industry is well supported by the area's community college system, offering training in word processing, electronics, accounting and lab technology.

**Neighborhoods:** Excuse us if we go on too long, but neighborhoods in San Francisco are fun to talk about. *Bayshore:* In southeast San Francisco, it contains Candlestick Park and many small groups of homes separated by warehousing and manufacturing sectors. *Buena Vista:* At the geographic center of the city, it includes Haight-Ashbury (one-time center of the dropout generation) and Ashbury Heights; it is famous for its contrasts, between the hilly summit and flatland and between the prosperous, conservative communities and the less elevated homes of the poor. *Downtown:* The heart of the city, it contains the major commercial districts (Market Street being the lower dividing line of the developed area; Montgomery Street, being the financial sector), major employers, government offices, tallest buildings, theaters, best restaurants and key historic sites. *Lake Merced District:* The most recently developed area, it was until recently farmland; it contains the campus of San Francisco State University, the zoo, golf courses and shopping centers. *Mission District:* This is an area strong in character and tradition. Its residents even have their own Brooklynese-type accent; however, the latest sounds are increasingly Latin as more Hispanics move in, displacing the older residents. Despite its working-class reputation, the area has many Victorian homes that attract well-heeled residents with the cash to invest in renovation. *Richmond District:* Located in northwest San Francisco and sometimes called the Presidio, it contains some elegant neighborhoods but is solidly middle-class. Amenities include good shopping and accessibility to parkland, the ocean and much open recreational space. *Sunset District:* Adjacent to Golden Gate Park and characterized by winding streets and look-alike row houses, this district is solidly middle-class and is considered a good place to raise children. *West of Twin Peaks:* Residential areas in this hilly, forested area constitute the most suburban settings in the city, with many detached single-family homes.

**Politics/Government:** San Francisco has a mayor-council form of government with a directly elected mayor serving a four-year term. The mayor does not sit on the city council, and has veto power over council bills. The council consists of eleven members elected at large to four-year overlapping terms; the city council meets weekly. A source of controversy in San Francisco is opposition to further downtown skyscrapers, which many residents believe have been spoiling the city's character; however, the price of this opposition is continued gains by Los Angeles, some at the expense of San Francisco's economic development. The difference in local attitudes could have been predicted somewhat by the 1980 electoral count—43 percent for Reagan in the San Francisco area (eleventh lowest of eighty-six metro areas) versus 51 percent for Reagan in the Los Angeles metro (forty-first out of eighty-six).

**Transportation:** Good public transportation (buses and cable cars and BART rapid transit to Berkeley, Oakland and outlying areas) eliminates the need for a car except for trips to enjoy the beauty of the surrounding areas.

**Health Care:** The overall quality of health care in San Francisco is high. With one of the finest medical schools in the country housed at the University of California at San Francisco (UCSF), the city draws exceptionally talented and committed physicians and students. Its number of physicians per 100,000 residents is a high 416. Six major teaching hospitals, seven cardiac rehabilitation centers and five general hospices are located in the Bay Area. In addition, the city has fluoridated water and only minimal air pollution.

**Child Care:** Women in the work force account for 44 percent of all employed, and day-care inquiries may be directed to a Bay Area reference and referral service called Bananas (415-658-0381 for referrals, 415-658-7101 for general information).

**Housing:** What's not to like in a city of many parks and gardens with springlike weather ten months every year? A very high cost of living, for one. High rents (averaging over $500 a month) discourage many otherwise would-be San Franciscans. The average price of a home has climbed beyond $160,000.

**Public Safety:** San Francisco has a fairly high crime rate, registering 678 reported robberies per 100,000 city residents in 1986.

**Cultural Attractions:** For aesthetic edification, San Francisco has many museums. The Museum of Modern Art, the M. H. de Young Museum, the Asian Art Museum and the California Palace of Legion of Honor are notable for their extensive collections.

The area's theaters are highly regarded; the American Conservatory Theatre, the new Eureka Theater, the Berkeley Repertory, Magic Theatre and Fugazi Theatre are all highly touted. Not to mention a major symphony orchestra and opera company, along with a quality ballet and scores of smaller dance companies (second only to New York in this department).

**Sports/Recreation:** Among the city's sports attractions are the Giants (baseball) and the 49ers (football).

**Taxes:** The price of high-quality municipal services and, often, of high central-city quality of life is high taxes. The "Queen of the

Pacific" is no exception, with a local tax burden amounting to over 4 percent of average annual household income.

## WHERE TO BREAK IN

Though the San Francisco economy is becoming more oriented to small business, the Bay Area has many large employers. For more information, contact the San Francisco Chamber of Commerce at 415-392-4511.

| Firm/Organization | Product/Service | No. Employees |
|---|---|---|
| Hewlett-Packard (Palo Alto) | telecommunications | 18,000 |
| Associated Indemnity Corp. (Novato) | insurance | 16,000 |
| Bechtel Group Inc. | engineering/surveying systems | 7,500 |
| Wells Fargo and Co. | state bank | 6,300 |
| Pacific Gas and Electric | electric utility | 5,000 |
| Varian Associates Inc. (Palo Alto) | electron tubes | 5,000 |
| Southern Pacific Co. (Menlo Park) | water, sewer pipe, power lines | 4,000 |
| Bechtel Power Corp. | engineering/surveying systems | 3,000 |
| Raychem Corp. | drawing, insulating nonferrous wire | 3,000 |
| Multi Benefit Realty Fund (Oakland) | building operations | 2,700 |
| SRI International (Menlo Park) | research and development labs | 2,650 |
| BankAmerica Corp. | national bank | 2,500 |
| Mervyn's | department store | 2,100 |
| Bechtel Civil and Minerals | engineering/surveying systems | 2,000 |
| Pacific Bell | telecommunications | 2,000 |
| Southern Pacific Transportation Corp. | railroads/line-haul operating | 2,000 |
| Levi Strauss and Co. | clothing | 1,600 |

| Firm/Organization | Product/Service | No. Employees |
|---|---|---|
| Chevron USA Inc. | crude petroleum/natural gas | 1,400 |
| Del Monte Corp. | canned fruits/goods | 1,300 |
| Watkins-Johnson Co. (Palo Alto) | transmitting equip. | 1,020 |
| American Building Maintenance Industries | cleaning services | 1,000 |
| Bechtel Constructors Corp. | heavy construction | 1,000 |
| Chevron Corp. | crude petroleum/natural gas | 1,000 |
| Fireman's Fund Insurance Co. (Novato) | insurance | 1,000 |
| Kaiser Aluminum (Oakland) | aluminum products | 1,000 |
| National Surety Corp. (Novato) | surety co. | 1,000 |
| TransAmerica Airlines Inc. (Oakland) | air carrier | 1,000 |

Nearly 48 percent of San Francisco's businesses employ four or fewer persons, and 76 percent have fewer than fifteen employees. The Bay Area is home to four of *Business Week* magazine's small hot-growth companies of 1987—Informix (database management and software), Adobe Systems (Palo Alto; software for laser printers/electronic software), 3COM (Mountain View; office communications systems) and McGrath Rentcorp. (San Leandro; rents modular offices).

---

## SUMMING UP: OPPORTUNITY FOR WHOM?

From its Victorian architecture to its lofty hills, San Francisco is a delight to look at. It's equally nice to look away from. With many vistas, the San Francisco Bay is readily visible and, on a clear day, aahh-inspiring. Situated on a narrow strip of land separating the Pacific Ocean and the bay, the city faces lush and luxe Marin County to the north, beyond which are the fertile Napa Valley vineyards, and to the east the university town of Berkeley and the industrial city of Oakland.

San Francisco often is likened to Boston. Each is a little sister to a larger city nearby (L.A. or New York), each is situated on a bay, each has a distinctive history, each maintains an air of provincialism and its concomitant, snob appeal. Despite their similarities, the differences are pronounced. One San Francisco native explains the two cities' differences this way: People in Boston care most about their work; people in San Francisco care about their whole life.

Possibly because the weather is so nice, life-style is a distinctive preoccupation here, and the city's history of progressivism and tolerance have encouraged many styles of life. San Francisco's population is 53 percent white, 21 percent Asian, 12 percent black and 12 percent Hispanic. Chinatown, Japantown and North Beach (Italian) are distinctive neighborhoods that add a great deal of ethnic (and culinary) flavor to the city. The Bay Area hosts the greatest number of Asians in the West; to accommodate this large minority, the city runs a Chinese hospital and publishes an Asian-American yellow pages.

The city also has a sizable homosexual population concentrated in the Castro area. One result of this is that of the total number of AIDS cases reported in the United States, 39 percent are concentrated in New York and San Francisco. Whereas a significant portion (30 percent) of New York's AIDS sufferers are intravenous drug users, 95 percent of San Francisco patients are homosexual. Because the homosexual community is large, well educated, relatively wealthy and politically organized, San Franciscans have been forced to focus on the AIDS tragedy. Groups of individuals, city government and local businesses have taken action together. San Francisco established the first hospice in the nation for patients dying of AIDS-related illnesses. The Coming Home Hospice, a nonprofit facility financed through community fundraising, offers constant care for about $140 a day—hospitals often charge up to ten times that amount. The city of San Francisco is spending $11 million a year on AIDS-related research, care and support services. Pacific Telesis and Levi Strauss are among local companies that support awareness measures at their offices and have devised specialized nondiscriminatory personnel policies to handle AIDS in the workplace.

San Francisco has a variety of pleasant sights: Coit Tower, the Golden Gate Bridge, Alcatraz, Fisherman's Wharf and snaking

Lombard Street are perennial tourist meccas. Each is structurally distinct and adds an element of interest to the urban landscape, while cable cars and pastel-colored houses add quaint charm.

If the dollars are not daunting, San Francisco is a great place to live and work. With singles making up 34 percent of the urban population, San Francisco has the third highest concentration (behind Boston and Washington, D.C.) of unmarried people in the United States. The straight singles scene is alive and well and concentrated along trendy, bar-soaked Union Street and increasingly south of Market Street. Numerous bars and clubs in the Castro area cater to the neighborhood's gay clientele.

# Seattle, Washington

SEATTLE–TACOMA, WASH. CMSA POPULATION (7/86): 2,284,500 (17th largest), of which Seattle PMSA population is 1,751,000.

POPULATION GROWTH 1980–86: 8.9%

COUNTY: King

EMPLOYMENT (9/87): 937,500

AVERAGE TEMPERATURE: 52.5°F

YEARLY RAINFALL: 35.65 inches

HUMIDITY: 62% (19th most humid)

COST OF LIVING: 108.1

---

## KEYS TO THE CITY

**Small Business Growth:** birth rate, growth rate, growth index (rank/86): 3.7   2.9   6.6   (33rd)

**Average Annual Job Growth (9/84–9/87):** 4.1% (15th/largest 100)

**Keys to Prosperity:** East–West trade, defense spending (aerospace).

**Key Developments:** Convention center, new tunnel.

**Key Life-Style Trends:** Support for the arts, trend toward suburbanization. Seattle residents take full advantage of a unique variety of nearby spectacular marine and mountain scenery.

---

## WHY OPPORTUNITY KNOCKS IN SEATTLE

Seattle is the business and financial center of the Great American Northwest. It is the center of the Puget Sound region in northern Washington state, the most heavily populated region in the state, and the hub of a highly advanced industrial, international trade and service economy. Seattle serves as a major distribution center for incoming and outgoing goods and is the closest entry for commerce with Asia's Pacific Rim.

The port of Seattle provides the city with much of its prosperity, as do the aerospace, forest products, food products, agricultural commodities and primary metals industries. The port is the second largest handler of container cargo in the country (over 21

345

million tons in 1980) and is investing a record $100 million in terminal improvements to accommodate the burgeoning East– West and tapering Alaskan peninsula trade. The city is, on the average, a day and a half closer to the Orient than the rival ports of Oakland and Long Beach and is generally the first port of call from Hong Kong, Korea and Taiwan.

Boeing is by far the area's largest business concern. Boeing has fueled the city's mid-1980s economic boom with employment rising from 57,000 in 1983 to 80,000 in 1986. Boeing provides employment for one out of every ten persons in the Seattle–Tacoma area, and 42 percent of its sales come from government contracts.

Downtown Seattle is in the middle of a construction boom. In addition to a new transit tunnel to link Highway I-90 with downtown, the $136 million Washington State Convention Center is under construction, and thirteen buildings, with a total of 6.6 million square feet of new office space, are being built presently or are in the design stages. Despite the current double-digit office vacancy rates, Seattle is expected to absorb the newly created space as the city continues its steady growth.

Like many growing cities, Seattle shows a trend toward suburbanization. The population of Seattle proper is about half a million and has been declining over the last several years as the population of the suburbs has steadily risen. While Mercer Island retains its insularity as a wealthy community of "quiet streets and expensive homes," Bellevue, once a small suburb of Seattle, is now the state's fourth largest city.

---

## QUALITY OF LIFE

**Weather:** People in Seattle don't have much to talk much about in the area of weather, because it's usually the same—cloudy or rainy, and mild. Because of its proximity to the ocean and to an inland lake, Seattle proper doesn't get much snow; so forget snow boots, but bring galoshes! The city has an average of 160 rainy days per year and annual rainfall of 39 inches. Be prepared for a yearly average of 229 cloudy days, 79 partly cloudy days and only 57 clear days.

**Education:** Seattle's public elementary and secondary school system is divided into thirty-four districts and consists of 481 schools enrolling over 260,000 pupils; the student/teacher ratio in the city's public schools is about 20 to 1. The area is served by 9 public community colleges, with combined enrollment of about 50,000 students, and 10 four-year colleges and universities (9 private, 1 public) enrolling roughly 48,000 students. With the heavy concentration of engineering and technical employment in the city, Seattle has a high proportion of college-educated people and a good availability of training for technical posts. Seattle's respect for education is shown by the fact that it has the fourth highest level of per capita spending for libraries among the top 100 U.S. cities.

**Politics/Government:** Seattle has a mayor-council form of government with a mayor elected directly to a four-year term. The mayor is a strong executive; he does not serve on the city council and can veto council bills. The city council consists of nine members elected at large to overlapping four-year terms; it meets weekly. Seattle politics is fairly independent, as shown by the fact that of the eighty-six largest metro areas it gave the seventh highest percentage of votes for John Anderson in the 1980 presidential election (the remaining votes were split: 47 percent Republican, 40 percent Democratic).

**Transportation:** Although Seattle's motorists face heavy commuter traffic, the city does have excellent mass transit, consisting of streetcars, buses and a ferry line. Amtrak runs four trains a day through Seattle, and the city's Henry M. Jackson Memorial Airport is served by twenty-eight airlines providing over 200 flights daily.

**Health Care:** Health care in Seattle is of high quality and low cost. Area facilities include five teaching hospitals, a medical school and specialized treatment centers for cardiac ailments and cancer.

**Child Care:** Working parents in need of child-care information or referral can call the United Way of King County at 206-447-3751.

**Housing:** The average cost of a house (1,800 square feet, 1/4-acre lot) is $97,000; a two-bedroom, one-bathroom (950 square feet, unfurnished) apartment averages $429 a month.

**Public Safety:** With 557 reported 1986 robberies per 100,000 city residents, Seattle has a higher than average crime rate.

**Cultural Attractions:** By way of sit-down entertainment, Seattle offers opera, symphony and several stage theaters, with the Seattle Symphony Orchestra, Seattle Repertory Theatre and Pacific Ballet among the premier performing groups.

**Sports/Recreation:** Seattle's location in the Great Northwest nets it plenty of the great outdoors. The city sits between a huge marine bay and a long freshwater lake. To the east and west are two towering mountain chains that provide Seattle residents with spectacular scenery. Two national forests in the area are readily accessible, and Mount Rainier (when visible) provides a distinctive spot on the horizon for the region's residents.

Seattle ranks high in availability and quality of recreation. The city's offerings include a zoo, an aquarium, two speedways for auto racing, one thoroughbred track and three professional athletic teams—the Mariners (baseball), the Supersonics (basketball) and the Seahawks (football).

**Taxes:** When the taxman darkens the doorway, Seattle residents have relatively little to fear, with a local tax burden of less than 1.5 percent of average annual household income.

---

## WHERE TO BREAK IN

Boeing is Seattle's largest employer, with 80,000 employees. The other large employers in the area are listed below. For more information, call the Seattle Chamber of Commerce at 206-461-7210.

| Firm/Organization | Product/Service | No. Employees |
|---|---|---|
| Pacific Northwest Bell | telephone utility | 3,300 |
| General Telephone Co. Northwest | telephone utility | 2,200 |
| Fluke John Mfg. Co. (Everett) | measuring instruments | 2,000 |
| Safeco. Corp. | insurance | 2,000 |
| Seafirst Corp. | national bank | 2,000 |
| Wright-Schuchart | holding company | 2,000 |
| Longview Fibre Co. | paperboard mill | 1,600 |
| Tacoma Boatbuilding (Tacoma) | shipbuilding/repairs | 1,540 |
| Alaska Airlines Inc. | air carrier | 1,200 |
| Eldec Corp. (Lynnwood) | electronics | 1,100 |

Seattle is a city of numerous small businesses as well. Nearly 50 percent of them might be considered tiny: Of the 45,885 firms in the area, 22,868 employ only one to four persons, and 76 percent of the total business concerns employ fewer than fifteen persons. The Seattle economy is highly dependent on the aerospace industry, but severe swings are buffered by the energetic entrepreneurial community of small businesses.

---

## SUMMING UP: OPPORTUNITY FOR WHOM?

Seattle today has retained much of its provincial charm in the preservation of Pike Place Market and older neighborhoods with well-appointed wooden houses. A strong hip element that grew up in the 1960s remains but has been eclipsed of late by the city's Yuppie contingent. In May of 1985, Seattle had its first ever "Yuppie Cotillion" with a "BMW" theme (Business, Money and Wealth) to raise money for the March of Dimes.

Hip is far from dead. It's just more respectable these days. Though somewhat isolated, Seattle is ambitiously cosmopolitan and supports a healthy and extensive artists' community to which dealers, critics and patrons are closely tied. From the Stellas and Rauschenbergs in the Seattle–Tacoma Airport to the grand site-generated sculpture project at the National Oceanic and Atmospheric Administration, Seattle residents find there's always something to look at (or bump into). Public support for art in the city is considerable: A new downtown home for the Seattle Art Museum is planned and, as part of Mayor Charles Royer's plan to make Seattle a "kids' city," art programs have been integrated extensively into the public schools. The West these days is more than wild and woolly.

The West is also more than western. It's eastern . . . East Asian, that is. Seattle has the largest Asian and Pacific Islander population in the Northwest, with approximately 7.5 percent of Seattle's residents falling into this category. The majority, however, are white (79.5 percent, 94.5 percent in the suburbs), while blacks (9.5 percent), Hispanics (2.6 percent) and Amerindians (1.3 percent) make up the rest of the population. In addition to the intercultural mix, Seattle women seem well established in the workplace, with 42.6 percent of the labor force consisting of females.

# Tampa–St. Petersburg, Florida

TAMPA–ST. PETERSBURG–CLEARWATER, FLA. MSA POPULATION (7/86): 1,914,300 (20th largest)

POPULATION GROWTH 1980–86: 18.6%

COUNTY: Hillsborough (Tampa), Pinellas (St. Petersburg and Clearwater)

EMPLOYMENT (9/87): 782,400

AVERAGE TEMPERATURE: 72.2°F

YEARLY RAINFALL: 49.38 inches

HUMIDITY: 70% (4th most humid)

COST OF LIVING: 105.2

---

## KEYS TO THE CITY

**Small Business Growth:** birth rate, growth rate, growth index (rank/86): 3.9  3.4  7.3  (15th)

**Average Annual Job Growth (9/84–9/87):** 3.8% (20th/largest 100)

**Keys to Prosperity:** Tourism, high-tech, finance, government (AFB), health care, publishing.

**Key Developments:** Airport, light rail.

**Key Life-Style Trends:** As industry grows relative to tourism and retirement, Tampa–St. Pete becomes trendy like other Florida growth centers, seeing the evolution of more activities for singles and DINKYs (Double Income No Kids Yet) and more attention to households with children.

---

## WHY OPPORTUNITY KNOCKS IN TAMPA–ST. PETERSBURG

The Tampa Bay area's greatest asset is its subtropical climate and miles of sandy gulf beaches. This has perpetuated the region's retirement/resort image. True, 3.2 million sunbathing tourists a year does explain a good deal of the region's growth. But a few miles in from the beach is a business community growing faster than any other in Florida.

Several companies involved in advanced electronics R&D and

350

manufacturing, such as Honeywell, IBM, General Electric and Sperry Microwave, maintain facilities in the area. Other high-tech corporations in the area are Electronics Communications, Critikon, Silor Optics and Concept Incorporated. Clearwater's HSC (Home Shopping Network), a specialty television retailer, is the Tampa Bay area's premier small company; with total 1986 sales of over $160 million, HSC's sales had increased 177-fold in the previous four years.

The fastest growing sector other than tourism in Tampa and St. Petersburg is finance, including insurance and real estate. This is no surprise, since Pinellas County alone has been gaining 16,000 new residents annually for the past six years. With about $21 billion in banking deposits, the Tampa–St. Petersburg metro area (including Clearwater) is gaining prominence as a financial market. Tampa is the ninth largest port in the country, handling about 44 million tons in 1986, with successful satellite industries such as packaging and warehousing. Other major industries are health services, printing and publishing.

But tourism is still the region's life force, with the services and retail sectors accounting for 50 percent of Tampa Bay employment; this steady and relatively resilient employment factor serves as a buffer against the cyclic influences that often batter the more manufacturing-dependent cities. Other anticyclic features of the local economy are a significant level of government (including the MacDill Air Force Base) and educational employment.

---

## QUALITY OF LIFE

**Weather:** Freezing temperatures (32°F and less) are a rarity in the Tampa Bay area, but 90° days abound. The average summer temperature is 82°, and the average winter temperature is 60.4°; the summer months are punctuated with frequent thunderstorms.

**Education:** The Tampa (Hillsborough County) public school system has a total K–12 enrollment of 136,559 pupils. The St. Pete (Pinellas County) public school system enrolls 84,000 pupils. While only 43 percent of Tampa's high school graduates go on to postsecondary education, the figure for St. Pete is 60 percent. Of 114 private schools in Tampa, 72 have some religious affiliation; 109 private and parochial schools in St. Pete have a total enrollment of 24,000 pupils.

The University of South Florida at Tampa enrolls 23,750 students and offers the B.A., B.S., M.A., M.S. and Ph.D. degrees in architecture, arts and literature, business administration, education, engineering, fine arts, medicine, natural sciences, nursing, public health and social sciences. The University of Tampa enrolls 2,000 students and offers curricula in nursing, fine arts, music and business administration. Tampa College offers bachelor's and master's degrees in business administration. Tampa also has two junior colleges, Hillsborough Community College and Florida College. St. Petersburg has seven four-year colleges and universities, one junior college on three campuses throughout Pinellas County, and a law school.

**Politics/Government:** Tampa has a strong mayor-council form of government. The mayor is directly elected to a four-year term, does not serve on the city council and has veto power over council bills. Three of the seven council members are elected at large, the other four according to districts; all serve four-year, nonoverlapping terms, and the council meets weekly. St. Petersburg, by contrast, has a council-manager form of government, with a "weak" mayor.

**Transportation:** While private automobile is the preferred form of transportation in and about the Tampa Bay area, municipal bus service is also available. Spurred by the area's booming population and economic growth in recent years, the Hillsborough County Planning Department is considering a light-rail commuter system, which could be in operation by the late 1990s. Intercity transit is provided by Amtrak, Greyhound and Trailways. Air transportation is conveniently accessible throughout the Tampa Bay area, facilitated by the St. Pete/Clearwater International Airport and the Tampa International Airport, served by twenty-three carriers.

**Health Care:** Health care in Tampa is provided by twenty-one Hillsborough County hospitals and medical centers, with 4,435 hospital beds. Area hospitals offer specialized facilities and care in cancer treatment, psychiatry and physically handicapped child rehabilitation. St. Pete is served by twenty-one Pinellas County hospitals, with over 5,000 beds; medical emergency service departments are maintained by fifteen medical centers.

**Child Care:** Working parents seeking information on the availability of child care should call United Way of Tampa (813-228-8359) or the United Way of St. Petersburg–Pinellas County (813-822-4183).

**Housing:** The average price of a three-bedroom, two-bathroom house is $81,000, while the average monthly rent for a two-bedroom, one-bathroom apartment is $367.

**Public Safety:** In 1986 there were 1,199 reported robberies per 100,000 city residents in Tampa, and 620 per 100,000 in St. Petersburg, placing this metro area among the most "unsafe" in our study.

**Cultural Attractions:** Cultural resources of the Tampa–St. Pete area include the Tampa Museum of Art, which specializes in contemporary American painting and American anthropological exhibits. The Museum of Science and Industry features technological exhibits, and St. Pete's Salvador Dali Museum has the world's largest collection of the Spanish surrealist painter's works. St. Pete's Museum of Fine Art features pre-Columbian and Far Eastern exhibits. Music, dance and dramatic attractions include the Florida Orchestra, with pop and classical repertoire, the Sarasota Opera, the Tampa Ballet, Playmakers (an experimental theater group) and the Tampa Players, a repertory company.

**Sports/Recreation:** Pro sports attractions include the Tampa Bay Buccaneers (football); also in the area are college basketball and spring training/minor-league baseball. Participant sports include golf, tennis and almost any type of water activity.

**Taxes:** Residential property in Tampa is taxed at a rate of between $22.285 and $27.285 for each $1,000 of assessed value.

---

## WHERE TO BREAK IN

For individuals interested in relocating to the Tampa–St. Petersburg area, we include a listing of major area employers. For more information, contact the Tampa Chamber of Commerce at 813-228-7777 or St. Pete's Downtown Improvement Corporation at 813-821-5166.

| Firm/Organization | Product/Service | No. Employees |
|---|---|---|
| Hillsborough County School Board | education | 14,800 |
| MacDill Air Force Base | military | 8,640 |
| Hillsborough County | government | 6,720 |

| Firm/Organization | Product/Service | No. Employees |
|---|---|---|
| General Telephone Company | telephone utility | 5,420 |
| University of Southern Florida | education | 4,310 |
| Tampa International Airport | transportation services | 4,170 |
| City of Tampa | government | 4,160 |
| Tampa/Electric Company | electric power utility | 3,550 |
| U.S. Postal Service Tampa Division | mail service | 3,540 |
| Tampa General Hospital | general medical & surgical hospital | 3,500 |
| Saint Joseph's Hospital | health care | 2,500 |
| Maas Brothers | retail trade | 2,200 |
| NCNB National Bank | banking | 1,750 |
| First Florida Bank | banking | 1,700 |
| IBM Corporation | computers | 1,600 |

## SUMMING UP: OPPORTUNITY FOR WHOM?

Located on Florida's "Sun Coast" on the Gulf of Mexico, Tampa Bay is one of the best protected harbors in the world. St. Petersburg, which lies on a peninsula that encloses Tampa Bay on the north and west, has a total area of 56.8 square miles and a population of 240,863; St. Pete's population density is 4,240 persons per square mile. Eastward across the bay lies the city of Tampa, larger than St. Petersburg in both area and population, but overall less densely populated—covering 84.4 square miles and sheltering 276,444 residents, Tampa has a density of 3,275 persons per square mile. The Tampa–St. Pete area's suburban population of 1,079,610 showed a 21.4 percent growth rate between 1976 and 1980.

Currently 5.9 percent unemployed, the combined work force of the Tampa–St. Petersburg metro area (Hillsborough and Pinellas counties) is 772,448. The area's major industries are tourism, finance, insurance, real estate and land development, electronics manufacturing, health services, printing and publishing. The

area's labor force is distributed as follows among the basic industrial groupings:

| Industry | Share of Work Force (in %) |
| --- | --- |
| Services/tourism | 30.1 |
| Retail trade | 18.9 |
| Manufacturing | 11.5 |
| Wholesale trade | 8.4 |
| Construction | 7.9 |
| Transportation, communication and utilities | 7.7 |
| Finance, insurance and real estate | 7.3 |
| Government | 5.0 |
| Agriculture | 3.2 |

The continued growth of the Tampa Bay economy should generate employment opportunities for engineers, bankers, clerical personnel, health-care professionals and educators.

# Tucson, Arizona

MSA POPULATION (7/86): 602,400 (62nd largest)
POPULATION GROWTH 1980–86: 13.4%
COUNTY: Pima
EMPLOYMENT (9/87): 242,100
AVERAGE TEMPERATURE: 67.8°F
YEARLY RAINFALL: 11.05 inches
HUMIDITY: 25% (41st most humid)
COST OF LIVING: 103.2

---

## KEYS TO THE CITY

**Small Business Growth:** birth rate, growth rate, growth index (rank/86): 4.3  3.7  8  (11th)

**Average Annual Job Growth (9/84–9/87):** 4.1% (15th/largest 100)

**Keys to Prosperity:** High-tech manufacturing, relatively low wages, defense (one air force base, one army base).

**Key Developments:** Tucson Economic Development Corporation is very active.

**Key Life-Style Trends:** As in other rapidly growing Sunbelt cities, the retirees are being joined by many new, younger people seeking work. Tucson provides ample leisure activities, but the large number of mobile homes (12 percent of all homes) and the large number of fast-food franchises (Taco Bell, etc.) is making Tucson more and more like "the road to the airport" all over. A pity.

---

## WHY OPPORTUNITY KNOCKS IN TUCSON

The second most populous and job-providing city in Arizona is the city of Tucson, in Pima County. Tucson residents hold 10 percent of all jobs and earn 20 percent of total personal income generated in the state. Tucson is located in the southeastern part of the state at an elevation of 2,390 feet. It has the Rincon Mountains to the east, the Tucson Mountains to the west and the Sierrita

Mountains to the south. Tucson was established by the Spanish in 1775, and was incorporated as a city in 1877.

This 600,000-person, 350-square-mile desert metro area was identified by Wharton Econometrics in 1985 as the sixth fastest growing U.S. employment center. Wharton Econometrics forecasted an average employment growth rate of 3.4 percent for the Tucson area. The Tucson Realty and Trust Company ranked Tucson fourth in the nation for land appreciation for the period 1984 to 1986. The city has grown rapidly over the last fifteen years. *The National Real Estate Investor* says that in 1982, when the Howard Hughes estate was opened, was when development really started growing rapidly. From 1970 to 1985, total wage and salary workers in Pima County grew by an average of 5.4 percent. Employment in the manufacturing sector showed an even more impressive growth rate of 8.7 percent, for a fifteen-year cumulative increase of 250 percent during a period when Pima County's population grew by 83.4 percent. Tucson has proved itself to be a worthy component of the southwestern Sunbelt, called the fastest growing region in the nation by the U.S. Department of Commerce.

According to a study conducted by the Federal Home Loan Bank of San Francisco, the region will see economic expansion and population growth far in excess of national trends at least until 1992. Tucson is expected to continue growing more rapidly than most other U.S. areas—so long as U.S. growth continues, a caveat with global implications.

The success of Tucson's high-tech manufacturing industry depends on the nation's ability to be competitive in world markets. Arizona is currently an important center for high-tech manufacturing, and will continue to be so while its labor is still relatively inexpensive. High-tech employment accounts for over 63 percent of all manufacturing in Tucson, and Tucson accounts for over 20 percent of Arizona's total high-tech employment. This sector of the industry became important when IBM decided to locate a plant in Tucson, since IBM's presence played a major role in bringing new companies to the area.

California's Silicon Valley is still the nursery for high-tech investment, and it originally depended on nearby university staff for research and development; now, as the computer firms become larger and better capitalized, they have research budgets and unexcelled facilities of their own. Silicon Valley's problems with costs point to good high-tech growth potential in low-wage, low-housing-cost Tucson.

Tucson has a sufficiently large urban area to offer attractive amenities and services to relocating executives and professionals. Both the University of Arizona and Pima Community College provide higher education opportunities and are aware of and responsive to the needs of high-tech employers. More people seem to be familiar with the high-tech environment, and trends show that this kind of worker can be easily attracted to Tucson.

An important amenity is the fact that Tucson is currently generating approximately 97 percent of its own electricity. Uninterrupted power is a must for high-tech manufacturing and development.

The Tucson Economic Development Corporation is an agency that aggressively searches for new business. Along with other organizations, it has made it possible for many companies to obtain financing to relocate to Tucson, thereby avoiding the astronomical housing costs and higher labor costs of California. Some may want to take full advantage of Tucson's proximity to Mexico for even lower labor costs at the border. These attractions have helped Tucson increase its labor force 57 percent over the last twelve years.

Tucson now has forty-eight major industrial parks, up from thirty-three in 1985. This major increase in industrial park construction has been matched by an equally large increase in the construction of major office buildings, from twenty in 1984 to thirty-two in 1986. The biggest of the thirty-two, the Great Western Bank Building, is soon to be matched by the equally large United Bank Tower.

This office construction has been matched by new facilities for meetings and conventions. In 1985, Tucson resorts reserved 329 meetings. Business people came to enjoy a city that receives more sunshine than any other area in the United States, with an annual high temperature of 81°F and an average low of 54°. So many have come, and are expected, that construction of smaller hotels has declined in favor of larger ones. There are currently 185 hotels and motels in the Tucson metro area. There are 270 meeting facilities, the largest of which holds 9,580 people.

Other growth indicators: Taxable retail sales between 1984 and

1986 increased 10.8 percent; postal receipts increased 19.3 percent; school enrollment is up 13.3 percent for the same period. According to the Arizona Department of Commerce, the net assessed valuation in Tucson grew a whopping 21.6 percent.

Retail sales have increased in Pima County through the last decade and represented close to $4 billion in 1986, up from $3.4 billion in 1984. Restaurant and bar sales totaled $354 million in 1984 and have been growing steadily, along with tourism, conventions and building construction.

## QUALITY OF LIFE

**Weather:** Tucson is warm and sunny throughout most of the year. Although there are an average of 139 days with temperatures in the 90s each year, the area's low humidity makes them more comfortable. In addition, temperatures fall after sunset, making summer evenings cool. There are roughly 20 days a year on which the temperature drops to freezing (32°F and less).

**Education:** Pima Community College, the University of Arizona and the University of Phoenix (Tucson office) had a combined undergraduate enrollment of 54,523 in 1986. The University of Arizona offers master's degrees in 122 fields and doctorates in 82. The University of Phoenix (Tucson office) offers master's degrees in 3 fields. Vocational and training facilities are available at Pima Community College, Pima County Private Industrial Council, Adult Vocational Training Project, Tucson Jobs Corps, Tucson Urban League, Jobs for Progress, Center for Employment Training, ABC Technical and Trade School, and the ITT Technical Institute. Tucson has 111 elementary schools, 28 junior high schools, 19 high schools, 27 parochial schools and 103 private schools.

**Politics/Government:** Tucson has a council-manager form of government. The city council consists of seven members, all of them elected at large. Council members serve as mayor in rotation, and lack veto power. Council members are elected to four-year overlapping terms.

**Transportation:** The Tucson area is served by six major highways, but commuter traffic is heavy. Intracity travel is assisted by a good network of municipal buses. For travel to points outside Tucson, the area is served by three major bus lines and Amtrak. Tucson

International Airport is served by sixteen air carriers, offering seventy daily flights.

**Health Care:** Tucson and Pima County are served by seventeen hospitals, with a combined capacity of 2,910 beds. Specialized hospitals or units exist for psychiatry, cancer treatment, cardiac rehabilitation and substance abuse.

**Child Care:** Working parents, no matter where they live or choose to move, will very likely encounter difficulty in locating dependable, high-quality day care. In Tucson, the local chapter of the United Way oversees a home care operation (602-881-8940). Parents specifically interested in day-care centers can contact D.S. Day Care (602-622-4601), a resource and information service.

**Housing:** Of the people in Tucson, 61 percent own their homes (including mobile homes, 12 percent of all homes), while 39 percent rent them. Many of the older population own mobile homes since they are cheaper to acquire and maintain, and they can be moved. Single-family-occupancy homes are 53 percent of the total, apartments and duplexes 26 percent, and townhouses/condominiums are 9 percent. The average cost of a three-bedroom, two-bathroom home is around $76,500; the average rent for a two-bedroom, one-bathroom apartment is $305.

**Public Safety:** With 262 reported 1986 robberies per 100,000 city residents, Tucson is among the cities in our study with the lowest crime rates.

**Cultural Attractions:** Main attractions include the Tucson Museum of Art, the Arizona Opera Company, the Tucson Community Center, San Xavier Mission, Arizona-Sonora Desert Museum, the Tucson Symphony Orchestra, the Arizona Theatre Company, Old Tucson Movie Set, the University Artist Series, Kitt Peak National Observatory, the Arizona Dance Theater and the Southern Arizona Light Opera Company. There are fifteen museums and fourteen libraries.

**Sports/Recreation:** Leisure fans will like the eleven parks, twelve bowling alleys, twenty-one municipal pools, 120 tennis facilities and twenty-eight golf courses. Also, the University of Arizona is a member of the Pacific Athletic Conference 10 as well as the National Collegiate Athletic Association. The Houston Astros baseball club has an AAA farm team—the Tucson Toros—and the

Cleveland Indians baseball club has spring training and playing facilities in Tucson. There is greyhound racing, rodeo sports (La Fiesta de los Vaqueros), a Ladies Professional Golf Association Open and a polo club (the Pima County Polo Club).

**Taxes:** Residential property in Tucson is assessed at 10 percent of market value and taxed at a rate of $13.35 per $100 of valuation.

---

## WHERE TO BREAK IN

For individuals interested in seeking employment in Tucson, we include a list of selected major employers in the area. For more information, contact the Tucson Chamber of Commerce at 602-792-1212.

| Firm/Organization | Product/Service | No. Employees |
|---|---|---|
| Hughes Aircraft | missiles and components | 8,000 |
| IBM | computer products | 5,500 |
| Burr-Brown Corporation | electronics | 1,200 |
| Krieger | air ventilation products | 1,100 |
| National Semiconductor | electronics | 770 |
| Gates Learjet | private jet aircraft | 550 |
| TEC, Inc. | computer displays | 350 |
| Hamilton Test Systems (United Technologies) | computerized test systems | 275 |
| Unitronics (Curtis Electronics) | printed circuit boards | 250 |
| Foster Grant | optical products | 200 |
| Lambda Electronics (Veeco Instruments) | power supplies | 200 |

Within the last five years many manufacturers have opened new plants and offices. The manufacturing industry's employment of 3,200 in 1986 was double what it was in 1976. Other major employers are: the service industry, 24.7 percent; retail/wholesale trade, 22.9 percent; government, 19.4 percent; construction, 9.3 percent; finance, insurance and real estate, 5.4 percent; and transportation, communications and public utilities, 3.9 percent. Davis

Monthan AFB employs 7,703 military and civilian employees. Fort Huachuca employs 11,731.

---

## SUMMING UP: OPPORTUNITY FOR WHOM?

Of metro Tucson's population, 29 percent are nineteen and younger, 28 percent are twenty to thirty-four, 31 percent are thirty-five to sixty-four, and 12 percent are sixty-five and older. This relatively high percentage of over-thirty-fivers reflects the fact that up until a few years back Tucson was a retirement haven. Even with the great influx of career-minded younger people, the older population is still very much a reality and helps to lend stability to the area. Certain zones (the city is divided into ten) have higher percentages of people sixty-five and older and have high median ages. Zone 10 is 48 percent sixty-five and older, and the median age is sixty-four. The zones with the higher median ages tend to have fewer persons per household.

With strong high-tech manufacturing and R&D, a healthy and growing services sector, and a thriving retail market, Tucson should be a good source of employment for health-care professionals, engineers and technicians, accountants, people with office and clerical skills, and educators.

# Washington, D.C.

Washington, D.C.–Md.–Va. MSA Population (7/86): 3,563,000 (10th largest)

Population Growth 1980–86: 9.6%

County: None, independent city

Employment (9/87): 2,048,700

Average Temperature: 53.3°F

Yearly Rainfall: 38.89 inches

Humidity: 59% (28th most humid)

Cost of Living: 132.1

## Keys to the City

**Small Business Growth:** birth rate, growth rate, growth index (rank/86): 4.2 4.4 8.6 (7th)

**Average Annual Job Growth (9/84–9/87):** 3.9% (19th/largest 100)

**Keys to Prosperity:** Federal government, high-tech (biotech, telecommunications, computers, defense), international business, tourism, trade associations.

**Key Developments:** Doubling of downtown office space in 1980s.

**Key Life-Style Trends:** Washington is a very international community and, because of its rapid growth, is young. The suburban areas have blossomed and spread as the central city (with its building restrictions) has seen a growth mostly in office space. More nightlife is shifting to suburban centers.

## Why Opportunity Knocks in Washington, D.C.

Washington, D.C., is a leading postindustrial city, where business is booming. The key to its economic prosperity is simple: As the seat of the federal government, the nation's capital concentrates national and international power. Easy access to the nation's key lawmakers gives a competitive edge to businessmen who wish to influence decisions concerning politics, finance, trade and indus-

363

try. It also means obtaining the most up-to-date information, one step ahead of everyone else in today's fast-paced business world.

Expanding most quickly are today's advanced growth industries, such as biotechnology, telecommunications, information and computer firms, and many service industries. Half of all research and development in the United States begins in Washington, D.C. High-tech is big business because the federal government is the biggest consumer of technology, equipment and services in the world. About 2,000 high-tech firms in the area employ 10 percent of the region's work force, including 107,000 engineers and scientists, 20,000 computer programmers and systems analysts, and 25,000 health technicians.

Eighty-five of the nation's top electronics firms have pinpointed the Washington–Baltimore area as the place to locate major operations, regional headquarters, entire divisions or subsidiaries. This region of the country is the most valuable computer market in the country, with an average value per site of $2.8 million. High-tech firms enjoy the advantages of being near research facilities such as the Institute of Defense Analyses in Prince George's County, the Aerospace Software Consortium in Northern Virginia and the Department of Defense. The Washington–Baltimore area is also a major communications center, with 225 domestic and international communications organizations, such as INTELSAT. These companies enjoy the benefits of having a close relationship with the Federal Communications Commission.

One of the most rapidly expanding industries is biotechnology, which is growing at the rate of 20 to 25 percent a year. By the year 2000, Washington is expected to become a $50 billion biotechnology center. Fifty-six of the nation's biotech firms, constituting one-quarter of the industry, are located in the metro area. An additional 220 local firms provide specialized supplies and services to this industry. The National Institute of Health, a preeminent research center for biology, provides information and financial assistance to these firms. The NIH provided $300 million worth of funds to biomedical research in 1984 alone.

Defense contracting is also a field that promises continued growth. From 1970 to 1985, contract awards climbed from $16 billion to $133 billion.

The District of Columbia is headquarters for the world's most influential financial institutions: the International Monetary Fund, the World Bank, the Inter-American Development Bank, the Export-Import Bank, the Securities and Exchange Commission, the Federal Reserve Board, the State Department and the Department of Commerce. These institutions maintain significant foreign exchange operations and correspondent services. They also handle large international lending and commercial transactions.

As a world city, Washington is the place to be if you're involved with international business. Of the largest international companies, over three-quarters have offices in the D.C. area. Of the largest U.S. multinational firms, 85 percent are in the city, and almost 75 percent of top foreign businesses investing in the United States own firms in D.C. or have investments in area corporations. These companies need to maintain a position at America's seat of power to stay on top.

Although D.C.'s area is small, less than seventy square miles, it boasts a $4 billion commercial market. The city is working hard to attract businesses by advertising its balanced budget, high bond ratings, highly educated labor force, resources, key location, prestige and probusiness attitude. Unlike other U.S. cities, Washington is free from state or county interference, which means that businesses need only one set of licenses and one set of permits.

In terms of market strength, greater Washington leads the nation with a median effective income of $36,002 per household and is the sixth largest market in the United States. The area's population of 3.4 million is also expected to rise by an additional 20 percent by 1990. In 1984, total retail sales amounted to $23 billion. Retail sales per household exceeded New York City's by $6,000 annually.

Washington's second largest industry is tourism. In 1984, 17.2 million domestic and international visitors spent more than $1 billion there. Between 1982 and 1985, the Washington region had a 25 percent increase in the number of hotel rooms. The nation's capital attracts tourists, conventioneers and business travelers.

The growth of construction and commercial real estate in D.C. reflects the city's economic prosperity. Dozens of commercial and multiuse buildings are going up in a center-city renaissance, adding almost 10 million square feet of office space during the last two years. Total office space in the city between 1980 and 1987 grew to more than 155 million square feet.

## QUALITY OF LIFE

**Weather:** With no 0°F days, about two months of freezing days and one month's worth of days in the 90s each year, D.C. has a mild winter and a livable summer; spring and autumn are said to be the climate's best assets.

**Education:** Washington prides itself on its exceptional academic resources. The area has the most highly skilled labor force in the country, with 28 percent of the adult population over twenty-five having completed at least four years of college. Eighty percent of all residents have completed high school.

D.C. ranks third nationally in investment per pupil, and the nearby Virginia communities of Falls Church and Alexandria's expenditure, respectively, of $5,090 and $4,794 per pupil is well above the national average of $3,429. D.C. public schools were the first in the country to make computer literacy a requirement for high school graduation. High school students in Washington participate in career internship programs in engineering, electronics, hotel management, computer science, health care, performing arts, communications and finance to prepare for future jobs.

The number of jobs requiring professional skills in D.C. increased by 29 percent during the 1970s. By 1980, 37 percent of the resident work force was highly skilled. The District of Columbia's nineteen universities and colleges have joint programs with industry and government in medicine, engineering, computers and other sciences. To meet the demands of the flourishing high-tech fields, 8,000 area college students annually graduate with degrees in either the sciences or engineering. Washington has twice as many Ph.D.s as Boston or New York City, and two and a half times as many as San Francisco. Major university research centers include Georgetown, George Washington and Howard universities. Within one hour's drive are sixty colleges and universities and more than 250 trade and technical schools. The District of Columbia's colleges and universities contribute $1.6 billion to the local economy each year. There are nearly 100,000 college students in D.C. Many decide to settle in the city after graduation.

**Neighborhoods:** The District of Columbia itself has a population of about 630,000, but Greater Washington is over twice that size, at 1.5 million. Much of the city's professional work force commutes from a sixteen-county area ranging down from southern Maryland through northern Virginia. The city itself offers a variety of neighborhood options, from the small, well-tended, restored homes of Georgetown, to the downtown apartment buildings and the new townhouse and apartment developments of southwest Washington, to the sprawling array of homes up from Cleveland Heights through upper Northwest Washington to Chevy Chase Circle. Many people employed in the District opt out of the congested city proper in favor of the rapidly growing cities of Alexandria, Fairfax, Falls Church, Manassas and Manassas Park in the Virginia counties of Arlington, Fairfax, Loudon or Prince William. Or they hike out in the other direction, to Bethesda, Chevy Chase, Columbia, Reston, Silver Spring or other communities in Maryland's Charles, Frederick, Montgomery or Prince George's counties (some even commute from Baltimore). The Washington area subway system is making commuting farther out much easier, whether for carless residents in the communities along the route, or farther-out commuters who drive as far as the subway and ride in the rest of the way.

**Politics/Government:** Once entirely dependent on congress for funding, the District of Columbia adopted a home rule charter in 1975, which gives citizens a much greater say in their future. The city has a strong-mayor system of government, in which the mayor is elected directly. The city council has thirteen members, five elected at large and the remaining eight elected by ward.

Three administrators work directly below the mayor and serve at his pleasure. They are the deputy mayor for operations (or city administrator); the deputy mayor for economic development, in charge of planning, the department of public housing, community development, business development and consumer affairs; and the deputy mayor for finance, in charge of the budget, the comptroller's office and revenue collection.

The government of the District of Columbia is probably the most comprehensive city government in the nation, incorporating all the normal functions of city, county and state governments: education, corrections, university budgets, police, fire control, and professional, occupational and motor vehicle licensing.

But this "full-service government" has a number of controversies facing it, such as prison overcrowding, homelessness (a homeless initiative was recently on the city ballot), AIDS and public safety issues, most recently stemming from drug-related violent crimes.

**Transportation:** Washington, D.C., is centrally located on the eastern seaboard, linking the industrial Northeast with the expanding Sunbelt. Transportation in the nation's capital is convenient and efficient. The city has three major airports—Washington National, Baltimore–Washington International and Washington Dulles International. These airports are modern, efficient and clean. They cater to 25 million passengers a year.

The Metrorail rapid transit system is among the most efficient and convenient in the world. With over sixty stations, it serves major parts of suburban Maryland, northern Virginia and the District of Columbia. In addition, there are more than 2,000 Metrobuses that make almost 800,000 trips a day.

**Health Care:** Washingtonians are cared for in some of the nation's finest medical and research facilities. There are fifty-four hospitals and four major medical schools. These include George Washington University, Georgetown University, Howard University and the University of Maryland. In addition, the National Institutes of Health, Bethesda Naval Hospital and Walter Reed Army Hospital pioneer much of today's advanced medical research.

**Child Care:** Call United Planning Organization National Child Care Program at 202-397-3800.

**Housing:** A three-bedroom, two-bathroom house in the Greater Washington area averages $185,000; the average rent for a one-bedroom apartment ranges between $350 and $550.

**Public Safety:** With 754 reported 1986 robberies per 100,000 residents, Washington has a fairly high crime rate.

**Cultural Attractions:** To enhance life in Washington is a rich store of cultural attractions. The Smithsonian Institution boasts thirteen museums and galleries, including the Hirschhorn Museum, the Sculpture Garden, the National Gallery of Art, the Museum of Natural History, and the Air and Space Museum. The Smithsonian also features the National Zoo, whose most famous inhabitants are America's cherished pandas, Ling Ling and Hsing Hsing, gifts from China. Private museums include the Corcoran Gallery of Art, the Phillips Collection and more than 200 art galleries.

The Kennedy Center for the Performing Arts is the home of the acclaimed National Symphony Orchestra, the Washington Opera, the new American National Theatre Company and the American Film Institute.

Theater is well represented by the National Theatre, the country's oldest; Arena Stage; the Folger Shakespeare Theatre, the Warner Theatre, Ford's Theatre and Lisner Auditorium, home of the Washington Ballet.

**Sports/Recreation:** Washingtonians are great sports enthusiasts and have every right to be proud of their teams. The Redskins won the Superbowl in 1983 and 1988 and recently captured two National Football League trophies. The Bullets (basketball) have brought home the NBA championship and three division titles. The Capitals (hockey) won four major awards in the 1984 National Hockey League ceremonies, including Coach of the Year. And the city has two powerhouse college basketball teams: the Georgetown University Hoyas, who were the 1984 national champions and 1985 runners-up, and the University of the District of Columbia Firebirds, who won the NCAA division championship in 1982.

**Taxes:** Residential property is assessed at full market value and taxed at a rate of $2.03 for each $100. The sales and use tax is 6 percent.

---

## WHERE TO BREAK IN

The District of Columbia has many organizations eager to help newcomers in the area. The following is a list to help you get started:

| | |
|---|---|
| Greater Washington Board of Trade | 202-857-5950 |
| Mayor Marion Barry, Jr. | 202-727-6319 |
| Deputy Mayor for Economic Development Curtis R. McClinton, Jr. | 202-727-6600 |
| One-stop center for business permits and licenses | 202-727-7089 |
| Employment Services—tax credits, job training, employment and referrals | 202-639-1000 |
| District of Columbia government procurement opportunities | 202-727-0171 |
| Minority Business Opportunity | 202-727-3817 |
| D.C. Public Schools Corporate Initiative Program | 202-724-4015 |

Washington Convention Center                          202-789-1600

Washington Convention and Visitors Association—       202-789-7000
  convention and meeting planning information

---

## SUMMING UP: OPPORTUNITY FOR WHOM?

The Washington area is predominantly a city of highly educated white-collar workers, although the central city has a large black population with its share of poverty. The area's greatest resource is its labor force of educated, young, adaptable talent. It boasts the highest concentration of scientists, engineers, economists, computer specialists, writers, management analysts, mathematicians and statisticians. D.C. is perhaps the best city in the country for professional women. A higher percentage of women, 51.5 percent, is employed in D.C. than in any other U.S. city. According to the U.S. Census Bureau, women hold almost half of the managerial and professional positions in the city.

The District of Columbia is also particularly favorable for black professionals. The city has always had a large, stable black community, currently totaling 70 percent of D.C.'s 627,400 residents. The reason for that stability lies in the fact that Washington, beneath the strata of national and international government, is a city run by blacks. Marion Barry, the city's mayor, who is black, is now serving his third term. He continues to be the major impetus driving minority programs. For example, he has strictly enforced the Sheltered Market Program, which requires District government agencies to give 35 percent of the dollar volume of their contracts to minority firms. In 1985, 529 minority contractors received $170 million in city contracts for goods. As a black lawyer said, "It's true that in Washington, where blacks have so much responsibility managing the city's affairs, there is a conscious effort to include black attorneys and other black professionals in business opportunities with the city."

According to a study published in 1985 by the District of Columbia Department of Employment Services, total employment is projected to grow by 2.3 percent annually in the Washington, D.C., MSA from 1980 to 1990, totaling 1,964,000 by 1990. The area's growth leader will be the service industry, expected to grow 4 percent annually. Within the services industry, hotels and other lodging places are projected to grow 5.5 percent. The area's largest industry, the government sector, will grow only by .3 percent annually. And the area's largest single employer, the federal government, will grow by only .1 percent annually.

By 1990, professional and technical workers will likely replace clerical workers as the area's largest occupational group. The slowest growing occupational group will likely be laborers. The single largest occupation is expected to be secretaries (102,180), followed by janitors (74,490), then general office clerks (56,220). The majority of these occupations require a twelfth-grade education. Over the decade of the 1980s, 97,720 job openings are expected to be created annually in the metro area. Professionals and technical workers will probably account for 27.2 percent (26,580) of all job openings. Laborers are expected to create the fewest job openings, 2,920 annually between 1980 and 1990.

Perhaps the most popular profession in Washington is law. Since 1979, Washington's legal sector has grown 38 percent, and there are law firms and lawyers to represent every interest, from corporate to environmental law.

Unlike other urban centers, D.C. is not a concrete jungle. The reason is that the Capitol is and will remain by law the city's tallest building. One-fourth of D.C.'s land is parks. The city's physical beauty, combined with a crime rate down 21 percent from 1981 to 1986, not to mention a rich store of cultural attractions, puts D.C. high on the scale of livability.

# West Palm Beach, Florida

MSA Population: 755,600 (51st largest)
Population Growth 1980–86: 31%
County: Palm Beach
Employment (9/87): 319,600
Average Temperature: 74.6°F
Yearly Rainfall: 69.79 inches
Humidity: 70% (4th most humid)
Cost of Living: 108

## Keys to the City

**Small Business Growth:** birth rate, growth rate, growth index (rank/86): 3.8  2.8  6.6  (33rd)

**Average Annual Job Growth (9/84–9/87):** 6.3% (3rd/largest 100)

**Keys to Prosperity:** Tourism, agriculture, high-tech (IBM, RCA, etc.), health care.

**Key Developments:** Airport expansion, growth of Florida Atlantic University, plans for R&D park near F.A.U., a new Zenith radio plant.

**Key Life-Style Trends:** High-tech is attracting more younger people, especially to the southern part of the metro area, around Boca Raton. Services to the elderly (law, medicine) are profitable and are protected by various professional devices to make entry more difficult.

## Why Opportunity Knocks in the Palm Beaches

A perusal of *New York Times* society wedding announcements will reveal that many of the brides' and grooms' parents have two addresses: Park Avenue/Central Park West and Palm Beach. This is the land of Jaguars and Mercedes, glitzy malls and posh galleries, luxury condos and stately seaside Spanish Colonial mansions. In short, greater West Palm Beach—Palm Beach County including Boca Raton and Delray Beach—is Florida's Gold Coast.

With miles of pretty beaches (available only to those who have purchased access: renters, owners and hotel guests), the county traditionally rings up a healthy volume of tourist revenue, to the tune of $1 billion annually. Agriculture is also still a major component of the area's economy, with the main cash crop being sugarcane. Fruit, vegetable, dairy and beef production also contribute their share to the highest dollar values for agricultural output of any area outside California. Recently, Palm Beach County has been trading in its Gold Coast reputation for "Computer Coast" and "Silicon-Sea." The coming out of high-tech to the Palm Beaches is represented by the significant presences of corporations such as IBM, Gould, Rodime, RCA, Motorola, Mitel, Burroughs, Siemans, United Technologies, Pratt & Whitney and Solitron, all of which have either regional headquarters or major facilities in the county.

In order to solidify its high-tech, light manufacturing growth, the county is planning a research-and-development park adjacent to the campus of its Florida Atlantic University, so area companies will be able to draw on faculty, students and facilities. Gould, Inc., has been instrumental, along with the county, in getting the 501-acre Florida Technoplex research park off the ground.

The combination of the county's probusiness attitude and natural amenities of beach and climate has proved nearly irresistible to corporations anxious to locate major facilities in an area where qualified and valuable employees will settle down. Efforts have paid off; the county's population has grown by 2,000 per month in the period from 1984 to 1987. Other factors attractive to business are the heavy concentration of highways (five in all), a $157 million expansion project at Palm Beach International Airport and railroad freight capabilities.

## QUALITY OF LIFE

**Weather:** What they will tell you is that South Florida's ample rainfall supports a wide variety of attractive subtropical plant life; what they won't tell you is that most of that rain comes in the form of thundershowers during the summer months. But with many sunny days and warm breezes, Palm Beach County, with an average winter temperature of 69.2°F and an average summer temperature of 82.2°, has a fairly pleasant climate.

**Education:** The Palm Beach County School Board enrolls a total of 80,642 pupils at its ninety-three elementary school, middle school and senior high school facilities. The area is served by seventy-five private and parochial schools, with a combined enrollment of 17,597 pupils. Of the area's high school graduates, 70 percent enter postsecondary educational institutions. There are five colleges and junior colleges within a thirty-mile radius of West Palm Beach, including Florida Atlantic University, Palm Beach Junior College, Palm Beach Atlantic College, the College of Boca Raton and Northwood Institute. Curricula in business, engineering, medicine, arts and sciences are offered.

**Politics/Government:** West Palm Beach has a council-manager form of government. Council members are elected at large to two-year overlapping terms. The five-member council meets weekly. It elects a mayor from among its members, and the mayor serves for one year. The mayor lacks veto power over council actions. West Palm serves as the seat of Palm Beach County.

**Transportation:** Palm Beach County has municipal bus service, but most mobile people own a car—all parts of the county are within thirty miles of the area's central and fastest artery, Interstate 95, which has heavy rush-hour commuter traffic. The more scenic and slower artery is coastal AIA. The area is served by Amtrak, which offers four departures daily, as well as Greyhound and Trailways. Palm Beach International Airport is served by twenty-two airlines offering 104 flights a day.

**Health Care:** The county's health-care facilities include eighteen hospitals, with a combined total of 3,500 beds, offering a full selection of surgical and clinical services. Not surprisingly, care for the elderly is widely available; twenty-two nursing homes supply 2,600 beds.

**Child Care:** Working parents in need of child-care options and solutions should call United Way of Palm Beach County at 305-863-1772.

**Housing:** The average cost in West Palm Beach of a new, 1,800-square-foot house on a quarter acre of property is $120,053; the average rent for a two-bedroom, one-bathroom apartment (excluding utilities, except water) is $465.

**Public Safety:** With 1,475 reported 1986 robberies per 100,000 city residents, West Palm Beach has the third highest rate of the forty-two metros, exceeded only by Las Vegas and Detroit.

**Cultural Attractions:** Palm Beach County has a number of museums, including the Morikami Museum, which features Japanese cultural exhibits, bonsai gardens and a 150-acre park. The Norton Gallery of Art specializes in French Impressionist, American and Chinese painting, and the Boca Raton Museum of Art exhibits traveling collections and local professional work. The South Florida Science Museum incorporates a planetarium, an aquarium and an observatory. Musical, dance and dramatic attractions include the Palm Beach Opera, Ballet Florida, the Florida Repertory Theater, the Caldwell Theater Company and the Royal Poinciana Playhouse. The county also has eighteen public libraries, numerous parks and public beaches and over 100 golf courses. The most popular tourist attraction is the Flagler Museum.

**Sports/Recreation:** Baseball fans have access to several minor-league pro teams; participants will enjoy the county's golf and tennis facilities and the opportunity to engage in almost every water sport, including surfing.

**Taxes:** Florida has no state income tax, and Palm Beach County's property, school and utility taxes are fairly low (not very many children in school); the state sales tax is 5 percent. Living costs, while some of the highest in the state, are reasonable by national standards.

---

## WHERE TO BREAK IN

For persons interested in moving to Palm Beach County, we provide a listing of the area's major employers. For more information, contact the West Palm Beach Chamber of Commerce at 305-833-3711.

| Firm/Organization | Product/Service | No. Employees |
|---|---|---|
| Palm Beach County School Board | education | 11,000 |
| IBM Corp. | computers | 8,300 |
| Pratt & Whitney | aircraft engines | 8,000 |

| Firm/Organization | Product/Service | No. Employees |
|---|---|---|
| State of Florida | government | 5,800 |
| Palm Beach County | government | 3,500 |
| Sugar Cane Growers | agricultural union | 2,900 |
| Florida Power and Light | electric utility | 2,700 |
| Motorola | mobile two-way radio equipment | 1,250 |
| Palm Beach Newspapers | printing/publishing | 1,000 |

## SUMMING UP: OPPORTUNITY FOR WHOM?

Located in southeast Florida, Palm Beach County covers 2,200 square miles and has a population of 752,115. The population of the entire metro area, which includes several surrounding counties, is 3,009,292. The population of West Palm Beach, Delray Beach and Boca Raton is 166,612; the county seat is at West Palm Beach. While there are thirty-seven municipalities in the county, most people choose to live in incorporated cities, which collectively account for 65 percent of the county's population.

The Palm Beaches' labor force of 339,845 is currently 6.3 percent unemployed. In spite of a "wrinkle city" retiree reputation, the median age of the county is not all that high. The number of people employed in the Palm Beaches rose by 70 percent between 1970 and 1980, and over a third of newcomers have been between the ages of eighteen and forty-five. Not everyone in the county is rich, either, although the area's per capita income is $18,900—40 percent higher than the statewide figure. In addition to tourism, agriculture and high-tech manufacturing, the county's major industries are health care, education, finance, land development and retail trade. The area's continued growth should generate employment opportunities for engineers, computer programmers, educators, health professionals and individuals with office expertise.

# 8

## A Note on Smaller Cities of Opportunity

It's easier to grow when you're little than when you're big. The prizes for most rapid growth tend to go to smaller cities rather than big ones. On the other hand, smaller cities lack certain amenities. They aren't for everyone. It may help to look at different types of smaller cities.

Leaving aside communities that are too small to deserve the name "city," the three main types of smaller cities in the United States are the exurban satellite, the company town and the regional center.

### The Exurban Satellite

The exurban satellite is typically a half hour or more by car or train from a major city, and may be within the city's metro area. An example is Stamford, Connecticut. The satellite is generally on the edge of commutability, although some people in the area may commute and others may visit the city frequently. Companies in the satellite city offer the potential of "reverse commuting"—living in the major central city and working in the smaller community.

Satellite cities seem to offer the best of both worlds—a small-town feeling and lower taxes in the smaller community, yet with access to the big city's cultural and specialized shopping facilities and commercial services. They offer the opportunity to stay in touch with the best of the city while avoiding its worst problems. As one disgruntled New Yorker put it: "They have their cake and eat our lunch, too."

Satellite cities can be an ideal solution to the urban dilemma. But the danger of satellite cities is that they will never fully enjoy their theoretical potential, because they will quickly be overrun with the same kinds of problems plaguing the larger cities: (1) traffic congestion; (2) need for new infrastructure to support more people (the building of new roads only worsens the congestion while the roads are under construction); (3) increased housing costs; and (4) either a shortage of inexpensive labor or the problem of coping with pockets of poverty in the area. New York City is everywhere. (Stamford office space, for example, is seriously over-built.)

The strongest protection against the dangers of satellite cities resides in the existence of what is coming to be called a healthy "civic infrastructure"—a community beyond that local govern-ment itself that cares about the quality of life and is prepared to spend the volunteer time and philanthropic money required to make a community work for everyone. Alas, satellite cities are too often the brainchildren of developers, and citizens bestir them-selves only in response to crises, after much damage has been done.

## Company Towns

The archetype of the benevolent company town is Hershey, Penn-sylvania, dominated by the chocolate factory. At one point, Procter & Gamble played that role in Cincinnati.

By extension, small state capitals are company towns—Olym-pia, Washington, for example. Albany and Sacramento are larger versions.

Yet another kind of company town is the university town. The problem is that universities are so much a magnet for certain types of businesses these days that university towns have to strug-gle to maintain their scale. Look at Princeton, New Jersey.

It's a strong team when a university town is also a state capital. This is a frequent occurrence. Look at Austin, Albany, Columbus

(Ohio), Lansing, Lexington, Madison. It's a powerful combination in the high-tech era, especially when the university has a medical center—as in Columbia, South Carolina.

## Regional Rural Centers

The other major type of smaller city is the regional rural center. A major metropolis such as Kansas City doesn't qualify because it is too big, but all over America exist smaller versions of Kansas City—the county seat, home of the county fair, the place where farmers bring their products to sell and visit to stock up on things they can't buy at their local general store.

The regional center has the down-to-earth feeling of a frontier town, taking its character from the type of industry it serves— wheat farming, fruit growing, cattle or sheep rearing, oil drilling, mining and so forth.

Trouble is, from an opportunity perspective, agriculture has not been a growth industry. Some farming communities have been hard hit in recent years, with real estate values suffering seriously.

Instead, growth in regional centers has mostly been coming from aerospace and defense, or from the creation of manufacturing facilities. Banking on job growth in high-tech defense areas should be cautious, given the potential for progress in arms-reduction talks. On the other hand, if a viable manufacturing base has been developed, the regional center has the potential of benefiting a great deal if oil or commodity prices rebound.

## A Sample City: Huntsville, Alabama

As an example of a city that was too small to make our minimum population size for this book, but which has been growing very rapidly, in large part with defense contract business, we offer Huntsville, Alabama, which has the fastest growing collection of small businesses among the smaller communities.

# Huntsville, Alabama

MSA POPULATION (7/86): 233,700 (not ranked)
POPULATION GROWTH 1980–86: 18.6%
COUNTY: Madison
EMPLOYMENT (9/87): 127,000
AVERAGE TEMPERATURE: 60.8°F
YEARLY RAINFALL: 52 inches
HUMIDITY: 63% (16th most humid)
COST OF LIVING: 98

## KEYS TO THE CITY

Huntsville's economy has long been linked to space and military contracts. However, it has a diversity of other businesses that should protect it somewhat from the consequences of possible major defense cuts.

## WHY OPPORTUNITY KNOCKS IN HUNTSVILLE

Huntsville is located in Madison County, Alabama, and has a population of 159,381, up significantly from the 1980 figure of 143,000. Madison County has a population of 223,424, and the outlying Huntsville area has about half a million residents.

Although our emphasis has been on larger metro areas, we include the small city of Huntsville because of its impressive growth record, its outstanding employment opportunities and the strong civic infrastructure that, since World War II, has shaped a depressed backwater into a center for high-tech research, development and manufacturing.

Huntsville's growth as a center for aerospace research and development began in 1950 with the federal government's election of the city as the base for Wernher von Braun and his companion rocketry scientists. The "Space Race" was in full swing, and Huntsville was in an ideal position to benefit from the new and unfamiliar technology that is so commonplace today. Since the 1950s, Huntsville has made contributions to every major U.S. space effort, from the Atlas through the Saturn rockets and, most recently, the Space Shuttle. As a result, the city's Cummings Research Park has grown both in size and prominence, gaining several significant new tenants in the last few years. The recent Challenger Space Shuttle disaster, which has embarrassed and frustrated NASA for nearly two years, was, for obvious reasons, a strong blow to Huntsville's economy. But it was in no way a death blow, since the shuttle program is slated to resume shortly, and because of other government aerospace programs that are patrons to the city's space- and rocket-oriented industries.

Still, it would be incorrect to suggest that Huntsville's economy, even its manufacturing sector, isn't diversified: The fastest growing components of the city's high-tech economy are in the manufacture of consumer products. Representatives of this new phase are Laser-Video, Inc., a manufacturer of compact discs, and Chrysler Corporation Electronics Division, which is constructing a facility at the Huntsville–Madison County airport/industrial park, known as the Jetplex. Gold Star of America, a subsidiary of the Korean electronics firm, is planning a VCR-manufacturing plant in Huntsville, and Intergraph Corp. has commenced construction of a new computer-manufacturing facility in the area. Huntsville is also a center for telecommunications development and manufacturing, and the area's 6,000 engineers are supported by several software concerns, such as McCormack and Dodge.

Huntsville's "the sky is not the limit" motto is intended to drive home a locally perceived prominence in and emphasis on space and defense technology, as well as a strong future in high-tech consumer products manufacturing. It is not surprising, then, that the city's chamber of commerce can celebrate with equal pomp the announcement of a VCR plant and ground-breaking for a facility for Electronic Warfare Association. But this city knows what side its bread is buttered on, and has known for a long time. It was in July of 1941 that the southern city saw the establishment of a chemical weapons manufacturing plant, known as the Huntsville Arsenal, by the U.S. Army. Although the facility was closed in 1949, the military presence returned, as mentioned, with the army's Rocket and Missile Agency in 1950. It is only natural that Huntsville unabashedly hedges its bets with this salvation-turned-boom, as the municipality promotes its piece of the SDI

("Star Wars") action, along with other forward-looking projects such as the proposed orbital space station.

---

## QUALITY OF LIFE

**Weather:** Huntsville's nicest season is the long autumn, whose cool dryness is in stark contrast with the hot, humid summer. The winter is mild, there are few extremely cold days and the temperature dips below 0°F about once a year.

**Education:** Huntsville's public education system, with a total enrollment of 25,017, consists of thirty-eight elementary schools, middle schools and senior high schools; the high school student/teacher ratio is an impressive 9.5 to 1. The Huntsville–Madison County area is also served by fifty private and parochial schools. Although the city has no two-year colleges, it does have two public universities. Alabama Agricultural and Mechanical University, with an enrollment of over 200 students, offers bachelor's and master's degree programs in agricultural and environmental sciences, home economics, arts and sciences, business, education and engineering sciences. The University of Alabama at Huntsville offers clinical and residency training for medical students, as well as bachelor's, master's and doctoral programs in engineering, music, physics, computer science and history.

**Transportation:** With no city buses or passenger rail service, a car is a must in Huntsville. The area is not yet troubled, however, by heavy commuter traffic. The Huntsville–Madison County Airport is served by four airlines, providing a total of thirty-two flights daily. The city is served by both Trailways and Greyhound, respectively providing fourteen and eight departures a day.

**Health Care:** Health care in Huntsville is very low-cost, and facilities include three full-service hospitals and four nursing centers.

**Housing:** The average resale cost of a house in the Huntsville area is $67,875.

**Public Safety:** The incidence of violent and property crime in Huntsville is proportionally below the national average for metro areas. In 1986 Huntsville registered a very low 136 reported robberies per 100,000 city residents.

**Cultural Attractions:** Huntsville's cultural assets are surprisingly good for such a small municipality. The city's von Braun Civic

Center houses the Huntsville Museum of Art and provides performance space for the Huntsville Symphony Orchestra. The Huntsville Concert Association books concerts by prominent bands and soloists, and the Broadway Theater League arranges local performances of plays and musicals by well-known national touring groups. Finally, the Huntsville Little Theater is the city's own professional repertory company.

**Sports/Recreation:** The Huntsville area has one state park, two county parks and twenty-eight city parks, offering facilities for a variety of recreational sports including golf, boating, tennis, basketball, swimming, soccer, softball and fishing.

**Taxes:** The Huntsville area offers low living costs: Low-cost electricity is provided by the Tennessee Valley Authority, Alabama state income taxes are the lowest in the nation, and food and housing costs are well below the national average. Within the city limits of Huntsville, property is taxed at a rate of $5.80 for each $100 of assessed value, and property is assessed at 10 percent of market value.

---

## WHERE TO BREAK IN

In addition to the Army Ballistic Missile Agency, NASA's George C. Marshall Space Flight Center and the Army Strategic Defense Command, which administers the "Star Wars" project, Huntsville has a variety of high-tech employers. For individuals interested in relocating in the Huntsville–Madison County area, we supply a list of selected major employers. For more information, contact the Chamber of Commerce at 205-535-2024.

| Firm/Organization | Product/Service | No. Employees |
|---|---|---|
| Intergraph Corp. | computer systems | 4,100 |
| Chrysler Corp., Electronics Div. | automotive electronics | 3,300 |
| SCI Systems Inc. | computer/electronics assy. | 3,100 |
| Boeing Co. | aerospace R&D engineering | 2,000 |
| Teledyne Brown Engineering | R&D engineering | 2,000 |

| Firm/Organization | Product/Service | No. Employees |
|---|---|---|
| AVCO Electronics Textron | electronic products | 1,200 |
| Dunlop Tire & Rubber Co. | automotive tires | 1,175 |
| Universal Data Systems | data transmission | 775 |
| M. Lowenstein Co. Huntsville Plant | textiles | 675 |
| Morton Thiokol, Inc., Huntsville Div. | solid propellant rocket | 650 |

## SUMMING UP: OPPORTUNITY FOR WHOM?

Huntsville–Madison County has a labor force of 127,000, with a mid-1987 unemployment rate of 7.3 percent, down considerably from the mid-1986 rate of 8.1 percent. The area's major industries are defense-oriented missile and weapons research and development, space-related development and manufacturing, textiles, trade and education. The general vicinity of Huntsville is also heavily agricultural. We provide a partial industrial distribution for the Madison County nonagricultural work force:

| Industry | Share of Work Force (in %) |
|---|---|
| Manufacturing | 26.2 |
| Services | 19.5 |
| Wholesale and retail trade | 18.8 |
| Transportation, communications and utilities | 2.1 |

Huntsville continues to attract new corporate citizens concentrated in the high-tech aerospace, defense, and computer science development and manufacturing industries. The growth of these industries should create employment opportunities for electrical, aeronautics and production engineers, electronic technicians and research technicians. The proliferation of high-tech satellite industries, such as software firms, will increase demand for computer specialists and office personnel.

# 9

## THE BOTTOM LINE:
## WHAT'S RIGHT FOR YOU

This book has attempted to show where economic growth is likely to occur most rapidly in the United States in the coming years. The kinds of things that must be taken into account in making an updated best estimate of a city's prospects are:

1. Behavior of oil prices.
2. Impact of changes in the value of the dollar—the effect of changes in foreign exchange rates on international competition in manufacturing and services (includes tourism).
3. Behavior of the stock market.
4. News about natural disasters (oil spills, fires, earthquakes, floods), water quality, toxic-waste developments.
5. Real estate prices and vacancy rates.

After adjusting for the news, the "hot spots" must be weighed against your own career objectives and the quality of life in the cities you are thinking of moving to.

Are we saying that you should care only about economic and survival issues? Not at all.

Someone might wish to move to a city of opportunity in order to minimize the amount of time he or she spends earning a living, so that more time is left to spend with family or friends, reading, or in leisure activities. The terrible situation is to have to give up leisure activities in order to maintain oneself on the margin of existence in a community that is stagnant.

People who move to areas where the need for people is great are performing a socially important activity. The economy is made more efficient. Areas less in need lose people; areas more in need gain people. This adds to the prosperity of everyone.

We appreciate that it is painful for someone to leave a community where his or her roots are set down. Parents with children have good reasons to wish to avoid changing school systems.

But life has checkpoints where a move is easier—college graduation, before marriage, after marriage but before child-rearing, mid-career within a company, mid-career as part of a career change.

Will this book give you all the answers for choosing a city to move to? No, but it will give some, and it will help you structure the questions to ask yourself.

The final decision should be based on a visit to the cities you are considering moving to. Find out what it will cost to rent or buy a home, what the time and money costs will be to get to work. Detailed assistance is available for the asking from the local Chamber of Commerce in most cities (the southern cities are much more helpful than other cities; Los Angeles imposes a charge for its publications), or from realtors, or from the relocation office of your company if it's a company move.

Whatever you decide . . . good luck!

## THE 1990s AND BEYOND

A recent federally funded study has identified some emerging trends that will certainly impact business in the 1990s and beyond. The Hudson Institute's "Workforce 2000" tells us that the U.S. economy is changing, with most of the new wealth coming from service industries like trade, education, health care, government finance and business services.

These service firms will be concerned about recruiting employees and new jobs in these areas will require a much higher level of skills than jobs today. Just as the workforce becomes older and minorities are more fully integrated into, and utilized by, the economy, we will see sixty percent of all women working by the year 2000, causing a real change in employee benefits programs, and the services needed to reflect these demographic changes.

As this book goes to press, the Democratic and Republican candidates are in the throes of primaries. The outcome of the struggle in November of 1988 will have regional implications. Some cities will be better off under a Democratic President, others under a Republican one.

The major issues hanging over the future opportunities to be found in American cities have to do with: (1) A possible recession brought on by higher interest rates to stem any serious outflow of dollars resulting from sale of U.S. debts by foreign debt-owners concerned about a string of American trade and budget deficits. (2) The price of oil, now at about $14 a barrel, $4 below what U.S. oil producers require to make a profit. (3) The American defense industry, especially the "Star Wars" component, which has already been scaled back from heavy increases early in the Reagan Administration. (4) The importance of education.

(1.) *Recession*. Whatever the origins of a recession, cities will bear the burden unevenly. Higher interest rates are a likely originating point for a recession, and the need to retain restless international money a reason for higher interest rates. Higher taxes (thereby reducing the budget deficit and the need for U.S. debt to foreigners) would be another approach, but, judging from reactions to the recommendations of one Presidential candidate in the 1988 campaign, the American public doesn't want to hear about higher taxes.

If you see recession in America's future, consider the following factors that will make for relative resistance to recession. First, does the city derive a lot of its income from taxation outside its borders? If so, this will help it through recession years. The key numbers to look for to determine these recession-resistant cities are provided in Chapter 2 in the section titled "Industry Dependence and Outlook." The cities of opportunity with more than one-fifth of their workers in government jobs were listed there as (in order of percentage in government): Sacramento, Washington, Austin, San Antonio, El Paso, Salt Lake City and Tucson. However, two cautionary notes: First, some of the government jobs are highly dependent on state tax revenues, and this could be a problem in oil-producing cities like Austin. Other cities in this category include Oklahoma City and New Orleans. Second, some of the government jobs may be in the defense contracting area, which may be subject to significant cuts during the next few years.

Another area to look at to protect yourself against recession is the construction field. Again, look back to Chapter 2. The metro areas that would be most affected by a turndown in construction activity are in the states of Arizona, California, and Florida. They are in the greatest danger of a construction slow-down from higher interest rates.

The remaining area to focus on is manufacturing. In a recession, sales of manufactured goods decline, which means layoffs back at the factory. The cities of opportunity that would be most affected are Greensboro, Charlotte, and Detroit, in that order. The key variable to watch for in these cities is the value of the dollar in world markets. If the dollar appreciates, foreign goods are expensive and U.S. manufactured goods more expensive, affecting demand for U.S. goods and therefore employment.

(2.) *Oil Prices.* As we go to press, oil prices are at $14 a barrel. This is not a good price for American producers, who need about $18 to make a profit. If prices stay at $14 a barrel, Texas, Louisiana and Oklahoma will stay depressed. The proposal to be considered by the Presidential candidates is for an oil import tax, which would bring in money to the U.S. government (thereby cutting the deficit) and would permit U.S. producers to raise their prices above world markets. A tax might even be devised that is between $18 and the world price. However, the losers from such a tax would be the residents of the Northeast and Midwest who need oil for heating in the long winter months; right now, they are benefitting from the low price of oil. So Presidential candidates must be careful what they say. The cities of opportunity most affected by oil prices are, again, shown in Chapter 2, in the category of mining: Houston, Denver, Dallas. Austin would have a derivative interest in oil prices because of its dependence on the revenues derived from taxes on oil. Texas in 1987 imposed on its residents the largest tax increase of any state, ever.

(3.) *Defense.* President Reagan, when he came to office, embarked on a program of strategic nuclear modernization, which was a large factor in the increased defense spending. As this program was coming to an end in 1983, he introduced the Strategic Defense Initiative, widely dubbed as "Star Wars." The Star Wars program as originally introduced is estimated to cost anywhere from $400 billion to $1 trillion over the next 20 years. The $10 billion spent to date has helped cushion the blow to many defense-oriented metro areas from the likely winding down of the nuclear modernization program.

As of press time, all the major Democratic presidential candidates favor ending the Star Wars program (though they might keep some elements of it that relate to other programs), and all the major Republican presidential favor continuing it, although the commitment of Senator Dole and Vice President Bush is weaker than that of Representative Kemp. President Reagan has scaled down his own appropriation request for 1988–89 from $6.3 billion to $4.5 billion.

The cities of opportunity that would benefit economically from cutting back or ending the Star Wars program, based on net federal tax subsidy to defense contractors elsewhere in the United States, are the metro areas of New York, Chicago, Philadelphia, Detroit, Houston, Miami, Kansas City and Atlanta. The New York metro area alone spent a net of $144 million to the rest of the country during the 1983–86 buildup phase of Star Wars.

On the other hand, the cities of opportunity that have been benefiting from Star Wars money and are net recipients of these tax dollars are the metro areas of Los Angeles, San Francisco, Boston, Seattle, San Diego, Dallas, Denver and Washington, D.C. They have taken in $2 billion from the rest of the country during the buildup phase.

Of course, economic considerations alone should not determine one's views on defense issues. On the other hand, one should know the regional impact of national decisions, especially when looking for a city of opportunity.

(4.) *Education.* Increasingly, people are becoming aware of the importance of education—or, more broadly, the "development of human resources"—in the growth of regions. The surprising growth of Massachusetts has been attributed to a single institution—the Massachusetts Institute of Technology—and the innovative research and development it has generated and fostered.

At least one southern governor looked north and decided that the South has been approaching its economic development strategy from the wrong end. According to William F. Winter, Mississippi's governor from 1979 to 1983, no longer can the South rely on the myth that "Yankee industry will move in to save us." Contemplating Mississippi, Winter recognized that "we could not have a competitive state unless we had human beings who had competitive skills." A major challenge for the South is to "eliminate the drastic disparities between [school] districts."

At the elementary and secondary school level, a crude measure of teaching resources is the public school pupil/teacher ratio, which is provided in the "Education" section for each of the cities of opportunity. But assessing the quality of education must go beyond such crude numbers to an examination of how the school system handles gifted pupils, what the dropout rate is, what the private schools are doing and so forth.

For the assessment of higher education in a community, no overall numbers will suffice. In our city write-ups we have also indicated local facilities. Resources are available for assessing these institutions; it's important to evaluate a city's present and future educational resources in assessing its future.

Cities exist to provide jobs. If the jobs that can be expected to open up require higher levels of skills, we should all do something about it. Individuals should focus on improving their skills, all the time. Governments should focus on helping people do just that. With skills in hand, we all have something to offer to the city of opportunity that we choose to settle in.

John Tepper Marlin
February 1988

# NOTES

PREFACE

**Intercity transfers.** Turned down by one-fifth of working couples. *Source:* Independent Relocation Consultants Association.

**Misery Index:** A nontechnical translation of data in Angus Campbell, Philip E. Converse, and Willard L. Rodgers, *The Quality of American Life: Perceptions, Evaluations, and Satisfactions* (New York: Russell Sage Foundation, 1976).

CHAPTER 1. WHY THIS BOOK NOW?

**Job mobility.** David Birch, *Job Creation in America: How Our Smallest Companies Put the Most People to Work* (New York: Free Press, 1987).

**When Americans Move.** U.S. Department of Commerce, Bureau of the Census, *Current Population Reports*. Series P-20. (Washington, D.C.: Government Printing Office).

**Marital Status and Job-Related Moves.** Consultant comments from Marcy Mann, president of Transfer Consultants, Inc., of Marietta, Georgia; quoted by Beth A. Gault in "Pulling Up Roots: Relocating the Family," *KNOW: The Relocation Guide for Atlanta*, vol. 1, no. 2 (Fall 1987), p. 22.

**Psychiatrist on the Trauma of Moving:** Dr. Harry W. Hollingsworth, Ridgeview, Georgia, cited in Gault, "Pulling Up Roots."

**Adjustment:** Joanne Atkinson, "Relocation: No Simple Exercise," *KNOW*, p. 28.

Thanks to attorney Howard Mindus, who helped avert a statistical error in this chapter.

CHAPTER 2. JOBS MEAN OPPORTUNITY

**Jobs as Opportunity.** Definition of metro areas: Since mid-1983, a metro area is federally defined as an area of at least 100,000 people of which at least 50 percent is urban. The big metro areas, however, get special treatment. At the smaller level, the Primary Metro Statistical Area (PMSA) basically has a population of at least 100,000, of which at least 60 percent are urban and less than 50 percent commute to work outside the area. At the larger level, the Consolidated Metro Statistical Area (CMSA) has at least 1 million people and has at least two PMSAs. For full metro area labor market definitions, see U.S. Department of Labor, Bureau of Labor Statistics (BLS), Establishment Survey Data, *Supplement to Employment, Hours, and Earnings, States and Areas, Data for 1980–84* (Washington, D.C.: Government Printing Office), pp. ix, 381–87.

**CMSA versus PMSA:** In the tabular material in Chapters 2 and 3, we basically opt for the PMSA as our unit of analysis, since the CMSA is too large an area—the New York CMSA has twelve PMSAs and a population as of mid-1986 of 18 million; Los Angeles has four PMSAs and a population of 13.1 million; Chicago has six PMSAs and a population of 8.1 million; and so forth. (However, we must reconcile the labor market data in Chapter 2 with the small business data in Chapter 3, which will in a few cases make tidy adherence to the new federal definitions impossible.) The latest (mid-1986) metro population data cited above are from U.S. Department of Commerce, Bureau of the Census, *News* (press release), "Dallas–Fort Worth Tops Houston as Eighth Largest Metro Area," embargoed for release July 24, 1987. We prefer to work with labor market data rather than population data because we are more interested in where people work than in where they live.

**Largest 100 Metro Areas, by number of jobs (September 1987):** Table 2.1. Data provided in a special printout prepared for this book by the BLS. We are grateful to the BLS for their assistance.

**Multiplier-Accelerator:** See Alvin H. Hansen, *Business Cycles and National Income* (New York: W. W. Norton, 1951), pp. 171–94.

**"Creative destruction":** Joseph A. Schumpeter, *Capitalism, Socialism, and Democracy*, 3rd ed. (New York: Harper & Brothers, 1950), pp. 81–86. Schumpeter was afraid that entrepreneurship would decline, pp. 131–34. Birch shows he is wrong so far.

**The Myth of the Steady Company/City:** Data from Birch, *Job Creation in America*, p. 45. Figure on 45 percent gain provided by William LeFevre of Advest, cited in Vartanig G. Vartan, "Market Place: Buying Laggards of Previous Year," *New York Times*, January 5, 1988.

**Strategic Recommendations:** Quote about playing it safest: Birch, *Job Creation in America*, p. 47.

**Manchester, New Hampshire, story:** Told in *Forbes* 70th anniversary issue and cited in *Reason* magazine, October 1987, p. 16.

**Change in Jobs:** Table 2.2. Data provided in a special printout prepared for this book by the BLS. We show just one decimal place. In fact, the numbers are provided to the BLS by the states, based on payroll record information submitted voluntarily by a representative sample of establishments (industrial, commercial, governmental), and the accuracy of the data—although very high because of the large sample coverage obtained by the BLS—is not so great that we should count on the validity of the second decimal place. See U.S. Department of Labor, BLS, Establishment Survey Data, *Supplement to Employment, Hours, and Earnings, States and Areas, Data for 1980–84* (Washington, D.C.: Government Printing Office), pp. 388–92, esp. Table 1.

**Industry Dependence:** Data for proportion of workers in each industry derived from printouts from the BLS, reprocessed via Lotus 1-2-3.

**Predictions by industry:** Based on "Business Outlook," *The New York Times*, January 4, 1988, pp. D-6–7.

Thanks to Betty Greenfield for timely assistance in processing data in this chapter and to Professor Howard Ross for bibliographic help.

CHAPTER 3. ENTERPRISE MEANS JOBS

**Cities of Opportunity, Ranked:** Table 3.2. The table has 86 cities instead of the 100 largest labor markets shown in Chapter 2. The reason, alluded to in the notes to Chapter 2, is that the Census Bureau (and, by extension, the Bureau of Labor Statistics) continually revises its definitions of metro areas and David Birch's small business data are organized according to older criteria. The BLS, for example, now tabulates Dallas and Fort Worth separately, but they are combined in Birch's statistics. Similarly, Birch combines San Jose with San Francisco; Oxnard–Ventura and Riverside, California, with Los Angeles (to extricate Anaheim, we reluctantly had to combine Birch's Greater Los Angeles data with BLS's Anaheim data); Gary, Indiana, with Chicago; Trenton, New Jersey, with Philadelphia; Jersey City, Newark and Passaic, New Jersey, and Nassau–Suffolk, New York, with New York City; Akron with Cleveland; and San Juan, Puerto Rico, was omitted by Birch. See Birch, pp. 207–34; he lists communities by county, not city, so to reconcile his figures with BLS data you need to know that San Jose is in Santa Clara County, Gary is in Lake County, Trenton is in Mercer County, Jersey City is in Hudson County, Newark is in Essex County and Paterson is in Passaic County.

CHAPTER 4. QUALITY-OF-LIFE CONSIDERATIONS

For background on community indicators, see the "Assessing Community Health" issue of the *National Civic Review*, 76:6 (November–December 1987), pp. 472–500.

Thanks to John Parr, Chris Gates and other National Civic League directors and staff for identifying the components of the League's National Civic Index, and to Jeffrey Buckner for taking the time to help the author formulate the CIVIC PRIDE and other mnemonics.

CHAPTER 5. BECOMING BETTER OFF

**Switching Careers:** Derived from Birch, *Job Creation in America*, pp. 169–70. He provides before-and-after salaries for job changes with comparable needed aptitudes.

CHAPTER 6. YOUR BEST MOVE

**Women:** Andrea Heil, "The Right Place," *Savvy*, November 1985, pp. 27–34, 82–83.

**Black businesses:** *American Demographics*, July 1987.

**Hispanic Small Businesses:** William O'Hare, "Best Metros for Hispanic Businesses," *American Demographics*, November 1987, pp. 30–33; Jack Lessinger, *Regions of Opportunity* (New York: Times Books), cited in *American Demographics*, June 1987.

**Whyte study:** William H. Whyte, "Central Cities' Value for Business," *National Civic Review*, 77:1 (January–February 1988), pp. 29–33.

**Less than 3 percent of jobs open up through death or retirement:** Birch, p. 176.

**Regional Projections Retirement:** Birch, *Job Creation in America*, pp. 148–49, 196.

**Moving:** Joe Schwartz, "On the Road Again," *American Demographics*, April 1987, pp. 39, 40.

CHAPTER 7. THE CITIES OF OPPORTUNITY

"Businesses Ranked Within State by Employee Size," *Dun's Business Rankings 1987*. Parsippany: Dun's Marketing Services, 1987.

"Hot Spots: *Inc.*'s List of the 50 Fastest-Growing U.S. Cities." *Inc.*, April 1987, pp. 50–64.

*Inter City Cost of Living Index* (Fourth Quarter, 1986), American Chambers of Commerce Researchers Association.

*Let's Go USA*, New York: St. Martin's Press, 1987.

Marlin, John Tepper, and Avery, James S., *The Book of American City Rankings*, New York: Facts on File, 1983.

"Metropolitan Statistical Areas by Population Rank," *United States Department of Commerce News,* July 1, 1986.

*Municipal Yearbook 1987,* Washington, D.C.: International City Management Association, 1987.

U.S. Department of Commerce, Bureau of the Census, *1980 Census of Population: Standard Metropolitan Statistical Areas and Standard Consolidated Statistical Areas: 1980,* Washington, D.C.: Government Printing Office, October 1981.

U.S. Department of Commerce, Bureau of the Census, *Supplementary Report, Provisional Estimates of Social, Economic and Housing Characteristics,* Washington, D.C.: Government Printing Office, March 1982.

### Albuquerque

*Absolutely Albuquerque.* Greater Albuquerque Chamber of Commerce, 1986.
*Albuquerque Metroplex: The Option.* Albuquerque Metroplex, Inc., 1986.
*Business Brief.* Albuquerque Economic Development, February–March 1987.
*Community Profile: Albuquerque's West Side,* Greater Albuquerque Chamber of Commerce, April 1986.
*New Mexico Business Journal,* vol. 11, no. 5 (May 1987), pp. 33–54.
*New Mexico Progress.* Sunwest Financial Services, May 1987.
Thanks for help to Tina Gonzalez of the City of Albuquerque.

### Anaheim

*Anaheim, California.* Windsor Publications/Anaheim Chamber of Commerce, 1986.
*Anaheim Update (March 1987),* Anaheim Area Visitor & Convention Bureau, March 1987.
Nimroody, Rosy. *Star Wars: The Economic Fallout.* Council on Economic Priorities, Cambridge, Mass.: Ballinger Publishing Company, 1988.
Reinhold, Robert, "Where Growth is King, a Move to Rein It In." *The New York Times,* August 19, 1987.

### Atlanta

Elie, L. Eric. "What It's Like to Live and Work in Atlanta." *Business Week Careers,* p. 60.
*Family and Child Care Statistics in Metropolitan Atlanta: 1987.* Child Care Solutions, a project of Save the Children, Southern States Office.
Toner, Robin. "Atlanta, City of Future, Meets Its Past." *The New York Times,* February 7, 1987.

### Austin

*Austin MSA Employment & Economic Forecast.* Austin Chamber of Commerce, 1986.
*Directory of Major Employees In the Austin Area Metroplex.* Austin Chamber of Commerce, 1986.

*Kaleidoscope: The Guide to Austin.* Austin Chamber of Commerce, Summer 1987.
Thanks for help to Professor Terrell Blodgett of the LBJ School.

## Baltimore

*Baltimore Report.* Pace Communications, Inc., 1987.

## Boston

*Boston Report.* Greater Boston Chamber of Commerce, September 1986.
Frailey, Fred W., and Delouise, Richard I. "Cities Where Business is Best." *U.S. News and World Report,* April 29, 1985, p. 52.
"The Inc. 100: America's Fastest-Growing Small Public Companies." *Inc.,* May 1987.
*Making the Grade.* The Corporation for Enterprise Development, March 1987.
Peirce, Neal. "Massachusetts: Distinction in Adversity." *The Book of America,* p. 164.
Thanks to Ernest B. Gutierrez, Jr., of the City of Boston and to several departments that provided new data: Boston Redevelopment Authority, Women's Commission, Fair Housing Commission, Arts and Humanities Commission, and the police department. Boston vacancy rate data from Tony Di Matteo, Boston Board of Realtors.

## Charlotte

*Charlotte in Detail* and *Charlotte Overview.* Charlotte Chamber of Commerce, 1987.
*New and Expanded Business in Charlotte/Mecklenburg.* Charlotte Chamber of Commerce, 1987.
Thanks to Ronnie Sorbin, Research Division, Charlotte Police Dept., for crime data.

## Chicago

"Chicago Bounces Back—A New Prosperity Eclipses An Industrial Decline" *Newsweek,* October 6, 1986.
Colby, Mary. "Leading Private Firms in Chicago." *Crain's Chicago Business,* February 24, 1986, p. 20.
Davis, Terry C. "Chicago: Absorption High But Suburbs Show About 30% Vacancy." *National Real Estate Investor,* February 1987, p. 66.
Goozner, Morill. "Post Industrial Blues: How Service Economy Strains Social Fabric." *Crain's Chicago Business,* November 3, 1986, p. 1.
Johnson, Dirk. "Urban Class Problem Stirs Chicago Debate." *The New York Times,* March 25, 1987, p. A-10.
McCarron, John. "Is Chicago Ready for Reform?" *Planning,* September 1984, p. 4.
Sniklo, Ken. "Chicago's the Second City that Pushes to Be No. 1 (5 Top Metros for Black Professionals)." *Black Enterprise,* May 1987, p. 50.

## Cincinnati

*Cincinnati Area Labor Force.* Greater Cincinnati Chamber of Commerce, March 1987.

*Greater Cincinnati.* Greater Cincinnati Chamber of Commerce, 1987.

*Greater Cincinnati Area Profile.* Greater Cincinnati Chamber of Commerce, 1987.

## Columbus

*Columbus City Guide (Columbus Monthly's Complete Guide to Central Ohio).* Columbus Monthly Publishing Company, 1986.

*Columbus Economic Review.* City of Columbus Development Department, Spring 1987.

*Growth Potential: 1985–1995.* City of Columbus Strategic Planning Office of Management and Budget, December 1985.

*Profile . . . Columbus, Ohio.* Department of Development, City of Columbus, in association with Columbus Area Chamber of Commerce, 1986.

Thanks for help to Patricia A. Ackerman of the Columbus Chamber of Commerce and Patrick Grady of the City of Columbus Development Department.

## Dallas–Fort Worth

*Dallas Area Employment Trends and Economic Indicators.* Research Department, The Dallas Chamber, December 1987.

*Dallas at a Glance 1987–88.* The Dallas Chamber, 1987.

*Fort Worth Community Profile.* Economic Development Division of the Fort Worth Chamber, 1985.

*Fort Worth Welcome Home: Fort Worth Chamber Newcomers' Guide.* Fort Worth Chamber, 1987.

Ross, Steven S. "Living and Working in Dallas–Ft. Worth." *Business Week's Careers,* 1987.

*Texas Labor Market Review.* Texas Employment Commission, April 1987.

Thanks for help to Cheryl Merryfield of the Fort Worth Chamber of Commerce and to Pat Svacina of the City of Fort Worth.

## Denver

*Colorado Labor Force Review.* Department of Labor and Employment, May 1987.

*Environmental Protection Agency Pollution Report,* 1987.

Hayes, Thomas C. "Hard Times Not Over for Texas Real Estate." *The New York Times,* March 24, 1988, p. D-1. (Cites Denver vacancy rate.)

*National Real Estate Investor,* February 1987.

*Occupational Employment Outlook: 1985–1990.* Colorado Division of Employment and Training, July 1985.

*Occupational Supply/Demand Outlook.* Colorado Department of Labor and Employment, Fourth Quarter, 1986.

U.S. National Oceanic and Atmosphere Administration (NOAA), National Weather Service, Local Climatological Data, 1981.

## Detroit

*Greater Detroit/Southeast Michigan: Welcome to Our World.* Greater Detroit Chamber of Commerce, 1986.

*Metropolitan Detroit Firms Employing 500 or More.* Greater Detroit Chamber of Commerce, June 1986.

*1987 Economic Fact Book.* Greater Detroit Chamber Foundation, Inc., Economic Education/Research Fund, 1987.

*1987 Economic Outlook for Greater Detroit.* Greater Detroit Chamber of Commerce, 1987.

Thanks for help to Gene Scott of the City of Detroit.

## El Paso

*El Paso Industrial Development Corporation Quarterly Report (April 1987),* El Paso Industrial Development Corporation, April 1987.

"El Paso/Juarez: Bordering on Success," supplement to *New Mexico Business Journal,* June 1987.

Statistical, economic, industrial and demographic data furnished by El Paso Industrial Development Corporation.

## Greensboro

*Greensboro Report.* Greensboro Area Chamber of Commerce, 1986.

*Greensboro Visions Environmental Scan.* Greensboro Visions, June 1987.

*North Carolina 1987 Profile: Greensboro/Guilford County,* North Carolina Department of Commerce Economic Development Office, 1987.

Thanks for help to Angie Macon, Greater Greensboro Chamber of Commerce.

## Hartford

*Greater Hartford Fact Pack.* Greater Hartford Chamber of Commerce, 1987.

Thanks for help to Beth Wood Kenworthy, Greater Hartford Chamber of Commerce.

## Houston

Carlson, Eugene. "Would You Believe Houston As a New Business Hot Spot?" *Wall Street Journal,* December 2, 1986, p. 1.

Erickson, R. "Trends for Economic Development." *American City and County,* October 1985, p. 53.

Hayes, Thomas C. "Hard Times Not Over for Texas Real Estate." *The New York Times,* March 24, 1988, p. D-1.

*Houston Economic Development Newsletter.* Houston Chamber of Commerce, May 1987.

*Houston Facts 1987.* Houston Chamber of Commerce, 1987.

## Indianapolis

*The Bare Facts.* Indianapolis Chamber of Commerce, 1987.

*City Guide.* Indianapolis: Capital Communications Corporation, 1986.

*Metropolitan Indianapolis.* Metropolitan Indianapolis Board of Realtors, 1984.

## Jacksonville

*Child Care Services Study.* Jacksonville Community Council, Inc., Summer 1987.

*First Coast Growth Report.* Jacksonville Chamber of Commerce, April 1986, January 1987.

"Jacksonville: Florida's Business City," supplement to *Business Facilities*, February 1987.

Linn, Alan. "A Big, Ol' Country Town." *USAIR*, December 1986.

Thanks for help to Mayor Thomas L. Hazouri, City of Jacksonville.

## Kansas City, Missouri–Kansas

*Greater Kansas City Resident Guide.* Metromark Publishing, 1987.

*Kansas City Today.* Kansas City Area Economic Development Council, 1985.

*1986: An Economic Review and Forecast.* Chamber of Commerce of Greater Kansas City, 1987.

*Profile of Kansas City, Missouri.* Kansas City Area Economic Development Council, 1986.

*This is Kansas City.* Kansas City Area Economic Development Council, 1987.

Thanks for help to Mary Novaria of the Greater Kansas City Economic Development Council.

## Las Vegas

Thanks for help to Richard Serfas, Clark County Economic Development Board.

## Memphis

*Guide to Memphis.* Memphis Area Chamber of Commerce, 1987.

*Memphis Area Major Employers 1987.* Memphis Light, Gas & Water Division, 1987.

*Memphis: Communications/Agriculture/Transportation/Education.* Memphis Area Chamber of Commerce, 1986.

*Taxes in Tennessee for Business Development and Individuals.* Memphis Area Chamber of Commerce/Memphis Light, Gas & Water Division, 1983.

Thanks for help to Leola Hansen, office of Mayor R. C. Hackett, City of Memphis.

## Miami

*Greater Miami and the Beaches Report.* Pace Communications, Inc., 1986.

*Miami: The State of the City 1986.* City of Miami Department of Communications, Public Affairs Division, 1986.

Sherrill, Robert. "Can Miami Save Itself?" *The New York Times Magazine.* July 19, 1987.

## Minneapolis–St. Paul

Borchet, John. *America's Northern Heartland.* Minneapolis: University of Minnesota Press, 1988.

Bosch, Michael. "Two Hot Towns in the Snow Belt." *U.S. News and World Report,* April 28, 1985, p. 54.

*The Good Life in the Twin Cities.* Merrill Lynch Realty/Burnet, Inc., 1986.

*Making the Grade.* Corporation for Enterprise Development, March 1987.

Thanks for help to Ted Kolderie of the Hubert H. Humphrey Institute. The statements about the region's population compared to Texas and the number of company head offices are from John Borchert of the University of Minnesota, via Kolderie.

## Nashville

*Nashville: A Gathering Place for American Culture.* Nashville Area Chamber of Commerce 1986 Business Directory, 1986.

*Tennessee Community Data: Nashville.* Tennessee Department of Economic and Community Development, March 1986.

*This is Nashville!* South Central Bell Telephone, 1983.

## New York

Breznick, Alan. "Corporate Exodus to Cost New York 10,000-Plus Jobs." *Crain's New York Business,* June 8, 1987, p. 1.

"Business Incentives: It's Koch and Carry." *Crain's New York Business.* June 15, 1987, p. 8.

*Comptroller's Report.* Comptroller of the City of New York, April 1987.

Fein, Esther B. "An Update on Dating: Distress in New York." *The New York Times,* June 3, 1987, p. B-1.

"Firm Bashing: New York City Still Corporate America's Most Likely Place to Set Up Shop." *Insight.* June 22, 1987, p. 45.

Gill, Brendan. "The Sky Line: On the Brink." *The New Yorker,* November 9, 1987, p. 126.

Hall, Trish. "The Dinner Party Quietly Bows." *The New York Times,* February 24, 1988, p. C-1.

Lambert, Bruce. "New York Lacks Spaces for Increase of the Homeless." *The New York Times,* May 28, 1987, p. B-2.

Leape, Martha P. *The Harvard Guide to Careers.* Cambridge: The Harvard University Press, 1983.

Marlin, John Tepper. "What the Market Crash Says About New York City." *The New York Times,* October 24, 1987, p. 31.

Scardino, Albert, "Changing Era for New York's Economy." *The New York Times,* May 18, 1987, p. B-1.

Spinola, Steven. "Reducing Costs the No. 1 Priority." *Crain's New York Business,* June 1, 1987, p. 10.

Stollman, Rita. "Despite Costs, Manhattan's Lure Still Potent." *Crain's New York Business,* February 9, 1987, p. 20.

————. "White Collars for Blue in Brooklyn and Queens." *Crain's New York Business*, February 9, 1987, p. 20.

Wagner, Robert, Jr., Chairman. *Report of the Committee on the Year 2000*. City of New York, 1987.

"Why the Big Apple is the Big Apple." *Crain's New York Business*, June 1, 1987, p. 8.

Whyte, William H. "New York City's Value for Business." *The New York Times*, May 16, 1987, p. 31.

Thanks for help to Perry Davis of Perry Davis Associates, Regional BLS Commissioner Samuel Ehrenhalt, Bernard Kabak and other staff members of the Special Deputy New York State Comptroller for New York City, New York Deputy Mayor Alair Townsend and City Club of New York chairman Stanley Turkel.

## Orlando

*Orlando Area Major Employers Directory*. Greater Orlando Chamber of Commerce, 1987.

*Orlando Today—Economic Profile*. Greater Orlando Chamber of Commerce, 1987.

## Philadelphia

*Economic Development Within the Philadelphia Metropolitan Area*. Greater Philadelphia Chamber of Commerce, 1986.

*Economic Report on the Philadelphia Metropolitan Area 1985*. Greater Philadelphia Chamber of Commerce, 1985.

*Executive Summary—Why Philadelphia?* Philadelphia International Network, Inc., 1986.

*The Greater Philadelphia Story*. Greater Philadelphia Chamber of Commerce, 1987.

*Southeastern Pennsylvania: A Prospectus for Growth*. Philadelphia Electric Company Area Development Department, 1987.

Thanks for help to David Boonin, City of Philadelphia, and Tom Whiting and Joan Welsch, Greater Philadelphia Chamber of Commerce.

## Phoenix

"Inside Phoenix." *Arizona Republic*, 1987.

Peirce, Neal R. "The Peirce Report." *Arizona Republic*. Februaryruary 8, 1987.

*Phoenix Facts 1987*. Phoenix Metropolitan Chamber of Commerce, 1987.

*Valley Growth: United or Fragmented?* Morrison Institute for Public Policy, Arizona State University, 1987.

Thanks for help to Phoenix City Manager Marvin A. Andrews and Phoenix Metropolitan Chamber of Commerce.

## Providence

*Business Profile*. Greater Providence Chamber of Commerce, 1987.

*City of Providence Monograph*. Rhode Island Department of Economic Development, December 1986.

*Major Companies in Rhode Island Employing 500 or More.* Greater Providence Chamber of Commerce, January 1987.

*Rhode Island, the Better Business State.* Rhode Island Department of Economic Development, 1987.

Thanks for help to James G. Hagan, Greater Providence Chamber of Commerce.


## Raleigh–Durham

*Development in the Triangle.* Pace Communications, Inc., 1987.

*Durham Executive Summary.* Greater Durham Chamber of Commerce, 1987.

*Durham, North Carolina, Economic Summary.* Greater Durham Chamber of Commerce, August 1986.

*Major Employers: Raleigh/Wake County/Research Triangle Park.* Greater Raleigh Chamber of Commerce, Februaryruary 1986.

*Raleigh, North Carolina Executive Summary.* Greater Raleigh Chamber of Commerce, 1987.

*Raleigh Report.* Pace Communications, Inc., 1986.

Thanks for help to Bill K. Baukom, Jr., Greater Durham Chamber of Commerce; Betsy Hinnant, Public Affairs Director of the City of Raleigh; and Paul Norby, Office of the Durham City Manager.


## Sacramento

*The Business Handbook—Sacramento on the Go 1986.* Publications Network in cooperation with Sacramento Metropolitan Chamber of Commerce, 1986.

*Business in Sacramento.* Sacramento Metropolitan Chamber of Commerce, 1987.

*Living in Sacramento.* Sacramento Metropolitan Chamber of Commerce, 1988.

*Sacramento Economic Forecast 1986.* Bank of America Regional Administration, 1986.

*Sacramento Region Business Profile.* Sacramento Area Commerce and Trade Organization, 1987.

Thanks for help to David R. Gross, Sacramento Metropolitan Chamber of Commerce.


## Salt Lake City

*1986 Baseline Projections.* State of Utah, 1985.

*Salt Lake Area Health Care and Medical Industry Profile.* Salt Lake Area Chamber of Commerce, July 1986.

*Salt Lake Area Major Employers.* Salt Lake Area Chamber of Commerce, 1987.

*Salt Lake Area Metropolitan Profile.* Salt Lake Area Chamber of Commerce, 1987.

U.S. Department of Energy. *Typical Electric Bills, January 1986,* Mountain Fuel Supply, October 1986.

*Utah Data Guide.* State Office of Planning and Budget, July 1986.

*Labor Market Information Services.* Utah Department of Employment Security, December 1985.

*Utah Economic and Business Review.* Bureau of Economic and Business Research, Graduate School of Business, University of Utah, vol. 46, no. 12 (December 1986).
Thanks for help to Cheryl Smith, Salt Lake Area Chamber of Commerce, and Natalie Gochnour, State of Utah Office of Planning and Budget.

## San Antonio

Martin, Carole. "A Businesswoman's Guide to San Antonio." *Working Woman,* March 1985, p. 150.
*San Antonio: A Look at Our Economy.* MARCOA Publishing, Inc., 1987.
*San Antonio Business' Guide to San Antonio.* Greater San Antonio Chamber of Commerce, 1987.
*San Antonio Facts.* San Antonio Chamber of Commerce, 1985.
*San Antonio 1986 Executive Summary.* San Antonio Economic Development Foundation, Inc., 1986.

## San Diego

*1988 Housing Guide.* Greater San Diego Chamber of Commerce, 1988.
*San Diego Welcomes You!* Windsor Publications in cooperation with Greater San Diego Chamber of Commerce, 1987.
*The Union-Tribune's Annual Review of San Diego Business.* San Diego: The Union-Tribune Publishing Company, 1986.
Thanks for help to Lonna R. Wilkes, San Diego Economic Development Corporation.

## San Francisco

Adams, Gerald. "The Neighborhoods of San Francisco." *California Living,* 1977.
*The Big 50: Bay Area's Biggest Publicly Held Corporations.* San Francisco Chamber of Commerce, 1986.
Lindsey, Robert. "No Longer Smug, San Francisco Looks Into Mirror and Ponders Future." *New York Times.* December 20, 1987.
*San Francisco: Its Economic Future.* Wells Fargo Bank, June 1987.
*SPUR Report.* San Francisco Planning and Urban Research Association, April 1987.
Thanks for help to Luis Espinoza, Mayor's Office of Housing and Economic Development.

## Seattle

Thanks for help to Jim Mayfield, Greater Seattle Chamber of Commerce.

## Tampa–St. Petersburg

*Florida's Suncoast: St. Petersburg and the Gulf Beaches.* St. Petersburg Area Chamber of Commerce, 1987.
*Population Projections, by Jurisdiction, Planning Area and Census Tract.* Hillsborough County Planning Commission, December 1986.

*St. Petersburg Skylines.* St. Petersburg Downtown Improvement Corporation, Winter 1985 and Winter 1986–87.

*Tampa—America's Next Great City.* Greater Tampa Chamber of Commerce, 1987.

Thanks for help to Martin J. Normile, St. Petersburg Downtown Improvement Corporation, and Sharon Hall Everidge, City of Tampa.

## Tucson

*About Tucson.* Economic Development Department, Tucson Metropolitan Chamber of Commerce, Fall 1985.

*Community Audit for the Metropolitan Tucson, Arizona, Area.* Tucson Economic Development Corporation, Spring 1987.

*Tucson.* Tucson Economic Development Corporation, 1986.

*The Tucson Area Economy and Housing Market: Outlook to 1992.* Federal Home Loan Bank of San Francisco, October 1983.

*Tucson Community Profile.* Arizona Department of Commerce, 1986.

*Tucson Trends.* Tucson Newspapers, Inc., and Valley National Bank of Arizona, 1986.

## Washington, D.C.

*A Capital Link.* Greater Washington Board of Trade, 1985.

*District of Columbia Office of Business and Economic Development 1986 Annual Report.* Office of Business and Economic Development, Government of the District of Columbia, 1986.

*Indices, A Statistical Index to District of Columbia Services.* prepared for the Government of the District of Columbia, July 1986.

Ruffin, David C. "Washington, D.C.: A Thriving Center of Power and Culture." *Black Enterprise.* May 1987.

*Washington Area Jobs and Occupations in the Year 1990.* District of Columbia Dept. of Employment Services, January 1985.

*Washington, D.C., is Business.* American Advance Research Corporation, 1987.

Thanks for help to Thomas P. Hoey, Government of the District of Columbia.

## West Palm Beach

*Palm Beach County Demographic Profile.* Chamber of Commerce of the Palm Beaches, 1987.

*The Palm Beaches.* Chamber of Commerce of the Palm Beaches, 1987.

Thanks for help to Eric Berlin, City of West Palm Beach.

### CHAPTER 8. A NOTE ON SMALLER CITIES OF OPPORTUNITY

*An Introduction to Huntsville and Madison County.* BellSouth Advertising and Publishing Company in association with Chamber of Commerce of Huntsville/Madison County, 1986.

*Business Headlines 1986: Huntsville.* Chamber of Commerce of Huntsville/Madison County, 1986.

*Community Data: Huntsville/Madison County.* Alabama Development Office, May 1987.

*Huntsville Business Report.* Chamber of Commerce of Huntsville/ Madison County, May, July, September, Novemberember 1986 and January 1987.

*Huntsville/Madison County.* Towery Publishing in association with Chamber of Commerce of Huntsville/Madison County, 1987.

*The Sky is Not the Limit: Huntsville, Alabama.* Chamber of Commerce of Huntsville/Madison County, 1987.

Thanks for help to Helen J. Berrisford, Chamber of Commerce of Huntsville/Madison County.

**AFTERWORD**

**Oil prices:** See Eliot Janeway, "The Oil Price Drop Victimizes Banks," *The New York Times,* February 23, 1988, p. A-31.

**Defense:** See Trish Gilmartin, "Revision Portends Possible Two-Year Delay in SDI Program Schedule," *Defense News,* February 22, 1988, p. 8; and Rosie Nimroody, *Star Wars: The Economic Fallout* (Cambridge, Mass.: Ballinger Publishing Company, 1988).

**Education:** William F. Winter quoted in Ferrel Guillory, "Mississippi's Elder Statesman Preaches the Gospel of Economic Reform," *Governing,* February 1988, pp. 36–40.

# ABOUT THE AUTHOR

**John Tepper Marlin** is an expert on urban America and is dedicated to improving the quality of life in cities. He has been president of the Council on Municipal Performance (COMP) since its founding in 1972, and in 1987 also became the vice president of the ninety-four-year-old National Civic League. He has edited the best-selling *Let's Go Student Guide to Europe* and has written six other books on cities: *Contracting Municipal Services, The Wealth of Cities, City Housing, The Book of American City Rankings, Book of World City Rankings* and *Privatization of Local Government: Lessons From Japan.* He is also the editor of two publications, *The Privatization Report* (monthly) and *The National Civic Review* (bimonthly). Dr. Marlin is an economist, previously employed by the Small Business Administration, the Federal Deposit Insurance Corporation and the Board of Governors of the Federal Reserve System. He received his Ph.D. from George Washington University. Dr. Marlin is a resident of New York City.

Additional copies of *Cities of Opportunity* may be ordered by sending a check for $13.95 (paper) and $24.95 (cloth), plus $1.50 for postage and handling of the first book and $.50 for each additional book, to:

> MasterMedia Limited
> 333 West 52nd Street
> Suite 306
> New York, NY 10019
> (212) 246-9500

John Tepper Marlin is available for keynote addresses, half-day and full-day seminars, and workshops. Please contact MasterMedia for availability and fee arrangements.

# OTHER MASTERMEDIA BOOKS:

*The Pregnancy and Motherhood Diary: Planning the First Year of Your Second Career*, by Susan Schiffer Stautberg, is the first and only undated appointment diary that shows how to manage pregnancy and career. ($12.95 paper)

*The Dollars and Sense of Divorce*, by Dr. Judith Briles, is the first book to combine practical tips on overcoming the legal hurdles of divorce and planning finances before, during and after divorce. ($10.95 paper)

*Out the Organization: Gaining the Competitive Edge*, by Madeleine and Robert Swain, is written for the millions of Americans whose jobs are no longer safe, whose companies are not loyal and who face futures of uncertainty. It gives advice on finding a new job or starting your own business. ($17.95 cloth)

*Aging Parents and You: A Complete Handbook to Help You to Help Your Elders Maintain a Healthy, Rewarding and Independent Life*, by Eugenia Anderson-Ellis and Marsha Dryan, is a complete guide to providing care to aging relatives. It gives practical advice and resources to the adults who are helping their elders lead productive and independent lives. ($9.95 paper)

*Beyond Success: How Volunteer Service Can Help You Begin Making a Life Instead of a Living*, by John F. Reynolds III and Eleanor Raynolds, CBE, is a unique how-to book targeted to business and professional people considering volunteer work, senior citizens who wish to fill leisure time meaningfully and students trying out various career options. The book is filled with interviews with celebrities, CEOs and average citizens who talk about the benefits of service work. ($19.95 cloth)

*Criticism in Your Life: How to Give It, How to Take It, How to Make It Work for You*, by Dr. Deborah Bright, offers practical advice, in an upbeat, readable and realistic fashion, for turning criticism into control. Charts and diagrams guide the reader into managing criticism from bosses, spouses, relationships, children, friends, neighbors and in-laws. ($17.95 cloth)

*Managing It All: Time Saving Ideas for Career, Family Relationships, and Self*, by Beverly Benz Treuille and Susan Schiffer Stautberg, is written for women who are juggling careers and families. Over 200 career women (ranging from a TV anchorwoman to an investment banker) were interviewed. The book contains many humorous anecdotes on saving time and improving the quality of life for self and family. ($9.95 paper)